Student Manual

Understanding Human Behavior and the Social Environment

EIGHTH EDITION

Charles H. Zastrow
George Williams College of Aurora University

Karen K. Kirst-Ashman
University of Wisconsin, Whitewater

Prepared by

Karen K. Kirst-Ashman
University of Wisconsin, Whitewater

Charles H. Zastrow
George Williams College of Aurora University

Vicki Vogel
University of Wisconsin, Whitewater

BROOKS/COLE
CENGAGE Learning

Australia • Brazil • Japan • Korea • Mexico • Singapore • Spain • United Kingdom • United States

ISBN-13: 978-0-495-80590-8
ISBN-10: 0-495-80590-4

Brooks/Cole
10 Davis Drive
Belmont, CA 94002-3098
USA

Cengage Learning is a leading provider of customized learning solutions with office locations around the globe, including Singapore, the United Kingdom, Australia, Mexico, Brazil, and Japan. Locate your local office at: **www.cengage.com/international**

Cengage Learning products are represented in Canada by Nelson Education, Ltd.

To learn more about Brooks/Cole, visit **www.cengage.com/brookscole**

Purchase any of our products at your local college store or at our preferred online store
www.ichapters.com

Printed in the United States of America
1 2 3 4 5 6 7 8 12 11 10 09

This *Student Manual* has two objectives. The first objective is to provide a study outline of the key concepts in each chapter of *Understanding Human Behavior and the Social Environment*. These chapter outlines are designed to help you learn the material in the text.

The second objective is to present classroom exercises. These exercises are designed to help you acquire knowledge, values, and skills related to content on human behavior and the social environment.

For each chapter the course outlines are presented first. These are followed by several exercises designed to help you understand the content. Each of the exercises in this manual has the following format: a brief description, a statement of objectives, and procedural instructions.

Text Objectives

A major thrust of this text is to provide content on the concepts identified in the Educational Policy and Accreditation Standards (EPAS) of the Council on Social Work Education (CSWE). CSWE is the accrediting body for social work educational programs.

Accredited social work programs need to provide content on human behavior across the life course; social systems in which people live; social systems that promote or deter people in maintaining or achieving health and wellbeing; theories and knowledge to understand biological, social, cultural, psychological, and spiritual development; and person and environment.

This text has the following thrusts:

- It presents a vast array of theories and research that seek to explain and describe human development and behavior. It focuses on individual functioning within systems of various sizes (including families, groups, organizations, and communities).
- It presents substantial information on human diversity, including material on groups distinguished by age, class, color, disabilities, ethnicity, culture, gender identity and expression, gender, marital status, political ideology, immigration status, race, religion, sex, and sexual orientation.
- It uses a life-span approach that allows for a description of human growth and development from conception through adulthood.
- It identifies biological, psychological, and sociological factors that influence development for each age group. Interactions among these systems are discussed in some depth. For many of the biopsychosocial theories described, content about values and ethical issues is included.
- It presents material on strategies that promote social and economic justice. Human rights are described.
- It describes normal developmental tasks and milestones for each age group.
- It describes the impact of social and economic forces on individuals, social systems, and societies.
- It presents material on the attainment and maintenance of optimal mental and physical health and well-being. It also describes the ways in which systems promote or deter health and well-being.
- It presents material, using a four-faceted approach, to evaluate theory, and describes how diverse theories can be applied to client situations.

This text presents the material in a readable fashion. Numerous case examples, photographs, and illustrations are used in presenting provocative and controversial issues about human behavior. As much as possible, jargon-free language is used so that the reader can readily grasp the theory.

How to Use the Study Outlines

Study outlines are provided for each chapter. The text covers a wide variety of topics and issues. The study outlines are intended to provide a structured overview of each chapter, thus making the material more manageable and coherent. They are aimed at helping you conceptualize the basic concepts addressed in the text. Such outlines provide a structure into which more specific details may be fit. Through teaching the course, we've found that an outline helps students learn and integrate the basic contents of the text. The outlines summarize what material you are expected to learn and acquire competence in.

The outlines can be used in two ways. First, they can help in your study of the material when you are on your own. One of the most common complaints we hear students make is that they "don't know what the instructor wants." That is, they don't understand which aspects of the course material are most important. Study outlines provide guidelines for what and how to study. Second, the outlines can help you take notes in class. Outlines may help you grasp more of the material. You can follow the basic organization of the material while your instructor lectures in class.

In summary, the study outline is designed to help you learn the material more efficiently. In class, outlines also should help decrease the need for "speed-writing" during lectures.

Exercises

The specific objectives of each exercise are listed in the text of this manual. It should be noted that class exercises are most often supposed to be fun and helpful in conveying the meaning of course content to you. (In reflecting on our own undergraduate and graduate courses, we have the most vivid and most positive memories of those courses in which classroom exercises were an integral part.)

The exercises in this manual have a variety of objectives. For example, there is an ice-breaker exercise to help you get acquainted and to foster group cohesion. There are a variety of value-clarification exercises to help you clarify your values in relation to controversial issues. These include surrogate motherhood, euthanasia, racism, sexism, homosexuality, ageism, and a variety of other issues. A number of exercises help you grasp the theoretical material presented in the text. We believe that theoretical material is best learned (and remembered) when you apply theoretical concepts and knowledge to real-world situations.

There are also a number of exercises designed to help you develop assessment skills. Since a primary focus of the text is assessment, a number of class exercises require you to assess real-life situations, using the theories and research presented in the text. Through such application of theory, you should not only improve your assessment skills but also be able to gauge the merits and shortcomings of the theoretical content.

Chapter 1
Introduction to Human Behavior and the Social Environment

Study Outline

I.   **Ethical Question 1.1**: Was it ethical for Dr. Itard and the others to remove Victor from the wild against his will?

II. **A Perspective**

III. **Foundation Knowledge and Social Work**

    A.   Social work has three thrusts

        1.   Help people solve problems and cope with situations

        2.   Work with large systems to improve people's access to resources

        3.   Link people with systems

    B.   Social workers are generalists

    C.   The Process of Social Work: The Importance of Assessment

        1.   Basic steps in the social work process

            a.   Assessment

            b.   Planning

            c.   Intervention/implementation

            d.   Evaluation

            e.   Termination

        2.   The importance of assessment

    D.   Identifying and evaluating alternative courses of action

        1.   Figure 1.1: Social Workers Help Clients Identify Alternatives and Evaluate the Consequences of Each

        2.   Highlight 1.1: Case Example: Unplanned Pregnancy

IV.   **The Organization of This Book: Lifespan Development**

    A.   Infancy and childhood

    B.   Adolescence

    C.   Young and middle adulthood

    D.   Later adulthood

    E.   Bio-psycho-social development

    F.   Human diversity

    G.   Figure 1.2: Organization of the Text

    H.   Common life events

    I.   Normal developmental milestones

    J.   Highlight 1.2: Bio-Psycho-Social Developmental Dimensions Affect Each Other

V.   **Important Concepts for Understanding Human Behavior**

    A.   Human diversity, cultural competency, oppression, and populations-at-risk

        1.   Human diversity: The vast range of differences among groups including those related to age, class, color, culture, disability, ethnicity, gender, gender identity and expression, political ideology, race, religion, sex, and sexual orientation

        2.   Highlight 1.3: Culture and the Importance of Cultural Competency

            a.   Culture: The configuration of shared attitudes, values, goals, spiritual beliefs, social expectations, arts, technology, and behaviors that characterize a broader society in which people live

            b.   Cultural competency: The mastery of a particular set of knowledge, skills, policies, and programs used by the social worker that address the cultural needs of individuals, families, groups, and communities

            c.   Cross-cultural understanding: The ability to appreciate and compare differences and similarities between and among different cultures including your own

        3.   Discrimination: The act of treating people differently because they belong to some group rather than on their own merit

        4.   Oppression: Putting unfair and extreme limitations and constraints on members of an identified group

5. People of color: A collective term that refers to the major groups of African, Latino, Asian, and First Nations Peoples [Native Americans] who have been distinguished from the dominant society by color

6. Population-at-risk: Any group of people who share some identifiable characteristic that places them at greater risk of social and economic deprivation and oppression than the general mainstream of society

B. Privilege, power, and acclaim

1. Power: The ability to achieve one's goals despite the oppression of others

2. Privilege: Entails special rights or benefits enjoyed because of elevated social, political, or economic status

3. Prestige: The amount of social respect or standing given to an individual based on occupation

4. Acclaim: Enthusiastic approval or praise

5. Poverty line: The annual cash income level that the federal government determines is necessary to maintain each individual or family at a minimal subsistence level

6. The inequality gap in the U.S. is the widest of all the industrialized nations

7. The powerful in society tend to come from backgrounds of privilege and wealth

8. Group membership and values

9. The societal perspective on group differences

   a. Prejudgments: Predetermined assumptions made without assessing facts

   b. Stereotypes: Standardized views, about people who belong to some group, that do not take into account individual qualities and differences

VI. Focus on Empowerment, the Strengths Perspective, and Resiliency

A. Empowerment: The process of increasing personal, interpersonal, or political power so that individuals can take action to improve their life situations

B. Strengths perspective: This orientation focuses on client resources, capabilities, knowledge, abilities, motivations, experience, intelligence, and other positive qualities that can be put to use to solve problems and pursue positive changes

   1. Principles involved in the strengths perspective

      a. Every individual, group, family, and community has strengths

      b. Trauma and abuse, illness and struggle may be injurious, but they may also be sources of challenge and opportunity

        c.   Assume that you do not know the upper limits of the capacity to grow and change, and take individual, group, and community aspirations seriously

        d.   Every environment is full of resources

2.   Multiple sources of strengths: A case example

        a.   Individual strengths

        b.   Family strengths

        c.   Group strengths

        d.   Community strengths

        e.   Natural support network: Also called a helping network, it is a group of people—including family, friends, neighbors, work colleagues, and fellow members in organizations such as churches and other community groups—who informally provide help and support

3.   Individual empowerment

        a.   Highlight 1.4: Assessing Your Strengths

            1)   Individual strengths

            2)   Family strengths

            3)   Group strengths

            4)   Organizational strengths

            5)   Community strengths

4.   Empowerment through groups

5.   Organizational and community empowerment

C.   Resiliency: Using strengths to fight adversity

1.   Resiliency: The ability of an individual, family, group, community, or organization to recover from adversity and resume functioning even when suffering serious trouble, confusion, or hardship

2. Two dimensions of resiliency

    a. Risk—involves stressful life events or adverse environmental conditions that increase the vulnerability of individuals or other systems

    b. Protection—concerns those factors that buffer, moderate, and protect against those vulnerabilities

3. Examples of resiliency at the individual, organizational, and community levels

D. Critical Thinking About Ethical Issues

1. Values: Perceptions and opinions held by individuals, professionals, and cultures about what is good and desirable

2. Ethics: Principles based on values that guide behavior and determine what is right and correct

3. National Association of Social Workers *Code of Ethics* basic ethical principles to guide practitioner's behavior

    a. Social workers' primary goal is to help people in need and to address social problems

    b. Social workers challenge social injustice

    c. Social workers respect the inherent dignity and worth of the person

    d. Social workers recognize the central importance of human relationships

    e. Social workers behave in a trustworthy manner

    f. Social workers practice within their areas of competence and develop and enhance their professional expertise

4. Ethical dilemmas: Situations where ethical principles conflict and all solutions are imperfect

5. Critical thinking: The careful examination and evaluation of beliefs and actions to establish an independent decision about what is true and what is not

6. Ethical decision-making involves critical thinking

E. Highlight 1.5: Application of Values and Ethics to Bio-Psycho-Social System Assessments

1. NASW Code of Ethics' ethical responsibilities

    a. To clients

    b. To colleagues

        c.   In practice settings

        d.   As professionals

        e.   To the social work profession

        f.   To the broader society

   2.   Critical thinking process suggestions

        a.   Put your theoretical and factual knowledge base about human behavior to work

        b.   Identify your own values concerning the issues and then distinguish between your values and professional ethics

        c.   Weigh the pros and cons of each alternative available to you and your client, and then proceed with the alternative you determine is the most positive

F.   Highlight 1.6: Ethics in Social Work at the International Level: Human Rights and Social Justice Issues

   1.   Human rights: The premise that all people regardless of race, culture, or national origin are entitled to basic rights and treatment

   2.   Social justice: The idea that in a perfect world all citizens would have identical rights, protection, opportunities, obligations, and social benefits

   3.   Two international organizations [International Federation of Social Workers (IFSW), and International Association of Schools of Social Work (IASSW)] developed an international social work code of ethics entitled *Ethics in Social Work, Statement of Principles*. It contains five parts

        a.   Preface

        b.   Definition of social work

        c.   International conventions (that refers to various organizations' statements of human rights)

        d.   Principles

        e.   Professional conduct

G.   Concept Summary Box

VII. A Theoretical Approach to Human Behavior and the Social Environment: Ecosystems Theory

A. Ecosystems theory: Systems theory used to describe and analyze people and other living systems and their transactions (fits well with the concept of person-in-environment)

B. Highlight 1.7: A Summary of Some of the Other Theoretical Perspectives Addressed in This Book

C. Understanding key concepts in systems theories

    1. System: A set of elements that are orderly and interrelated to make a functional whole

    2. Boundaries: The borders or margins that separate one entity from another

    3. Subsystem: A secondary or subordinate system that is a component of a larger system

    4. Homeostasis: The tendency for a system to maintain a relatively stable, constant state of balance

    5. Role: The culturally established social behavior and conduct expected of a person in any designated interpersonal relationship

    6. Relationship: A reciprocal, dynamic, interpersonal connection characterized by patterns of emotional exchange, communication, and behavioral interaction

    7. Input: The energy, information, or communication flow received from other systems

    8. Output: The response of a system, after receiving and processing input, that affects other systems in the environment (not to be confused with the term outcome, which refers to a specified variable that is measured for the purpose of evaluation)

    9. Feedback: A special form of input in which a system receives information about its own performance

        a. Negative feedback: The system can choose to correct any deviations or mistakes and return to a more homeostatic state

        b. Positive feedback: A system receives information about what it is doing correctly in order to maintain itself and thrive

    10. Interface: The point where two systems (including individuals, families, groups, organizations, or communities) come into contact or communicate

    11. Differentiation: A system's tendency to move from a more simplified to a more complex existence

12.   Entropy: The tendency of a system to progress toward disorganization, depletion, and death

13.   Negative entropy: The process of a system toward growth and development

14.   Equifinality: The fact that there are many different means to the same end

D.   Applications of systems concepts to a case example of child abuse

    1.   The presenting problem

    2.   The investigation

    3.   The children

    4.   Parental history and current status

    5.   The assessment of human behavior

        a.   Physical indicators of abuse

        b.   Behavioral indicators of abuse

        c.   Family social functioning

    6.   Making connections with available resources

    7.   Commentary

    8.   Ethical question 1.2: When child maltreatment is suspected, should children be allowed to remain in their own home? How much risk of child maltreatment is too much risk? What effect does it have on children to be removed from their home?

VIII.   The Ecological Perspective: Important Concepts

A.   Ecosystems theory tends to place greater emphasis on individuals and individual family systems' functioning within their environments; systems theories can assume a broader perspective such as the dynamics in a social service agency or government

B.   Major terms in the ecological perspective

    1.   Social environment: Involves the conditions, circumstances, and human interactions that encompass human beings

    2.   Transactions: People communicating and interacting with others in their environments

    3.   Energy: The natural power of active involvement between people and their environments

4.   Interface: The exact point at which the interaction between an individual and the environment takes place

5.   Adaptation: The capacity to adjust to surrounding environmental conditions

6.   Coping: A form of adaptation that implies a struggle to overcome problems

7.   Interdependence: The mutual reliance of each person upon every other person

C.   Concept Summary Box: Systems and Ecological Perspective Concepts Prominent in Ecosystems Theory

IX. People's Involvement with Multiple Systems in the Social Environment

A.   Figure 1.3: Human Behavior Involves Multiple Systems

B.   Micro, mezzo, and macro systems

    1.   System: Set of elements that are orderly and interrelated to make a functional whole

    2.   Micro: Individuals

    3.   Mezzo: Small groups, including family, work groups, and other social groups

    4.   Macro: Systems larger than small groups focusing on the social, political, and economic conditions and policies that affect people's overall access to resources and quality of life

C.   Interactions between micro systems and macro systems

    1.   Community: A number of people who have something in common that connects them in some way and that distinguishes them from others

    2.   Organizations: Structured groups of people who come together to work toward some mutual goal and perform established work activities that are divided among various units

    3.   Organizational theory: Specific attempts to understand how organizations function, what improves or impairs the ability of an organization to accomplish its mission, and what motivates people to work toward organizational goals

    4.   Community theory: Involves perspectives on the nature of communities, and how social workers practice within the community context

X. Human Behavior and Community Macro Systems

A.   Community: A number of people with something in common that connects them in some way and that distinguishes them from others

B. Theoretical perspectives on communities

1. Structural perspective—focuses on how individuals fit into their community environment and are linked to those who govern them

2. Three dimensions of communities

   a. Political entities

   b. Power

   c. Geographical organization

3. Sociopsychological perspective—involves how its members feel about themselves and how they interact with one another

   a. Similar concerns and a sense of identity

   b. Sense of well-being

   c. Ethical question 1.3: Was it right that Fabian was allowed to continue to sell his flowers? To what extent were his neighbors' rights violated? What would the best solution have been?

4. Human ecology perspective—considers how the environment affects human development, interaction, and quality of life

   a. Additional ecological concepts that apply to community macro systems

      1) Competition: How community members vie for the use of land and seek an advantage of place for commercial, industrial, institutional, and residential purposes

      2) Segregation: The detachment or isolation of some group having certain common characteristics (such as race, ethnicity, or religion) through social pressure, restrictive laws, or personal choice

      3) Integration: The process of bringing together and blending a range of groups (including people of different races and ethnic backgrounds) into a unified, functional whole

      4) Ethical question 1.4: To what extent is economic inequality fair? Did Doug have the right to vent his anger in such a violent manner? What, if anything, could be done to improve Doug's economic and ecological status?

5. Social systems perspective—the emphasis is on analyzing how the various social subsystems within the community interact with each other

C.   Models of community

    1.   Highlight 1.8: Characteristics of Three Models of Community Planning

    2.   Locality development model (also called community development): This model asserts that social change can best be brought about through broad participation of a wide spectrum of people at the local community level

    3.   Social planning model: This model emphasizes a technical process of problem solving

    4.   Social action model: This model assumes there is a disadvantaged segment of the population that needs to be organized to pressure the power structure for increased resources or more democratic treatment

        a.   Saul Alinsky—well known social activist

        b.   Spotlight on Diversity 1.1: Latino and Hispanic Communities Promote Strengths and Empowerment

            1)   La Raza Unida: A political movement and party, comprising mostly Mexican American people and others of Spanish-speaking heritage, that advocates for policies and candidates favorable to the needs of Hispanic people

            2)   Communidad de Bienestar (community of wellness): A community-sponsored initiative in the middle of the Chicago Puerto Rican community

            3)   Alianza Escolar: A school alliance program in Virginia that seeks to provide educational services that promote learning and encourage youth to stay in school while also assisting parents to participate in their children's education and expand their own potential

            4)   Brief note on terms

                a)   Hispanics—term was introduced in the 1970s and used by the U.S. Census Bureau; however, many people do not accept this label to represent themselves

                b)   Latino—some people prefer this label as more representative of the amalgam of people linked by the Spanish colonial history. Given the extensive diversity among the people grouped under this label, it is preferable to use terms based on national origin

                c)   Latina—used when referring exclusively to women

                d)   Chicano/Chicana has often been used to refer to people of Mexican descent

XI.   Human Behavior in and with Organizational Macro Systems

A.   Social agency: An organization providing social services overseen by a board of directors and usually staffed by various personnel including social workers, members of other professions, paraprofessionals, and clerical staff

B.   The terms social services, human services, and sometimes social welfare are often used interchangeably when referring to organizations, agencies, and agency personnel

C.   What are organizations?

   1.   Social entities that are goal-directed, are designed as deliberately structured and coordinated activity systems, and are linked to the external environment

   2.   Social workers are expected to have expertise in surviving and thriving in organizations

D.   The exceptional problems of social service organizations

   1.   The shifting environment

   2.   Vagueness of process

   3.   Vagueness of goals

      a.   Accountability: A practitioner's responsibility to clients, community, and agency for ethical and effective practice

      b.   Evaluating outcomes of an entire organization or a program are much more difficult than evaluating the outcomes of micro or mezzo interventions

E.   Goal displacement

   1.   Goal displacement: This occurs when an organization continues to function but no longer achieves it goals

   2.   An example of goal displacement

   3.   Systems theory, organization, and goal displacement

XII.   Social Worker Roles in Macro Systems

A.   Enabler: A worker who helps a client cope with various stresses ranging from crisis situations like divorce or job loss to community issues such as inadequate housing or day care

B.   Mediator: A worker who resolves arguments or conflicts among micro, mezzo, or macro systems

C.   Integrator/Coordinator: A generalist social worker can function as an integrator/ coordinator in many ways, ranging from advocacy and identification of coordination opportunities, to provision of technical assistance, to direct involvement in the development and implementation of service linkages

D.   Manager: A worker who has some level of administrative responsibility for a social agency or other unit in order to accomplish various tasks

E.   Educator: A worker who gives information and teaches skills to client and other systems

F.   Analyst/Evaluator: A worker who analyzes how systems function and evaluates how well programs and systems work; in addition, they can evaluate the effectiveness of their own interventions

G.   Broker: A worker who helps link clients (individuals, groups, organizations, or communities) with community resources and services

H.   Facilitator: A worker who guides and directs a group encounter or gathering

I.   Initiator: The person or persons who call attention to an issue

J.   Negotiator: One who represents an organization, a group, or an individual that is trying to gain something from another group or system

K.   Advocate: One who steps forward and speaks on the behalf of the client system

XIII. Summary

Experiential Exercises and Simulations

Four exercises are presented here. The first is an ice-breaker. In the second, you will create a symbolic representation of major positive and negative events in your life. The third pertains to social histories, and the fourth is a writing exercise. Each of the exercises in this manual has the following format: A brief description, a statement of objectives, and procedural instructions.

Exercise 1.1: Introductory Ice-Breaker

A.   Brief Description
In this introductory exercise, you will introduce yourself and share something about yourself with other members of the class.

B.   Objectives
You will:
1.   Express some basic information about yourself.
2.   Practice participating in class activities.
3.   Examine some basic feelings about yourself.

C.   Procedure
1.   Arrange yourselves in a circle to allow for maximum eye contact among all group members.
2.   On an 8" x 5" notecard or a piece of scratch paper, draw six equal divisions and fill in the following information:

Upper Left-hand Corner: Write three adjectives that describe what you like about yourself.

Upper Right-hand Corner: Write three adjectives that describe what you dislike about yourself.

Left Center: State briefly why you are taking this course.

Right Center: State briefly what you expect to be doing five years from now, both personally and professionally.

Lower Left-hand Corner: State briefly what makes you angry.

Lower Right-hand Corner: State briefly what makes you happy.

You have approximately five minutes to jot down this information. You should self-disclose only the information you feel comfortable in sharing.

Exercise 1.2: This Is Your Life

A.   Brief Description
In this exercise, you are asked to create a symbolic representation of major positive and negative events in your life.

B.   Objectives
You will:
1.   Identify normal life events.
2.   Develop a perspective on the types of issues and simulations that will be examined throughout the course.
3.   Examine the effects of various life events and relate them to the ways that similar life events may affect clients.

C.   Procedure
1.   Take a few moments to reflect on the most memorable occasions in your life. Think about the most positive happenings. These may include happy occasions, special activities, awards, achievements, special relationships, or graduations. Then focus on some of the major negative happenings. These might include illnesses, deaths, accidents, job losses, or significant disappointments.
2.   Break into small groups of four to six. You may join any group you wish, but the groups should be the appropriate size.
3.   Share as many of the positive and negative happenings in your life as you choose to. Focus on the effects of these happenings on your life. You will have approximately 10 minutes for the small-group discussion.
4.   After you finish your discussion, have a representative summarize some of the happenings discussed in the group and share them with the entire class.
5.   As a take-home assignment, create a symbolic picture of your life. Incorporate the major positive and negative happenings. Anything you feel is too personal to share should either be excluded from the life picture or stated in vague, general terms. You may be as

creative as you like in illustrating your life. Examples of different types of formats include: a line or bar graph illustrating various highs and lows; a fan that is divided into different life stages and has different colors that portray positive and negative times; a piano keyboard on which the white keys reflect positive times and the dark keys refer to negative ones; a time chart with magazine cut-outs to emphasize various life events.

The projects will not be evaluated for artistic ability but rather on such elements as depth of insight, creativity, amount of detail, and completeness. Regardless of the format, specific information needs to be clearly incorporated.

Exercise 1.3: Social History Assignment

A.   Brief Description
You will select and interview an individual while following an outline that indicates the information you need to solicit. The information reflects the types of information typically gathered by social workers in practice when doing a social history. Social histories reflect the important aspects of an individual's development and help social workers assess the nature of a client's problems.

B.   Objectives
This exercise will enable you to:
1.   Identify those aspects of human development that are important in shaping an individual's life situation and issues.
2.   Recognize the complexity and necessity of assessment in social work practice.
3.   Experience the process of interviewing and recognize the need to develop interviewing skills.

C.   Procedure
1.   Choose a person to interview. This could be a friend, a relative, or an acquaintance. Describe this assignment to the person, and ask the person for permission to do the interview. Feel free to show the person these guidelines or your proposed outline ahead of time. Make it clear that his or her real name will not be used and that the information will be kept confidential. Your instructor will provide additional information regarding how to conduct the interview.

In practice, a social history involves "an in-depth description and assessment of the current and past client situation, often included in the case records and medical records of clients" (Barker, 2003, p. 404). The purpose is not to learn every intimate detail of the client's personal life but rather to gain a generalized understanding of what a client's life is like in addition to gaining more specific information related to the client's problem.

The Social History Outline developed for this assignment is not a complete social history, but only portions of one. There are no sections that relate to problems or to recommendations. This assignment does not focus on a client's problem, because you have neither client nor problem to work with. However, this assignment is designed to give you practice to interview someone, obtain developmental and social information, and summarizing this information in an organized, informative manner.

One requirement of the assignment is to go to the library and do some related research on interviewing techniques. Look for information on what is involved in interviewing and how to do it. Summarize the research and information you reviewed and include it in the "Research Application" section of the paper. Apply this research and information to your own interview where possible. For example, which techniques did you find useful or could you have used? How were they, or might they have been, helpful in your interview situation?

Include a brief <u>bibliography</u> of all your references at the end of the paper.

3. Use the following outline when conducting the interview. Note that, at times, the outline includes specific questions you might want to ask.

This is simply a guideline for you to use. In some cases you might have to ask more questions to get sufficient information. In other cases, the questions may not apply. In these cases, you should state that they don't apply. You should also make it clear when information is unavailable.

SOCIAL HISTORY OUTLINE

I. <u>Basic Data</u>

Client: (Legal name plus nickname)   Date of Birth:

Chronological Age: Race:

Religion: School and Grade:

Place of Employment: (if appropriate)   Address:

Telephone Number:

II. <u>Individual Client Profile</u>

    A. <u>Brief Physical Description of Client—Personality Picture</u>

        1. Describe the person's physical appearance (e.g., tall or short; color of hair). You might include information about dress, posture, and facial expressions.

        2. Mention anything that's striking about the individual.

        3. Describe your impression of the person's personality (e.g., outgoing; soft-spoken; nervous).

        4. Mention specific behaviors, if appropriate, that describe exactly what you mean (e.g., "She seemed nervous, as she constantly fidgeted in her chair and rapped her knuckles on the desk"). This might include information about motor activity, unusual mannerisms, and the client's reactions to you, the interviewer.

        5. Be brief, clear, and specific.

    B. <u>Developmental History Questions</u>

        1. <u>Pregnancy</u>

            a. Was your mother's pregnancy normal; uneventful; problematic?

            b. Describe any problems or unusual circumstances.

---

2. <u>Delivery</u>

    a. Was the delivery normal; routine; difficult/problematic?

    b. Identify difficulties, problems, or unusual circumstances.

    c. Provide APGAR score, if available.

    d. Type of delivery (e.g., vertex; breech).

    e. Were you born at full term or prematurely? If premature, by how many months?

    f. Where were you born?

3. <u>Medical Problems</u>

    a. Did you experience any significant medical problems as a child that were out of the ordinary?

    b. If so, please describe the problems and any treatment you might have received.

4. <u>Developmental Milestones</u>

    a. Sat alone

    b. Walked

    c. First words

    d. Toilet trained

5. <u>Parental Care</u>

    a. Do you think that your parents found it difficult or easy to care for you as a child? Explain.

6. <u>Social/Emotional Aspects</u>

    a. What were your peer relationships like during childhood?

    b. How would you have described yourself as a child (e.g., outgoing; shy; bright)?

    c. What types of play, activities, and hobbies did you participate in as a child?

> d. How would you describe your childhood (e.g., happy; uneventful; turbulent)?
>
> e. Were there any events that occurred during childhood that you feel significantly affected you? If so, describe the events and their effects.

    7. <u>Other</u>

        Is there any other information about your childhood that is important?

C. <u>School History</u>

    1. Schools attended (names, dates, and locations)

    2. Current school status (e.g., high school graduate; college sophomore)

    3. Academic progress in schools (was school difficult for you?)

    4. Attendance

    5. Courses taken

    6. Participation in school-related activities

    7. Peer relationships (e.g., did you have friends in school? Did you feel liked by your classmates?)

    8. Parental involvement with schools

    9. Vocational history (special non-college job training)—type of training, dates, jobs, work record

D. <u>Military Service</u>

If applicable, describe the branch, rank, dates of service, duties, and type of discharge.

E. <u>Employment History</u>

    1. Place, types, and dates of employment

    2. Primary job responsibilities

    3. Likes and dislikes about each job

    4. Attendance record

    5. Are you happy with your current employment? Explain.

F. Current Social/Emotional Elements

1. What are your social relationships like now? Would you say you are the type of person who has many friends or only a select few? Would you call yourself a lonely person?

2. Do you have any special relationships (e.g., girl/boyfriend; spouse)? If so, describe them. If married, elaborate under the following section, "Family History."

3. What are your major interests, activities, and hobbies? Describe them.

4. In summary, how would you describe your overall "fit" into a social context (e.g., generally popular; shy except with close friends)?

G. Self-Description

1. What do you like about yourself? What are your strengths?

2. What do you dislike about yourself?

3. Describe your current fears or worries.

4. What do you see as your personal accomplishments?

5. What is the most difficult thing you've accomplished? Why do you think this is so?

6. Describe the most painful event in your life.

7. What things would you like to change in your life and about yourself?

III. Family History

A. Family of Origin

1. Describe each family member in your family of origin. Include the following information:

a. Relationship and name

b. Date of birth and age

c. Occupation

d. Education

e. Vocation and employment

f. Current marital status

g.   Any major medical/psychological problems

h.   Brief description of physical appearance, personality, and how the person relates to other family members.

2.   Use the following format:

Mother: (continue with above information)

Father:

Sister:

Brother:

Etc.

3.   Family function

a.   What are marriage dates and current status (e.g., married; divorced)?

b.   Describe your parents' relationship.

c.   What types of family planning/birth control did your parents use?

d.   How does each of the other family members feel toward you?

e.   How do you get along with and relate to each of the other family members?

f.   Are there any problems currently operating within the family? Were there any in the past? If so, explain.

g.   Describe the socioeconomic (overall financial/living) conditions of your family now and during your childhood.

h.   Did you have any special care situations during childhood (e.g., adoption; foster care)? If so, when did they occur and what were they like?

i.   Did any significant stressful event occur in your family during your childhood? These might include deaths, domestic violence, drug/alcohol abuse, physical abuse, job loss, or other traumas. If so, explain.

j.   How would you summarize the quality of your family life during your childhood?

k.   Is there anything else about your family life during your childhood that you'd like to add?

4.   Extended family

   a.   Briefly describe all people living or dead who are or were related to you. Include more detail for those relatives who are especially meaningful or significant to you.

   b.   Use the following format:

   Maternal Grandmother:

   Maternal Grandfather:

   Paternal Aunt:

   Etc.

B.   <u>Current Family Relationships</u>

1.   Marital status

   a.   Married, separated, single, widow/widower, divorced

   b.   Length of present marriage

   c.   How would you describe the quality of your present marriage (e.g., bad communication; enjoyable; full of conflict)?

   d.   Were you or your spouse married before?

   e.   If so, what were the dates, lengths of marriages, and reasons for terminating the marriage?

   f.   What are your socioeconomic (overall financial/living) conditions currently like?

2.   Children

   a.   Names

   b.   Ages

   c.   Grade in school

   d.   Brief description of physical appearance and personality

   e.   How would you describe each child's behavior? How easy or difficult is each child to manage?

   f.   Relationships with peers and siblings.

4.   Write a paper that summarizes the information you've gathered. The paper should be typewritten, double-spaced, and eight to twelve pages in length. Use an outline form for topic headings followed by a narrative presentation of information for each heading. Make sure each underlined topic heading is included in your paper.

5.   The following provides an example of what your final social history might look like:

SOCIAL HISTORY EXAMPLE

I.   Basic Data:
Client: Prudence Dill
Nickname: Pickles
Chronological Age: 18
Date of birth: August 31, 1992
Race: Caucasian
Religion: Roman Catholic
School: University of Wisconsin-Madison
Grade: Freshman
Place of Employment: Buster's Burger Palace
Address: 709 Main Street, Apt. 4, Nomansland, Wisconsin
Telephone: (414) 208-0009

II.   Individual Client Profile:

A.   Brief Physical-Personality Picture:

Prudence is a tall, thin, attractive young woman who has an energetic and responsive manner. She seemed interested in the interview and eager to provide information.

B.   Gestation, Delivery, and Post-Natal Period:

Prudence is the third born in a family of five children. To her knowledge, her delivery was without any complications. She had no physical problems at birth or shortly thereafter. As far as she knows her parents had planned for her. Both parents had indicated they always wanted a large family. She felt they were very happy with her when she was born.

C.   Underline{Development:}

1.   Underline{Medical:}

Prudence was a consistently healthy child. She never had any serious diseases, allergies, accidents, or broken bones. She is up-to-date on her immunizations and has no sensory impairments. She avoids engaging in health hazards such as smoking, drugs, or unhealthy eating habits. However, she does engage in some moderate drinking. She lifts weights three times a week in addition to participating in other sports. These sports include wrestling and ice hockey. In summary, Prudence appears to be a healthy individual.

6.   Following are some suggestions you might consider for improving the writing of professional reports such as social histories. They are in no particular order of importance or priority.

Use paragraphs to divide content into different topics/points/issues (avoid one-sentence paragraphs).

Avoid slang. Slang doesn't sound very professional. Don't use "guys." Use "young men" or "boys." Don't use "mom." Use "mother." Don't use "fizzled out." Use "didn't succeed" or something similar.

Avoid using words such as "always," "average," "perfect," or "all." (Who is "average"? Are you? What is perfect? Is someone "always" a happy person even after getting a D- on an exam for this course?)

Avoid sexist language. Use "Ms." instead of "Mrs." Use "woman" instead of "lady." Use "homemaker" or "woman who does not work outside of the home" instead of "housewife." Don't call adult women "girls."

Avoid using acronyms. Some people may not understand them. Spell the term out the first time and put the acronym in parentheses right after it. Thereafter, you can use just the acronym. For example, "The National Association of Social Workers (NASW) is the major professional organization for social work practitioners. NASW is a good organization to join."

Be as concise as possible. Look at a sentence and see if you could use fewer words. Consider dividing giant sentences into two or more smaller ones.

Distinguish between fact and your impression of what's going on. Ways to phrase your impressions include "My impression is . . .," "It appears that . . .," or "It seems that . . .".

Use apostrophes to indicate possession. For example, "Underline{Ronald's} pet monkey is named Bonzo," or "Underline{Freddy's} girlfriend jilted him when he was age 11."

It's shorter to state ages by saying, "Matilda, 108, . . ." instead of "Matilda was a woman who was 108 years old."

Spell correctly.

Avoid labeling people with terms like "low-life dirtball," "Mongoloid," "sleazy," or "abnormal."

Stress confidentiality. Don't use real names in this practice interview. Change some minor facts such as the specific community the person comes from if they are too revealing of her/his identity.

If you take notes during the interview, ask the client's permission first.

When you begin the interview, review its purpose and generally what you plan to do.

Exercise 1.4: Writing Exercise

A.   Brief Description
You will be asked to do a brief role-play in class to practice a portion of the social history. You will then practice a portion of the social history. You will then write up your findings and have a peer critique them.

B.   Objectives
This exercise will enable you to:
1.   Dramatize a portion of an interview through a role-play.
2.   Evaluate a peer's and your own writing.
3.   Employ suggestions to improve your writing.

C.   Procedure
1.   Your instructor will discuss Exercise 1.3, entitled Social History Assignment, and will specify a small portion of the assignment for use during a practice role-play.
2.   Form pairs; one person will be the interviewer and one the interviewee. You will be given 10 minutes to collect and write down as much information as you can. The information should follow the portion of the social history outline that you've been instructed to address. This is to give you the chance to practice how to do your real social history interview. The interviewee should not give truthful information about her- or himself but should make up information to protect confidentiality.
3.   After 10 minutes, exchange roles. The interviewer will now be the interviewee and vice versa. For the next 10 minutes, do the same role-play with your roles reversed.
4.   You will be given another 10 minutes to write down the information you've gathered as if you were writing a real portion of a social history. Try to utilize the good writing suggestions you've been given.
5.   Stop writing after 10 minutes have passed regardless of whether you've finished writing about all of the information. Exchange summaries with your role-play partner. Take another 5 minutes to critique each other's writing. Give constructive criticism regarding (a) writing style (grammar, spelling, clarity), and (b) accuracy of information, professional objectivity. Make suggestions to your partner, if you can, about how s/he might better present the information.
6.   If there is time, your instructor may choose to critique some of the information summaries before the entire class. This may be done either by asking for volunteers, or by collecting all of the paragraphs anonymously and arbitrarily selecting one or two. The instructor will copy the information on the board and ask for constructive feedback from the class during the subsequent discussion.

REFERENCES: Barker, R. L. (2003). *The social work dictionary* (5th ed.). Washington, DC: NASW Press.

Chapter 2
Biological Development in Infancy and Childhood

Study Outline

I.   **A Perspective**

II. **The Dynamics of Human Reproduction**

    A.   Conception: The act of becoming pregnant

        1.   A woman is born with about 400,000 immature eggs

            a.   Ovulation: The ovaries' release of a mature egg into the body cavity near the end of one of the fallopian tubes

            b.   Fimbriae: Fingerlike projections at the end of the fallopian tubes

            c.   Cilia: Fingerlike projections inside the fallopian tubes that move eggs toward the uterus

        2.   Sperm

            a.   Ejaculation: Discharge of semen by the penis

            b.   The typical ejaculate usually contains about 200 million sperm

            c.   Sperm are healthiest during the first 24 hours after ejaculation, although remain viable up to 72 hours

            d.   An egg's peak fertility is within the first 8 to 12 hours after ovulation, although it may remain viable for fertilization up to 24 hours

            e.   As some sperm remain viable up to 5 days after ejaculation, it is possible to become pregnant if intercourse occurs up to 5 days before ovulation

        3.   Fertilization process

            a.   Zygote: Genetic material in the egg and sperm combine to form this single cell

            b.   Blastocyst: Within a week of the zygote cell dividing into more cells, this new mass forms and attaches itself to the lining of the uterus

            c.   Conceptus: Product of conception

            d.   Embryo: Term of the conceptus from the point of attachment until 8 weeks of gestation

            e.   Fetus: Term used from 8 weeks of gestation until birth

B.   Diagnosis of pregnancy

1.   Human Chorionic Gonadotropin (HCG): A hormone secreted by the placenta; most pregnancy tests work by detecting this in a woman's urine or blood

2.   Home pregnancy tests (EPTs)

   a.   Procedure—can be used as early as the first day a menstrual period was supposed to start

   b.   Accuracy—one study found that the majority of HPT brands are up to 85 percent inaccurate if taken on the first day of a missed period; however, most do provide accurate results if taken a week after a missed period

C.   Fetal development during pregnancy

1.   First trimester—sometimes considered the most critical

   a.   Fetal development

      1)   By the end of the first month, a primitive heart and digestive system have developed

      2)   Begins to resemble human form more closely during the second month

      3)   The third month involves the formation of arms, hands, legs, and feet

   b.   Mother's symptoms

      1)   Tiredness, breast enlargement and tenderness, frequent urination, food cravings, and morning sickness

      2)   These are primarily due to the tremendous increase in the amount of hormones her body is producing

2.   Second trimester

   a.   Fetal development

      1)   Toes and fingers separate

      2)   Skin, fingerprints, hair, and eyes develop, and a regular heartbeat emerges

      3)   Begins to sleep and wake at regular times

      4)   Its thumb may be inserted into its mouth

b. Mother's symptoms

    1) Most of the unappealing symptoms occurring during the first trimester subside

    2) More likely to feel the fetus's vigorous movement, and abdomen expands significantly

    3) Some women suffer edema (water retention)

3. Third trimester

    a. Fetal development

        1) Involves the completed development of the fetus

        2) Fatty tissue forms underneath the skin and internal organs complete their development

        3) The brain and nervous system become completely developed

        4) Viability: The ability of the fetus to survive on its own if separated from its mother

        5) Although a fetus reaches viability by about the middle of the second trimester, many infants born at 22-25 weeks do not survive, or if they do many experience chronic health or neurological problems

        6) The viability issues becomes especially critical when referring to abortion

    b. Mother's symptoms

        1) This may be a time of some discomfort—the uterus expands, and the abdomen becomes large and heavy, which may exert pressure on other organs

        2) Some of the weight is from the baby itself, amniotic fluid, and the placenta

D. Prenatal influences

1. Nutrition

2. Drugs and medication

    a. Teratogens: Substances, including drugs, that cause malformation in the fetus (e.g., Thalidomide babies)

    b. Prescription, nonprescription, and street

        c.   Caffeine

        d.   Drug addiction

        e.   Ethical Question 2.1: Should a pregnant woman who consumes illegal drugs that damage her child be punished as a criminal? Should her child be taken from her? If so, with whom should the child be placed?

   3.   Alcohol

        a.   Fetal Alcohol Syndrome: Alcohol consumption during pregnancy that produces grave effects on a fetus

        b.   Fetal alcohol effects: Condition that manifests relatively less severe problems, presumably resulting from lower levels of alcohol consumption during pregnancy

   4.   Smoking—including secondhand smoke

   5.   Age

        a.   Women between ages 16 and 35 tend to provide a better uterine environment for the developing fetus and to give birth with fewer complications than do women under 16 or over 35

        b.   Down Syndrome: A congenital condition resulting from a chromosomal abnormality

        c.   Teen mothers account for slightly over 10 percent of all U.S. births, and are more likely to experience premature births and stillbirths than are other mothers

   6.   Other factors

        a.   Income and socio-economic class

        b.   Illness during pregnancy

        c.   Sexually transmitted infections, including AIDS

E.   Prenatal assessment

   1.   Ultrasonography (ultrasound): It uses high frequency sound waves to produce the image of a fetus on a television-like screen

        a.   The most common method of fetal diagnosis

        b.   Test can be performed as early as the fifth week of pregnancy, and can determine the fetus's gender, its position in the uterus, any gross physical abnormalities

2. Amniocentesis: Involves the surgical insertion of a needle through the abdominal wall and into the uterus to obtain amniotic fluid for determination of fetal gender or chromosomal abnormalities

    a. Muscular dystrophy: A group of hereditary diseases characterized by progressive wasting of muscles

    b. Spina bifida: A condition in which the spinal column has not fused shut and, consequently, some nerves remain exposed

    c. Recommended for women who:

        1) Are over 35

        2) Are genetic carriers of defects

        3) Have already given birth to child with defects

    d. Disadvantage—the test is usually performed between 15 and 20 weeks of pregnancy, results take 2 to 3 weeks, and, if a serious problem is discovered, people don't have much time to decide whether to terminate the pregnancy

3. Chorionic villi sampling (CVS): Insertion of a thin plastic tube or a needle through the abdomen into the uterus to obtain samples of chorionic villi to analyze potential genetic irregularities

    a. Chorionic villi: Tiny fingerlike projections on the membrane that surrounds the fetus

    b. Advantages—It can be performed by the eighth or ninth week of pregnancy, and results can be obtained within 24 hours

    c. Disadvantages—There is an increased risk of miscarriage

4. Maternal blood tests

    a. Done between the fifteenth to twentieth weeks of gestation

    b. Alpha-feto protein (AFP) can be measured

5. Fetoscopy: A procedure usually performed after the 16th week, in which a tiny instrument called a fetoscope is inserted into the amniotic cavity, making it possible to see the fetus

F. Highlight 2.1: Access to Prenatal Care: Obstacles in the Macro Environment

G. Problem pregnancies

1. Ectopic pregnancy (tubal pregnancy): This occurs when a fertilized egg begins to develop somewhere other than in the uterus, in most cases in the fallopian tube

2. Toxemia (preeclampsia): An abnormal condition involving a form of blood poisoning

    a. In the last 2 to 3 months of pregnancy, 6% to 7% of women experience this

    b. Eclampsia: If toxemia is allowed to progress, it can result in this, which involves convulsions, coma, and, in approximately 15% of cases, death

    c. Eclampsia is a leading cause of maternal and fetal death in the U.S. today (African American women are at higher risk)

3. Rh incompatibility: This occurs when the mother has Rh+ blood and the fetus has Rh-, the consequence to an affected fetus can be cognitive disability, anemia, or death

4. Spontaneous abortion (miscarriage): The termination of a pregnancy due to natural causes before the fetus is capable of surviving on its own

5. Concept Summary Box: Problem Pregnancies

H. The birth process

1. Causes of labor

    a. Prostaglandins: Chemical substances that appear to stimulate the uterine muscles thereby causing contractions

    b. Oxytocin: A substance released by the pituitary gland late in pregnancy, apparently causes the powerful uterine contractions late in the birth process that are necessary to expel or push out the fetus

2. Indications of labor

    a. First, there is usually a small bloody discharge of mucus

    b. Second, the bag of water that acts as a cushion to protect the fetus is released in varying amounts from a trickle to a gush

    c. Third, the beginning of uterine contractions, initially about 10 to 20 minutes apart

    d. Braxton-Hicks contractions (false labor): Unlike in true labor, they occur very irregularly and frequently far apart, there is no hardening of the abdominal muscles in preparation for the birth

3. Stages of labor

    a. First stage: Dilation—the cervix is dilated in preparation for the baby to pass through it. Contractions begin

b.   Second stage: Expulsion marks the time when the baby is actually born

         1)   Begins when contractions are about 2 to 3 minutes apart and last for about 60 to 70 seconds each

         2)   Episiotomy: Involves making a small incision in the skin just behind the vagina, to relieve pressure on the strained tissues and help to provide a larger opening through which the baby can emerge. Many women question the necessity of this procedure

c.   Third stage: Afterbirth—the placenta and other fetal material making up the afterbirth detaches itself from the uterine walls and is expelled

4.   Birth positions

a.   Vertex presentation: Babies are born with their heads emerging first (95 percent of babies are born in this position)

b.   Breech presentation: The buttocks and feet appear first and the head last

c.   Transverse presentation: The baby lies crossways in the uterus (either the baby must be turned during labor, or a Cesarean section must be performed)

d.   Cesarean section: A surgical procedure in which the baby is removed by making an incision in the abdomen through the uterus

e.   Figure 2.1 Forms of Birth Presentation

5.   Natural childbirth—the emphasis is on education for the parents. The intent is to maximize her understanding of the process and to minimize her fear of the unknown. The Lamaze method is currently popular in the United States

6.   Newborn assessment

a.   Apgar scale—evaluation of signs usually occurs twice, at 1 minute and at 5 minutes after birth. A maximum score of 10 is possible

         1)   Heart rate (ranging from no heart rate to at least 100 beats per minute)

         2)   Respiration (ranging from not breathing to normal breathing and crying)

         3)   Reflex response (ranging from no response while the airways are being suctioned to active grimacing, pulling away, and coughing)

         4)   Muscle tone (ranging from limpness to active motion)

         5)   Skin color (ranging from bluish-gray to good color everywhere)

b. Brazelton Neonatal Behavioral Assessment Scale: Assesses the functioning of the central nervous system and behavioral responses of a newborn

    1) Usually administered 24 to 36 hours after birth

    2) Includes a range of 28 behavioral items and 18 reflex items

7. Birth defects—refer to any kind of disfigurement or abnormality present at birth

a. Miscarriage—Provides a means for the body to prevent seriously impaired or abnormal births

b. Down syndrome: A disorder involving an extra chromosome that results in various degrees of cognitive disability

c. Spina bifida: A condition in which the spinal column has not fused shut and consequently some nerves remain exposed

d. Hydrocephalus: This frequently occurs along with spina bifida. An abnormal amount of spinal fluid accumulates in the skull, possibly resulting in skull enlargement and brain atrophy

8. Low birth weight and preterm infants

a. Low birth weight is defined as 5 pounds 8 ounces or less

b. Very low birth weight is defined as newborns weighing 3 pounds 5 ounces or less

c. Approximately 7.6 percent of babies born in the U.S. have low birth weight

d. Causes include certain fetal defects, being part of a multiple-birth scenario, prematurity, and the pregnant mother's behavior and experience

e. Preterm or premature babies born before the 38th week of gestation often experience low birth weight

f. Full-term pregnancy is considered to last between 37 and 42 weeks, with most being born at about 40 weeks

g. The lower the birth weight, the greater the potential for developmental delays and long-term disabilities

h. Low birth weight children are more likely to experience a learning disability or breathing problems

i. Social work roles used to help pregnant women bear healthy infants might include broker, educator, and/or counselor

9. Other factors at birth affecting the neonate

    a. Phenylketonuria (PKU): Genetic condition where a neonate is unable to metabolize milk properly

    b. Anoxia: Deprivation or absence of oxygen during birth

III. Early Functioning of the Neonate

A. The average full-term newborn weighs about 7½ pounds and is approximately 20 inches long

B. Reflexes that characterize newborns

    1. Sucking response: Facilitates babies' ability to take in food

    2. Rooting reflex: Automatic movement toward a stimulus

    3. Moro's reflex (startle response): When infants hear a sudden loud noise, they will automatically react by extending their arms and legs, spreading their fingers, and throwing their heads back. It seems to disappear after a few months of life

    4. Stepping reflex: Involves infants' natural tendency to lift a leg when held in an upright position with feet barely touching a surface

    5. Grasping reflex: Refers to a newborn's tendency to grasp and hold objects such as sticks or fingers when placed in the palms of their hands

    6. Babinski reflex: Involves the stretching, fanning movement of the toes whenever the infant is stroked on the bottom of his or her feet

    7. Swimming reflex: Involves infants making swimming motions when they're placed face down in water

    8. Tonic neck reflex (fencer pose): The infant's turning of the head to one side when laid down on its back, the extension of the arm and leg on the side its facing, and the flexing of the opposite limbs

IV. Developmental Milestones

A. Human development: The continuous process of growth and change involving physical, mental, emotional, and social characteristics that occur over a lifespan

B. Growth as a continuous, orderly process

    1. Growth always follows a pattern from simple to complex

    2. Aspects of development progress from more general to being more specific

3. Cephalocaudal development: Refers to the development from the head to the toes (that is, infants begin to learn how to use the parts of their upper body such as the head and arms before their legs)

4. Proximodistal development: Refers to the tendency to develop aspects of the body trunk first and then later master manipulation of the body extremities

C. Specific characteristics of different age levels—capabilities tend to be similar for all people within any particular age category

D. Individual differences—although people tend to develop certain capacities in a specified order, the ages at which particular individuals master certain skills may show a wide variation

E. Nature-nurture controversy: Involves how much the environment affects development compared to how much development is affected by heredity

F. Relevance to social work—in order to assess human needs and human behavior accurately, the social worker must know what is considered normal or appropriate

G. Profiles of normal development for children ages 4 months to 11 years

1. Age four months

a. Motor: Are able to balance their heads at a 90-degree angle, and can lift their heads and chests when placed on their stomachs in a prone position. They frequently watch their hands, keep their fingers busy, and place objects in their mouths

b. Adaptive: Are able to recognize their bottles and often this stimulates bodily activity. Sometimes teething begins, although the average age is closer to 6 or 7 months

c. Social: Are able to recognize their mothers and other familiar faces. They imitate smiles and often respond to familiar people by reaching, smiling, laughing, or squirming

d. Language: Will turn his/her head when a sound is heard. Verbalizations include gurgling, babbling, and cooing

2. Age eight months

a. Motor: Are able to sit alone without being supported. They can stand by pulling themselves up on a chair or crib. They can reach for an object and pick it up with all their fingers and a thumb. Crawling efforts have begun. These babies can usually begin creeping on all fours, displaying greater strength in one leg than the other

b. Play: The baby is capable of banging two toys together. Many can also pass an object from one hand to the other. These babies can imitate arm movements such as splashing in a tub, shaking a rattle, or crumpling paper

c. Adaptive: Can feed themselves pieces of toast or crackers. They will be able to munch instead of being limited to sucking

d. Social: Can begin imitating facial expressions and gestures. They can play "pat-a-cake," "peek-a-boo," and wave "bye-bye"

e. Language: Babbling becomes frequent and complex. Most babies will be able to attempt copying the verbal sounds they hear. Many can say a few words or sounds such as "mama" or "dada." However, they don't yet understand the meaning of words

3. Age one year

a. Motor: Most babies can crawl well. Although they usually require support to walk, they can stand alone without holding on to anything. They can open drawers, undo latches, etc.

b. Play: Like to examine toys and objects both visually and by touching them. Objects are frequently dropped and picked up again one time after another. Babies this age like to put objects in and out of containers

c. Adaptive: Because of their mobility, 1-year-olds need careful supervision. Parents need to scrutinize their homes and make them as safe as possible. Babies are able to drink from a cup. They can feed themselves with their fingers. They begin to cooperate while being dressed by holding still or by extending an arm or a leg. Regularity of both bowel and bladder control begins

d. Social: Are becoming more aware of the reactions of those around them. They often vary their behavior in response to these reactions. They enjoy having an audience. They will tend to repeat behaviors that are laughed at. They will also seek attention by squealing or making noises

e. Language: Begin to pay careful attention to the sounds they hear. They can understand simple commands. They begin to express choices about the type of food they will accept or about whether it is time to go to bed or not. They are imitating sounds more frequently and can meaningfully use a few other words in addition to "mama" and "dada"

4. Age eighteen months

a. Motor: A baby can walk. Although these children are beginning to run, their movements are still awkward and result in frequent falls. Walking up stairs can be accomplished by a caregiver holding the baby's hand. These babies can often descend stairs by themselves but only by crawling down backwards or by sliding down by sitting first on one step and then another. They are also able to push large objects and pull toys

b. Play: Like to scribble with crayons and build with blocks. However, it is difficult for them to place even three or four blocks on top of each other. Dolls or stuffed animals frequently are carried about as regular companions. These toys are often shown affection such as hugging. Babies begin to imitate some of the simple things that adults do such as turning pages of a book

c. Adaptive: Ability to feed themselves is much improved by age 18 months. These babies can hold their own glasses to drink from, usually using both hands. They are able to use a spoon sufficiently to feed themselves

d. Social: Children function at the solitary level of play. It is normal for them to be aware of other children and even enjoy having them around; however, they don't play with other children

e. Language: Children's vocabularies consist of more than three but less than fifty words. These words usually refer to people, objects, or activities with which they are familiar. They frequently chatter using meaningless sounds as if they were really talking like adults. They can understand language to some extent. For instance, children will often be able to respond to directives or questions such as "Give Mommy a kiss," or "Would you like a cookie?"

5. Age two years

a. Motor: Can walk and run quite well. They also can often master balancing briefly on one foot and throwing a ball in an overhead manner. They can use the stairs themselves by taking one step at a time and by placing both feet on each step. They are also capable of turning pages of a book and stringing large beads

b. Play: Very interested in exploring their world. They can stack up to six or seven blocks. They like to play with and push large objects such as wagons and walkers. They also enjoy exploring the texture and form of materials such as sand, water, and clay. Adults' daily activities such as cooking, carpentry, or cleaning are frequently imitated. They also enjoy looking at books and can name common pictures

c. Adaptive: Begin to be capable of listening to and following directions. They can assist in dressing rather than merely cooperating. They may at least try to button their clothes, although they are unlikely to be successful. They attempt washing their hands. A small glass can be held and used with one hand. They use spoons to feed themselves fairly well. Two-year-olds have usually attained daytime bowel and bladder control with only occasional accidents. Nighttime control is improving but still not complete

d.   Social: Play alongside each other, but not with each other in a cooperative fashion. They are becoming more and more aware of the feelings and reactions of adults. They begin to seek adult approval for correct behavior. They also begin to show their emotions in the forms of affection, guilt, or pity. They tend to have mastered the concept of saying "No," and use it frequently

e.   Language: Can usually put two or three words together to express an idea. Their vocabulary usually includes more than fifty words. Over the next few months, new vocabulary will steadily increase into hundreds of words. They can identify common facial features such as eyes, ears, nose, and so on. Simple directions and requests are usually understood. Although 2-year-olds cannot yet carry on conversations with other people, they frequently talk to themselves or to their toys. It's common to hear them ask "What's this?" in their eagerness to learn the names of things. They also like to listen to simple stories, especially those with which they are very familiar

6.   Age three years

a.   Motor: Can walk well and also run at a steady gait. They can stop quickly and turn corners without falling. They can go up and down stairs using alternating feet. They can begin to ride a tricycle. Three-year-olds participate in a lot of physically active activities such as swinging, climbing, and sliding

b.   Play: Begin to develop their imagination. They use books creatively such as making them into fences or streets. They like to push toys such as trains or cars in make-believe activities. When given the opportunity and interesting toys and materials, they can initiate their own play activities. They also like to imitate the activities of others, especially those of adults. They can cut with scissors and can make some controlled markings with crayons

c.   Adaptive: Can actively help in dressing. They can put on simple items of clothing such as pants or a sweater, although their clothes may turn out backwards or inside out. They begin to try buttoning and unbuttoning their own clothes. They eat well by using a spoon and have little spilling. They also begin to use a fork. They can get their own glass of water from a faucet and pour liquid from a small pitcher. They can wash their hands and face by themselves with minor help. They can use the toilet by themselves, although they frequently ask someone to go with them. They need only minor help with wiping. Accidents are rare, usually happening only occasionally at night

d. Social: Tend to pay close attention to the adults around them and are eager to please. They attempt to follow directions and are responsive to approval or disapproval. They also can be reasoned with at this age. They begin to develop their capacity to relate to and communicate with others. The play is still focused on the parallel level where their interest is concentrated primarily on their own activities. However, they are beginning to notice what other children are doing. Some cooperation is initiated in the form of taking turns or verbally settling arguments

e. Language: Can use sentences that are longer and more complex. Plurals, personal pronouns such as "I," and prepositions such as "above" or "on" are used appropriately. Children are able to express their feelings and ideas fairly well. They are capable of relating a story. They listen fairly well and are very interested in longer, more complicated stories than they were at an earlier age. They also have mastered a substantial amount of information including their last name, their gender, and a few rhymes

7. Age four years

a. Motor: Tend to be very active physically. They enjoy running, skipping, jumping, and performing stunts. They are capable of racing up and down stairs. Their balance is very good, and they can carry a glass of liquid without spilling it

b. Play: Have become increasingly more creative and imaginative. They like to construct things out of clay, sand, or blocks. They enjoy using costumes and other pretend materials. They can play cooperatively with other children. Simple figures can be drawn, although they are frequently inaccurate and without much detail. Four-year-olds can also cut or trace along a line fairly accurately

c. Adaptive: Tend to be very assertive. They usually can dress themselves. They've mastered the use of buttons and zippers. They can put on and lace their own shoes, although they cannot yet tie them. They can wash their hands without supervision. They demand less attention while eating with their family. They can serve themselves food and eat by themselves using both spoon and fork. They can even assist in setting the table. Four-year-olds can use the bathroom by themselves, although they still alert adults of this and sometimes need assistance in wiping. They usually can sleep through the night without having any accidents

d. Social: Are less docile than 3-year-olds. They are less likely to conform, in addition to being less responsive to the pleasure or displeasure of adults. Four-year-olds are in the process of separating from their parents and begin to prefer the company of other children over adults. They are often social and talkative. They are very interested in the world around them and frequently ask "what," "why," and "how" questions

e. Language: The aggressiveness manifested by 4-year-olds also appears in their language. They frequently brag and boast about themselves. Name calling is common. Their vocabulary has experienced tremendous growth; however, they have a tendency to misuse words and some difficulty with proper grammar. Four-year-olds talk a lot and like to carry on long conversations with others. Their speech is usually very understandable with only a few remnants of earlier, more infantile speech remaining. Their growing imagination also affects their speech. They like to tell stories and frequently mix facts with make-believe

8. Age five years

a. Motor: Are quieter and less active than 4-year-olds. Their activities tend to be more complicated and more directed toward achieving some goal. For example, they are more adept at climbing and at riding a tricycle. They can also use roller skates, jump rope, skip, and succeed at other such complex activities. Their ability to concentrate is also increased. The pictures they draw, although simple, are finally recognizable. Dominance of the left or right hand becomes well established

b. Play: Games and play activities have become both more elaborate and competitive. Games include hide-and-seek, tag, and hopscotch. Team playing begins. Five-year-olds enjoy pretend games of a more elaborate nature. They like to build houses and forts with blocks and to participate in more dramatic play such as playing house or being a space invader. Singing songs, dancing, and playing records are usually very enjoyable

c. Adaptive: Can dress and undress themselves quite well. Assistance is necessary only for adjusting more complicated fasteners and tying shoes. These children can feed themselves and attend to their own toilet needs. They can even visit the neighborhood by themselves, needing help only in crossing streets

d. Social: Have usually learned to cooperate with others in activities and enjoy group activities. They acknowledge the rights of others and are better able to respond to adult supervision. They have become aware of rules and are interested in conforming to them. They tend to enjoy family activities such as outings and trips

e. Language: Continue to develop and become more complex. Vocabulary continues to increase. Sentence structure becomes more complicated and more accurate. They are very interested in what words mean. They like to look at books and have people read to them. They have begun learning how to count and can recognize colors. Attempts at drawing numbers and letters are begun, although fine motor coordination is not yet well enough developed for great accuracy

9. Ages six to eight years

   a. Motor: Are physically independent. They can run, jump, and balance well. They continue to participate in a variety of activities to help refine their coordination and motor skills. They often enjoy unusual and challenging activities, such as walking on fences, which help to develop such skills

   b. Play: Participate in much active play such as kickball. They like activities such as gymnastics and enjoy trying to perform physical stunts. They also begin to develop intense interest in simple games such as marbles or tiddlywinks and collecting items. Playing with dolls is at its height. Acting out dramatizations becomes very important, and these children love to pretend they are animals, horseback riders, or jet pilots

   c. Adaptive: Much more self-sufficient and independent, these children can dress themselves, go to bed alone, and get up by themselves during the night to go to the bathroom. They can begin to be trusted with an allowance. They are able to go to school or to friends' homes alone. In general, they become increasingly more interested in and understanding of various social situations

   d. Social: In view of their increasing social skills, they consider playing skills within their peer group increasingly important. They become more and more adept at social skills. Their lives begin to focus around the school and activities with friends. They are becoming more sensitive to reactions of those around them, especially those of their parents. There is some tendency to react negatively when subjected to pressure or criticism; for instance, they may sulk

   e. Language: Continue to become more refined and sophisticated. Good pronunciation and grammar are developed according to that which they've been exposed to. They are learning how to put their feelings and thoughts into words to express themselves more clearly. They begin to understand more abstract words and forms of language. They also begin to develop reading, writing, and numerical skills

10. Ages nine to eleven years

   a. Motor: Continue to refine and develop their coordination and motor skills. They experience a gradual, steady gain in body measurements and proportion. Manual dexterity, posture, strength, and balance improve. This period of late childhood is transitional to the major changes experienced during adolescence

   b. Play: Frequently becomes the finale of the games and play of childhood. If it has not already occurred, boys and girls separate into their respective same-gender groups

c. Adaptive: Become more and more aware of themselves and the world around them. They experience a gradual change from identifying primarily with adults to formulating their own self identity. They become more independent. This is a period of both physical and mental growth. These children push themselves into experiencing new things and new activities. They learn to focus on detail and accomplish increasingly difficult intellectual and academic tasks

d. Social: The focus of attention shifts from a family orientation to a peer orientation. They continue developing social competence. Friends become very important

e. Language: A tremendous increase in vocabulary occurs. These children become adept at the use of words. They can answer questions with more depth of insight. They understand more abstract concepts and use words more precisely. They are also better able to understand and examine verbal and mathematical relationships

H. A concluding note: the developmental milestones provide a general baseline for assessment and subsequent intervention decisions

V. Significant Issues and Life Events

VI. The Abortion Controversy: Impacts of Social and Economic Forces

A. Highlight 2.2: Case Example: Single and Pregnant

B. Functioning within mezzo and macro environments

C. National Association of Social Workers (NASW) policy statement is based on the principle of self-determination

1. Every individual (within the context of his or her value system) must be free to participate or not participate in abortion, family planning, and other reproductive health services

2. Opposes government restrictions on access to reproductive health services

3. Opposes any special conditions and requirements, such as mandatory counseling or waiting periods, attached to the receipt of any type of reproductive health care

D. The impacts of macro system policies on practice and access to services

1. Anti-abortion belief is that human life, and therefore personhood, begins at conception, and so an embryo, at any stage of development, is a person. Therefore abortion is murder, and the government should make all abortions illegal

2. Pro-choice advocates focus on a woman's right to choose whether to have an abortion. A woman has the right to control what happens to her own body, to navigate her own life, and to pursue her own current and future happiness

3. Political controversy

a. *Roe v. Wade*, 1973—U.S. Supreme Court overruled state laws that prohibited or restricted a woman's right to obtain an abortion during the first 3 months of pregnancy. States were allowed to impose restrictions in the second trimester only when such restrictions related directly to the mother's health. States could forbid abortions during the third trimester, excluding those necessary to preserve a woman's life and health

b. *Harris v. McRae*, 1980—The court confirmed that both Congress and individual states could legally refuse to pay for abortions. This significantly affected poor women

c. *Webster v. Reproductive Health Services*, 1989—The Supreme Court upheld a restrictive Missouri law prohibiting abortions in public hospitals unless the mother's life is in danger, forbidding spending state funds for counseling women about abortion; and required doctors to add an expensive layer of testing before performing abortions after twenty weeks

d. *Planned Parenthood v. Cosey*, 1992—The Supreme Court ruled that states had the right to restrict abortions as they saw fit, except that they could not outlaw all abortions

e. Unborn Victims of Violence Act, 2004—President Bush signed this into law which gives legal status or personhood to a fetus hurt or killed when a federal crime is committed. Some consider this a back-door attack on reproductive rights

f. Child Custody Protection Act—under debate which would criminalize an adult who accompanies a young woman seeking an abortion out-of-state if the home state's rules for parental consent have not been meet

g. Most states require minors to notify or obtain permission from an adult, usually a parent, before obtaining an abortion

h. Spotlight on Diversity 2.1: International Perspectives on Abortion Policy

1) Brazil—About 30% of all pregnancies end in abortion, which is illegal

2) Egypt—Abortion is illegal unless the woman's life is in danger, although they are performed surreptitiously in private Cairo clinics

3) France—The national health care system pays for abortions in government-approved clinics for any reason up to the tenth week of pregnancy

4) Great Britain—Women seeking abortions must be authorized by two physicians; abortion was legalized in 1967 and is no longer a major political dispute

5)   Ireland—Although abortion is illegal, thousands of women go to other countries each year for the procedure

6)   Japan—Abortions are usually legal up to 22 weeks of gestation, the husband's or partner's consent is usually necessary

7)   Latin America—Abortion is illegal in all countries but Barbados and Cuba

8)   Latvia—Abortion is the primary form of birth control

9)   Poland—Abortions were deemed illegal in 1992, since then self-induced abortions have become rampant

10)   Russia—Abortions are legal and used to terminate about two-thirds of pregnancies. Typically, Russian women will have a number of abortions over their lifetimes

11)   Turkey—Any woman can have an abortion up to the tenth week of gestation

4.   Restricting access

    a.   Enacting mandatory delays before an abortion can be performed

    b.   Requiring women to receive negative material on abortion or counseling prior to the abortion

    c.   Requiring teenagers to either notify one or both parents or receive consent from one or both parents

    d.   Restrictions on military personnel

5.   Limiting financial support

    a.   Only 16 states provide Medicaid funding for all medically necessary abortions

    b.   The Hyde Amendment in 1977 abolished federal funding for abortion unless a woman's life was in danger

    c.   Since 1993, Medicaid can fund an abortion only in the case of rape, incest, or a life-threatening situation, even when a woman's health is jeopardized by her pregnancy to the extent that it will leave her incapacitated

    d.   Gag rule—banning federal funding to agencies that allow staff to talk to pregnant women about abortion as an alternative

    e.   Four states forbid private insurance plans from covering abortion

6. Condition of the mother

7. Fetal condition

8. Ethical Question 2.2: What are your personal views about abortion? Under what, if any, circumstances do you think it might be performed?

9. Declining number of abortion facilities

    a. Seventy-one percent of abortions are performed in abortion clinics instead of hospitals or physicians' offices

    b. Number of abortions performed in hospitals or physicians' offices has sharply declined

    c. Anti-choice harassment and violence are significant factors in discouraging medical personnel from performing abortions

    d. Fewer than half (46%) of residency training programs in obstetrics and gynecology routinely provide training in first-trimester abortions

10. Violence against clinics

    a. Highlight 2.3: Violence against Abortion Clinics and Staff

        1) Eric Rudolph—bombing of abortion clinics, the 1997 bombing of a lesbian nightclub, and the attack at the Centennial Olympic Park during the 1996 Olympics

        2) The Nuremberg Files—a website listing abortion providers, and drawing a line through the names of those who have been killed; comparing them to Nazi war criminals

    b. *Madsen et al. v. Women's Health Center, Inc.* (1994)—The Supreme Court allowed a buffer zone around clinics to permit patients and employees access and to control noise around the premises

    c. Freedom of Access to Clinic Entrances (FACE) Act made it a federal crime to block access, harass, or incite violence in the context of abortion services

11. Stem cell research

    a. Stem cells are cells extracted from embryos created for fertility treatments but not used to produce children

    b. Fetal cells in contrast to mature adult cells keep growing rapidly after being transplanted and have a talent for secreting a cocktail of chemicals that help restore and replace damaged tissue

    c. Potential for using stem cells to combat spinal cord injuries, Parkinson's disease, juvenile diabetes, heart disease, and Alzheimer's disease

d. Religious conservatives argue that using those stem cells means deriving benefit from the destruction of human embryos

e. Federal funding is provided only for research on the existing stem cell lines that have already been harvested or prepared for use

f. Therapeutic cloning (nuclear transfer)—The process of extracting an egg from a woman's ovary, hollowing it out, and fusing it with a nucleus from a patient's own DNA

g. Ethical Question 2.3: What is your opinion about using stem cells for research? Should the possibility of helping many seriously ill people through stem cell research be pursued? Or is an embryo several days old a human being that should be respected as such? How do you feel about embryonic tissue that is discarded after use at fertility clinics?

12. Partial-birth abortion

a. President Bush signed into law the first ban on a specific abortion procedure called intact dilation and extraction. Opponents refer to it as partial-birth abortion

b. This law was passed even though in June 2000 the U.S. Supreme Court in *Stenberg v. Carhart* struck down a Nebraska law that banned partial-birth abortions because it denied women their constitutional right to have an abortion

c. Eighty-eight percent of abortions are performed by the 12th week of gestation (58% are performed at less than 9 weeks)

d. Only 12 percent of abortions are performed at week 14 or beyond (fewer than 2% of them are performed 21 weeks or after)

e. Commentary—Social workers need to understand the issues and the context in which opposing views are raised in order to help clients make difficult decisions

E. Incidence of abortion

1. Table 2.1: Facts About Women Having Abortions

2. One-third of all abortions were performed for women age 20 to 24

3. The largest number of women having abortions (41 percent) had not had any children

4. The majority had had no previous abortions (53 percent)

5. Eighty-one percent of women having abortions were single

6. Eighty-eight percent lived in metropolitan versus rural areas

7.	African-American women are more than three times as likely as white women to have an abortion, and Hispanic women are almost twice as likely

8.	Women who report no religious affiliation are more than four times as likely to obtain an abortion as other women

F.	Reasons for abortion

1.	Three-quarters say that having a baby would interfere with their work, education, or other responsibilities

2.	Approximately two-thirds say they cannot afford a child

3.	Half say they do not want to be a single parent or are having problems with their husband or partner

4.	Approximately 14,000 abortions occur because women have become pregnant as a result of having been raped

G.	Methods of abortion

1.	Vacuum aspiration (vacuum curettage or vacuum suction)

a.	A procedure used up to 12 weeks into a pregnancy

b.	Cervical entrance is enlarged and the contents of the uterus are evacuated through a suction tube

c.	Curettage is sometimes used afterward which involves scraping with a curette (a small, spoon-shaped instrument)

d.	This procedure is considered very safe and rarely has complications

2.	Medical abortion (an abortion induced by taking certain drugs)

a.	Mifepristone (RU 486)

1)	It was approved by the U.S. Federal Drug Administration for use as an abortion drug in 2000

2)	The process involves taking three mifepristone pills and then taking a dose of misoprostol (a prostaglandin that triggers uterine contractions)

3)	The uterine lining will break down, which makes it unable to support a fetus, then causes uterine contractions that expel the fetus

4)	Most women abort within four hours of taking misoprostol, and 95 percent expel the fetus within a week

          5)   The pregnancy is successfully terminated 92 percent of the time

          6)   This is used effectively up to 7 weeks after the last menstrual period

    b.   Methotrexate

          1)   This drug blocks production of the hormone progesterone and thereby prohibits embryonic cell division and subsequent development

          2)   It should be administered within 7 weeks after the last menstrual period

          3)   The woman usually gets an injection (although it can be taken orally), then takes misoprostol a few days later to cause uterine contractions and expulsion of the fetus

          4)   Abortion usually occurs within 2 weeks for 80 to 85 percent of women

          5)   This drug was initially approved for treating cancer and is also used to treat psoriasis and rheumatoid arthritis

3.   Dilation and Evacuation (D & E)

    a.   Second trimester abortions are more complicated and involve greater risks

    b.   D & Es are used during the fourth and fifth months of pregnancy

    c.   Similar to vacuum aspiration, however more fetal material needs to be removed

    d.   General anesthesia is used instead of local

4.   Intact Dilation and Evacuation (referred to as late-term abortion or partial-birth abortion)

    a.   This is performed during the third trimester or sometimes during the late second trimester

    b.   It is reserved for situations when serious health risks to the woman or severe fetal abnormalities exist

    c.   The cervix is dilated, the fetus emerges feet first out of the uterus, and the fetal skull is collapsed to permit passage of the head through the cervix and vagina

    d.   This accounts for fewer than 1 percent of all abortions in the U.S.

5. Illegal abortion

    a. Approximately 25 percent of women around the world are residents of countries that prohibit abortion

    b. Each year 80,000 women die from dangerous illegal abortions

H. Importance of context and timing

    1. The risk of dying from an abortion is between 0.4 and 1 in 100,000

    2. Major physical complications are uncommon, occurring in fewer than 1 percent of all abortions

    3. There is no relationship between abortion and breast cancer

I. Spotlight on Diversity 2.2: Effects of Abortion on Women and Men

    1. Most women experience no long-term psychological effects

    2. Many men experience a sense of powerlessness and feelings of residual guilt, sadness, and remorse, and many clinics now provide counseling for male partners

    3. Both partners should receive the counseling they need to make the decisions

J. Arguments for and against abortion

    1. For abortion:

        a. Permitting women to obtain an abortion corresponds with the principle of self-determination and allows women to have greater freedom of choice concerning their own bodies and lives

        b. If abortions were prohibited, women would seek illegal abortions as they did in the past. No law has ever stopped abortion and no law ever will. Performed in a medical clinic or hospital, an abortion is relatively safe; but performed under unsanitary conditions, perhaps by an inexperienced or unskilled abortionist, the operation is extremely dangerous and may even imperil the woman's life

        c. If abortions were prohibited, some women would attempt to self-induce abortions. Such attempts can be life-threatening. Women have tried such techniques as severe exercise, hot baths, and pelvic and intestinal irritants, and have even attempted to lacerate the uterus with such sharp objects as nail files and knives

        d. No contraceptive method is perfectly reliable. All have failure rates and disadvantages. Contraceptive information and services are not readily available and accessible to all women, particularly teenagers, the poor, and rural women

e.   Abortions are necessary in many countries with soaring birth rates. Contraceptives may be inadequate, unavailable, or beyond what people can afford. Abortion appears to be a necessary population-control technique to preserve the quality of life. (In some countries the number of abortions is approaching the number of live births.)

2.   Against abortion:

a.   The right of a fertilized egg to life is basic and should in no way be infringed

b.   A woman who chooses to have an abortion is selfish. She prefers her own pleasure over the life of her unborn child

c.   In a society where contraceptives are so readily available, there should be no unwanted pregnancies and therefore no need for abortion

d.   Abortion is immoral and against certain religious beliefs. For example, Pope John Paul II condemned abortion as a sign of the encroaching "culture of death" that threatens human dignity and freedom

e.   People supporting abortion are antifamily. People should take responsibility for their behavior, cease nonmarital sexual intercourse, and bear children within the family context

K.   Social worker roles and abortion

1.   Enabler

2.   Educator

3.   Broker

4.   Advocate

L.   Highlight 2.4: Abortion-Related Ethical Dilemmas in Practice

1.   Loewenberg and Dolgoff's hierarchy of ethical principles

a.   Principle 1: Protection of life

b.   Principle 2: Equality/inequality

c.   Principle 3: Autonomy, independence, and freedom

d.   Principle 4: Least harm

e.   Principle 5: Better quality of life for all people

      f.   Principle 6: Privacy and confidentiality

      g.   Principle 7: Honesty and full disclosure

    2.   Illustrations of ethical dilemmas

VII.   Infertility

    A.   Infertility: The inability to conceive despite trying for one year

    B.   It is estimated that infertility affects 6.1 million Americans, or about 10 percent of people of reproductive age

    C.   Causes of infertility

        1.   Female infertility

            a.   Pelvic inflammatory disease (PID): Infection of the female reproductive tract (especially the fallopian tubes) that can cause inflammation and scar tissue that blocks tubes

            b.   Failure to ovulate or decreased frequency of ovulation

            c.   Hostile mucus—abnormally thick mucus on the cervix that acts as a barrier, preventing sperm from entering the uterus

            d.   Endometriosis: The growth of tissue resembling that of the uterine lining outside the uterus, often resulting in severe pain, can cause infertility

            e.   Hormonal defects

            f.   Smoking

            g.   Exposure to toxic substances

        2.   Male infertility

            a.   Low sperm count and decreased sperm motility

            b.   Damaged veins in the scrotum or testes

            c.   Undescended testes

            d.   Drugs, alcohol, and cigarettes

        3.   Couple-related causes of infertility

    D.   Psychological reactions to infertility

    E.   Treatment of infertility

F.   Assessment of infertility

  1.   Assessment of the male entails tests that evaluate the number, normality, and motility of sperm

  2.   Assessment for the female usually involves first evaluating whether she is ovulating each month, and after that the fallopian tubes and uterus are x-rayed

  3.   Laparoscopy: A thin, tubular instrument is inserted into the body cavity to examine the female reproductive organs directly

G.   Alternatives available to the infertile couple

  1.   Adoption

  2.   Surgery and fertility drugs

  3.   Artificial insemination (AI): The relatively simple procedure of injecting a sample of specially treated sperm from the male partner into the female partner's reproductive tract

     a.   Intrauterine insemination (IUI): Sperm is deposited directly into the uterus instead of the vagina

     b.   Artificial insemination by husband (AIH)

     c.   Artificial insemination by donor (AID)

     d.   Surrogate motherhood

     e.   Ethical and legal issues

     f.   Ethical Question 2.4: Does a child resulting from artificial insemination by an unknown donor have the right to know who that donor was? What if this knowledge is necessary for some medical reason such as diagnosing a hereditary disease? What if the donor does not want the child to know who he is?

  4.   Assisted reproductive technology (ART): Involves procedures to promote pregnancy that involve handling both the sperm and the egg. The results of ART procedures are often referred to as test-tube babies

     a.   In vitro fertilization (IVF): The process in which eggs are removed from a woman's body, fertilized with sperm in a laboratory, and then implanted in the woman's uterus

     b.   Gamete Intrafallopian Transfer (GIFT): A doctor places collected eggs and sperm directly into a fallopian tube

c. Zygote Intrafallopian Transfer (ZIFT): Eggs and sperm are first combined in a laboratory dish. The fertilized egg is then immediately transferred to the fallopian tube

d. Direct sperm injection [intracytoplasmic sperm injection (ICSI)]: A physician, using a microscopic pipette, injects a single sperm from a man's ejaculate into an egg. The resulting zygote is subsequently placed in the uterus

5. Surrogate motherhood

6. Ethical Question 2.5: What if the surrogate mother changes her mind shortly before birth or right after birth and decides to keep the baby?

If the child is born with severe mental or physical disabilities, who will care for the child and pay for the expenses? Should it be the surrogate mother, the contracting adoptive couple, or society?

Should the best interests of the children instead of their procreators be taken into account? At some point in the children's lives, should they be told that they have a surrogate mother somewhere? How might this affect their own psychological well-being?

7. Acceptance of childlessness

H. The effects of macro systems on infertility

1. New developments are rapidly advancing

2. These alternatives are very expensive and not available to poor people and the uninsured

I. Social work roles and infertility

1. Enabler

2. Mediator

3. Educator

4. Broker

5. Analyst/evaluator

6. Advocate

J. Spotlight on Diversity 2.3: A Feminist Perspective on Infertility Counseling and Empowerment

VIII. Summary

The following four exercises are designed to help you examine the various alternatives available in the situations of unplanned pregnancy and infertility and apply knowledge of human development to making assessment decisions.

Exercise 2.1: The Abortion Decision

A.   Brief Description
      You will be provided with a vignette describing a case of unplanned pregnancy. You will determine your own personal opinions concerning abortion and then form small groups to discuss the various options available to the person described in the case. Finally, you will break into pairs and participate in a role-play that focuses on distinguishing between personal and professional values.

B.   Objectives
      You will:
      1.   Become aware of the alternatives available to a person in the situation of unplanned pregnancy.
      2.   Examine your own opinions toward the controversial issue of abortion.
      3.   Evaluate the distinction between personal and professional values.

C.   Procedure
      1.   Read the following vignette:

      > Marge is a 16-year-old high school sophomore who is two months pregnant. The father is Homer, a 17-year-old high school junior.
      >
      > Marge and Homer have been "going steady" for two years. They think they love each other. Marge is a cheerleader and Homer is a quarterback on the varsity football team. They're both involved in school activities and have never really thought much about the future. Marge hasn't told Homer yet. She's confused about what to do. She doesn't know how he'll react. Marge hasn't told her parents yet either. They're religious, and she's afraid they'll be terribly disappointed in her. What should she do?

      2.   After reading the vignette, imagine yourself in Marge's position. Determine what you would do according to your own value system and jot this decision down on a piece of scrap paper.
      3.   Break into groups of four to six persons. Discuss the various alternatives available to Marge and the possible positive and negative consequences of each alternative. Select one member of your group to write down each alternative and the positive and negative consequences of each alternative. <u>DO NOT</u> share your personal opinion about what Marge should do with the rest of your group.
      4.   You will have 10 to 15 minutes of small-group discussions. Then come together for a full class discussion. Share what you discussed about the available alternatives. As you do so, each alternative, along with its potential positive and negative consequences, will be written on the board so that all may see them.

5. Now form pairs for a role-play. In each pair, one person plays Marge and the other a school social worker. The scene of the role-play is Marge talking to the social worker about her problem and what to do. The social worker should help Marge identify the various alternatives available to her and the consequences of each. The client should be helped to come to HER OWN DECISION. The role-play may continue for 15 to 20 minutes.

6. Come together once again for a full class discussion. The following questions may be used to initiate discussion:
   a. How did it feel being in the place of the client or the school social worker?
   b. Did any of the people playing social workers have opinions concerning abortion that differed from the client's decision? If so, in what respect?
   c. How difficult was it to remain objective in view of having your own personal opinions?
   d. What did you learn about professional values from doing this exercise?
   e. What did you learn about what counseling might be like?

Exercise 2.2: Abortion Related Ethical Dilemmas in Practice

A. Brief Description

This exercise presents you with a variety of scenarios dramatizing ethical dilemmas concerning the abortion issue. In small groups you will discuss how a hierarchy of ethical principles might be applied, followed by a full-class discussion.

B. Objectives
You will:
1. Become aware of some of the ethical dilemmas that may be encountered in social work practice concerning the abortion issue.
2. Examine how a hierarchy of professional ethics can be applied.

C. Procedure
1. Review the following material (also presented in the text):

> Picture yourself as a professional social worker in practice. What happens when your own personal values seriously conflict with those expressed by your client? A basic professional value clearly specified in the National Association of Social Workers (NASW) Code of Ethics is the right of clients to make their own decisions. Or, what happens when there are problems regardless of which solution you choose? What happens when, whatever you do, you are placed in the position of violating some professional ethic?
>
> By definition, an ethical dilemma involves conflicting principles. When two or more ethical principles oppose each other, it's impossible to make a "correct" decision that satisfies both or all principles involved. There is no perfect solution.
>
> For instance, if your 15-year-old client tells you that he plans to murder his mother, you are caught in an ethical dilemma. It is impossible to maintain confidentiality with your client (a basic social work professional value) and yet do all you can to protect his mother from harm.

A wide range of situations involving abortion can place workers in situations involving ethical dilemmas. Dolgoff, Loewenberg, and Harrington (2005) have formulated a hierarchy of ethical principles to provide a guide for making difficult decisions. When two ethical principles conflict, they suggest which principle should have priority. Principle 1 should take priority over principles

2 through 7, principle 2 should take priority over principles 3 through 7, and so on. The hierarchy can be helpful in working through difficult situations.

The hierarchy of ethical principles involves the following (p. 65-67):

Principle 1: **"Protection of life"** should be met first. This might include food, clothing, shelter, adequate income, and access to health services.

Principle 2: After basic survival needs, the principle of **"equality and inequality"** suggests that equal persons have the right to be treated equally and non-equal persons have the right to be treated differently if the inequality is relevant to the issue in question. It follows that people with lesser power or people in vulnerable positions may need special treatment.

Principle 3: Social workers should strive to make decisions that foster people's right to **"autonomy and freedom."** People have the right to make decisions about how to behave and live their own lives as long as these decisions do not hamper other people's autonomy and freedom.

Principle 4: People should experience the **"least harm"** possible in any situation. This principle straightforwardly states that people have the basic right to be saved from injury. Furthermore, in the event of potential injury, social workers should choose the route causing the least injury possible, the least lasting harm or injury, and, finally, "the most easily reversible harm."

Principle 5: People have the right to pursue a good **"quality of life."** Social workers should choose options that enhance the quality of life for individuals and communities.

Principle 6: People's **"privacy and confidentiality"** should be fostered and maintained. However, these are less important than the well-being of all.

Principle 7: Practice decisions should allow workers to maintain **"truthfulness and full disclosure."** Social workers should be able to provide any information that they deem necessary in any particular situation. However, the truth should not be told for its own sake when it violates a client's confidentiality.

---

2. Break up into small groups of four to six persons. Eight scenarios depicting ethical dilemmas are presented below (the first provides an example of how to proceed). For each scenario, discuss how Dolgoff and his colleagues' hierarchy of ethical principles for decision making might be applied. Starting with principle 1 and continuing through principle 7, evaluate how the ethical principles can be involved in each dilemma. Remember, there are no easy or "perfect" answers.

3. Read the following situation and its subsequent discussion of ethical principles as an example of how to discuss the others.

SCENARIO A: A 16-year-old young woman is raped and impregnated by a 40-year-old man as she is walking home from school one night. Both she and her parents are horrified and plagued with worry. They come to you for help. The girl desperately wants an abortion.

APPLICATION OF ETHICAL PRINCIPLES TO SCENARIO A: Consider Principle 1, the need to protect life. If you *personally* adopt an antiabortion stance and feel that abortion is murder, what do you do? A professional social worker's personal values must be acknowledged yet put aside in professional situations. In this case, the young woman and her parents want her to have the abortion.

We then look at Principle 2, which calls for the nurturance of equality and the combating of inequality. According to this principle, people should be treated equally. In this case they should have equal access to services. A neighboring state, its border only 25 miles away, allows abortions for all women who want them within the first trimester. Is this fair? Is this ethical? Should you help the young woman and her parents seek an abortion in a state that has different rules? Or should you work actively in your own state to advocate for change so that abortion would be a legal alternative for clients such as this?

Now consider Principle 3, which stresses people's right to autonomy, independence, and freedom. The young woman has the right to make her own decision. Your state might legally allow abortions for all women seeking them, or it might restrict them to only those women who have been raped or sexually abused. Or your state might ban all abortions unless the life of the mother is critically endangered.

If an abortion is legal in your state for a teenager like this, you as a worker can help her get one. She has made her decision. It is her legal right. However, if your state does not allow her to have a legal abortion, you are confronted with another dilemma.

Another potential issue to explore with women experiencing unwanted pregnancy concerns a woman's spiritual beliefs. What are her beliefs about this situation and how do they affect not only her ultimate decision, but also the psychological results of that decision?

Principle 4 refers to choosing options that result in the least harm to those involved. What kind of harm or potential harm might each of the people involved suffer? How might you measure the severity of harm?

Principle 5 reflects the importance of maintaining an optimum quality of life. If this young woman is prevented from having an abortion, how might her future be affected? In what ways might she lose control over her life? How will her short-term and long-term quality of life be affected?

Does Principle 6, the right to privacy and confidentiality, concern this situation? It is your responsibility to maintain your client's confidentiality.

How does Principle 7 concerning truthfulness and full disclosure apply? Can you provide the young woman and her parents with information that will help them pursue their chosen alternative? Should you share with them your personal views about what should be done? Or should you strive to maintain professional objectivity?

This discussion raises questions and issues. Each case is unique. Circumstances and attitudes vary widely. It is a professional social worker's ethical responsibility to resolve dilemmas and help clients solve problems to the best of that worker's ability. Each client should be helped to identify alternatives, evaluate the pros and cons of each, and come to a final decision. There are no absolute answers or perfect solutions.

Abortion provides an especially difficult issue because of people's strong opinions either against abortion or in favor of free choice. For this specific issue, the National Association of Social Workers (NASW) has established a policy statement to help provide direction (NASW, 2006). It states:

"The NASW Code of Ethics (NASW, 1999) states that 'social workers promote clients' socially responsible self-determination' (p. 5). Self-determination means that without government interference, people can make their own decisions about sexuality and reproduction. It requires working toward safe, legal, and accessible reproductive health care services, including abortion services, for everyone" (p. 147).

4. In a similar manner, discuss the following scenarios, one by one. Apply the hierarchy of ethical principles to each.

SCENARIO B: A 45-year-old grandmother becomes pregnant. She already has seven children. Her personal physician refused to prescribe birth control pills for her because of her age and other health reasons. Nor did he discuss other forms of birth control with her or offer her the alternative of sterilization. Physically, it would be hazardous for her to have any more children. She comes to you, distraught and crying. She doesn't know what to do.

SCENARIO C: A woman of 32 who has a severe cognitive disability becomes pregnant. She is not capable of taking care of herself independently. However, she is easy prey and has a history of numerous sexual encounters. Her genetic background indicates that there is a high probability that she would have a child with a cognitive disability. It is clear that she would be unable to care for any child herself.

SCENARIO D: A 19-year-old college student is six weeks pregnant. She's been going with her boyfriend for the past seven months. For the past three months they have been seeing only each other, but don't consider themselves "serious" as yet. She had been using a diaphragm and contraceptive cream, but they failed to protect her. She doesn't want a baby right now. However, she feels terribly guilty about getting pregnant.

SCENARIO E: A married 24-year-old woman is pregnant. She already has one child with genetic defects. She and her husband have been through genetic evaluation and counseling at a local university. The conclusion is that since both parents have significant genetic problems, the chances for a normal child are extremely unlikely. The couple was deciding on a sterilization procedure when she became pregnant.

SCENARIO F: A married 28-year-old medical technician has been unaware of being pregnant until now, the seventh week of gestation. Throughout her entire pregnancy she has been exposing herself to dangerous X-ray radiation. The possibility that her fetus has been damaged from the radiation is very high. She and her husband want children at some time, but they dread the thought of having a baby who has serious impairments.

SCENARIO G: Four months ago a married man of 42 had a vasectomy. His 41-year-old wife just found out she is five weeks pregnant. Some sperm apparently had still been evident in his semen. They already have three teenage children. They adamantly do not want any more.

SCENARIO H: A 14-year-old high school student is pregnant. It just happened one night when she was out drinking. She never really considered using contraception. She's shocked that she's pregnant and is having difficulty thinking about the future.

5. After approximately one-half hour, your instructor calls you back together to participate in a group discussion. Individuals have an opportunity to share either their own feelings or issues discussed in the small groups. Address the following questions:

a. What ethical principles did you find to be the most useful for each case?
b. For each case, what do you think should be done?

  c. To what extent was the ethical hierarchy helpful for thinking each scenario through?

  d. To what extent do you think that the ethical hierarchy would be helpful in addressing other ethical dilemmas encountered in social work practice?

  e. To what extent do you agree with the hierarchy of ethical principles?

  f. Which situations were the most difficult to address and why?

Exercise 2.3: The Infertility Crisis

A. Brief Description

Within a small group format, you will explore your own feelings about infertility and delineate the alternatives available to infertile couples.

B. Objectives

You will:

1. Become aware of the alternatives available to infertile couples and evaluate the consequences of each.

2. Identify your own feelings about infertility.

3. Recognize the need to employ empathy toward clients in this position.

C. Procedure

1. Complete the following statement:

  If I were infertile, I would _____.

Record your answer on a piece of scratch paper. You have a few minutes to think about and write down your feelings.

2. Form groups of four to six persons. Discuss the following questions within your group.

  a. What are the alternatives available to infertile couples and the respective advantages and disadvantages of each?

  b. How would you feel if you found that you were infertile?

  c. What feelings do you think infertile couples might experience?

  d. What types of information and support do you think would be most helpful for an infertile couple?

3. You will have 15 minutes of small-group discussion, then come together and summarize and discuss the groups' findings.

Exercise 2.4: Developmental Assessment

A. Brief Description

The instructor will present a series of vignettes that profile children of various ages. You will discuss whether each child is normal or is experiencing developmental lags.

B. Objectives

You will:

1. Relate motor, play, adaptive, social, and language milestones that characterize various ages.

2. Apply this information to making assessment decisions.

C. Procedure

    1.   One at a time, you are provided with the following vignettes. After each vignette, evaluate the extent to which each child fits the "normal" developmental profile. Focus on whether the motor, play, adaptive, social, and language milestones are appropriate for the child's age level. What types of referrals might be appropriate for those children who display developmental lags in various areas?

    a.   Kenji, age 2 years, can walk well but still runs with an awkward gait. He likes to play with and push large objects such as wagons and walkers. He also likes to play alongside other children but is not able to play with them in a cooperative fashion. His vocabulary includes about twenty-five words, but he is not yet very adept at putting two to three words together in order to express an idea.

    b.   Chaniqwa, age 4 years, is very active physically. She enjoys running, skipping, jumping, and performing stunts. She can use the bathroom by herself. She has a substantial vocabulary, although she has a tendency to misuse words and use improper grammar.

    c.   Wyanet, age 1 year, is able to balance her head at a 90-degree angle. She can also lift her head when placed on her stomach in a prone position. She is not yet able to sit alone. She can recognize her bottle and her mother. Verbalizations include gurgling, babbling, and cooing.

    d.   Sheridan, age 5 years, can draw simple, although recognizable, pictures. Dominance of her left hand has become well established. She can readily dress and undress herself. She enjoys playing in groups of other children and can cooperate with them quite well. She has a vocabulary of about fifty words. She can use pronouns such as *I* and prepositions such as *on* and *above* appropriately. She can put two or three words together and use them appropriately, although she has difficulty formulating longer phrases and sentences.

    e.   Luis, age 18 months, can crawl well but is unable to stand by himself. He likes to scribble with crayons and build with blocks. However, it is difficult for him to place even three or four blocks on top of each other. He can say a few sounds, including *mama* and *dada,* but cannot yet understand the meaning of words.

REFERENCES

Dolgoff, R., Loewenberg, F. M., & Harrington, D. (2005). *Ethical decisions for social work practice* (7th ed.). Belmont, CA: Brooks/Cole.

National Association of Social Workers (NASW). (1999). *Code of Ethics of the National Association of Social Workers.* Retrieved on September 23, 2008 from http://www.naswdc.org/pubs/code/code.asp?print=1 .

National Association of Social Workers. (2006). *Social work speaks: National Association of Social Workers policy statements 2006-2009* (7th ed.). Washington, DC: Author.

I. **A Perspective**

II. **Theories of Psychological Development**

    A.   Personality: The complex cluster of mental, emotional, and behavioral characteristics that distinguish a person as an individual

    B.   Psychodynamic theory

        1.   Freud's conception of the mind was two-dimensional—(1) the conscious, the preconscious, and the unconscious; (2) the id, superego, and ego

        2.   The repressed barrier—a barrier under which disturbing material (primarily thoughts and feelings) had been placed by the defense mechanism of repression

        3.   Repression: A process in which unacceptable desires, memories, and thoughts are excluded from consciousness by sending the material into the unconscious under the repressed barrier

        4.   The id, superego, ego

            a.   Id: The primitive force hidden in the unconscious

            b.   Ego: The rational component of the mind

            c.   Superego: The conscience, consisting of the traditional values and mores of society interpreted to a child by the parents

        5.   Figure 3.1 Freud's Conception of the Mind—Conscious, preconscious, unconscious

        6.   Psychosexual development

            a.   Libido: Energy of the id's biological instincts

            b.   Fixation: The partial halt of personality development at some developmental stage

            c.   Defense mechanism: Any unconscious attempt by the mind to adjust to painful conditions

7. Highlight 3.1 Definitions of Common Defense Mechanisms Postulated by Psychoanalytic Theory

    a. Compensation: Struggling to make up for feelings of inferiority or areas of weakness

    b. Repression: Mechanism through which unacceptable desires, feelings, memories, and thoughts are excluded from consciousness by being sent down deep into the unconscious

    c. Sublimation: Mechanism where consciously unacceptable instinctual demands are channeled into acceptable forms for gratification

    d. Denial: Mechanism where a person escapes psychic pain associated with reality by unconsciously rejecting reality

    e. Identification: Mechanism through which a person takes on the attitudes, behavior, or personal attributes of another person whom he had idealized

    f. Reaction formation: Blocking out threatening impulses or feelings by acting out an opposite behavior

    g. Regression: Mechanism where a person falls back to an earlier phase of development in which he or she felt secure

    h. Projection: Mechanism through which a person unconsciously attributes his own unacceptable ideas or impulses to another

    i. Rationalization: Mechanism by which an individual, faced with frustration or with criticism of his actions, finds justification for them by disguising from himself (as he hopes to disguise from others) his true motivations

8. Stages

    a. Oral (Birth to 18 months): People fixated at this stage were thought to have severe personality disorders, such as schizophrenia or psychotic depression

    b. Anal (1½ to 3 years old): People fixated at this stage have such character traits as messiness, stubbornness, rebelliousness; or they may have a reaction formation and have such opposite traits as being meticulously clean and excessively punctual

c.   Phallic (3 to 5 years old): People fixated at this stage are apt to show characteristics of pride, promiscuity, and self-hatred

    1)   Boys:

        a)   Oedipus complex: The dilemma faced by every son at this age when he falls sexually in love with his mother and feels antagonism toward his father

        b)   Castration anxiety: A son's fear that his father will discover his "affair" with his mother and remove his genitals

    2)   Girls—Electra complex: The dilemma faced by every daughter at this age, where she falls sexually in love with her father and feels antagonism toward her mother

d.   Latency (Resolution of Oedipus/Electra complexes to puberty): The child can now be socialized and become involved in the education process and in learning skills

e.   Genital (Puberty to death): The person reaching this stage is fully able to love and to work

    1)   The work ethic was highly valued, and viewed as important in life

    2)   Freud theorized that personality development was largely completed by the end of puberty, with few changes hypothesized

9.   Psychopathological development

a.   Sources of disturbances

    1)   Unresolved traumatic experiences

    2)   Internal unconscious processes

    3)   Sexuality frustrations

    4)   Obsessions: A recurring thought such as a song repeatedly on your mind

    5)   Compulsions: An act a person feels driven to repeat, often against his or her will

C.   Critical thinking: Evaluation of psychodynamic theory

    1.   Critical thinking: The careful examination and evaluation of beliefs and actions to establish an independent decision about what is true and what is not

    2.   Research does not support either the existence of Freud's theoretical constructs or the effectiveness of his therapeutic method

    3.   Another criticism is Freud's lack of clarity regarding Oedipus complex and Electra complex

    4.   Another criticism is that essentially women are left in the disadvantaged position of feeling perpetual grief at not having a penis

D.   Neo-Freudian psychoanalytic developments

    1.   Carl Jung (1875-1961)

        a.   Swiss psychologist who proposed the idea of an inherited "collective unconscious" that gave people a sense of their goals and directions

        b.   Jung developed his analytic psychology approach

        c.   He was fascinated with people's dreams and the interpretation of their meaning

        d.   He minimized the role that sexuality plays in emotional disorders

    2.   Erich Fromm

        a.   He came to the United States from Germany in 1934

        b.   Unlike Freud's biological orientation in his analysis of human behavior, Fromm had a social orientation—he focused on how people interact with others

        c.   He used psychoanalysis as a tool for understanding various social and historical processes and the behavior of political leaders

    3.   Alfred Adler

        a.   Rejected Freud's libidinal theory and developed "individual psychology" that emphasized social interaction. He saw people as creative, responsible individuals who guide their own growth and development through interactions with others in their social environment

b. Adler theorized that each person's unique striving process or lifestyle is sometimes self-defeating because of inferiority feelings. The individual with "psychopathology" is discouraged rather than sick

c. Social interest, an inborn trait, guides each person's behavior and stresses cooperation with others

4. Harry Stack Sullivan (1892-1949)

a. An American, who made perhaps some of the most radical deviations from Freudian theory

b. Like Adler, he emphasized that each individual personality developed on the basis of interpersonal relationships

c. People generally have two basic needs (1) security, and (2) satisfaction—whenever a conflict arose between these two needs, the result was some form of emotional disturbance

d. Sullivan placed greater emphasis upon developmental child psychology than did Adler and proposed six developmental stages ranging from infancy to late adolescence

5. Limitations

E. Behavioral theories

1. Behavioral theories differ from many other personality theories because instead of focusing on internal motivations, needs, and perceptions, they focus on specific observable behaviors

2. Social learning or social behavioral theory: Involves people's perceptions about different situations and their ability to distinguish between one and another. More credit is given to people's ability to think, discriminate, and make choices

F. Phenomenological theories

1. Phenomenological or self theories of personality focus on the way the world appears to particular individuals and how they attach meanings to their experiences and feelings

1. Carl Rogers' person-centered (previously known as client-centered) therapy

a. Self-concept: A person's perception of and feelings about him- or herself including his or her personality, strengths, weaknesses, and relationships with others

b. Self-actualization: The tendency for every person to develop capacities that serve to maintain or enhance the person

c. Sense of self-regard: The learned perception of self-worth that is based on the perceived attention and esteem received from others

d.   Real self: The person one actually is

e.   Ideal self: The person one would like to be

f.   Conditions of worth: A person's perceptions that he or she is only valuable when behaving as others expect and prefer him or her to act

g.   Incongruence: The circumstance where a discrepancy exists between a person's ideal self, real self, self-concept, and experience, the result of which is tension, anxiety, and internal confusion

h.   The person-centered therapist focuses on the constructive side of human nature, on what is right with the person, and on the assets the individual brings to therapy

G.   Feminist theories: Based on the concept of feminism and the basic themes in that definition

1.   Feminism is the doctrine advocating social, political, and economic rights for women equal to those of men and the movement for the attainment of such rights

2.   Referred to as feminist theories because of the multiple origins and ongoing nature inherent in their development

3.   Nine principles of these approaches:

a.   Emphasize the elimination of false dichotomies

1)   Critically evaluate the way thought and behavioral expectations are structured within the culture

2)   Feminist perspective emphasizes attending to a balance between autonomy and relationship competence for both genders

b.   Rethinking knowledge

1)   Critically evaluating not only *how* you think about something, but also *what* you think about

2)   What ideas and thoughts are considered to reflect "facts" and which are thought to have value

c. Recognition that *differences exist in male and female experiences through their lifespans*

    1) Impacts of gender role socialization

        a) Gender role: Cluster of socially defined expectations that people of one gender are expected to fulfill

        b) Socialization: Development process of teaching members of a culture the appropriate and expected pattern of values and behavior

d. The *end of patriarchy*: The doctrine maintaining that men hold positions of power and authority, head families, and provide the basis for tracing descent in family lineage

e. *Empowerment*: The process of increasing personal, interpersonal, or political power so that individuals can take action to improve their life situations

f. *Valuing process equally with product*: Focus on decision-making based on equality and participation by all

g. The personal is political

    1) Personal experience is integrally intertwined with the social and political environment

    2) Sexism: The prejudice or discrimination based on sex, especially discrimination against women that involves behavior, conditions, or attitudes that foster stereotypes of social roles based on sex

    3) The political environment can be changed and improved by personal actions

h. *Unity and diversity*

    1) Related concepts are "sisterhood" and "solidarity"

    2) Women working together can achieve a better quality of life for all. Diversity is viewed as a source of strength

i. *Consciousness raising*: the development of critical awareness of the cultural and political factors that shape identity, personal and social realities, and relationships and of one's position and opinions with respect to these issues

4. Ethical Question 3.1: What are your views about the various approaches to feminism? What is the fair way to treat women and men? What kinds of efforts, if any, do you think should be undertaken to improve current conditions?

5. Feminist identity development

    a. Passive acceptance

    b. Revelation

    c. Embeddedness

    d. Synthesis

    e. Active commitment

6. Commentary

7. Spotlight on Diversity 3.1: Diversity in Feminism

    a. Liberal feminism: Holds that women should have opportunities and rights equal to those of men

        1) The National Organization for Women (NOW) generally reflects a liberal feminist perspective

        2) Glass ceiling: A barrier involving psychological perception and decision making by those in power that prevents women from progressing higher in a power structure just because they are women

    b. Cultural feminism: Claims that women have special, unique qualities that differentiate them from men

    c. Marxist or socialist feminism: Views the oppression of women as just one instance of oppression, women being downgraded as one of various classes of people devalued by a capitalistic society

        1) Seeks a total transformation of the current capitalist system, where the wealth would be spread much more equally across classes including women and other oppressed populations

        2) One implication might be that women working in the home should be paid for that work because it is work, just as others are paid for working outside the home

    d. Radical feminism: Perceives liberal feminism and cultural feminism as entirely too optimistic about the sources of women's oppression and the changes needed to end it

      e.   Postmodern feminism: Is not focused on social action, but rather is an academic movement that seeks to reform thought and research within colleges and universities

          1)   Epistemology: Concerns the question of how people—whether laypeople or scientists—know. How do we know about truth and reality?

          2)   Deconstruction: Involves analysis of underlying meanings and assumptions when presented with an occurrence, trend, or so-called fact. In a way, it is a form of critical thinking

H.   Critical thinking about the relevance of theory to social work

    1.   Theory: A coherent group of principles, concepts, and ideas organized to explain some observable occurrence or trend

    2.   Medical model

        a.   Views clients as patients

        b.   Conceptualizes emotional and behavioral problems as mental illnesses

        c.   In the 1960s, social work shifted at least some of its emphasis to a reform approach

    3.   Systems theory

        a.   In the past two decades social work has increasingly focused on using a systems approach

        b.   Human beings are viewed as being in constant interaction with other micro, mezzo, and macro systems within their social environment

    4.   Highlight 3.2: Critical Thinking and Evaluation of Theory

        a.   Evaluate the theory's application to client situations

        b.   Evaluate the research supporting theory

        c.   Evaluate the extent to which the theory coincides with social work values and ethics

        d.   Evaluate the existence and validity of other comparable theories

        e.   Some theories have similarities

5. Spotlight on Diversity 3.2: Being Sensitive to Diversity When Examining Psychological Theories

    a. It is important to view transitions, life events, and other life issues as outcomes of person(s), environment processes rather than as separate segments of life confined to predetermined ages and stages of experience

    b. The Dual Perspective: All people adapt to and interact with two environments: (1) the family and community labeled the *nurturing environment*, and (2) the larger environment of white people, the *sustaining environment*

    c. Socialization: The process by which individuals become competent, participating members of a society, that is, the process by which adults prepare children for competent adulthood in their own social group

    d. Seriation: The ordering of events in a temporal sequence before they can develop an understanding of the past, present, and future

    e. Worldview: Concerns one's perceptions of oneself in relation to other people, objects, institutions, and nature. It relates to one's view of the world and one's role and place in it

    f. Spirituality: Includes one's values, beliefs, mission, awareness, subjectivity, experience, sense of purpose and direction, and a kind of striving toward something greater than oneself

    g. Strengths-based social work practice: Focuses on helping client systems tap into the strengths within them

III. Cognitive Development: Piaget

A. Cognition: Involves the ability to take in information, process it, store it, and finally retrieve and use it. In other words, cognition involves the ability to learn and to think

B. Piaget postulates that each stage of cognitive development is characterized by certain principles or ways in which an individual thinks

    1. Conservation: The concept that a substance can be changed in one way (e.g., shape) while remaining the same in another (e.g., quantity)

    2. Schema: Ways of thinking about and organizing ideas and concepts depending on one's level of cognitive development

    3. Adaptation: The capacity to adjust to surrounding environmental conditions

    4. Assimilation: The taking in of new information and the resulting integration into the schema or structure of thought

    5. Accommodation: The process by which children change their perceptions and actions in order to think using higher, more abstract levels of cognition

C.   Four major stages of cognitive development

1.   Sensorimotor period (birth to age 2): Child progresses from simple thoughtless reflex reactions to a basic understanding of the environment

   a.   Children learn that they have various senses through which they can receive information

   b.   Goal-directed behavior: Instead of displaying simple responses randomly, the child will purposefully put together several behaviors in order to accomplish a simple goal; however, the ability to plan very far ahead is extremely limited

   c.   Object permanence: The concept that objects continue to exist even when they are out of sight and hearing range. This is the most important schema acquired during the sensorimotor period

   d.   Representation: The visual imagining of an image in one's mind which allows one to begin solving problems

2.   Preoperational thought period (ages 2 to 7): A child's thinking continues to progress to a more abstract, logical level

   a.   Barriers to the development of logical thinking

      1)   Egocentrism: The inability to see things from anyone else's point of view

      2)   Centration: A child's tendency to concentrate on only one detail of an object or situation and ignore all other aspects

      3)   Irreversibility: A child's ability to follow and think something through in one direction without being able to imagine the relationship in reverse

   b.   Developing cognitive ability

      1)   Classification: A child's ability to sort items or stimuli into various categories according to certain characteristics

      2)   Seriation: A child's ability to arrange objects or stimuli in order according to certain characteristics

      3)   Conservation: The concept that a substance can be changed in one way while remaining the same in another

3. Period of concrete operations (ages 7 to 11): A child develops the ability to think logically on a concrete level. In other words, a child has mastered the major impediments to logical thinking that were evident during earlier stages of cognitive development

   a. More complex thinking is developed

   b. A child develops the ability to conceptualize in terms of reversibility

   c. A child gains much flexibility in thinking about situations and events

   d. Children develop their use of symbols to represent events in the real world

   e. Their focus is on thinking about things instead of ideas

4. Period of formal operations (ages 11 to 16): The final stage of cognitive development; it characterizes cognitive development during adolescence

   a. Culmination of abstract thought

   b. Three characteristics of adolescent thought

      1) Identification of numerous variables affecting situations

      2) Hypothesize about relationships and think about changing conditions

      3) Hypothetical-deductive reasoning: An adolescent can systematically and logically evaluate many possible relationships in order to arrive at a conclusion

D. Critical thinking: Evaluation of Piaget's theory

   1. The vast majority of his suppositions are based on observations of his own children instead of under laboratory conditions

   2. Piaget focused on the "average" child

   3. Considered only limited dimensions of human development

   4. His idea that cognitive growth through these stages stops at adolescence

      a. Some suggest a fifth stage of post-formal thought

      b. Post-formal thought is characterized by dialectical thinking (an organized means of evaluating issues that considers many perspectives and potential possibilities

      c. Formal analysis: Tends to be linear in nature with the goal of logically determining a definite conclusion

5.   Piaget's responses

    a.   An individual's social environment may influence cognitive development

    b.   Individual differences might have to be taken into account

    c.   Even if a person develops a capacity for formal operational thought, this capacity may not be versatile in its application to all problems

6.   Questions have been raised regarding the meaning and appropriate age level attributed to some of Piaget's specific concepts

7.   Piaget's examination of egocentricity has also received some criticism

8.   Egocentricity: Involves the concept that a child is unable to see things from anyone else's perspective but his own

9.   Piaget has provided us with a foundation for thinking about cognitive development and has tremendously influenced research in this area

IV.   Emotional Development

A.   Emotion: The complex combination of feelings and moods that involves subtle psychological reactions and is expressed by displaying characteristic patterns of behavior

B.   Infants' emotions

    1.   Crying

        a.   Hungry cry: Also referred to as the basic cry, this is a rhythmic sequence consisting of a focalization, a pause, an intake of air, and another pause

        b.   Angry cry: An exceptionally loud cry where the baby forces a large column of air through the vocal cords

        c.   Cry of pain: This is characterized by an initial loud wail with no preceding sniffling or moaning. It may be followed by the baby holding its breath for a long period

    2.   Smiling and laughing

        a.   Reflex smiling: Almost immediately after birth, infants can be observed smiling. At one time this was thought to be related to gastrointestinal gas. However, research indicated that it occurs automatically as a function of central nervous system development and frequently just before a baby falls asleep

        b.   Social smiling: Infants smile in response to someone they see or hear; displayed by their fourth week

       c.   Selective social smiling: Children smile in reaction to people and sounds they recognize; begins by about 3 ½ months

       d.   Laughing: The older they get, the more frequently babies laugh and the more they find to laugh at; begins at about the fourth month

C.   Infants and temperament

    1.   Temperament: Each individual's distinguishing mental and emotional nature that results in a characteristic pattern of response to people and situations

    2.   Emotionality: The intensity of an infant's reaction to circumstances, how easily the infant is provoked, and how quickly the emotional reaction can be subdued

    3.   Activity: The pact and energy with which an infant undertakes action

    4.   Sociability: The extent to which an infant prefers interaction and involvement with others

    5.   Three categories of temperament characterizing children

       a.   Easy children—Those whose lives have a relatively predictable, rhythmic patterns. They are generally cheerful and easy to get along with

       b.   Difficult children—These children are frequently irritable, have much irregularity in their daily patterns of activities, and have much difficulty adapting to new situations

       c.   Slow-to-warm-up children—They tend to have a generally low level of activity, a mild temperament, and moderate reactions to new situations and experiences

       d.   Over a third of children do not fit neatly into one category of temperament or the other

    6.   Temperament and parenting

    7.   Spotlight on Diversity 3.3: Cross-Cultural Diversity in Expectations and Temperament

       a.   Malaysian infants tend to be less flexible and responsive to new situations, and more reactive to outside stimuli than do American infants

       b.   Among the Masai in East Africa during famine, babies with difficult temperaments outlived easy babies

c.   Findings from one study of Canadian and Chinese 2-year-olds

       1)   Chinese children were generally much shyer and more withdrawn than Canadian children

       2)   Canadian mothers were much more punitive and overprotective in orientation with shy children, whereas Chinese mothers supported and encouraged introverted behavior

d.   The Zinacantecos (a group of Mayans in southern Mexico) reinforce the innate predisposition toward restrained motor activity by swaddling their infants and by nursing at the slightest sign of movement

D.   Attachment: A strong affectional tie that binds a person to an intimate companion

    1.   Stages of attachment

       a.   Stage 1: During the first 3 months of life, infants learn to distinguish between people and things

       b.   Stage 2: From age 3 to 6 months, infants learn to distinguish between primary caregivers and strangers

       c.   Stage 3: From age 6 to 9 months, infants search out their caregivers and try to stay close to them

       d.   Stage 4: From about age 9 to 12 months, infants develop a more detailed internal picture of the caregiver, her behavior, and her expectations

       e.   Stage 5: Beginning at age 12 months, the child will develop increased sensitivity to his dynamic interaction with the caregiver

    2.   Qualities of attachment

       a.   Significant amount of time spent together

       b.   Alert reactions to the child's needs and the provision of attentive care

       c.   The caregiver's emotional responsiveness and depth of commitment to the child

       d.   Being readily available in a child's life over a long period of time

    3.   Patterns of attachment

       a.   Secure attachment: Infants actively explore their environment and interact with strangers while their mothers are present

       b.   Anxious-avoidant attachment: Infants avoid contact with their mothers after separation or ignore their efforts to interact

     c.   Anxious-resistant attachment: Infants are very cautious in the presence of the stranger

     d.   Disorganized attachment: Babies' responses are particularly notable in the reunion. They behave in contradictory, unpredictable ways that seem to convey feelings of extreme fear or utter confusion

4.   Long-term effects of attachment

     a.   Children who manifested secure attachment with caregivers early on tended to have more positive social interactions with peers as they got older

     b.   Children who learn how to trust and interact positively as young children can apply these skills when they develop other social relationships later on

5.   Attachment and day care

     a.   Small staff-child ratio so that children receive adequate personal attention

     b.   Size of total group present should be no more than 12 to 15 children

     c.   Caregivers should be trained in various relevant areas such as child development and child management

     d.   Staffing should be stable with little turnover

     e.   The daily experience should be steady and predictable

6.   Spotlight on Diversity 3.4: Cross-Cultural Differences in Attachment

     a.   German infants show considerably more avoidant attachment than American babies do, which may be an intended outcome of cultural beliefs and practices

     b.   Infants of the Dogon people of Mali, Africa showed no avoidance attachment to their mothers

     c.   A high proportion of Japanese infants demonstrate anxious-resistant attachment. Japanese parents value infants' dependence on them and expect infants to resist separation

     d.   Secure attachment still tends to be the norm in most infant-caregiver relationships

V.   Self-Concept, Self-Esteem, and Empowerment

A.   Self-concept: All individuals form impressions about who they think they are, as if each person develops a unique theory regarding who exactly she feels she is

B.   Self-esteem: A person's judgment of his or her own value

C.   Highlight 3.4 The Effects of Positive and Negative Self-Concepts

D.   Global self-worth: An overall view of how positively they feel about themselves, in two ways—how competent children perceive themselves, and that their self-esteem depends on the amount of social support they receive from those around them

   1.   How competent children perceive themselves in five different areas of their lives

      a.   Scholastic

      b.   Athletic

      c.   Social

      d.   Behavioral

      e.   Physical appearance

   2.   Findings

      a.   Most significant variable: how much positive regard children felt from people around them

      b.   For both younger children (grades 3 through 5) and older children (grades 6 through 8), physical appearance was the most important, and behavioral conduct was the least important

      c.   Children who felt a more positive global self-worth tended to be happier, and more likely to involve themselves in activities, express a high level of self-confidence, and handle criticism better

E.   Spotlight on Diversity 3.5: A Cross-Cultural Perspective on Self-Esteem

   1.   Rotheram-Borus and Phinney research

      a.   Mexican-American children were more oriented to working in groups

      b.   African-American children were more comfortable with individual, action-oriented activities

      c.   Both groups were responsive and somewhat submissive to people in authority

2. Native American study

    a.   The older the child the less relationship between self-esteem and good health attitudes

    b.   Pueblo and Navajo children demonstrated the strongest relationship between self-esteem and health attitudes, whereas Apache children exhibited no correlation

3. Asian and Pacific American study

    a.   More negative self-concepts, physically and racially, than Anglo children

    b.   Third generation (Sansei) and fourth-generation (Yonsei) Japanese-American children received lower scores on all the measures of physical self-concept

    c.   The research points to a need for increased sensitivity to the physical self-concepts of Japanese-American children, such as emphasizing their many positive physical attributes

VI. Significant Issues and Life Events

A. Intelligence and intelligence testing

1. Intelligence: The ability to understand, to learn, and to deal with new, unknown situations

2. Cattell's fluid and crystallized intelligence

    a.   Fluid intelligence: An individual's natural aptitude for solving highly conceptual and other problems, remembering facts, attending to the task at hand, and calculating numerical figures

    b.   Crystallized intelligence: Intellectual abilities that emphasize verbal communication and involve the ability to learn from others in the social environment through education and interaction

3. Sternberg's Triarchic theory of intelligence

    a.   Componential element of intelligence: How people think about, process, and analyze information to solve problems and evaluate their results

    b.   Experiential element of intelligence: A person's actual doing of a task; it is the insightful, perceptive facet of intellect that enables an individual to put together information in new and creative ways

    c.   Contextual element of intelligence: The practical aspect of how people actually adapt to their environment

4.   Intelligence testing

      a.   Stanford-Binet IQ Test

            1)   First used in 1905, and has continued to be refined

            2)   Five areas of scores that measure both verbal and nonverbal ability, including various aspects of reasoning

            3)   Newly designed approaches stress nonverbal performance for people with limited English, deafness, or communication disorders

            4)   About two thirds of all scores fall between 84 and 116, with the average IQ score of 100

      b.   Wechsler tests

            1)   The Wechsler Preschool and Primary Scale of Intelligence (for children age 4 to 6 ½)

            2)   The Wechsler Intelligence Scales for Children (for children age 6 to 16)

            3)   The Wechsler Adult Intelligence Scales (for adults age 16 to 74)

            4)   The Wechsler tests provide a single overall IQ score in addition to separate verbal and performance scores, which is useful in detecting specific learning problems

            5)   About two thirds of all people score between 85 and 115, with the average score of 100

5.   Ethical Question 3.2: Should children be informed of their IQ? Should parents be told of their child's results? What are the reasons for your answers?

6.   Targeting special needs

      a.   Giftedness—five dimensions:

            1)   Excellence

            2)   Rarity

            3)   Demonstrability

            4)   Productivity

            5)   Value

7.   Other potential problems with IQ scores

      a.   Spotlight on Diversity 3.6: Cultural Biases and IQ Tests

            1)   Biases can involve the use of words, concepts, and contexts that are more familiar to some children than to others

            2)   What is considered significant by members of a culture can influence how children respond to questions posed by IQ tests

            3)   Testing situations and children's comfort level in them can affect IQ test results

            4)   Culture-fair in IQ tests try to include test items and terms that are familiar to children from as many cultural and socio-economic backgrounds as possible. It is impossible to achieve a totally culture-free test

      b.   The definition of IQ is arbitrary—it does not provide a reliable indication of competence in the real world

      c.   Placing IQ labels on people may become self-fulfilling prophecies

      d.   IQ scores do not take motivation into account

B.   People Who have Cognitive Disabilities: A Population-at-Risk

    1.   Cognitive disability: A condition characterized by intellectual functioning that is significantly below average and accompanying deficits in adaptive functioning, both of which occurred before age 18; the more negative term is mental retardation

    2.   Spotlight on Diversity 3.7: What Are People with Cognitive Disabilities Like?

      a.   Seven possible areas of deficiency

            1)   Attention

            2)   Memory

            3)   Self-regulation

            4)   Language development

            5)   Academic achievement

            6)   Social development

            7)   Motivation

b.   Percentage of people with cognitive disabilities by category

        1)   Mild—85%

        2)   Moderate—10%

        3)   Severe—3 to 4%

        4)   Profound—1 to 2%

3.   Defining cognitive disability

     a.   Must score significantly below average in intellectual functioning on IQ tests—generally 70 or below

     b.   Must have deficits in adaptive functioning

     c.   Must manifest itself between birth and 18

4.   Four categories of cognitive disability (approximate levels)

     a.   Mild: 50-55 to approximately 70

     b.   Moderate: 35-40 to 50-55

     c.   Severe: 20-25 to 35-40

     d.   Profound: below 20 or 25

5.   Eleven adaptive skills used to evaluate an individual's ability to function independently

     a.   Communication

     b.   Self-care

     c.   Home living

     d.   Social/interpersonal skills

     e.   Use of community resources

     f.   Self-direction

     g.   Functional academic skills

     h.   Work

     i.   Leisure

j.   Health

k.   Safety

6.   Ethical Question 3.3: Do people with cognitive disabilities have the right to have children?

7.   The significance of empowerment by support systems

    a.   Intermittent support: Occasional provision of support whenever needed

    b.   Limited support: Intensive help or training provided for a limited time to teach specific skills, or to assist in major life transitions

    c.   Extensive support: Long-term, continuous support that usually occurs on a daily basis and affects major areas of life both at home and at work

    d.   Pervasive support: Continuous, consistent, and concentrated support necessary for ongoing survival

8.   Support systems perspective coincides with social work values

    a.   Stresses ability to function and achieve instead of labeling

    b.   Moderates the historical "medical" aspects

    c.   Shifts primary assessment focus from IQ to adaptive skills

    d.   Provides for cultural and linguistic diversity in assessment

9.   Macro system responses to cognitive disabilities

    a.   Deinstitutionalization: The process of relocating people who need a significant level of care (e.g., people with cognitive disabilities, physical disabilities, or mental illness) from a structured institutional residence into a typical community setting

        1)   Spotlight on Diversity 3.8: The Americans with Disabilities Act: A Macro System Addresses a Population-At-Risk

            a)   Title 1 prohibits job and employment discrimination

            b)   Title 2 prohibits public facilities, organizations, and transportation discrimination

            c)   Title 3 prohibits discrimination in public accommodations and services operated by private entities

            d)   Title 4 requires that telecommunication relay services allow access for the hearing impaired

      e)   Title 5 includes miscellaneous provision relating to more specific aspects

      f)   Only about one-third of people with disabilities are employed—same as before the ADA passed

   b.   Community-based services

     1)   Settings should be structured to maximize clients' autonomy

     2)   Normalization: Arranging the environmental context for people with cognitive disabilities so that it is as "normal" as possible

   c.   Ethical Question 3.4: Should people with cognitive disabilities be *mainstreamed* (that is, be integrated into regular school classes) or be provided separate special education to meet their special needs? What are the pros and cons of each approach?

10.   Social work roles

   a.   Enabler — *helping people & families to make decisions & solve problems.*

   b.   Broker — *link clients to resources*

   c.   Educator — *information about employment or personal Hygiene*

   d.   Coordinator — *oversee a range of services*

   e.   General manager — *providing services to clients & family.*

   f.   Initiator —

   g.   Negotiator   *can work w community, government to change policies where services are not avail.*

   h.   Advocate

C.   People with Learning Disabilities: A Population-at-Risk

1.   Learning disability: A disorder in one or more of the basic psychological processes involved in understanding or using language which may manifest itself in an imperfect ability to listen, think, speak, read, write, spell, or do mathematical calculations

2.   Spotlight on Diversity 3.9: People with Developmental Disabilities: A Population-at-Risk

   a.   Developmental disabilities: Functional impairment as a result of disease, genetic disorders, or impaired growth pattern before adulthood. Cognitive disabilities and learning disabilities are among a number of developmental disabilities

b.   Five aspects common to developmental disabilities

    1)   Result from specific mental and/or physical problem

    2)   Appear before age 22

    3)   Conditions are permanent

    4)   Result in substantial functional limitations

    5)   Demonstrate need for lifelong supplementary help and services

c.   Autism: Condition characterized by intense inner directedness, behavior is often bizarre

d.   Cerebral palsy: Disability involving problems in muscular control and coordination resulting from damage to the brain's muscle control centers before or during birth

e.   Orthopedic problems: Physical conditions that interfere with the functioning of the bones, muscles, or joints, such as congenital malformations of the spine, bone deformities, and missing extremities such as arms or toes

f.   Hearing problems: Range from mild to total deafness

g.   Epilepsy: Commonly referred to as seizure disorders, and consists of various disorders marked by disturbed electrical rhythms of the central nervous system and manifested in convulsive attacks

h.   Concurrent disabilities are common

3.   Four basic characteristics of learning disabilities in general

a.   Distinct discrepancies between expected performance according to his or her IQ test results and actual performance

b.   Some central nervous system dysfunction results in a problem in psychological processing. This involves potential structural and functional differences in the brain

    1)   Structure refers to differences in such aspects as the size of various parts of the brain

    2)   Function involves brain-waive activity

c.   The deficits will come together to form a convergence or focus in how information is processed

d.   Nonacceptance of other causes to explain the problem

4. Five to 6 percent of school children ages 6 to 17 and more than half of all students identified as needing placement in special education classes

5. Learning disabilities involve problems in processing

   a. Inability to grasp the meanings of words or how words relate to each other in terms of grammatical position

   b. Auditory processing difficulties, such as problems in focusing on sounds

   c. Trouble saying what they mean or would like to say

   d. Visual perception problems such as difficulty seeing things as they really are

   e. Problems concerning memory and recall

6. What causes learning disabilities

   a. Neurological malfunction or deficits

   b. Genetic factors

   c. Teratogens (substances such as drugs that can cause malformation in the fetus)

   d. Medical conditions such as premature birth or childhood AIDS

7. Effects of learning disabilities on children

   a. Highlight 3.5: The Effects of a Learning Disability

   b. Fear of failure results in almost the complete avoidance of new experiences

   c. Learned helplessness reaction: Using the fact that they cannot do some things in order to get out of doing other things they are capable of doing

   d. Low self-esteem

   e. How people with learning disabilities are treated and accepted is critical in terms of their satisfaction and achievement as adults

8. Treatment of learning disabilities

   a. Educational treatment

      1) Cognitive training: Focuses on procedures to teach children with learning disabilities how to change their patterns of thinking

         a) Self-instruction: The process of making students aware of the various stages of problem-solving tasks while they are performing them and to bring behavior under verbal control

        b)   Direct instruction: Emphasizes drilling and practicing, and is usually used to improve math and reading skills

        c)   Behavior modification: Focuses on specifying and reinforcing good behavior and decreasing poor behavior

    b.   Family and other social settings

      1)   Positive things children do should be emphasized

      2)   Children should feel loved for who they are

      3)   Comparisons to others and what they accomplish should be avoided

      4)   Structure in the form of clear guidelines for behavior is helpful

9.   Macro system responses to empowering people with learning disabilities

    a.   Education for All Handicapped Children Act

    b.   Inclusion concept: Students with disabilities are assimilated into regular classrooms with same-age peers, but also receive the special attention and help they need

D.   Attention-Deficit Hyperactivity Disorder (ADHD): A syndrome of learning and behavioral problems beginning in childhood that is characterized by a persistent pattern of inattention, excessive physical movement, and impulsivity that appear in at least two settings (including home, school, work, or social contexts)

E.   Social work roles

    1.   Broker

    2.   Advocate

VII.   Summary

Experiential Exercises and Simulations

The following five exercises are designed to help you relate psychological concepts to real-life situations, examine the effects of various conditions on people, and evaluate your own perspectives and values about certain psychological conditions. Emphasis is placed on learning disabilities, self-concept, and cognitive disability.

Exercise 3.1: To See or Not to See

A.   Brief Description
You will be asked to read an exercise designed to simulate some of the visual perceptual problems experienced by people with this type of learning disability. Discussion follows regarding the difficulty and frustration involved.

B.   Objectives
You will:
1.   Recognize some of the difficulties facing people with visual perceptual problems.
2.   Examine your own feelings and frustration during such an experience.
3.   Employ empathy toward people with learning disabilities that involve visual perceptual problems.

C.   Procedure
1.   Read the following from this manual (or on a handout):

INSTRUCTIONS: The wollofgni alanogies have been belevopeb to ehnance ruoy aditily to unberstanb adsrtatc nocpects. Fro aech hter aeret wo se patare tastements. The fristil lusrtates woh wot se patare nocpects ro ibae s rae rael teb to aech ohter. The seco nb pari rp ovibse an popro tuni yt for yuo to lerate hte adsr tatc nocpect to anohter nocgif uratoin of wrobs. The byabs rae srtutcureb to rpe se nt vraoiusl evles ofb fificulyt. It si ver yim pr

o

t

n

a

t ht at yuobo not llif ni nay fo hte dl ank ps acse utnil yuo rae ins rtutceb to boso. In hte e vetn htat yuow riet an yhtgni no htis hse et defore degni insrtutceb to boso, uyo lliw imme biateyl cerie vea liafgni grabe for htis cuo rse:

    1.   Birds have xxxxx; people have ———.

    2.   xxxxx are mammals; ostriches are ———.

    3.   A yard has feet; a ——— has xxxxx.

    4.   A banana is xxxxx; an apple is ———.

    5.   Tigers are xxxxx; pets are ———.

    6.   xxxxx is cold; ——— is hot.

    7.   A volleyball is ———; a pickle is xxxxx.

    8.   ——— are brave; xxxxx are docile.

2.   This activity simulates several aspects of what a person with a learning disability involving a visual perceptual problem may experience. Read the instructions and follow them very carefully. You will have 5 to 10 minutes.

3.   Discuss what it is like to be a person with a learning disability. The following questions may be asked:

    a.   How did it feel to attempt following the instructions?

    b.   What adjectives might you use to describe your feelings during the activity?

    c.   How might a person react if placed in a similar situation in real life?

    d.   How might you react if you were placed in a situation where everyone else appears to know what to do, but you don't?

    e.   What might be done to help a person in such a situation?

4.   After voicing your feelings and opinions, read the following from this manual (or from a handout):

INSTRUCTIONS: The following analogies have been developed to enhance your ability to understand abstract concepts. For each there are two separate statements. The first illustrates how two separate concepts or ideas are related to each other. The second pair provides an opportunity for you to relate the abstract concept to another configuration of words. The dyads are structured to present various levels of difficulty. It is very important that you do not fill in any of the blank spaces until you are instructed to do so. In the event that you write anything on this sheet before being instructed to do so, you will immediately receive a failing grade for this course.

    1.   Birds have beaks; people have ——.

    2.   Rhinoceroses are mammals; ostriches are ——.

    3.   A yard has feet; a —— has inches.

    4.   A banana is yellow; an apple is ——.

    5.   Tigers are wild; pets are ——.

    6.   Winter is cold; —— is hot.

    7.   A volleyball is ——; a pickle is oblong.

    8.   —— are brave; sheep are docile.

    9.   Plants have stems; trees have ——.

    10.   Doctors have patients; social workers have ——.

---

5.   After you have read these instructions, discussion may be continued by asking the following questions:

    a.   How have your perceptions changed regarding how difficult the material is for you to understand?

    b.   What types of information were lacking? What became unclear?

    c.   How many of you began completing the first analogy sheet, even though the instructions told you not to?

    d.   What might it feel like to fail at an assignment considered fairly simple by your peers?

Exercise 3.2: I Don't Hear Anything, Do You?

A. Brief Description
    You will be given verbal instructions to perform a complicated task under distracting conditions. After you try to do so, discuss the difficulties and frustrations you experienced.

B. Objectives
    You will:
    1. Recognize some of the difficulties facing people with auditory perceptual problems.
    2. Examine your own feelings and frustration during such an experience.
    3. Employ empathy toward people with learning disabilities that involve auditory perceptual problems.

C. Procedure
    1. An audiotape of some type of muffled or distracting noise is prepared. The tape may be of the entire class holding small-group discussions, freeway traffic, or jazz music.
    2. You are asked to complete a task by following verbal instructions. Meanwhile, the instructor plays the prerecorded tape at a relatively loud volume.
    3. Have a pen or pencil ready. Do not begin work until the instructions have been completely read.
    4. You have a few minutes to struggle with the exercise. The instructions will not be repeated. This activity simulates what a person with a learning disability involving an auditory perceptual problem may experience.
        a. How did it feel to attempt to follow the instructions?
        b. What adjectives might you use to describe your feelings during the activity?
        c. To what extent do you feel that the instructions and the learning situation were fair?
        d. What exactly might have made you confused during this exercise?
        e. How might a person with a learning disability feel in a similar situation in real life where all of his or her peers are capable of performing the task?

Exercise 3.3: Developing a Positive Self-Concept

A. Brief description
    You will explore your self-concepts and then relate your findings to the general idea of a positive self-concept. Small group discussions follow.

B. Objectives
    You will:
    1. Identify those aspects of your own circumstances and personality that act to enhance or degrade your self-concept.
    2. Relate this information to how others might develop and maintain their self-concepts.
    3. Examine possible strategies for strengthening your self-concept.

C. Procedure
    1. Review the material in the text concerning self-concept and self-esteem. Jot down your answers to the following questions:
        a. What things (that people tell you; that you achieve; that you like about yourself) make you feel good about yourself?
        b. What things make you feel bad about yourself?
        Take 5 to 10 minutes to think and write down your ideas.

2. Break into groups of four to six persons. Discuss the following questions:
   a. What types of things can be done to enhance a person's self-concept?
   b. What types of things act to harm a person's self-concept?
3. After 10 to 15 minutes, the small-group discussions will end. Designate someone to share the findings of your group with the class. Have another person record the main points on the board so that everyone can focus on them. Be specific.
4. Summarize the findings of the entire group. Focus on both similarities and differences concerning how self-concepts are maintained. Relate findings to social work practice by discussing how social workers might act to enhance the self-concepts of clients. Examine what types of things discourage clients and harm their self-concepts.

Exercise 3.4: Who's the Smartest of Them All?

A. Brief description
You will be given questions concerning the differences and similarities among persons with varying levels of intelligence. Discussion will follow.

B. Objectives
You will:
1. Describe your perceptions of the effects of a person's intelligence on his or her behavior and the interaction between intelligence and personality.
2. Examine preconceived notions and stereotypes concerning persons of various levels of intelligence.
3. Recognize basic similarities and differences between people based on intellectual ability.

C. Procedure
1. The following three incomplete statements will be written on the board:
   a. People who have cognitive disabilities are:
   b. People with normal intelligence are:
   c. People with very high (far above normal) levels of intelligence are:
2. Break into groups of four to six. Discuss the feelings you think many people might have about persons of various levels of intelligence. Discuss not only your opinion but also stereotypes you think are frequently held. Record your findings. You will have 10 to 15 minutes for the small-group discussions.
3. Share your findings and record them on the board.
4. Continue with a discussion involving the entire class. Use the following questions to initiate this discussion:
   a. What major differences exist concerning the ideas about people of different levels of intelligence?
   b. How are people of all levels of intelligence thought to be similar?
   c. How do the following concepts relate to varying levels of ability:
      1) Emotional needs
      2) Intimate relationship need
      3) Self-concept
      4) Structure and supervision
      5) Work
      6) Right of free choice
   d. How should people with very high levels of intelligence be treated? Should they be given more leadership responsibility? How do they interact with people of average intelligence?

e.   What areas of life are most affected by levels of intelligence (e.g., family relationships, relationships with significant others, work, social life)?

f.   From a social work perspective, how should people of different levels of intelligence be treated?

Exercise 3.5: Everyday People

A.   Brief description

After reading about a child who has an IQ that is significantly below average attempting to interact with children of normal intelligence, you will be asked to discuss the alternatives.

B.   Objectives

You will:

1.   Recognize some of the effects of cognitive disability on an individual's self-concept and social interaction.

2.   Examine alternatives for enhancing the social situation of a person who has such a cognitive disability.

3.   Propose strategies for helping to integrate such an individual into a normal social setting.

C.   Procedure

1.   Bring this manual to class so that you might have the following material available:

> SITUATION:
>
> Mike, age 7, has been diagnosed as having a mild cognitive disability. He is a quiet, pleasant child who has difficulty keeping up with peers in schoolwork and in play/sport activities. He and his parents have moved into a new neighborhood filled with children of various ages.

QUESTIONS:

a.   How do you think Mike might feel about himself in relationship to his peers?

b.   How might the following people help to integrate Mike into the neighborhood:

1)   Mike's parents
2)   Neighbors
3)   Other children
4)   The school
5)   Mike himself

2.   Break into groups of four to six. After the situation is read aloud, discuss the subsequent questions. You will have 15 minutes for discussion.

3.   A representative from each group summarizes what his or her group talked about. Then the class discusses the small groups' findings.

4.   Summarize the conclusions of the entire group.

Study Outline

I.   **A Perspective**

II.   **Socialization:** The process whereby children acquire knowledge about the language, values, etiquette, rules, behaviors, social expectations, and all the subtle, complex bits of information necessary to get along and thrive in a particular society

III. **Family Environment**

    A.   Membership in family groups: Variations in family structures

        1.   Family structure: The nuclear family as well as those non-traditional alternatives to nuclear family which are adapted by persons in committed relationships and the people they consider to be "family"

        2.   Family is a primary group and members have significant influence on each other

        3.   Single-parent family: A family household where one parent resides with the children but without the other parent

        4.   Stepfamilies: Families in which one or both parents reside with children from prior marriages or unions

        5.   Blended family: Any nontraditional configuration of people who live together, are committed to each other, and perform functions traditionally assumed by families

        6.   Marrying later: Both men and women are waiting much longer to marry. Over 21 percent of all women and almost 28 percent of men never marry

        7.   Unmarried cohabitation: The proportion of unmarried-partner households rose from 3.5 percent in 1990 to 5.2 percent in 2000

        8.   Increased births to single women: Thirty-four percent of all births in 2002 were to unmarried mothers

        9.   Increased employment of mothers: Over 73 percent of single women with children and over 69 percent of married women with children are employed outside the home

B.   Positive family functioning

       1.   Family functions

       2.   Communication

       3.   Negotiation

C.   Macro systems, families, and empowerment

       1.   Unemployment

       2.   Day care

       3.   Ethical Question 4.1: As a student social worker, what do you think about the nation's day-care situation? How critical is it, especially for women? To what extent might you be willing to seek out answers for how to solve this problem and others like it?

IV.   Dynamics of Family Systems

A.   Highlight 4.1 The Application of Systems Theory Principles to Families

       1.   System: A set of elements that form an orderly, interrelated, and functional whole

       2.   Homeostasis: The tendency of a system to maintain a relatively stable, constant state of equilibrium or balance

       3.   Subsystem: A secondary or subordinate system

       4.   Boundaries: Invisible barriers that surround individuals and subsystems, controlling amount of contact with others

       5.   Input: The energy, information, or communication flow received from other systems

       6.   Output: Energy, information, or communication emitted from a system to the environment or to other systems

       7.   Feedback: A system's receipt of information from an outside source about its own performance or behavior

       8.   Entropy: The natural tendency of a system to progress toward disorganization, depletion and, in essence, death

       9.   Negative entropy: The process of a system toward growth and development

       10.   Equifinality: Many different means to the same end

       11.   Differentiation: A system's tendency to move from a more simplified to a more complex existence

B.   Family therapy: Intervention by a social worker or other family therapist with members of a family to improve communication and interaction among members and to pursue other changes and goals they wish to pursue

V.   The Family Life Cycle

A.   Traditional family life cycle stages

    1.   Separating as an unattached young adult from his or her family of origin

    2.   Marrying and establishing an identity as part of a couple versus as an individual

    3.   Having and raising young children

    4.   Dealing with adolescent children striving for independence and refocusing on the couple relationship as adolescents gain that independence

    5.   Sending children forth into their own new relationships, addressing midlife crises, and coping with the growing disabilities of aging parents

    6.   Adjusting to aging and addressing the inevitability of one's own death

B.   Carter and McGoldrick suggest a newer way of thinking about families that these stages can and do occur, but not necessarily in that order or at all

C.   Spotlight on Diversity 4.1: Diverse Perspectives on the Family Life Cycle

    1.   Separating from family of origin

        a.   Gay young adults face an extra readjustment in their relationships with their families of origin if they are coming out (identifying themselves as being gay and sharing this information with others) to them for the first time

        b.   Young lesbians also do not usually come out until young adulthood. They tend to bond earlier into stable couples than do gay men

    2.   Marrying and establishing an identity as a couple

        a.   National origin: Involves individuals', their parents', or their ancestors' country of birth

        b.   Displaced people: Those people who have been uprooted within their own country

        c.   Refugees: People who have crossed national boundaries in search of refuge

        d.   Immigrants: Individuals who have been granted legal permanent residence in a country not their own

        e.   Migrants: People, usually workers, who have temporary permission to live in a country, but plan to return to their country of origin

f.   Illegal aliens: People who migrate illegally to another country

g.   The tradition of arranged marriage versus love marriage is a source of conflict for many Asian Americans

h.   Outmarriage: Children marrying a person outside their ethnic community

3.   Having and raising young children

a.   Cultural values significantly affect how children are socialized, what values they acquire, and what behaviors they learn

b.   In Russian society, children are surrounded by female caretakers, whereas men are relatively little involved in family and household matters

c.   Russian society expects women to be as involved in the work force as are men and to also take over most of the housework. However, the Russian stereotype expects women to be passive and obedient; active, masculine behaviors are viewed as highly undesirable

d.   Russian boys have few opportunities to practice active, dominant behavior

4.   Dealing with adolescent children

a.   Most Latina mothers go into high gear to guard their daughters' virginity, especially as they reach adolescence

b.   Latinas tend to be supervised more closely when they go out with friends; dating doesn't take place until much later; and it is not unusual for chaperones to be present on dates

5.   Addressing midlife crises

a.   African American families in later life are likely to consist of a child generation, a young adult parent generation, a middle-aged grandparent generation, and one or even two elderly great-grandparent generations. Many continue working to make ends meet in spite of poor health

b.   Increasing numbers of African American grandparents are assuming responsibility for their grandchildren

c. Empowerment practice for grandparents

    1) Introduction to empowerment

    2) Importance of self-esteem

    3) Communicating with grandchildren

    4) Dealing with loss and grief

    5) Helping grandchildren deal with loss

    6) Dealing with behavior problems

    7) Talking to grandchildren about sex, HIV/AIDS, and drugs

    8) Legal and entitlement issues

    9) Developing advocacy skills

    10) Negotiating systems

    11) Making presentations (so that they might share their knowledge with others)

6. Adjusting to aging and dealing with eventual death

a. Native American elderly, those aged 65 and above, are more traditional in their philosophy and values and have a deeper understanding of racism and oppression against Native people as a result of having a longer history of experience with these forces

b. Through the elderly, traditional values are sustained; the ancient languages are spoken and taught, traditional ceremonies are observed and baskets are woven

c. Generally Native American traditional values consist of sharing, cooperation and a deep respect for elders

d. Lebanese families are generally very expressive in their response to death, even after several generations of living in the United States

e. In recent times Lebanese American reactions to death are less dramatic but still highly emotional and demonstrative. Calmness at wakes is perceived as a lack of love for the deceased, and emotional outbursts are perceived as respect for the deceased

f. Death is a particularly potent symbolic event among Hindus, given their beliefs about karma. Mourning cycles vary, but customs include a 10- to 12-day mourning ritual in addition to requiring extensive absence from work

g.   Judaism, regardless of denomination—Reform, Conservative, or Orthodox—has the overriding values of honoring the dead and comforting the mourners

h.   A Jewish burial is usually within twenty-four hours after the death and the funeral service begins with the cutting of a garment or a black ribbon attached to the mourners, the immediate family of the deceased. This ritual is a visual representation of the individual being separated—cut away—from the loved one

i.   Shiva (Hebrew word for seven) is the period of mourning at home after the burial, lasting for one week. Friends, family, and neighbors visit the mourners in the home, which provides the opportunity to share stories about the deceased

j.   The first thirty days (Sheloshim, the Hebrew word for thirty) after the funeral is a time when the family might attend morning and evening services

k.   Mourning ends after the first year, the Yahzeit, the family lights a special twenty-four-hour memorial candle

VI.   Learning Theory

A.   Critical thinking: Evaluation of theory

       1.   Learning theory: Theoretical orientation that conceptualizes the social environment in terms of behavior, its preceding events, and its subsequent consequences

             a.   Emphasizes the social functioning of people within their environments

             b.   Emphasizes the importance of assessing observable behaviors

             c.   Provides a positive approach

B.   Respondent conditioning: The emission of behavior in response to a specific stimulus. Also referred to as classical or Pavlovian conditioning

       1.   Unconditioned stimulus: Respondent behavior that is unlearned; a response is naturally emitted after exposure to a stimulus

       2.   Conditioned stimulus: Respondent behavior which occurs when a person learns to respond to a new stimulus that does not naturally elicit a response

       3.   Figure 4.1 A Stimulus-Response Relationship

       4.   Figure 4.2 Respondent Conditioning

5.   Systematic desensitization

    a.   The client is exposed very gradually to the thing he fears

    b.   While the client is being exposed to the fearful item or event, he or she is also taught an incompatible response

C.   Modeling: The learning of behavior by observing another individual engaging in that behavior (also called observational learning)

1.   Important within the context of practical parenting

2.   Important in social work intervention to model appropriate behavior through role playing

3.   Modeling behavior can be affected both by consequences to the model and to the observer

D.   Operant conditioning: A type of learning in which behaviors are influenced primarily by the consequences that follow them

1.   Many treatment applications are based on the principles of operant conditioning

2.   Highlight 4.2 Consequences and Recurring Behavior

E.   ABCs of behavior

1.   Antecedents: The events occurring immediately before the behavior itself

2.   Behavior: Any observable and measurable response or act. Behavior is occasionally broadly defined to include cognitions, psychophysiological reactions, and feelings, which may not be directly observable but are defined in terms that can be measured by means of various assessment strategies

3.   Consequences: Something that is given or something that is withdrawn or delayed. Consequences are best described in terms of reinforcement and punishment

F.   Reinforcement: A procedure or consequence that increases the frequency of the behavior immediately preceding it

1.   Positive reinforcement: Positive events or consequences that follow a behavior and strengthen it *get allowance if Room is cleaned.*

2.   Negative reinforcement: Removal of a negative event or consequence that serves to increase the frequency of a particular behavior *Seat Belt Buzzer. Becus increases the freq of Buckling*

G.   Punishment: The presentation of an aversive event or the removal of a positive reinforcer which results in the decrease in frequency of a particular behavior

H. Extinction: The process whereby reinforcement for a behavior stops, resulting in the eventual decrease in frequency and possible eradication of that behavior

    1. Extinction burst: When reinforcement initially is stopped, a brief increase in the frequency or intensity of the behavior may occur

    2. Figure 4.3 Positive Reinforcement, Negative Reinforcement, Punishment, and Extinction

VII. Applications of Learning Theory to Practice

A. The use of positive reinforcement

B. Types of positive reinforcers

    1. Primary or unconditioned reinforcers: Are rewarding in themselves, without any association with other reinforcers

    2. Secondary reinforcers: Have values that are learned through association with other reinforcers

        a. Material reinforcers and non-food consumables

        b. Activities

            1) Tangible events whose value has been learned

            2) Premack Principle: The opportunity to engage in a high-probability behavior (a preferred behavior) as a consequence for a low-probability behavior (a less-preferred behavior) will increase the low-probability behavior, but never vice versa

[Handwritten note in left margin: Person prefers garden work over laundry. Allow them to plant a garden after they finish the laundry. He/she will be more likely to do the laundry.]

        c. Social reinforcers: Include words and gestures used to indicate caring and concern toward another person

            1) Verbal praise

            2) Physical praise

        d. Token reinforcers: Designated symbolic objects reflecting specific units of value that an individual can exchange for some other commodity that he or she wants

C. Reinforcers versus rewards

    1. Reward: Something that is given in return for a service or a particular achievement

    2. Reinforcers: Increase the frequency of a behavior

D.   Suggestions for using positive reinforcement

   1.   Quality of positive reinforcement

   2.   Immediacy of positive reinforcement

   3.   Frequency of positive reinforcement

      a.   Continuous

      b.   Intermittent

   4.   Shaping behavior: Refers to the reinforcement of successive approximations, that is, small steps of progress, made toward the final desired behavior

E.   The use of punishment

   1.   Potential negative consequences

      a.   Tends to elicit a negative emotional response

      b.   Avoidance of the punishing person or situation

      c.   Teaches children to be aggressive

      d.   Possibility of physically harming the child

      e.   Teaches people what they should <u>not</u> do rather than what they <u>should</u> do

   2.   The nature of punishment

      a.   Relatively quick decrease in frequency of behavior

      b.   Effects are often temporary

      c.   Effects are frequently limited to the conditions where the punishment occurred

   3.   Effectiveness of punishment

      a.   Curb or eliminate self-injurious behavior when used in conjunction with positive reinforcers

      b.   The potential side effects of punishment should be cautiously considered

   4.   Suggestions for using punishment

      a.   Should be administered as soon as possible after the behavior that is to be punished occurs

      b.   Administer the punishing consequences every time the behavior occurs

      c.   Most important—reinforce appropriate behaviors at the same time

[Handwritten margin notes: "elec. 1yr old. Socket divert attent. instead."]

[Handwritten note: "If Behavior doesn't decrease prob never will."]

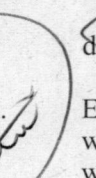

d. Remain calm while administering punishment

5. Ethical Question 4.2: What are your thoughts about punishing children? What was your experience with punishment as a child? If punishment was used, in what ways were you punished? Did punishment work or not? Why?

VIII. Additional Issues

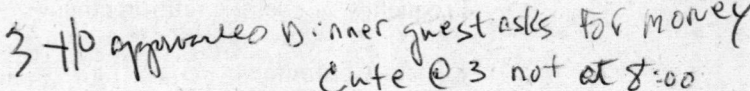

A. Accidental training

1. Negative attention is frequently an effective means of providing accidental training

2. Highlight 4.3 Accidental Training

B. Behaviorally specific terminology

C. Measuring improvement

1. Baseline: Refers to the frequency with which behavior occurs before behavior modification begins

2. Table 4.1: Behavior Chart: Number of Times Jessica Raises Her Hand

D. The importance of parental attention

1. A criticism of the application of learning theory has been that it is a rigid and somewhat cold dissection of human behavior

2. Active listening: The process in which the receiver of a communication pays close attention to what the sender of the communication is saying, and subsequently reflects back what was heard to make sure the message has been accurately understood

3. Feelings and communication occur simultaneously with the ongoing management of children's behavior

IX. A Specific Treatment Situation: Time-out from Reinforcement

A. Time-out: Previous reinforcement is withdrawn, with the intended result being a decrease in the frequency of a particular behavior. It is a form of extinction

B. Improving effectiveness

1. Should be applied immediately after the targeted behavior occurs

2. Should be applied consistently

3. Should extend from 1 to 10 minutes

4. Should take place in a very boring place

5. Avoid giving positive reinforcement—attention

6. Tell the child ahead of time which specific behaviors will result in a time-out, and the length of the time-out

7. Use gentle physical restraint if necessary and little emotion

8. After the time-out, replace behavior with positive reinforcement and praise it when it occurs

C. Ethical Question 4.3: What are your thoughts about using time-outs in child management? To what extent, if any, do you think they work? If they should be used, under what circumstances are they appropriate? Should any caregiver (for example, day-care providers, teachers, and babysitters) be allowed to administer them, or should parents be the only ones to do so? What are the reasons for your answer?

D. Grounding

1. Might resemble time-outs, but they don't seem to be very effective

2. Ethical Question 4.4: To what extent, if any, do you think grounding works? What were your experiences with grounding if you had any? What were the results? Would you consider grounding as a means of disciplining your own children? Why?

X. Impacts of Common Life Events on Children

A. Membership in family systems

1. Parenting styles

a. Permissive parenting: Encourages children to be independent and make their own decisions

b. Authoritarian parenting: Emphasizes control and conformity

c. Authoritative parenting: Provides control and consistent support

d. Ethical Question 4.5: What type of parenting style do you think is best, and why? What style did your parents use? To what extent was it effective, and why?

e. Spotlight on Diversity 4.2: Cultural Context and Parenting Style

1) Chinese American parents are generally viewed as more demanding concerning control of their children's behavior

2)   In Hispanic and Asian Pacific Island families, firm insistence on respect for parental authority (especially the father) is paired with high parental involvement

3)   African American mothers tend to require immediate and rigorous compliance with their directions, combined with caring and affection

B.   Spotlight on Diversity 4.3: Ethnic and Cultural Differences in Families: Empowerment through Appreciation of Strengths

1.   Three important factors when assessing the dynamics of families from various cultures

    a.   Cultural variations involving expectations and values reflect each culture

    b.   People of different cultures living in the United States and Canada experience varying degrees of assimilation into the majority culture simply by living there

    c.   People not having a white European origin frequently experience discrimination and oppression because of their differences

2.   Think in terms of cultural pluralism instead of a melting pot

3.   Respect and appreciate the differences within large groups

4.   Hispanic families

    a.   58 percent are of Mexican heritage

    b.   10 percent are Puerto Rican

    c.   3.5 percent are Cuban

    d.   28 percent are other Hispanic or Latino

    e.   Cultural themes

      1)   Common language

      2)   Family relationships

        a)   Great value on maintaining original two-parent family

        b)   Commitment to extended family

        c)   Community support systems

            (1)   Botanicas: Shops that sell herbs as well as records and novels in Spanish

            (2)   Bodegas: Grocery stores, also serve as information centers

            (3)   Club sociales: Provide recreation and links to community resources

            (4)   Como familial: Special friends who furnish reciprocal support

            (5)   Compadrazo: People who participate in baptisms, first communions, etc. and often serve as parent substitutes

      3)   Strict division of gender roles (although there is debate as to the extent to which Latinos adhere to traditional gender roles in contemporary U.S. society)

5.   Native-American families

    a.   Sensitivity to differences among tribes

    b.   Importance of extended family—sense of self is secondary to family and tribe

    c.   Emphasis on individualism—respect for individual opinion

    d.   Harmony with nature—one part of a greater whole

    e.   Concept of time—time considered aspect of nature and should not control how you live

    f.   Spirituality—involving both tribal religion and Christianity

6.   Asian-American families

    a.   There is great variation among the many groups clustered under this umbrella

        1)   Asian Americans (Japanese, Chinese, Filipinos, Asian Indians, and Koreans)

        2)   Asian Pacific Islanders (Hawaiians, Samoans, and Guamanians)

        3)   Southeast Asian refugees (Vietnamese, Cambodians, and Laotians)

    b.   Tend to consider the family as the primary unit

       c.   Interdependence—emphasis is on family harmony, adapting to the needs of others, and adherence to "correct" values

       d.   Hierarchical relationships—communication flows down from parent to child, who is expected to defer to the adults

       e.   Generally adhere to patriarchal hierarchy, fathers are the breadwinners, protectors, and ultimate authorities. Male children are highly prized, and older daughters are expected to play a caretaking function with younger siblings

   7.   A note on difference: Cultural themes of values and behavior are in general terminology

   C.   Membership in sibling subsystems

       1.   The coming of a new baby

       2.   Sibling interaction

       3.   The effects of birth order, family size, and family spacing

   D.   Gender role socialization

       1.   To what extent are males and females inherently different and in what ways

       2.   Nature/nurture argument about why people become the people they do

XI.   The Social Environment: Peers, Television, and School

   A.   The social aspects of play with peers

       1.   Purposes of play

          a.   Physical development

          b.   Fantasizing and creative thinking

          c.   Learning to relate to peers

          d.   Major avenue of socialization

       2.   Five qualities of play

          a.   Done purely for enjoyment

          b.   An end in itself

          c.   Done by choice

[Handwritten annotations:]

K76
Dr. Spock
1/ Children should be told in advance about the changes coming.

2/ Sharing a bed, baby using same crib/high chair.

3/ Tell child how much they're loved & valued.

3/ Encourage to express their feelings.

Some young children may regress
Some hostile
" happy & proud.

80% of U.S. child have at least 1 or more sibs.

1st Borns — parents may have higher expectations
↑ scores on achievemt Tests, go to College, conform to parent request, more self-controlled

only child — more achievemt oriented

106

      d.   Involves active participation

      e.   Enhances socialization and creativity

3. Play and interaction—social play and fantasy play

      a.   Social Play: Involves the extent to which children interact with other children as they play

            1)   Unoccupied behavior: Involves little or no activity

            2)   Onlooker play: Simply observing the playing behavior of other children

            3)   Solitary play: Playing independently, no attention given to other children and what they are doing

            4)   Parallel play: Playing independently, however child is playing in a similar manner or with similar toys as other children

            5)   Associative play: Playing together, but play is not organized

            6)   Cooperative play: Playing with each other in order to attain a similar goal

      b.   Fantasy play: Involves what children think about and how they imagine their pretend games as they play

4. Gender differences in play

      a.   Aggressiveness

      b.   Toy preference

[handwritten: Pink & Blue.]

[handwritten: Nature/nuture/socialization]

5. The peer group and popularity

[handwritten: Childs equals.]

      a.   Sociometry: Technique for examining children's interaction, involving asking children questions about their relationships and feelings toward other people

      b.   Sociogram: A diagram illustrating the relationships of children toward other people

      c.   Figure 4.4 Sociograms of a Special Education Class

      d.   Social skills provide a primary basis for popularity

B. Influence of television

I. Research indicates that television does influence and increase children's violent behavior

a. May model violent behavior they see

b. More likely to lose control and become more violent

c. Can influence a child's value system and beliefs about how the world really is

2. Relationship between amount of violent television viewed and amount of aggressiveness manifested by viewers

3. Children's cartoons among the most violent, followed by toy commercials

4. Explicitness of sex on television

5. Inaccurate portrayal of ethnic and other diversity

6. Underrepresentation of women

7. Many programs convey positive ethical messages about the value of family life, the need to work hard and sacrifice in order to achieve important goals, the value of friendship, the importance of loyalty and commitment in relationships, and many other cultural values

8. President Clinton's pleas to media after Columbine High School massacre

a. Movie studios stop showing guns in ads and previews that children can see

b. Theaters and video stores more rigorously enforce rules barring unchaperoned children under 17 from viewing R-rated movies

c. Re-evaluation of the ratings system

9. American Academy of Pediatrics suggest that children under two years old should not watch television, older children should not have television sets in their bedrooms, and pediatricians should have parents fill out a "media history" on office visits

10. Ethical Question 4.6: Is there too much violence on television? Should the amount of violence be monitored? If so, who should be responsible for setting standards and scrutinizing content? Should children's viewing of television be limited? If so, in what ways?

C. The school environment

    1. The teacher's impact

    2. The classroom environment

(handwritten: Group 2)

    3. Ethical Question 4.7: What type of classroom do you believe is most effective, and why?

    4. Spotlight on Diversity 4.4: Educational Programming that Responds to Cultural Values

(handwritten: Self-Fulfilling prophecy — Children preform at the level they are expected)

        a. The Kamehameha Early Education Program (KEEP)—developed to focus on the cultural values of Native Hawaiians

        b. KEEP is built on the principle of collaborative classroom work that complies well with Hawaiian cultural values

        c. Talk story—a manner of speaking that is common in Hawaiian communities, where a group of individuals all contribute to the reiteration or creation of a story by contributing small pieces

    5. Race, ethnicity, and schools

        a. External factors pertaining to gaps between the educational attainment of whites and some other ethnic groups

            1) Socioeconomic status

            2) Neighborhood resources

        b. Internal factors pertaining to gaps between the educational attainment of whites and some other ethnic groups

            1) Social atmosphere

            2) Inadequate cultural values and ethnicity depicted in instructional materials

            3) Low expectations and biases of educators

XII. Child Maltreatment

A. Maltreatment: Physical abuse; being given inadequate care and nourishment; deprivation of adequate medical care; insufficient encouragement to attend school consistently; exploitation by being forced to work too hard or too long; exposure to unwholesome or demoralizing circumstances; sexual abuse; and emotional abuse and neglect

B. Incidence of child maltreatment

    1.   Nearly 3 million cases of child maltreatment were reported in one year; 63 percent were neglect, 20 percent were physical abuse, 10 percent were sexual abuse, and 8 percent were psychological maltreatment

    2.   It is estimated that less than half of all maltreatment cases come to the attention of authorities

C. Physical child abuse

    1.   Spotlight on Diversity 4.5: Diverse Cultural Contexts: Discipline or Abuse?

    2.   Characteristics of physically abused victims

        a.   Bruises

        b.   Lacerations

        c.   Fractures

        d.   Burns

        e.   Head injuries

        f.   Internal injuries

    3.   Questions if you think abuse has occurred

        a.   Does this child get hurt too often for someone his or her age?

        b.   Does the child have multiple injuries?

        c.   Do the injuries occur in patterns, assume recognizable shapes, or look like some of the injuries described earlier?

        d.   Are the injuries such that they don't seem possible for a child at that stage of development?

        e.   Do the explanations given for the injuries make sense?

    4.   Behavioral indicators of possible physical abuse

        a.   Extremely passive, accommodating, submissive behaviors aimed at preserving a low profile and avoiding potential conflict with parents that might lead to abuse

            1)   If they are invisible, the parent may not be provoked

            2)   Hypervigilance: Abused children will avoid playing because it draws too much attention to themselves

        b.   Notably aggressive behaviors and marked overt hostility toward others caused by rage and frustration at not getting needs met

c. Developmental lags—these may appear in the form of language delays, poorly developed social skills for their age level, or lags in motor development

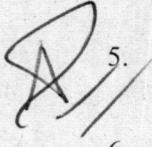

5. Ethical Question 4.8: Do parents have the right to spank their children? When does discipline become abuse?

6. Characteristics of abusers

   a. Need for personal support and nurturance

   b. Social isolation

   c. Communication and relationship difficulties

   d. Poor parenting skills

   e. Poor general coping skills

   f. Extreme external stress and life crises

D. Child neglect

   1. Child neglect: A caregiver's failure to meet a child's basic needs, and may involve depriving a child of physical, emotional, medical, mental health, or educational necessities

      a. Physical neglect: The failure to protect from harm or danger and provide for the child's basic physical needs, including adequate shelter, food, and clothing

      b. Inadequate supervision: Situations in which children are without a caretaker or the caretaker is inattentive or unsuitable, and therefore the children are in danger of harming themselves or possibly others

   2. Characteristics of neglected children

      a. Physical health care—illnesses are not attended to or proper dental care is not maintained

      b. Mental health care—children's mental health problems are either ignored or left unattended

      c. Educational neglect—parents fail to comply with laws concerning school attendance

      d. Supervision—children often or almost always are left alone without adequate supervision

      e. Abandonment and substitute child care—most blatant form of neglect is abandonment where parents leave children alone and unattended. Closely related to abandonment is when parents fail to return when they're expected

f. Housing hazards—inadequate heat, ventilation, or safety features. Dangerous substances such as drugs or weapons may be left in children's easy reach

g. Household sanitation—food may be spoiled, home filled with garbage or excrement, plumbing might not work

h. Personal hygiene—children's clothing may be ripped, filthy, and threadbare. Their hair might be unkempt and dirty. They themselves might be unbathed and odorous

i. Nutrition—children who frequently complain that they're hungry and searching for food, receiving food that provides them with inadequate nutrition. Significant delays in development result from malnutrition

j. Social and attachment difficulties—children may have problems interacting with parents, and they may fail to maintain secure attachment relationships

k. Cognitive and academic deficits—children may exhibit language deficits, poor academic achievement, low grades, deficits in intelligence, decreased creativity, and difficulties in problem-solving

l. Emotional and behavioral problems—neglected children may exhibit indifference, withdrawal and isolation, low self-esteem, physical and verbal aggression, difficulties in paying attention, and psychiatric symptoms such as those characterizing anxiety or depression

3. Physical conditions resulting from extreme neglect

a. Nonorganic failure to thrive syndrome (NFTT): Infants who are below the fifth percentile in weight, and sometimes in height

b. Psychosocial dwarfism (PSD): Emotional deprivation promotes abnormally low growth. PSD children (18 months to 16 years) are also below the fifth percentile in weight and height, exhibit retarded skeletal maturation, and a variety of behavioral problems

4. Characteristics of neglectful parents

a. Types of mothers who neglected their children

1) Indifferent, lethargic mother

2) Impulsive, irresponsible mother

3) Depressed mother

4) Mothers with mental retardation

5) Mothers with serious mental illnesses such as psychosis

5. Ethical Question 4.9: Should parents who neglect their children be punished or receive treatment? How should this be accomplished?

E. Psychological Maltreatment

1. Psychological abuse: Belittling, humiliating, rejecting, undermining a child's self-esteem, and generally not conducive to creating a positive atmosphere for a child

2. Psychological neglect: Passive or passive/aggressive inattention to the child's emotional needs, nurturing, or emotional well-being

3. Basic categories of behavior involved in psychological maltreatment

   a. Rejection: Abandoning the child, failing to acknowledge the child, scapegoating the child (i.e., placing unjustified blame on a child for some behavior or problem or criticizing a child unfairly), and verbally humiliating the child

   b. Isolation: Keeping the child away from a variety of appropriate relationships

   c. Terrorizing: Threatening and scaring the child

   d. Ignoring: Failing to respond to a child or simply pretending that the child isn't there

   e. Corrupting: Encouraging or supporting illegal or deviant behaviors

4. Characteristics of psychologically maltreated children—low self-esteem, anxiety, depression, a negative view of life, increased suicide potential, emotional instability, difficulties with impulse control, substance abuse, eating disorders, relationship difficulties, violence, criminal behavior, school problems, and poor performance on intelligence and achievement tests

5. Characteristics of perpetrators of psychological maltreatment—usually suffer serious emotional problems or deficits themselves. They may lack coping skills, their own emotional needs may not have been met in childhood, their own parents may have lacked nurturing skills, they may also be dealing with personal problems such as mental illness or alcoholism

F. A macro system response: Child Protective Services

G.	Treatment of physical abuse, neglect, and psychological maltreatment: Social work role

1.	Variables affecting a worker's decision regarding agency intervention

a.	Clearly visible proof of abuse or environmental characteristics which obviously endanger a child

b.	The degree of the child's helplessness and vulnerability

c.	Self-destructive behavior on the part of the child

d.	A long history of severe abuse

e.	Abusers who show no or little regret for their child's abuse and have difficulty accepting responsibility

f.	Abusers who openly reject the child or blame the child for the problem

g.	Serious emotional disturbances on the part of parents

h.	Lack of cooperation on the part of the parents

i.	Families who are exposed to numerous and severe psychological and social pressures

j.	Isolation of the family and lack of social support systems

2.	Parents need to learn how to prevent future abuse

H.	A macro system response: Involvement of the courts

1.	Petition: A written complaint being submitted to the court that the alleged abuse or neglect has occurred

2.	Adjudication: A hearing where the alleged abuse or neglect is proven or discounted

3.	Disposition: A hearing where the court determines what is to be done with the child

I.	Sexual abuse: Any sexual activity with a child where consent is not or cannot be given. This includes sexual contact that is accomplished by force or threat of force, regardless of the age of the participants, and all sexual contact between an adult and a child, regardless of whether there is deception or the child understands the sexual nature of the activity. The sexually abusive acts may include sexual penetration, sexual touching, or noncontact sexual acts such as exposure or voyeurism

1.	Incest: Sexual activities between a child and a relative, defined fairly broadly as a parent, stepparent, parent's live-in partner or lover, foster parent, sibling, cousin, uncle, aunt, or grandparent

2. Dynamics of child sexual abuse

   a. Greater danger from people they know than from strangers

   b. Children are easy victims

   c. The vast majority of offenders are male, although boys are more likely than girls to be abused by women, and 40 percent of the reported cases of day care sexual abuse involve female offenders

   d. Pedophile: Someone who prefers children for sexual gratification

   e. Phases of sexual abuse

      1) Engagement

      2) Sexual interaction

      3) Secrecy

      4) Disclosure

      5) Post-disclosure

3. Risk factors for sexual abuse

   a. Child risk factors

      1) Being a girl

      2) Being at an age slightly before puberty

      3) Having a disability

   b. Family risk factors

      1) Absence of a biological parent from the home

      2) Family conflict and communication problems

      3) Family isolation

      4) Having a mother who is not readily available to children

4. Characteristics of sexual abuse victims

   a. Physical indicators

      1) Sexually transmitted diseases

      2) Problems with throat or mouth

      3) Difficulties with urination

4)   Penile or vaginal discharge

5)   Bruises in the genital area

6)   Pregnancy

b.   Psychological indicators of sexual abuse

    1)   Low self-esteem

    2)   Emotional disturbance

    3)   Anger

    4)   Fear

    5)   Anxiety

    6)   Depression (sometimes suicidal)

c.   Behavioral indicators of sexual abuse

    1)   Withdrawing from others

    2)   Experiencing difficulties in peer interaction

    3)   Engaging in excessive sexual activity and inappropriate sexual behavior

    4)   Odd behavior related to sex

        a)   Knowledge or gestures inappropriate for age of child

        b)   Touching oneself or others inappropriately in a sexual manner

        c)   Desperate fears about being touched, undressing, taking showers in gym class, or being alone with a particular gender

    5)   Statements that seem odd

5.   Long-term effects of sexual abuse—not necessarily destined to be poorly adjusted for life

a.   Posttraumatic stress disorder: A condition where a person continues to reexperience an excessively traumatic event like a bloody battle experience or a sexual assault

b.   Variables that increase the risk of more serious problems in adulthood for survivors of sexual abuse

    1)   Closer relationship to the perpetrator

2)   Duration of the abuse

3)   Use of force and the intensity of abuse

4)   Lack of presence of parental and other support

5)   Inadequate coping ability of the survivor

6.   Highlight 4.4 Suggestions for Talking to Children Victimized by Sexual Assault

a.   Always believe the child

b.   Be warm and empathic

c.   Don't react with shock or disgust

d.   Encourage child to share all feelings, including negative ones

e.   Listen to the child

f.   Talk to the child in a private place

g.   Tell the child he or she is not the only child who has had this experience

h.   Allow child to express feelings of guilt

i.   Talk in language that the child can understand

j.   Tell the child you are very glad he or she told you about the incident(s)

k.   Ask if the child would like to ask you any questions and be sure to answer them honestly

l.   Do not treat the child any differently after he or she has told you

m.   If the child asks you to keep the abuse secret, answer honestly

n.   Don't let the issue drop

7. Treatment of sexual abuse: Social work role

    a. Phases of treatment of the incestuous family

        1) Disclosure-panic

        2) Assessment-awareness

        3) Restructure

    b. Duration

    c. Objectives

    d. Treatment themes

8. Prevention of sexual abuse: The need for a macro system response

9. Educating children about sexual abuse

    a. Right to privacy

    b. Right to say "no"

    c. Learn correct sexual terminology

    d. Open communication

XIII. Summary

Experiential Exercises and Simulations

Three exercises are described. In the first, you will analyze families in terms of systems concepts. In the second, you will describe certain behaviors in specific, measurable terms. In the third, you will evaluate the potential effectiveness of a variety of behavioral intervention programs for children.

Exercise 4.1: The Family System

A. Brief description
You are presented with a description of a family and its members, followed by a series of situations occurring within the family. Discussion focuses on the direct application of systems concepts to this family and its situations.

B. Objectives
You will:
1. Examine the meanings of various systems theory concepts.
2. Apply these concepts to a series of concrete family life situations.

C.   Procedure
1.   After reviewing the systems theory concepts, join other students in a circle. This allows maximum observation of the activity.
2.   The instructor describes the following family configuration:

WARD: Ward, age 41, is the husband and father. He can generally be described as calm and level-headed. He makes most of the family's decisions. Professionally, he's an accountant, earning an upper-middle-class income.

JUNE: June, age 35, is the wife and mother of the family. She can generally be described as pleasant, attractive, and warm. Although she is bright, she sometimes has difficulty asserting herself. She usually defers to Ward's opinions and decisions. She does not work outside the home.

WALTER: Walter is a pleasant, generally cooperative 16-year-old son. He has numerous friends, maintains a B+ grade average in school, and is interested in sports, especially football. He also loves cars and works on old wrecks whenever he has a chance in his free time.

BEVERLY: Beverly is 8 years old, and in third grade. She can generally be described as "cute." Although she is usually pleasant and cooperative, she has a tendency to get into minor trouble.

3.   The instructor asks for volunteers to play each of the family members. The roles are written on 5" x 8" notecards and given to each role-player. The family members sit together inside the class circle. The role-players are given a series of situations. Each is asked to respond as if he or she really was that family member. Role-players can add any additional details they wish about the family member.
4.   The instructor presents the following situations to the family members:

a.   Ward loses his job. The family faces a financial crisis.
b.   The school principal calls and reports that Beverly was caught smoking in the school restroom.
c.   Walter tells the family that he wants to drop out of school to earn some money. He says he has a great offer to work at the local garage as a mechanic earning $4.13 an hour.
d.   June tells Ward that she's having an affair with the mailman.

5.   Each family member tells how he or she feels about the situation and describes how the situation might affect the family.
6.   After receiving feedback from the individual role-players, discuss the situations using systems theory concepts. Relate each systems theory term to the dynamics that might be occurring in the family. For example, any of the situations might upset the family's homeostasis. Other examples include how June's affair might affect the parental subsystem and how Ward's losing his job affects the amount of input (in this case, financial input) into the family.

A.   Brief description
You will be asked to select, describe, observe, and determine the frequency of a behavior manifested by someone else in the room over a designated period of time. Discussion will focus on the importance of specificity in describing behavior.

B.   Objectives
You will:
1.   Describe a behavior in specific, measurable terms.
2.   Examine the difficulty involved in behavioral definition.

C.   Procedure
1.   Arrange yourselves in a circle to allow for optimum observation of other students' behavior.
2.   Take a few moments and select a specific behavior manifested by a particular individual in the room. Examples of such behaviors include blinking eyes, tapping feet, nodding heads, yawning, or swinging feet.
3.   Describe your chosen behavior in writing.
4.   You will have three minutes to count the number of times the specific behavior occurs. You will be told when to begin and when to stop your counting. Upon completion of your observation, write down the frequency of the behavior.
5.   Discuss the specific behaviors selected. What difficulties did you encounter in attempting to complete this task? Select particular behaviors and illustrate how an arbitrary decision is sometimes involved in deciding whether a behavior did or did not occur. For example, how far must one's head move before it is considered a head turn? How distinctly must an eyelid flutter before the movement is considered to be a blink? Relate this task to problems of description and of monitoring child-behavior management. Emphasize the importance of behavioral specificity in order to measure improvements in behavior and to enhance accountability.

A.   Brief description
Several behavioral programs for children are described; you are to evaluate their potential effectiveness.

B.   Objectives
You will:
1.   Recognize potential problems in attempting to control behavior.
2.   Assess the potential effectiveness of various behavioral techniques.
3.   Propose effective alternative child-behavior management techniques.

C.   Procedure
1.   Several child-behavior management situations are described on small slips of paper, which are placed in an envelope. The situations may include, but are not limited to, the following:

a.	Virgil, age 6, wets his pants an average of eight times a day. His mother decides to try to stop this behavior. She tells him that if he doesn't wet his pants the whole day he can have his dessert after dinner.

b.	Koko's father is disgusted with Koko's childish behavior. Koko is 9 years old. He says that he will give her a nickel every time she acts her age.

c.	Ahmed, age 11, is a sloppy eater. His mother states that if he doesn't change his eating habits, he'll have to go without supper.

d.	Susie, age 7, teases her sister Karen, age 3. Susie takes Karen's Barbie doll and holds it high above her head so Karen can't reach it. As a result, Karen cries and screams. Their father decides this behavior has to stop. He tells Susie that if she doesn't stop it, he'll take her own favorite doll and give it to Karen.

e.	Shirley, age 8, likes to jump off the tool shed into a big bale of hay. Her mother thinks this is much too dangerous and wants her to stop it. Her mother can usually see Shirley start climbing on the tool-shed roof from the kitchen window. Every time Shirley's mother sees Shirley climbing, she runs out of the house, grabs Shirley by the hand, pulls her into the house, and pleads with her to stop that climbing or she'll kill herself.

f.	Rick, age 10, likes to annoy his brother Kevin, age 6. Rick does this by shooting an air gun at Kevin. Even though the air gun just shoots air, it makes a loud noise, and sometimes Rick aims it right into Kevin's ear. Their parents want this to stop, so they ignore the behavior, hoping that it will go away.

2.	After reviewing the learning theory concepts and applications presented in the text, you will critique the behavioral situations. A volunteer draws one of the slips from the envelope, comments on the pros and cons of the program, and makes suggestions for improving it. After the student has a chance to comment, the rest of the class has an opportunity to evaluate the adequacy of the behavioral program.

3.	The envelope is handed to the next student. This person follows the same procedure as the first, and then the discussion is again resumed by the entire class.

4.	Repeat this procedure as frequently as time, numbers of situations, and interest allow.

Chapter 5
Ethnocentrism and Racism

Study Outline

I. **A Perspective**

II. **Ethnic Groups and Ethnocentrism**

    A.   Ethnic group: A distinct group of people who share a common knowledge, set of customs, history, culture, race, religion, and/or origin

    B.   Ethnocentrism: An orientation or set of beliefs that holds one's own culture, ethnic or racial group, or nation is superior to others

    C.   Spotlight on Diversity 5.1: Violence Against Minorities in the United States

        1.   Chinese Americans—frequent massacres of Chinese mining and railroad workers

        2.   African Americans

            a.   Slavery

            b.   Race riots

        3.   Native Americans

            a.   Extermination of many tribes

            b.   Bounties for Native American scalps

        4.   Racist groups

        5.   Police brutality

III. **Race and Racism**

    A.   Racial groups and ethnic groups are not necessarily the same

    B.   Race: A group of people believed to have a common set of physical characteristics

    C.   Racism: Stereotyping and generalizing about people, usually negatively because of their race; commonly a basis of discrimination against members of racial minority groups

IV. Aspects of Social and Economic Forces: Prejudice, Discrimination, and Oppression

A. Discrimination: The prejudgment and negative treatment of people based on identifiable characteristics such as race, gender, religion, or ethnicity. This involves physical actions, unequal treatment of people because they belong to a category

B. Prejudice: A combination of stereotyped beliefs and negative attitudes, so that prejudiced individuals think about people in a predetermined, usually negative, categorical way

C. Four types of people in terms of prejudice

1. Unprejudiced nondiscriminator: In both belief and practice, upholds American ideals of freedom and equality

2. Unprejudiced discriminator: Is not personally prejudiced but may sometimes, reluctantly, discriminate against other groups because it seems socially or financially convenient to do so

3. Prejudiced nondiscriminator: Feels hostile to other groups but recognizes that law and social pressures are opposed to overt discrimination

4. Prejudiced discriminator: Does not believe in the values of freedom and equality and consistently discriminates against other groups in both word and deed

D. Types of discrimination

1. *De jure* discrimination: Legal discrimination (Jim Crow laws)

2. *De facto* discrimination: Discrimination that actually exists, whether legal or not

E. Oppression: The unjust or cruel exercise of authority or power

V. Racial and Ethnic Stereotypes

A. Stereotypes: Preconceived and relatively fixed ideas about an individual, group, or social status

B. Racial and ethnic stereotypes: Involve attributing a fixed and usually inaccurate or unfavorable conception to a racial or ethnic group

VI. Racial and Ethnic Discrimination Is the Problem of Whites

A. From its earliest days, our society has singled out certain minorities to treat unequally

B. Minority: A group, or a member of a group, of people of a distinct racial, religious, ethnic, or political identity that is smaller or less powerful than the community's controlling group

C. Minority relationships become recognized by the majority as a social problem when the members of the majority disagree as to whether the subjugation of the minority is socially desirable or in the ultimate interest of the majority

VII. White Privilege

A. Examples of white privilege

1. White people can go shopping alone and be pretty well assured that they will not be followed or harassed

2. White people have no problem finding housing to rent or purchase in an area they can afford and want to live in

3. White people can feel assured that their children will be given curricular materials in school that testify to the existence of their race

4. White people can go into any supermarket and find the staple foods that fit with their cultural traditions

5. When white people use checks, credit cards or cash, they can be sure that their skin color is not being taken into account when their financial reliability is questioned

6. White people are never asked to speak for all white people

7. White people can go into any hairdresser's shop and find someone who can cut their hair

8. White people in affluent neighborhoods are generally confident that their neighbors will be neutral or pleasant to them

9. White people can assume that police officers will provide protection and assistance

10. White people can be sure that if they need legal or medical help, their race will not work against them

B. Hate crimes

1. Hate crimes have been added to the penal codes in nearly every state

2. With hate crimes, judges can impose a higher sentence when they find a crime was committed with a biased motive

VIII. Race Is a Social Concept

A. The concept of race is considered to be one of the most dangerous and tragic myths in our society

B. There are no clearly delineating characteristics of any race

C. Social definition of race is based on the way in which members of a society classify each other by physical characteristics

D. Ethical Question 5.1: Do you believe that some ethnic groups are more intelligent than other ethnic groups?

E. Dangerous myth that physical traits are linked with mental traits and cultural achievements

F. Most scientists, both physical and social, now believe that in biological inheritance all races are alike in everything that really makes any difference (such as problem-solving capacities, altruistic tendencies, and communication capacities)

IX. Institutional Values and Racism: Discrimination in Systems

A. Institutional racism: Discriminatory acts and policies against a racial group that pervade the major macro systems of society, including the legal, political, economic, and educational systems

B. Institutional values form the foundation for macro system policies

C. Individual racism: The negative attitudes one person has about all members of a racial or ethnic group, often resulting in overt acts such as name-calling, social exclusion, or violence

D. Discrimination and oppression in organizational macro systems

E. Institutional discrimination: Prejudicial treatment in organizations based on official policies, overt behaviors, or behaviors that may be covert but approved by those with power

F. Discrimination and oppression in community macro systems

   1. Educational macro system—schools in white neighborhoods generally have better facilities and more highly trained teachers than do those in minority neighborhoods

   2. History on Native American children—they learn that Indians were mere parts of the landscape and wilderness which had to be cleared out, to make way for the great "movement" of white population across the land

   3. Criminal justice macro system—although African Americans compose only about 12 percent of the population, they make up about 50 percent of the prison populations

X. Sources of Prejudice and Discrimination

A. Theories about why racial and ethnic discrimination occurs

   1. Projection: A psychological defense mechanism in which one attributes to others characteristics that one is unwilling to recognize in oneself

   2. Frustration-aggression: When unable to achieve or obtain something we desire, we sometimes retaliate against another person or group of people (sometimes called a scapegoat—anyone who bears the blame for others)

3.   Countering insecurity and inferiority: Insecure people seek to feel better about themselves by putting down another group

4.   Authoritarianism: Being inflexible and rigid and having a low tolerance for uncertainty. An authoritarian personality has a great respect for authority figures and quickly submits to their will

5.   History: Groups now viewed by white prejudiced persons as being second class are groups that have been either conquered, enslaved, or admitted into our society on a subordinate basis

6.   Competition and exploitation: In our society, once whites achieved dominance, they then used (and still are using) their power to exploit nonwhites through cheap labor. Throughout history in most societies, the dominant group (which has greater power and wealth) has sought to maintain the status quo by keeping those who have the least in an inferior position

7.   Socialization patterns: Prejudice is also a learned phenomenon and is transmitted from generation to generation through socialization processes

8.   Belief in the one true religion: A person with such a belief system comes to the conclusion that he or she is one of "God's chosen few." Feeling superior to others often leads a person to devalue "heathens," and then to treat them in an inferior way

9.   Ethical Question 5.2: If a social worker believes his or her religion is the one true religion, can that social worker fully accept clients who are members of some other religious faith? If your answer is no, do you believe that person should seek a different career?

B.   Evaluation of discrimination theories

C.   Spotlight on Diversity 5.2: Is Racial Discrimination Based on Criminal Thinking?

1.   Social Darwinism: The belief that the superior race must dominate all other races in order to ensure survival

2.   Concept of criminal thinking derives from rational therapy

3.   An Overview of Criminal Thinking and Thinking Errors Common to Racist Beliefs

     a.   Power thrust:

         1)   Criminal thinking: The criminal inflates low self-esteem by viewing himself or herself as an all-powerful, unique individual whose needs must come first and who can force others to meet those needs. The criminal rejects legitimate authority

2)   Racist thinking: Everything we know about racial discrimination allows us to acknowledge that it is based on a power thrust—control of one person over others and a resulting sense of power or triumph

b.   Ownership:

1)   Criminal thinking: An extreme form of control over others based on the criminal's attitude that his or her rights are unlimited; allows criminal to disregard all personal and social boundaries

2)   Racist thinking: Slaveholding is ownership by definition, and it is human control carried to the extreme

c.   Failure to consider injury to others:

1)   Criminal thinking: The criminal minimizes or denies injuring victims by an immediate criminal act or its far-reaching effects on the victims and others in society in order to maintain his or her self-image

2)   Racist thinking: People of color are forced to suffer (by comparison to their white counterparts) from lower grades of service, fewer opportunities for advancement, higher rates of infant mortality, longer periods of incarceration, and fewer options for neighborhoods in which they may live

d.   Lack of empathy:

1)   Criminal thinking: The criminal can maintain feelings of uniqueness only by refusing to consider the experiences or feelings of others

2)   Racist thinking: Oppression—if we believe that others are inferior to us, it reduces our motivation to empathically consider how they might feel or otherwise be affected by unequal treatment

e.   Good person self-image:

1)   Criminal thinking: The criminal has a distorted view of self as a good person who can do no wrong and may offer examples of "goodness" as evidence

2)   Racist thinking: Racists, like criminals, put considerable effort into building a good person self-image. The good person self-image was held by slave owners who asserted that they treated their slaves well. This self-image is reclaimed by white society every time it adopts a benevolent social policy, such as affirmative action. The error in thinking occurs when individuals hold this belief on the basis of a few good deeds and do not acknowledge their other destructive behaviors

f. Closed channel thinking:

    1) Criminal thinking: The secretiveness, closed-mind, and self-righteous attitude of the criminal do not allow for an open channel of communication or for being receptive to other points of view. Criminals acknowledge the faults of others but are not self-critical

    2) Racist thinking: Anyone who has tried to reason with a bigoted relative or colleague is aware of the impossibility of finding a receptive listener. Closed channel thinkers tend to overgeneralize and to see the world in absolute terms; good and bad, right and wrong, black and white

g. Victim stance:

    1) Criminal thinking: The criminal avoids taking responsibility for behavior by blaming others and by viewing himself or herself as a victim of others; often includes blaming the victim

    2) Racist thinking: Assuming an attitude of being victimized by "heavy tax burdens that force us to support people who are taking advantage of us—and who are undeserving." Racists blame the politicians and government for making people of color dependent on social welfare programs. They blame the victim by classifying people of color as lazy, illiterate, and irresponsible; and they point to high rates of school failure, unemployment, illegitimate births, and crime in the inner cities to support this characterization

h. Disregard for responsible performance:

    1) Criminal thinking: The criminal's energy and motivation are directed toward self-serving goals rather than socially responsible activities. The criminal avoids and disregards personal obligations in order to maintain a power position

    2) Racist thinking: Society has created a no-win situation for oppressed people of color, because many whites also believe themselves to be victimized by people of color who compete for their jobs, their educational scholarships, and their tax dollars to upgrade housing and public services in the inner cities. It is used by the racist to justify discrimination and promotes a disregard for responsible performance. After all, if we can convince ourselves that people of color are already taking advantage of a too-benevolent society, then there is no need to support social welfare programs or to make any effort toward improving their opportunities for success

       i.   Lack of a time perspective:

             1)   Criminal thinking: Refers to several aberrations in time concepts, including the failure to make positive changes based on past experiences and the tendency to live for the moment (instant gratification) rather than anticipate future benefits or outcomes

             2)   Racist thinking: Failure, or refusal, to consider the long-term benefits of providing all people with equal opportunities to be successful, contributing members of society demonstrates a lack of time perspective

       j.   Fear of fear:

             1)   Criminal thinking: Fear reactions are not used as a guide to responsible living, but are taken as threats to the criminal's self-esteem. Criminals often have irrational fears

             2)   Racist thinking: There is an irrational fear that equality, shared power, integrated living, and racial blending (intermarriage) somehow threaten the worth and well-being of white society

       k.   Lack of trust:

             1)   Criminal thinking: Trust of others is seen as a weakness and interferes with the criminal's need for power and control

             2)   Racist thinking: A lack of trust, which is implicit in all areas of racism, fosters the desire of many in the dominant mainstream society to retain their power position

XI. Impacts of Social and Economic Forces: The Effects and Costs of Discrimination and Oppression

    A.   Racial discrimination is a barrier in our competitive society to obtaining the necessary resources to lead a contented and comfortable life

    B.   Heavy psychological costs—Cooley's looking-glass self: Our idea of who we are and what we are is largely determined by the way others relate to us

    C.   Effects on children—African American children who have been subjected to discrimination even display a preference for white dolls and white playmates over black

    D.   Creation of a victim system—barriers to opportunity and education limit the chance for achievement, employment, and attainment of skills. This limitation can, in turn, lead to poverty or stress in relationships, which interferes with adequate performance of family roles. Strains in family roles cause problems in individual growth and development and limit the opportunities of families to meet their own needs or to organize to improve their communities

    E.   High costs for the majority group—it impairs intergroup cooperation and communication

F. Life expectancy rates—the life expectancy of nonwhites is 6 years less than that of whites in the United States

G. Undermining of the nation's political goals—many other nations view us as hypocritical when we advocate human rights and equality. We must first put our own house in order by eliminating racial and ethnic discrimination. With most of the nations of the world being nonwhite, our racist practices severely damage our influence and prestige

XII. The Effects of Discrimination on Human Growth and Development

A. History and culture of African Americans

    1. Slavery

    2. Economic dependence

    3. A rigid caste system in the South—"Jim Crow laws": prescribed how African Americans were supposed to act in the presence of whites, asserted white supremacy, embraced racial segregation, and denied political and legal rights to African Americans

    4. New employment opportunities during World War II

    5. *Brown v. Board of Education* (1954): Ruled that racial segregation in public schools was unconstitutional

    6. Wide-ranging civil rights legislation passed to protect rights in areas such as housing, voting, employment, and use of public transportation and facilities

    7. Current status of African Americans in the U.S.

        a. African Americans have advanced in formal schooling to a remarkable degree, although in most areas residential patterns have left many public schools predominantly Black or White

        b. Higher education also reflects the legacy of one for Blacks and another for Whites

        c. Gains in earning power have barely kept pace with inflation

        d. Housing in many areas remains segregated, despite growing numbers of Blacks in suburban areas

        e. African Americans are more likely to be victims of crimes and to be arrested for violent crimes

        f. African Americans have made substantial gains in elective office but still are underrepresented compared with their numbers in the general population

8. A middle class has emerged that is better educated, better paid, and better housed than any group of African Americans that has gone before it; however, the group left behind generates a disproportionate share of the social pathology that is associated with a deteriorating urban neighborhood

9. More than half of all African American children are being raised in single-parent families

10. Five strengths identified by the National Urban League that allow African American families to function effectively in a racist society

    a. Strong kinship bonds: Blacks are more likely than whites to care for children and the elderly in an extended family network

    b. Strong work orientation: Poor blacks are more likely to be working, and poor black families often include more than one wage earner

    c. Adaptability of family roles: In two-parent families, the egalitarian pattern of decision making is the most common. The self-reliance of black women who are the primary wage earners best illustrates this adaptability

    d. High achievement orientation: Working-class blacks indicate a greater desire for their children to attend college than working-class whites. Even a majority of low-income African Americans desire to attend college

    e. Strong religious orientation: Black churches since the time of slavery have been the source of many significant grassroots organizations

11. Schools have erroneously perceived African Americans as being less capable of developing cognitive skills

B. Effects of discrimination on development of self-concept

    1. Self-concept: The positive and negative thoughts and feelings that one has towards oneself

    2. If African American adults accept society's label of inferiority, they are likely to convey such thoughts and feelings to their children

    3. The importance of one's immediate social and physical environment in overcoming obstacles to developing positive self-esteem

    4. Celebrations, such as Kwanzaa, are ways of promoting pride for African Americans in their racial identity

C.   Spotlight on Diversity 5.3: Kwanzaa

1.   Means "first fruits of the harvest" in Swahili: Seven-day festival observed by some African Americans in late December and early January

2.   Originated in 1966 by M. Ron Karenga and it encourages the following seven qualities:

a.   *Umoja* (unity): African Americans strive for unity within family, community, and the world as a whole

b.   *Kujichagulia* (self-determination): African Americans define themselves and have the determination not to accept or internalize negative definitions

c.   *Ujima* (collective work and responsibility): African Americans live, work, and are responsible for harmonizing personal wants and needs with the collective wants and needs of the race

d.   *Ujamaa* (cooperative economics): African Americans become their own economic bosses through owning and supporting African American businesses

e.   *Nia* (purpose): African Americans contribute distinct gifts to the world, and they propose to develop those gifts and talents

f.   *Kuumba* (creativity): African Americans are creative, and all that they touch is made more beautiful through the contact

g.   *Imani* (faith): African Americans remain alive, giving, and compassionate people because of their faith that, though African Americans suffer in their todays, they will succeed in their tomorrows

D.   The Afrocentric perspective and Worldview

1.   Afrocentric perspective: Acknowledges African culture and expressions of African beliefs, values, institutions, and behaviors. It recognizes that African Americans have retained, to some degree, a number of elements of African life and values

2.   Worldview: Involves one's perceptions of oneself in relation to other people, objects, institutions, and nature

XIII.   **Community Strategies to Promote Social and Economic Justice**

A.   Mass media appeals: Striving to change institutional values

B.   Greater interaction between minority groups and the majority group

C. Civil rights laws: Changing the legal macro system

    1. Proponents of civil rights legislation make these assumptions

        a. New laws will reduce discriminatory behavioral patterns

        b. Laws will be used (civil rights laws were enacted after the Civil War but were seldom enforced and gradually were eroded)

D. Activism

    1. Politics of creative disorder: Operates on the edge of the dominant social system and includes school boycotts, rent strikes, etc. at businesses that are alleged to discriminate; public marches, and product boycotts. This type of activism is based on the concept of nonviolent resistance

    2. Politics of disorder: Reflects alienation from the dominant culture and disillusionment with the political system. Those being discriminated against resort to mob uprisings, riots, and other forms of violence

    3. Politics of escape: Engages in rhetoric about how minorities are being victimized, focus is not on arriving at solutions. The principal value seems to be the stimulation of public awareness of the discrimination

    4. Spotlight on Diversity 5.4: Rosa Parks' Act of Courage Sparked the Civil Rights Movement

E. School busing: A community initiative

    1. Ethical Question 5.3: Do you believe our society should expand or decrease the use of school busing to attempt to achieve racial integration?

    2. In some areas, school busing has become accepted and appears to be meeting the stated objectives. In other areas, however, the approach is highly controversial and has exacerbated racial tensions

    3. Three decades of school busing have failed to deliver all the benefits its boosters hoped for and its critics demanded

    4. African Americans who attended elementary and high schools with whites are substantially more likely to attend white-majority colleges, get jobs in desegregated workplaces that offer higher pay, and have white friends as adults

    5. African American students who go to integrated suburban schools rather than segregated city ones are less likely to drop out of high school, get in trouble with the police, drop out of college, or bear a child before age 18, and they are more likely to have white friends and live in integrated neighborhoods

    6. Whites also benefit from attending school with African American students because they learn more about diversity and tend to more thoroughly confront their racial stereotypes

7.   Are the benefits of school busing worth the costs?

8.   Surveys indicate a majority of Americans (including a large number of African Americans) oppose busing for integration purposes. The main reason for the growing opposition to busing is that it often has not raised educational achievement of students of color

9.   In 1991 the U.S. Supreme Court ruled that busing to achieve integration, when ordered, need not be continued indefinitely

F.   Affirmative action: A macro system response

1.   Reverse discrimination: Alan Bakke and the University of California at Davis

2.   Critics of affirmative action assert that it is a highly politicized and painful remedy that has stigmatized many of those it was meant to help

3.   1996 California Proposition 209: Explicitly rejects the idea that women and other minority group members could get special consideration when applying for jobs, government contracts, or university admission

4.   In 2003 the U.S. Supreme Court affirmed the right of colleges to consider race in admissions; however, it rejected the university's use of a point system to do so

5.   Supporters of affirmative action believe that if we abandon affirmative action, we return to the old-boy network

6.   Policies based on evenhandedness for individuals rather than for group

7.   Ethical Question 5.4: Do you believe affirmative action programs should be (1) expanded to give greater preferential treatment to minorities, (2) reduced to give less preferential treatment to minorities, or (3) eliminated?

G.   Confronting racist remarks and actions

1.   Racist jokes and sarcastic remarks help shape and perpetuate stereotypes and prejudices

2.   Ethical Question 5.5: Are you aware that if you listen to (and laugh at) racist jokes, you are involved in perpetuating stereotypes and prejudices?

H.   Minority-owned businesses

1.   Since the 1970s, federal, state, and local governments have attempted to assist minority-owned businesses in a variety of ways

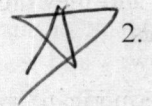

2.   Ethical Dilemma 5.1: Are Native American Casinos a Benefit or a Detriment?

     a.   Indian Gaming Regulatory Act (1988)—recognized the right of Native American tribes in the United States to establish gambling and gaming facilities on their reservations as long as the states in which they are located have some form of legalized gambling

b.　About one third of the recognized Native American tribes have casinos, those who have casinos have greatly reduced their rate of unemployment

c.　The revenues generated have helped spur economic development on land owned by the tribe and welfare rates on reservations with casinos have dropped.　They are using their profits for the betterment of the reservation and its people

d.　One negative effect is that in many communities where casinos have been built, there are dramatic increases in the number of people addicted to gambling.　Those who can least afford to gamble usually are the most affected

e.　Some Native Americans fear losing their traditional values to corruption and organized crime.　Some feel that casinos trivialize and cheapen their heritage

f.　Non-Native American critics sharply question the special economic status being given to Native Americans in being able to operate casinos, and demand that there be an even playing field

I.　Grassroots approaches to improving deteriorating neighborhoods

1.　Deteriorating neighborhoods in cities are a national disgrace

2.　One of the most comprehensive undertakings to assist inner cities was the Model Cities Program which was part of the War on Poverty in the 1960s

3.　To date, practically all programs that have endeavored to improve deteriorating neighborhoods have had, at best, only short-term success

4.　Grass-roots organizations: Community groups, composed of community residents who work together to improve their surroundings

5.　Cochran Gardens, St. Louis, Missouri was once a low-income housing project strewn with rubbish, graffiti, and broken windows until Bertha Gilkey and her group started with small projects.　Today it is a public housing project with flower-lined paths, trees, and grass, with trusting people who have a sense of pride in their community

XIV.　Social Work Practice with Racial and Ethnic Groups

A.　Ethnic-sensitive practice: Seeks to incorporate understanding of diverse ethnic, cultural, and minority groups into the theories and principles that guide social work practice

B.　Dual perspective: All people are a part of two systems: (1) the dominant or sustaining system (the society that one lives in), which is the source of power and economic resources; and (2) the nurturing system, composed of the physical and social environment of family and community

XV. Empowerment

A. People who work with an ethnic or racial group can help empower members of those groups by countering the negative image of the group with a positive value or image and an emphasis on the ability of each group member to influence the conditions of his or her life

B. Empowerment counters hopelessness and powerlessness with the belief that each person is able to address problems competently, beginning with a positive view of one's self

XVI. Strengths Perspective

A. Strengths perspective: Emphasizes people's abilities, interests, aspirations, resources, beliefs, and accomplishments

   1. Culturally competent practice

      a. Become aware of culture and its pervasive influence

      b. Learn about her or his own culture

      c. Recognize her or his own ethnocentricity

      d. Learn about other cultures

      e. Acquire cultural knowledge about the clients she or he is working with

      f. Adapt social work skills and intervention approaches to the needs and styles of the cultures of these clients

   2. Ethical Question 5.6: How culturally competent are you?

   3. National Association of Social Workers' standards for cultural competence in social work practice

      a. Ethics and values: Social workers shall function in accordance with the values, ethics, and standards of the profession, recognizing how personal and professional values may conflict with or accommodate the needs of diverse clients

      b. Self-awareness: Social workers shall seek to develop an understanding of their own personal cultural values and beliefs as one way of appreciating the importance of multicultural identities in the lives of people

      c. Cross-cultural knowledge: Social workers shall have and continue to develop specialized knowledge and understanding about the history, traditions, values, family systems, and artistic expressions of major client groups that they serve

      d. Service delivery: Social workers shall be knowledgeable about and skillful in the use of services available in the community and broader society and be able to make appropriate referrals for their diverse clients

e. Empowerment and advocacy: Social workers shall be aware of the effect of social policies and programs on diverse client populations, advocating for and with clients whenever appropriate

f. Diverse workforce: Social workers shall support and advocate for recruitment, admissions and hiring, and retention efforts in social work programs and agencies that ensure diversity within the profession

g. Professional education: Social workers shall advocate for and participate in educational and training programs that help advance cultural competence within the profession

h. Language diversity: Social workers shall seek to provide or advocate for the provision of information, referrals, and services in the language appropriate to the client, which may include use of interpreters

i. Cross-cultural leadership: Social workers shall be able to communicate information about diverse client groups to other professionals

4. Learning the culture of the group

a. When working with Native Americans it is considered rude—and an attempt to intimidate, in fact—to maintain direct eye contact

b. Chicano men, as contrasted to Anglo men, have been described as exhibiting greater pride in their maleness

c. Machismo: A strong sense of masculine pride

d. Familism: The belief that the family takes precedence over the individual

e. Folk healers: In Chicano communities, some use treatments that blend natural healing methods with religious or spiritual beliefs

f. Religious organizations that are predominantly African American usually have a social and spiritual mission

B. Self-awareness of values, prejudices, and stereotypes

C. Application of theory to practice: Techniques of intervention

1. Social workers should seek to use their own patterns of communication and avoid the temptation to adopt the client's accent, vocabulary, or speech

2. A social worker with an urban background who has a job in a small rural community needs to live his personal life in a way that is consistent with community values and standards

3. Use all of the formalities in initial meetings with adult clients of diverse racial and ethnic groups

4. Agencies and social workers should establish working hours that coincide with the needs of the groups being served

5. Membership in group services should be selected in such a manner that no one race vastly outnumbers the others

6. In working with adult clients who are not fluent in the English language, it is generally a mistake to use bilingual children of the clients as interpreters

7. Native Americans place a high value on the principle of self-determination. This sometimes provides a perplexing dilemma for a social worker who wonders "How can I help if I can't intervene?"

8. In establishing rapport with African American, Hispanic, Native American, or clients of other groups who have suffered from racial oppression, a peer relationship should be sought in which there is mutual respect and mutual sharing of information

D. Social work roles to counter discrimination

1. Professional commitment to work towards ending discrimination—National Association of Social Workers *Code of Ethics*

2. Council on Social Work Education's Educational Policy and Accreditation Standards requires that content on racism be included in the social work curriculum. EPAS also require that accredited programs must provide considerable content on populations-at-risk, on diversity, and on the promotion of social and economic justice

3. Association of Black Social Workers has been very active in combating racial prejudice and discrimination

4. Social work roles to help end racial and other forms of discrimination

    a. Advocate

    b. Initiator of action

    c. Educator

    d. Integrator/coordinator

    e. Counselor

    f. Broker

XVII. The Future of U.S. Race and Ethnic Relations

    A.   Three possible patterns of intergroup relations

        1.   Anglo-conformity: Assumes the desirability of maintaining modified English institutions, language, and culture as the dominant standard in American life. In practice, "assimilation" in America has always meant Anglo-conformity, and the groups that have been most readily assimilated have been those that are ethnically and culturally most similar to the Anglo-Saxon group [early British colonists]

        2.   The melting pot: Views the future American society not as a modified England but rather as a totally new blend, both culturally and biologically, of all the various groups that inhabit the United States. In practice, the melting pot has been of only limited significance in the American experience.

        3.   Cultural pluralism: Implies a series of coexisting groups, each preserving its own tradition and culture but each loyal to an overarching American nation. Although the cultural enclaves of some immigrant groups, such as the Germans, have declined in importance in the past, many other groups, such as the Italians, have retained a strong sense of ethnic identity and have resisted both Anglo-conformity and inclusion in the melting pot. This appears to be the form that race and ethnic relations are presenting taking

    B.   Spotlight on Diversity 5.5: A Dream of the End of Racism

XVIII. Summary

Experiential Exercises and Simulations

Five exercises are described. The first four exercises in this section are values-clarification exercises designed to help you identify your prejudices and stereotypes toward various racial and ethnic groups. The fifth is designed to test your knowledge of several diverse cultural groups.

Exercise 5.1: Stereotyping

A.   Brief description
Some vignettes will be read, and you will be asked to identify the racial or ethnic groups described in the vignettes.

B.   Objectives
You will:
    1.   Become aware that you, like everyone else, hold stereotypes about racial and ethnic groups.

C.   Procedures
    1.   The instructor begins by reading to you, or asking you to read, the vignettes that follow. Write down the name(s) of the racial or ethnic group(s) you think the characters involved in the action belong to as soon as you get a mental picture of the group(s).

a. While I stop at a gas station in the country to fill my car with gas, a pick-up truck stops at a gas tank near mine. I notice an emblem of a Confederate flag on the truck and a gun on the dashboard. A man with a large belly and a tattoo on his right arm gets out of the pick-up and yells, "Hey boy, fill'er up!"

b. I'm sitting in the family room in a house. The children are polite and well behaved. They bow when the grandfather enters the room and treat him with considerable respect. The children indicate we're having rice for dinner. They are setting the table and ask whether I want a fork or chopsticks.

c. While walking down an inner-city street, I observe some people sitting in front of a housing project listening to loud music and occasionally getting up to perform some fancy dance steps. A Cadillac stops in front of the project, and an attractive woman gets out. I hear someone say to her, "What's happenin', Momma?"

d. I'm sitting in the dining room at a table. Several other people are seated around the table, and they're having a great time—drinking wine, eating spaghetti, and laughing loudly. There is opera music playing softly in the background.

2. Probable responses to the vignettes listed above are: (a) poor white; (b) Chinese or other Asian; (c) African American; and (d) Italian. Discuss the following questions:

a. Were your images and responses based on stereotypes?
b. How are such stereotypes learned?
c. When are stereotypes useful? When are they destructive?

3. Read the following "actual" events in each vignette.

a. The pick-up truck driver is a Native American who borrowed his friend's truck to pick up her daughter, a junior at the university, at the airport. She's studying to be a genetic engineer. The gas station attendant is the man's nephew, an honor student in high school. He is working at the gas station to earn money for college. The man loves his nephew, and the greeting "Hey boy, fill'er up" is his way of relating to his nephew in a loving, joking manner.

b. The grandfather entering the room is attending his seventy-fifth birthday party. He is a person of German descent who loves Chinese food. He worked as an engineer in Taiwan for a number of years and is adept with chopsticks.

c. The people sitting on the steps are of Hispanic descent and are preparing for a neighborhood block party. Some of the young people doing "fancy dance steps" are high school students who belong to a folk dance group that will be performing at the block party. The attractive woman stepping out of the Cadillac is the mayor, an Anglo woman who has been invited to the party. The young person who says, "What's happenin', Momma?" does so as a friendly joke. The mayor is sponsoring three children in a South American country by sending them money every month.

d. The family is an African American family that loves pasta and wine. This is a close-knit, three-generation family. Members enjoy each other and laugh at each other's jokes. The hostess hates loud music while visiting with the relatives, so she turns down the CD player.

4.   After you have read the "real" stories, discuss the following questions:

    a.   Does the exercise demonstrate that you hold stereotypes?
    b.   Do negative stereotypes about ethnic or racial groups lead to prejudice and discrimination?
    c.   How can we identify the negative stereotypes we hold so that we do not discriminate against members of the groups that we negatively stereotype?

Exercise 5.2: Identifying My Prejudices and Stereotypes

A.   Brief description
Identify racial and ethnic groups into which you would hesitate to marry, and list reasons for your choices.

B.   Objective
You will:
1.   Become aware that you hold certain racist and ethnic stereotypes that you need to be aware of in order to develop an objective approach to social work practice with diverse groups.

C.   Procedures
1.   Since we have been raised in a society in which racist and ethnocentric beliefs flourish, it is likely that we have some racial and ethnic prejudices. It is important that these beliefs be identified. A person who is aware of them can take steps to remain objective in interactions with members of other racial and ethnic groups.
2.   The following questionnaire is distributed:

> Assume that you are single. Place an <u>X</u> by the name of each group into which you would hesitate to marry. Do not write your name on this sheet, so that you will remain anonymous.
>
> | | | | |
> |---|---|---|---|
> | _____ | Russian | _____ | White American |
> | _____ | Cuban | _____ | Arab |
> | _____ | French | _____ | Israeli |
> | _____ | Mexican | _____ | Chinese |
> | _____ | African American | _____ | Japanese |
> | _____ | Native American | _____ | Filipino |
> | _____ | Puerto Rican | _____ | Eskimo |
> | _____ | Italian | _____ | Brazilian |
> | _____ | German | _____ | Hungarian |
> | _____ | Polish | _____ | Vietnamese |
> | _____ | Norwegian | _____ | Pakistani |
> | _____ | Samoan | _____ | Korean |

3.   After you complete the first step, write (in the space following the groups that you checked) the reasons why you would hesitate to marry those that you have indicated. This is the part of the exercise that is important in identifying the specific stereotypes you hold. Go beyond writing something like "My parents wouldn't approve" or "I can't see myself marrying such a person" to include the reasons your parents wouldn't approve or the reasons why you can't see yourself marrying such a person.

4. Hand in your responses anonymously. The instructor will read many of the responses to the class. Discuss what a person needs to do to remain objective in interactions with members of ethnic and racial groups about which he or she has negative stereotypes.

Exercise 5.3: *Star Track* to New Venus

A. Brief description
You will form subgroups. Each subgroup has the task of selecting ethnic and racial groups to continue the human race on a new planet.

B. Objective
You will:
1. Identify some of your positive and negative stereotypes about various racial and ethnic groups.

C. Procedures
1. Form subgroups of about five persons. The instructor reads the following to the subgroups.

You are living in the year 2013. In 2010, the United States discovered a planet in a distant galaxy that appears to have a climate and atmosphere remarkably similar to Earth's. Scientists are virtually assured this planet, named New Venus, can support human life. In 2011 the United States began building a new spaceship, named *Star Track*, that will be capable of transporting 20 people to New Venus. *Star Track* has recently been completed. In the year 2013 a new comet, Dark Vadim, is discovered, and found to be headed on a collision course for Earth. Scientists predict it will strike at the end of this year. A huge explosion, much worse than a nuclear war, is expected, and many scientists are predicting Earth will disintegrate. The president of the United States has commissioned your subgroup to choose the ethnic and racial backgrounds of the twenty people who will soon board *Star Track* to fly to New Venus in order to continue the human race. The president informs your subgroup that it may select the racial and ethnic backgrounds from the following list. Everyone may come from one ethnic or racial background or from a variety of backgrounds. After you provide your selections, the president will select, consistent with your choices, people in their twenties, including ten men and ten women. All the people selected will be fluent in the English language.

Chinese	German
Japanese	French
Vietnamese	Polish
Filipino	Hungarian
Irish	Portuguese
Egyptian	Italian
White American	Saudi Arabian
African American	Iranian
Israeli	Eskimo
Native American	Cuban
Puerto Rican	Australian
Pakistani	Hawaiian
Mexican	Russian

2. While you are making your choices, the instructor lists the names of the racial and ethnic groups on the chalkboard. After you are finished, a representative from each subgroup marks its choices on the board.

3. State the reasons for your choices and why you did not choose people from the racial and ethnic backgrounds that you excluded.

4. The instructor summarizes racial and ethnic stereotypes that are expressed and may end the exercise by asking you what you feel you learned.

Exercise 5.4: Stranded in Komsa, Russia

A. Brief description
You will visualize your fears about being stranded in the middle of Russia.

B. Objectives
You will:
1. Understand how racial and ethnic groups feel about living in a country that has oppressed them.

C. Procedures
1. Visualize the following:

> You have a passport and are traveling alone by train in Russia. You have a number of exhilarating experiences. The train stops in Komsa, in the heart of Russia, far from any major city. Komsa is a medium-sized city, and you decide to spend a few days in this area. On your first day of shopping and sightseeing, you lose your passport, all your money and traveler's checks, and all your identification. You had all of these in your backpack. You think someone may have stolen these important documents from you, but you don't know who, nor do you know where it happened. You are aware that there is no American embassy in Komsa.

2. The instructor asks the class the following questions. Discuss each question.
   a. If this happened to you, what would be your fears?
   b. To whom would you turn for help?
   c. Do you fear you may be discriminated against or victimized because you are an American?
   d. Are the fears and concerns that you have similar to the concerns of racial and ethnic minorities who live in a country where the majority group has a history of discriminating against them?
   e. If you were a worker at a social welfare agency that is identified with the white power structure in our society, how might you seek to reduce the fears and concerns that nonwhite clients may have in asking for help?

Exercise 5.5: Multicultural Sensitivity

A. Brief description
A cultural sensitivity test is administered. It is designed to test your knowledge of several diverse cultural groups. Understanding diverse cultures is essential for effective work with clients.

B. Objectives
You will:
1. Examine your own levels of understanding of some basic aspects of several diverse cultures.
2. Recognize the importance of learning more about cultures that may be different from your own.

C. Procedure
1. The following questions are designed to test your understanding of some important aspects of four diverse cultural groups. Answer them to the best of your ability.

A. **AFRICAN AMERICAN CULTURAL DIFFERENCES TEST**

1. What does NAACP stand for?

2. In what year was NAACP established?
    a. 1865
    b. 1889
    c. 1909
    d. 1935

3. What does NABSW stand for and when was it established?

4. How does African American music express African American culture?

5. When did slavery end?

6. Kwanzaa is:
    a. A starchy grain originally imported by African slaves abducted in West Africa.
    b. An African American festival held in late December.
    c. An African American dance.
    d. A Muslim prayer sequence originally brought from Africa by abducted slaves.

Note: Donnise Bartholomew, Holly Lambert, Stephan Jurgen, Johnathan Greene, Geri McKinney, Nicole Leonard, Tameka Hinton, Janet Bonvillian, Lili Largent, and Rufus Brown, all social work majors at Clark Atlanta University, suggested questions #1, #5, and #6 on this test.

B. CHICANO CULTURAL DIFFERENCES

1. The Treaty of Guadalupe Hildago ceded to the United States what is now known as:
   a. The state of Texas
   b. The state of New Mexico
   c. The state of California
   d. The southwestern United States

2. Cinco de Mayo is a Mexican holiday that commemorates:
   a. Mexico's independence from France
   b. The battle of Puebla
   c. The death of the Frito Bandito
   d. The decline of the Diaz regime

3. A "frajo" is a:
   a. Short handled hoe
   b. Car
   c. Cigarette
   d. Pachuco

4. A "curandera" is a:
   a. Healer
   b. Witch
   c. Curious person

5. The 12th of December is:
   a. Cesar Chavez's birthday
   b. The day of the Virgin of Guadalupe
   c. The anniversary of "pachuco" riots

6. To Chicanos, the term "carnal" means:
   a. Brother
   b. Butcher
   c. Sports car
   d. Enemy

7. A "tio taco" is:
   a. A Mexican dish
   b. An individual who rejects his culture
   c. A Cuban
   d. An uncle from Spain

8. The most valued institution in Chicano culture is:
   a. The school
   b. The church
   c. The government
   d. The family

C. NATIVE AMERICAN CULTURAL DIFFERENCES

1. Which of the following is <u>not</u> a Native American invention?
    a. Canoe
    b. Kayak
    c. Parka
    d. Tomahawk

2. The words "Kemo sabe," popularized by the Lone Ranger's sidekick, Tonto, mean:
    a. White Friend
    b. Blue Eyes
    c. Honky
    d. Nothing at all

3. The phrase "The only good Indian is a dead Indian" is attributed to:
    a. Gen. Philip Sheridan
    b. Gen. Wm. T. Sherman
    c. Col. Henry B. Carrington
    d. Lt. Col. George A. Custer

4. Which of the following was not a member of the League of Six Nations (Iroquois Confederacy)?
    a. Oneida
    b. Seneca
    c. Kiowa
    d. Onondaga

5. Which of the following colleges was first instituted primarily to educate Indians?
    a. Yale
    b. Harvard
    c. Dartmouth
    d. Princeton

D. ASIAN CULTURAL DIFFERENCES

1. Buddha-Dharma is ____
   a. The teachings of Judo
   b. The practice of Oriental cooking
   c. The teachings of the Buddha
   d. The wife of the Buddha

2. The art of bonsai refers to ____
   a. Japanese silk screening
   b. Chinese wrestling
   c. Growing miniature trees
   d. None of the above

3. The "koto" is ____
   a. A Korean word for house
   b. A thirteen-string Japanese musical instrument
   c. The newest Oriental dance to hit the West Coast
   d. The Vietnamese national anthem

4. Which word sometimes means a Japanese ghetto? ____
   a. Nihon machi
   b. Sakana
   c. Kanji
   d. Ghettuloheli

5. Third generation Japanese are called ____
   a. Issei
   b. Nisei
   c. Yonsei
   d. Sansei

A.   ANSWERS TO THE AFRICAN AMERICAN CULTURAL DIFFERENCES TEST:

1.   National Association for the Advancement of Colored People
2.   c
3.   National Association of Black Social Workers, 1968
4.   African American music expresses African American culture as it "represents the combining of African characteristics with the content and conditions of being Black in the United States;" additionally, it "is a concrete demonstration of culture as dynamic and changing with African musical characteristics and Afro-American musical forms incorporating new technology (i.e., brass and piano) after the Civil War and creating additional Afro-American musical forms (i.e., blues, jazz, gospel)". (This question was posed and answered by Jualynne E. Dodson in *An Afrocentric Educational Manual: Toward a Non-Deficit Perspective in Services to Families and Children* [Knoxville: University of Tennessee School of Social Work Office of Continuing Social Work Education, 1983], 57)
5.   "The Civil War began in 1861, and on January 1, 1863, President Abraham Lincoln issued the Emancipation Proclamation, proclaiming that all slaves would be free. With the defeat of the Confederate army, slavery was ultimately made illegal in 1865 with the adoption of the 13th amendment" (Bogart R. Leashore, "African Americans Overview" in *The Encyclopedia of Social Work*, 19th ed. (Washington, D.C.: National Association of Social Workers Press, 1995), 103)
6.   b (*Webster's Ninth New Collegiate Dictionary* (Springfield, MA: Mirriam-Webster, 1991), 667)

B.   ANSWERS TO CHICANO CULTURAL DIFFERENCES TEST:

1.   (d) The treaty of Guadalupe Hildago was signed by the United States and Mexico in 1848. With this treaty, Mexico accepted the Rio Grande as the Texas border and ceded the Southwest (which incorporates the present-day states of Arizona, California, New Mexico, Utah, Nevada, and parts of Colorado) to the United States in return for $15 million.

2.   (b) This celebration commemorates a battle in which a small Mexican army defeated a French army battalion. Cinco de Mayo celebrations are still held in Mexico and in the United States where there are a significant number of Chicanos.

3.   (c) The term "frajo" is a slang word for cigarette, which is commonly used in the barrio.

4.   (a) The "curandera" is a person who is able to relieve people of their physical sickness. Many elderly Chicano people do not believe in the "doctor" as they are known in this country. They prefer to be attended by the curandera, or healer.

5.   (b) Chicanos are a very religious people. The 12th of December is the day of the patron saint of the Chicano people—the Virgin of Guadalupe.

6.   (a) "Carnal" means brother. It is usually used as a greeting between males.

7.	(b) Many individuals reject their culture due to the educational system in this country. Chicanos have been taught that their culture is inferior and that the Anglo-American culture is superior. Therefore, many Mexican Americans (especially second and third generation) do not identify with their cultural heritage and the term "Chicano."

8.	(d) Chicano families are traditionally very, very close. The total Chicano existence revolves around the family.

**C.	ANSWERS TO THE NATIVE AMERICAN DIFFERENCES TEST:**

1.	(d) The tomahawk was a French invention later copied and used extensively by Native Americans.

2.	(d) No one knows where this phrase comes from; there are no known languages that this can be traced to—it's another Hollywood gimmick.

3.	(a) Gen. Sheridan's direct quote: "The only good Indians I ever saw were dead." The phrase was later simplified.

4.	(c) The Six Nations was composed of: Oneida, Seneca, Tuscarora, Onondaga, Cayuga, and Mohawk.

5.	(c) Dartmouth.

**D.	ANSWERS TO THE ASIAN CULTURAL DIFFERENCES TEST:**

1.	c
2.	c
3.	b
4.	a
5.	d

2.	Discuss reactions to the test. You can begin with the following questions:
   a.	How easy or difficult was it to answer these questions?
   b.	How did you feel when you didn't know the answers?
   c.	Were any of the answers surprising to you and, if so, which ones? Explain why.
   d.	How might your ignorance of these and other significant aspects of a diverse culture hinder your work with clients in that cultural group?
   e.	What concrete steps can you take to enhance your knowledge of various cultural groups?

Study Outline

I.   **A Perspective**

II.   **Adolescence**

     A.   Adolescence: The transitional period between childhood and adulthood during which young people mature physically and sexually

     B.   Puberty: A physical concept that refers to the specific time during which people mature sexually and become capable of reproduction

         1.   Girls begin puberty between 9 and 12 years of age, and reach full height by about age 16

         2.   Boys begin maturing between ages 11 and 14—later than girls, and may continue to grow until age 18 to 20

         3.   Hormones: Chemical substances secreted by the endocrine glands; they stimulate growth of sexual organs and characteristics

     C.   Growth spurt: A sharp increase in height, typically characterizing the initial entrance into puberty

         1.   During this spurt the typical growth is from 2 to 5 inches

         2.   Because girls start the spurt earlier, they tend to be taller, to weigh more, and to be stronger than boys during ages 11 to 13; however, by the time both sexes have completed the spurt, boys once again are larger than girls

         3.   There is a tendency toward unequal and disproportionate growth in the body, causing motor awkwardness and clumsiness

     D.   Secular trend: Tendency for people to reach sexual maturity and their adult height faster than in the past   ↑ *Standard of Living, Better health & Nutrition*

     E.   Primary and secondary sex characteristics

         1.   Primary sex characteristics: These are related to the sex organs and reproduction

         2.   Secondary sex characteristics: Traits that distinguish the sexes from each other, but play no direct role in reproduction

3.   Proof of puberty

   a.   Girls: First menstruation; the average age is 12½ years

   b.   Menstruation: The monthly discharge of blood and tissue debris from the uterus when fertilization has not taken place. This is also called menarche

   c.   Boys: Hormones cause the testes to increase in size and to begin producing semen by age 14 on average

   d.   Spotlight on Diversity 6.1: Diversity and Menarche

      1)   African American girls begin menstruating significantly earlier than white girls and Hispanic girls

      2)   Hispanic girls begin menstruating earlier than white girls

      3)   Between ages 13½ and 14, a total of 90 percent of girls in all three groups have begun menarche

4.   Hair growth

5.   Development of breasts

6.   Voice changes: This occurs fairly late in puberty, and not as noticeable in girls as in boys

7.   Skin changes: An increased activity of the sebaceous glands (which manufacture oils for the skin) begins

8.   Nocturnal emissions: The ejaculation or emission of semen while a male is asleep

   a.   Approximately 90 percent of all males have nocturnal emissions at one time or another

   b.   Nocturnal emissions are a natural means of relieving sexual tension

   c.   Females have orgasms during sleep, however, not as frequently or as early as male nocturnal emissions

III.   Psychological Reactions to Physical Changes

A.   Body image and self-concept

   1.   Perception of body image and attractiveness is related to level of self-esteem

   2.   Girls generally tend to be more critical of and dissatisfied with their physical appearance than boys; 85 percent of girls worry about weight control compared to 30 percent of boys

3.   Before puberty, boys and girls display similar levels of depression; however, during adolescence girls are more likely to experience depression

4.   Ethical Question 6.1: Is it right or fair to place so much importance on external physical appearance, especially as such emphasis concerns weight? Is it equitable that the burden of weight control rests more heavily on women than on men? How have these concerns about weight and physical appearance affected you and your own aspects of biological, psychological, and social development?

B.   Early and late maturation in boys

     1.   Early maturers

        a.   Advantages are increased size and athletic ability, leadership opportunities, social status, and self-esteem

        b.   Disadvantages are they are more likely to experience hostility, nervousness, and depression. They are more likely to get in trouble with drugs, alcohol, truancy, fighting, and antisocial behavior

     2.   Studies found that boys who matured late had feelings of inferiority due to their smaller size and younger appearance, and therefore lower self-esteem. They may be denied the respect and attention given more mature-looking boys

     3.   When late maturers reached their 30s, they established a stronger and more robust sense of identity than did those in other maturation groups

     4.   By adulthood, the differences between early and late maturers become much less clear

C.   Early and late maturation in girls

     1.   Early-maturing girls are initially disadvantaged; they tend to have lower self-esteem and a lower self-concept in terms of body image. They tend to be less popular with peers who have not yet entered puberty, and tend to get into more trouble. They tend to experience more problems in school

     2.   Late-maturing girls may experience some anxiety as they wait to mature. Later-developing girls outperform other students on school achievement tests

     3.   The differences between early- and late-maturing girls in adulthood is uncertain

D.   Brain development during adolescence

     1.   Adrenal glands release hormones that attach themselves to receptor sites throughout the brain and play an important role in regulating mood and excitability

     2.   Adolescents' emotions easily reach a flash point and they are more motivated to seek out intense experiences—the brain regions that inhibit risky, impulsive behavior are still maturing, so there often is an insufficient internal brake on teenagers' sensation-seeking desires and roller-coaster emotions

[handwritten margin notes:] Located Near the Kidneys Directly influence Neurotransmitters such as: serotonin, Dopamine which play a role in regulating Mood + excitability

[handwritten note:] ☆ the Brain areas that inhibit risky behavior are still maturing. (pre frontal Lobes of the) Cerebral Cortex ☆ complicated Cognitive activities planning, decision making, goal setting

3. Parents are recommended to serve as the external brake while the adolescent brain is in this new phase of development

4. During adolescence, boys experience greater changes in their brains than girls

E. Adolescent health, and substance use and abuse

1. Use of mind-altering substances

a. The 1960s and 1970s displayed a significant increase in the adolescent use of drugs, followed by a decline in the 1980s. Another escalation in the 1990s. Use by high school seniors has declined somewhat every year since 2000

b. Despite the current slight decrease, teenage drug use is extensive in industrialized nations

c. Over 45 percent of high school seniors, almost 40 percent of tenth graders, and over 17 percent of eighth graders in the U.S. say they have drunk alcohol

d. By the time they finish high school, 17 percent of young people say they smoke often, 28 percent have drunk alcohol heavily in the past two weeks, and approximately 20 percent say they've tried a highly addictive substance such as cocaine, Ecstasy, inhalants, or heroin

e. Adolescent behavior in Canada concerning alcohol and other drug use is comparable

2. Use of alcohol

a. Immediate dangers from alcohol consumption include potential death when used with other drugs and accidents while driving

b. A recent research study has established that extensive alcohol use as a teenager can cause impairment of mental functioning later on in life

↑ Alcohol use damage Brain cells

c. Four categories for risk

1) Environmental factors including poverty, inadequate education, high unemployment, lack of positive role models, and absence of opportunity can place pressure on young people

2) Peer pressure—if everybody's doing it, it may be more tempting

3) Parental factors include lack of involvement with children and parents' failure to monitor adequately their children's behavior

4) Personal characteristics of adolescents include poor coping skills in response to the powerful emotional pain often experienced in adolescence, relationship and achievement problems at school, and a desire for excitement and self-gratification

d. Case scenario of Joe, an at-risk adolescent

e. Ethical Question 6.2: To what extent should efforts be made to make Joe a productive member of society? Whose responsibility is it to help Joe? His parents'? The community's? His school's? To what extent is a 13-year-old like Joe responsible for improving his own behavior?

3. Use of tobacco

a. Adolescent cigarette smoking, although still a serious problem, continues to be on the decline after peaking in 1996 and 1997

b. In 2006, 21.6 percent of high school seniors, 14.5 percent of tenth-graders, and 8.7 percent of eighth-graders indicated they smoke—down from 33.5 percent for seniors, 27.9 percent for tenth-graders, and 19.1 percent for eighth-graders in 1995

c. Smoking is related to heart disease and lung cancer

d. Risk factors for adolescents include lack of parental attention and support, having friends who smoke, and disinterest in education and school

4. Spotlight on Diversity 6.2: Ethnic Diversity and Alcohol, Substance, and Tobacco Use

a. Adolescents of color do not abuse alcohol and other substances more than do their white counterparts. White U.S. adolescents are significantly more likely to use cigarettes, alcohol, and other mind-altering substances than are African American youth

b. However, in eighth grade, Latino youth have the highest incidence for that age group of all substance use except amphetamines

c. American Indian and Canadian Aboriginal adolescents also have high levels of all substance use

IV. Significant Issues and Life Events

A. Highlight 6.1: Masturbation

   1. By the time they reach the end of adolescence, almost all males and about three quarters of all females have masturbated

   2. African American and Latino youths are less likely to masturbate than white teens

   3. Boys who masturbate do so about three times more frequently than do girls who masturbate

   4. Adolescents need to understand that masturbation is not abnormal or harmful, and is a normal means of relieving sexual tension and other stress

   5. Masturbation is even a prescribed means of treatment for sexual dysfunction

B. Sexual activity in adolescence

   1. The proportion of teenagers who have sexual intercourse increased dramatically from the 1950s to the 1970s; however, the rising rates of teenage intercourse have leveled off and even decreased somewhat over the last 2 decades

   2. The age at which first intercourse occurs has become younger

   3. Motivation for engaging in sexual intercourse—men for pleasure, fun, and physical reasons, whereas women's motives are more often based on love, commitment, and emotions

   4. Spotlight on Diversity 6.3: Racial and Other Differences in Adolescent Sexual Activity

      a. African-American teenagers are more likely to have sexual intercourse than their white and Hispanic counterparts

      b. By twelfth grade, 74.6 percent of African American males, 57.6 percent of Hispanic males, and 42.2 percent of white males report having had sexual intercourse

      c. By twelfth grade, 61.2 percent of African American females, 44.4 percent of Hispanic females, and 43.7 percent of white females have had sex

      d. Differences in patterns of sexual activity may relate more to poverty than to race or ethnicity

e. Other variables include alcohol use, high stress levels, having mothers who had sex at an early age, lower grade point average, and spending greater amounts of unsupervised time at home

f. Factors related to having intercourse at a later age include living in an intact family, having a highly educated mother, attending church regularly, and living in a neighborhood with high incomes and low unemployment rates for women

5. Ethical Question 6.3: At what age do people have the right to have sexual intercourse? What are the reasons for your answer?

C. Unplanned pregnancy in adolescence

1. The United States has the highest rate of teenage pregnancy among Western industrialized nations. It is over twice that of Canada, four times that of France, and almost six times greater than that of Sweden

2. About 9 percent of all teenage girls become pregnant each year, over 90 percent of these are unintended

3. Of all teenage pregnancies, about 51 percent result in live births, 35 percent in abortion, and 14 percent in miscarriages or stillbirths

4. Although it is still high, the actual birthrate has declined since its high point in 1991

5. In 1950 only 13 percent of teen mothers were not married, whereas in 2001, almost 80 percent were single

6. The majority of babies born to single teens remain at home with their young mothers. Only 8 percent of the children are placed for formal adoption and 5 percent live informally with someone in the mother's extended family

7. Other negative consequences

a. Increased physical risks in pregnancy

b. Long-term effects on mothers

1) Less likely to finish school

2) More often poor and dependent on social services

3) More likely to be unemployed or underemployed

4) Greater responsibility and stress

5) Potential serious impacts on mental health and daily functioning

         c.   Long-term effects on children

             1)   More likely to have a low birth weight and higher mortality rate

             2)   More emotional, intellectual, and physical problems

8.   Long-term follow-up studies indicate that 2 decades after giving birth, most former adolescent mothers are not welfare-dependent; many have completed high school, have secured regular employment, and do not have large families

9.   Comprehensive adolescent pregnancy programs seem to contribute to good outcomes, as do home-visitation programs

D.   Teenage fathers

1.   Variables making a person more likely to become a teen father include living in an inner city, doing poorly in school, being poor, and being involved in delinquent acts

2.   They typically remain physically and psychologically involved throughout the pregnancy and for at least some time after the birth

3.   Most have a lower income, less education, and more children compared to men who postpone having children until age 20 or older

4.   Many teenage fathers are the sons of absent fathers, although most do want to learn to be fathers

5.   Highlight 6.2: Portrait of a Single Father

E.   Why do teens get pregnant?

1.   Adolescents often do not use contraception conscientiously, and frequently don't use it at all

2.   Forty-five percent of women under age 16 failed to use contraception the first time they had intercourse, whereas 30 percent of women age 19 or older used no contraception during their first experience

3.   Reasons for not using adequate contraceptives

         a.   Deep sense of privacy and feeling uncomfortable talking about it

         b.   Fear of the wrong impression—that knowing about contraception means knowledgeable and experienced

         c.   Many adolescents express that most teenagers have neither ample knowledge about birth control methods nor adequate access to contraception

d.   Psychological avoidance—if they ignore the issue, it will cease to exist

e.   May simply think that they want to get pregnant

F.   Sex education and empowerment

1.   Fallacies about the assumption that adolescents won't think about sex or be interested in it unless someone around them brings up the subject

     a.   Assumption that adolescents have no other access to sexual information

     b.   That adolescents will automatically try anything they hear about

2.   One primary source of sexual information is friends, who probably don't know much more about sex than they do

3.   Sex education by parents

     a.   Adolescents feel uncomfortable talking about sex with parents

     b.   Some parents avoid the issue

     c.   Public opinion polls in the United States and Canada indicate that 93 percent of parents who have junior high-age students and 91 percent of parents who have high school-age students indicate that it is very or somewhat important to have sexuality education as part of the school curriculum

     d.   When parents were asked about the sexual behavior of their own teenager, 83 percent believed that the teen had gone no further sexually than kissing

4.   Current policy and sex education programs

5.   Abstinence-only-before-marriage sex education programs

     a.   Bush administration has strongly supported the development of such programs and over the past 25 years the government has spent over $1.5 billion on this type of program

     b.   Supporters say this approach drives home the point to young people that there is no choice when it comes to nonmarital sexuality

     c.   Participants in abstinence-only programs had the same rate of sexually transmitted infections (STIs) or sexually transmitted diseases (STDs) as their peers who did not participate in these programs

     d.   Studies found that in communities where more than 20 percent of youth had taken virginity pledges, there was an STI rate of 8.9 percent compared with 5.5 percent in communities with fewer pledgers

e. Many sexuality education experts believe that these programs may do more harm than good

f. Report sponsored by the U.S. House of Representatives list five criticisms of these programs

    1) Abstinence-only curricula contain false information about the effectiveness of contraceptives

    2) Abstinence-only curricula contain false information about the risks of abortion

    3) Abstinence-only curricula blur religion and science

    4) Abstinence-only curricula treat stereotypes about girls and boys as scientific fact

    5) Abstinence-only curricula contain scientific errors

g. Emphasizing how important it is to wait for sexual interaction until heterosexual marriage tends to alienate lesbian and gay youth even more than they already are

    1) Over twice as many lesbian and gay high school students than heterosexual students are threatened or harmed with a weapon

    2) Ninety-two percent of lesbian and gay students in middle and high school report that they frequently or often hear homophobic remarks

    3) Almost one in five of these students heard homophobic remarks from faculty or staff at their school

6. Comprehensive sex education programs

a. Empowers young people by teaching them about both abstinence and ways to protect themselves from STDs, HIV, and unintended pregnancy

b. Goals of a comprehensive sex education program

    1) Information

    2) Attitudes, values, and insights

    3) Relationships and interpersonal skills

    4) Responsibility

c. Characteristics of effective sex education programs

    1) Focus on decreasing specific risk-taking behavior

    2) Based on social learning theory that emphasizes assuming responsibility for behavior, recognizing consequences

    3) Provide vital, practical, and accurate information about the risks of sexual behavior, how to avoid risks and protect oneself

    4) Address how the media encourages young people to become involved in sexual behavior

    5) Provide examples of practice with communication, negotiation, and refusal skills

    6) Reinforce values that address the worth of postponing sexual activity and avoiding risky sexual behavior

    7) Employ teaching methods designed to involve the participants and induce them to personalize the information

7. Spotlight on Diversity 6.4: Empowerment through Sex Education for Native Americans

    a. A case study of a small community in the Cherokee Nation, involving 3 phases

        1) Phase 1: Developers of curricula should explore the community's needs by actively communicating with residents and observing interaction, expectations, and activities

        2) Phase 2: Developers should talk with community members about what principles and values preside over community customs and behavior, thereby identifying recommendations for change. During this phase, community members should be actively recruited to lead discussions and provide input

        3) Phase 3: Developers should take action to solve identified problems

8. Ethical Question 6.4: What type of sex education do you support? What specific content should and should not be taught?

G. Sexually transmitted infections (STIs)—or sexually transmitted diseases (STDs), are infections that people can contract through sexual relations. In the past they were referred to as venereal diseases (VD). About 19 million new cases of STIs develop every year

1. Chlamydia

    a. 2,291,000 non-institutionalized civilians in the U.S. have Chlamydia

    b. It is caused by a bacterium called Chlamydia trachomatis which is transmitted via vaginal, oral, or anal sexual contact

    c. Causes nongonococcal urethritis (NGU) in men. NGU is any inflammation of the male urethra that is not caused by gonorrhea [also called nonspecific urethritis (NSU)]

    d. About 75 percent of women and 50 percent of men experience no symptoms after infection

    e. Symptoms in women may be an infection of the lower reproductive tract, specifically irritation of the urethra or a cervical infection that results in vaginal discharge or burning sensations during urination. Women may get pelvic inflammatory disease (PID) which is an infection in the uterus, the fallopian tubes, and possibly the ovaries that results in a buildup of scar tissue

    f. Untreated or consecutive cases of PID can result in pelvic pain and possibly sterility. Chlamydia makes women up to 5 times more likely to contract HIV

    g. Male symptoms may include a discharge from his penis or burning sensations during urination. They may also develop ipididymitis, an infection of the epididymis (the structure along the back of each testis in which sperm maturation occurs)

    h. If a man or woman contracts chlamydia in the throat or rectum, they may experience pain in those areas

    i. Diagnosis includes laboratory tests examining urine or a specimen of infected cells. Treatment comprises antibiotics, usually azithromycin or doxycycline

    j. Infections can easily be passed back and forth between sexual partners even when one of the partners has been cured

    k. People contracting chlamydial infections are supposed to refer all previous sexual partners for treatment

2. Gonorrhea

    a. It is estimated that in the U.S. 700,000 people contract gonorrhea each year

    b. Also called "clap" and "drip," it is caused by a bacterium that can grow and multiply easily. It is easily transmitted by various sexual contacts including intercourse, oral stimulation of the genitals, and possibly even kissing. A woman has a 40 percent and a man 10 percent chance of contracting gonorrhea by having intercourse with a contagious person one time

    c. A man's symptoms include a yellowish, puslike discharge secreted from the opening at the tip of the penis. Urination is usually quite painful. About 5 to 10 percent of men have no symptoms. Symptoms may first appear as early as 2 days or as late as a month after infection

    d. Most women (as many as 80 percent) have mild or no noticeable symptoms because the infection most frequently invades the cervix

    e. If unchecked, gonorrhea usually spreads from the cervix, up the uterus, and into the fallopian tubes, and occasionally causes sterility

    f. Diagnosis of gonorrhea involves obtaining a sample of the discharge and laboratory tests. Treatment entails administering antibiotics. Increasingly resistant strains are evolving, making treatment increasingly more difficult. People remain contagious to others until they are cured

3. Syphilis

    a. Syphilis is much more deadly than gonorrhea or chlamydial infections, and is contracted by approximately 36,000 people each year in the United States

    b. It is transmitted during sexual intercourse by touching a syphilis sore that can occur on genitals, vagina, anus, rectum, mouth, or lips. A fetus may become infected by its mother

    c. Symptoms progress through four phases

        1) Primary stage: The appearance of a round, crater-like sore, which during this stage is painless. The chancre marks the spot where the bacteria initially penetrated the body, most frequently around the tip of the penis, in the vagina, or at the cervix, or through a cut anywhere on the skin. This usually appears from 10 to 90 days (an average of 21 days) after infection and disappears after 3 to 6 weeks

2) Secondary stage: Begins with lesions in mucous membranes and a rash appears and can spread all over the body. It neither itches nor hurts. This stage usually begins 3 to 6 weeks after the chancre disappears. Other symptoms include sore throat, hair loss, headaches, weight loss, nausea, joint pains, and fever

3) Latent stage: No symptoms occur during this stage, and begins sometime after all secondary-stage symptoms have disappeared. The bacteria concentrate in some organ of the body like the brain, spinal cord, or bones. After about 1 year in this stage, they are no longer contagious. One exception is a pregnant woman, who may pass the disease on to her child

4) Late stage: About 15 percent of the people who progress to the latent stage and remain untreated enter this stage. During this phase the bacteria viciously attack the organs where they've concentrated. The heart, eyes, brain, spinal cord, digestive organs, liver, or endocrine glands may be involved. Even death may result

d. Blood tests are usually used to diagnose syphilis, although a number of other tests can also be used. Penicillin or other antibiotics are common treatments and can be very effective if administered within a year after becoming infected

4. Pubic lice

a. Sometimes called crabs, they are tiny insects that cling to pubic hair and feed off the blood vessels in the skin of the pubic area. People become infected through direct contact

b. The primary symptom is itching and can be diagnosed by visual observation

c. Treatment involves applying Kwell, a prescription ointment or shampoo for a period of 12 hours. All clothing, towels, and sheets coming into contact with lice should be boiled or washed in very hot water

5. Scabies

a. Caused by the mite Sarcoptes scabiei, and become infected through direct contact with the organism

b. Symptoms include a red skin rash and severe itching. Diagnosis is through visual observation of the rash

c. Various creams are available for treatment

d. Like pubic lice, scabies are highly contagious so all material coming into contact must be thoroughly cleaned

6. Trichomoniasis

   a. There are about 7.4 million new cases of trichomoniasis in the U.S. each year

   b. Caused by a single-celled protozoan parasite, it can be contracted through sexual intercourse or by genital-to-genital area contact

   c. Women usually experience a vaginal discharge that is yellow-green in color. Men either experience no symptoms or mild burning in the urethra after urination

   d. Diagnosis requires a laboratory test, and is treated by prescription drugs such as metronidazole or tinidazole taken by mouth in a single dose

7. Genital herpes

   a. At least 45 million people in the U.S. ages 12 or older (one of five people) have had a genital herpes infection

   b. Most genital herpes is herpes simplex viruses type 1 (HSV-2), which causes outbreaks of painful blisters that break open and become sores. HSV-1 traditionally causes fever blisters or cold sores. Either type infecting the genitals is considered genital herpes

   c. The first outbreak occurs within 2 weeks of infection, although it may not happen for years. May last for 2 to 4 weeks before healing. Most people experience 4 to 5 outbreaks within the first year then tend to decrease in frequency over time

   d. Other symptoms may resemble the flu, and it may be passed on to a developing fetus. Often a cesarean section is performed at birth

   e. Diagnosis is performed by visual observation, testing tissue specimens, or administering blood tests. Because it is a virus, it cannot be cured; oral antiviral medications can shorten episodes, decrease their severity, or prevent them from occurring while the medication is being taken

   f. Psychological stress may also be related to outbreaks

8. Human Papillomavirus (HPV)

   a. About 20 million people in the U.S. currently have human papillomavirus (HPV)

   b. Some people develop genital warts—soft, moist, pink, or flesh-colored swellings, and can be single or multiple, small or large, and sometimes cauliflower shaped. They are transmitted through sexual contact with the infected area

c.   Genital warts can be treated with chemicals applied directly to the affected area, removed by laser surgery, electrosurgery, freezing with liquid nitrogen, or surgical excision

d.   HPV becomes imperceptible for 90 percent of women within two years after infection

e.   Well over 90 percent of cervical cancers are also infected with the virus; it can also lead to penile and anal cancers in men

9.   HIV (Human Immunodeficiency Virus)

a.   AIDS (acquired immunodeficiency syndrome) is caused by HIV. Its progression can be slowed down, but cannot be cured and eventually usually leads to death

b.   The largest percentage of AIDS cases in the U.S. occurs among people in their 20s and 30s who were infected with HIV in their teens or 20s

c.   Having another STI increases one's vulnerability to HIV. HIV becomes more concentrated in bodily fluids of people with an STI

10.   Preventing STDs

a.   Be informed

b.   Be observant

c.   Be selective

d.   Be honest

e.   Be cautious

f.   Be promptly tested and treated

H.   Major methods of contraception

1.   The pill

a.   Combined pill: Combines a synthetic estrogen and progestin. The most commonly used brands of combined pills are sold in packages of 21 pills. A woman then refrains from starting her next monthly pack of pills for 7 days. During this time she will have her menstrual period. Combined pills are theoretically 99.7 percent effective; however, the actual effectiveness rate is approximately 92 percent

b.   Mini-pill: Provides a lower dosage of hormones than the combined pill. They contain only progestin. Forty percent of women taking these pills fail to ovulate at all and another 20 percent ovulate inconsistently. They provide a useful alternative for women who are breast-feeding. The theoretical effectiveness rate is 99 percent, but its actual effectiveness rate can be as low as 92 percent

    c.   Both types of pills should be taken regularly at approximately the same time each day. If you forget more than one pill, it is best to consult your health-care practitioner

    d.   Advantages: They are effective and easy to use. They can decrease menstrual cramping, produce lighter menstrual periods, and provide some defense against PID. It has been found to decrease the risk of endometrial and ovarian cancer, and the risk of developing benign breast growths, iron deficiency anemia, acne, ectopic pregnancy, and symptoms occurring prior to menstruation

    e.   Disadvantages of taking birth control pills include undesirable side effects such as nausea, vomiting, bleeding between menstrual periods, and breast tenderness. These symptoms usually disappear after 2 to 3 months, like they do in pregnancy. They provide no help in preventing STIs. They also have interactive effects with some other drugs.

    f.   Serious problems are rare; they might include cardiovascular problems involving a heart attack, stroke, blood clots in the legs, lungs, heart, or brain, or developing high blood pressure. Several variables can increase risk

2.   The birth control patch and vaginal ring

    a.   Both were introduced in 2003 and use the same hormones as the combination birth control pill

    b.   Ortho Evra (the brand name) consists of a thin patch of material that sticks to the skin and releases hormones into the body to prevent pregnancy. Applied once a week for 3 weeks and then a week passes without a patch application. Can be placed on the buttock, abdomen, upper outer arm, or upper torso

    c.   The NuvaRing is a 2-inch diameter soft and transparent flexible ring that's inserted into the vagina between day 1 and day 5 of a menstrual period and left in place for 3 weeks. After insertion, vaginal moisture and body heat activate the release of hormones. It is removed for a week and then replaced with a new ring

    d.   Effectiveness rates and most of the advantages and disadvantages of both are the same as the combination birth control pill

3.   Depo-Provera injections

    a.   The most commonly used hormonal injection method. It is a long-acting progestin that is injected once every 12 weeks, although it probably provides an even longer period of protection. Theoretical effectiveness is over 99 percent, and actual effectiveness is 97 percent

b. Advantages include avoiding the use of estrogen, decreased risk of endometrial and ovarian cancer, decreased risk of PID, and the absence of menstrual bleeding

c. Disadvantage is the lack of protection against STIs, disturbances in the menstrual cycle, weight gain, breast tenderness, headache, nausea, and depression

d. Only 24 to 70 percent of women continue them after 1 year

4. Hormonal implants

a. Implanon has recently been approved for use in the U.S. and consists of a thin, flexible plastic implant about the size of a cardboard matchstick that is placed under the skin of the upper arm, where it can remain effective for up to 3 years

b. It is a progestin-only hormonal method with actual effectiveness rate of over 99 percent

c. Advantages include easy to use, is an appropriate option for women who can't use estrogen or who are breastfeeding, and can be removed by a health care provider at any time

d. The most common complaint is irregular bleeding including spotting between periods, periods may be longer and heavier, fewer and lighter, or may stop altogether. It can interact with certain medications, and it provides no protection against STIs. Warning signs of rare but potentially serious side effects include arm pain, bleeding or pus at the insertion site, severe headache, development of a breast lump, severe abdominal pain, or unusually heavy vaginal bleeding

5. Emergency contraception (EC)

a. This is typically used when unplanned, unprotected intercourse has occurred; when another method of contraception fails; or after a sexual assault

b. Two types are available—Plan B is a progestin-only brand available in the U.S. since 1999, consists of 2 pills and is available over the counter. Only 1 percent of women will become pregnant after taking Plan B if taken within 3 days

c. The second type includes regular birth control pills, usually containing both progestin and estrogen. A health care provider should be consulted, and they are administered in 2 doses 12 hours apart. As with Plan B, the sooner they are taken the better. Only two percent will become pregnant if taken within 3 days. This has been used for more than 3 decades

d. Common side effects for either involve nausea and vomiting which generally go away within 1 or 2 days, also may include breast tenderness, irregular bleeding, dizziness, or headache

e. There is debate about whether pharmacists have the right to refuse to fill these prescriptions if they have personal objections to its use

f. A potential form of EC is the ParaGard intrauterine device; if inserted by a health care professional within 5 days of unprotected intercourse, it is 99.9 percent effective

g. Ethical Question 6.5: Do pharmacists have the right to refuse to fill a prescription if they have personal moral objections to it?

6. Vaginal spermicides

a. The chemicals act to kill sperm, and the substance itself acts as a barrier that inhibits sperm from entering the uterus

b. Advantages include relative ease of use, ready availability, low cost, and their use only when needed

c. The theoretical effectiveness rate is only 85 percent, with an actual effectiveness rate of 71 percent when used alone. Effectiveness increases significantly when used in conjunction with another form of contraception

7. Condoms for men

a. Also called a prophylactic or rubber, it is a thin sheath made of latex or plastic that fits over the penis and serves as a barrier form of contraception

b. The theoretical effectiveness is 98 percent. The actual effectiveness rate of the condom is 85 percent. This significantly increases if used together with a spermicide or if the penis is withdrawn from the vagina prior to ejaculation

c. Advantages include a nonsurgical means of giving the male some direct responsibility for contraception. Their use has been given much publicity and encouragement to help prevent STIs

d. The disadvantage is the minor intrusion of spontaneity when placing it on the penis. It is also important that it be withdrawn shortly after ejaculation to avoid spilling semen

8. Female condom

a. This vaginal barrier form of contraception consists of two rings connected by latex. One ring fits over the cervix; the latex protects the cervix from contact with either the penis or semen. The other ring rests outside the vagina; here the latex forms a pouch for the penetrating penis, thus protecting the penis from vaginal contact. The theoretical effectiveness rate is 95 percent, although the actual rate is 79 percent

b.   Advantages include a woman being able to take responsibility for contraception and protection from STIs

c.   Disadvantages may involve reactions such as rashes resulting from a latex allergy or minor problems like skin irritation. Also the possibility of slippage during intercourse, the potential reduction of sensation, and the noise sometimes produced

9.   Diaphragm, cervical cap, and shield

a.   Cervical cap has the brand name FemCap, and the shield has a brand name of Lea's Shield, and each is available in the U.S. with a prescription

b.   The diaphragm is a circular thin piece of rubber stretched over a flexible ring of wire and shaped like a dome. A woman inserts it by pushing it with her fingers up into the vagina to cover the cervix. A woman must be fit for the correct size diaphragm

c.   FemCap is a silicone cup shaped like a sailor's hat that snugly covers the cervix with the rim of the hat conforming to the contours of the vagina. The 3 sizes vary depending on whether a woman has experienced a pregnancy

d.   Lea's Shield is a cervical cap that allows the one-way release of cervical fluids and air and fits snugly over the cervix

e.   Each of the devices should be used with spermicidal cream or jelly that is placed inside the bottom of the cup or dome and spread around the edges

f.   The diaphragm can be inserted up to 6 hours before intercourse and left in place for no more than 24; both FemCap and Lea's Shield can be inserted up to 8 hours prior to sexual intercourse and remain in place for no more than 48 hours. If any devices are left longer, there is danger of toxic shock syndrome, a potentially fatal bacterial infection

g.   The diaphragm has a theoretical effectiveness rate of 94 percent and an actual rate of 86 percent. FemCap has an actual rate of 86 percent for women who have never been pregnant and 71 percent for women who have given birth vaginally. Lea's Shield has an actual effectiveness rate of 85 percent

h.   The advantages are they are easy to carry with you, they don't interfere with normal hormones, they are effective right away, and they can be inserted hours before intercourse so they don't have to interfere with spontaneity

i.   The disadvantages include they can't be used while menstruating, some women have trouble putting them in correctly, they may be pushed out of position during some sexual positions, they don't help prevent STIs, and some women experience recurrent bladder infections when using the diaphragm or a cervical cap, and pain when using a cervical cap or shield

10.   The birth control sponge

   a.   This goes by the brand name of Today Sponge, and is a soft, cuplike sponge that can be inserted into the vagina and covers the cervix. It is saturated with a spermicide to provide additional protection. It should be left in the vagina at least 6 hours after sexual intercourse, but no longer than 30 hours because of the potential of toxic shock syndrome

   b.   It acts like a barrier to prevent sperm from entering the cervix, the chemical spermicide acts to kill sperm, and its potential for absorbing sperm is also beneficial

   c.   The theoretical and actual effectiveness for women who have not had children are 91 and 84 percent, respectively; the respective rates for women who have borne children are 80 and 68 percent

   d.   Most advantages resemble those of other barrier methods, disadvantages include the fact that some women find insertion difficult, notice vaginal irritation, and find it messy because liquid must be added prior to insertion

11.   IUD (intrauterine device)

   a.   A plastic device that is placed in a woman's uterus by a physician or trained health professional

   b.   ParaGard, introduced here in 1988 as the Copper T, and contains a fine copper wire wrapped around the base of the T. Once inserted, it is effective for up to 12 years

   c.   The second, brand name Mirena, has been available in the U.S. since 2000. It also assumes a T shape and this releases a small amount of progestin, and remains effective for up to 5 years

   d.   They both alter how sperm move and prevent sperm from fertilizing the egg, they change the interior lining of the uterus, the endometrium

   e.   Advantages include its high effectiveness rates, convenience, and no restrictions on spontaneity

   f.   Disadvantages include altered or irregular menstrual bleeding patterns, cramping. ParaGard may cause a 50-70 percent increase in menstrual flow; they don't help prevent STIs, slight possibility of slipping out unnoticed

12.   Withdrawal

     a.   Coitus interruptus refers to withdrawing the penis before ejaculating into the vagina. Theoretical effectiveness is 96 percent and actual effectiveness 73 percent

     b.   Advantages are that no extraneous devices or substances are needed and it's free

     c.   Disadvantages include that a few drops of semen are expelled by a pair of glands called the Cowper's glands before the full ejaculation, and can be transported out through the tip of the penis and still impregnate a woman. Effectiveness depends largely on the man's ability to withdraw prior to ejaculation

13.   Fertility awareness methods

     a.   Fertility awareness methods were formerly referred to as the rhythm method, which involves monitoring a woman's ovulation cycle and initiating sexual relations only during the safe times of her cycle

     b.   Calendar method: Involves counting the days of the menstrual cycle and trying to determine when ovulation occurs

     c.   Basal body temperature method: Involves taking the woman's temperature every morning as soon as she wakes up. A woman's body temperature undergoes minor predictable variations depending on where she is in her ovulatory cycle

     d.   Cervical mucus (or ovulation) method: A woman must examine her cervical mucus throughout her menstrual cycle. The consistency, amount, and clarity of the mucus tends to change predictably depending on where she is in her ovulatory cycle

     e.   Symptothermal method: Using any or all of the methods together, this tends to be more effective than one method used alone

     f.   The actual effectiveness rate for using any of these methods is 80 percent, the theoretical effectiveness rates with perfect use for the calendar method is 98 percent, the basal body temperature method 98 percent, and the cervical mucus method 97 percent

     g.   The advantage is that there is no manipulation of hormones and nothing must be done directly prior to sexual intercourse. A major disadvantage is that using any of the FAM methods requires conscientious attention to gathering data everyday, and do not help prevent STIs

14. Sterilization

    a.   Tubal ligation: The fallopian tubes leading from the ovaries to the uterus are severed

    b.   Vasectomy: A small section of the vas deferens is removed from the male near the place where the scrotum is attached to the body. The vas deferens is the tube that transports sperm from the testicles to the urethra; thus sperm are not ejaculated

    c.   Neither has any effect on the person's ability to respond sexually or enjoy sexual activity

    d.   An advantage and disadvantage of sterilization is that it is considered permanent. It also has nothing to do with preventing STIs

15. Ethical Question 6.6: To what extent should contraception be made readily available to anyone who wants it? What kinds of contraception should be offered, if any? Who should pay for contraception (for example, individuals using it or the government)?

16. Contraceptive methods of the future

    a.   Male implant: In 2002 the FDA approved the Vasclip, a tiny implantable clip that blocks the flow of sperm. No cutting or cauterizing

    b.   Hormones to suppress sperm production: Injecting males with hormones linked to decreased sperm production or to inhibiting the ability of sperm to fertilize an egg effectively. Hormonal implants in men provide another potential avenue of contraception

    c.   Contraceptive vaccines for women: A vaccine that would immunize women against the hormonal changes necessary to make the uterus hospitable for implantation of a fertilized egg

    d.   Vaginal barrier devices: Some made of polymers that release spermicide, a custom-molded cap, and modifications of the contraceptive sponge

    e.   Microbicides: New substances that would more effectively kill sperm as well as bacteria and viruses causing STIs

    f.   New IUDs: A number of IUDs are being developed in other countries

    g.   Fallopian-tube plugs: A liquid silicone would be injected into the fallopian tubes and would harden and form a stopper to prevent sperm from entering the tube

V.   **Summary**

Experiential Exercises and Simulations

The following four exercises are intended to help you understand the physiological changes during adolescence and the effects of these changes on adolescents' personalities. Special attention is focused on sexual development and decision-making.

Exercise 6.1: Self-Portrait

A. Brief description
Draw a picture of yourself as an adolescent and examine your own perceived physical strengths and weaknesses. Small-group discussions and a large-group discussion follow.

B. Objectives
You will:
1. Identify specific areas of concern that you had when you were an adolescent.
2. Relate these concerns to the concerns of adolescents in general.
3. Examine the impacts of physical changes and the perceptions of these changes on the individual personality.
4. Relate the physical changes you experienced to the factual material presented in the text.

C. Procedure
1. You are given a sheet of paper and asked to draw a clothed illustration of yourself at age 13 in the center.
2. Label the upper-left-hand portion of the paper "Strengths" and the upper-right-hand portion "Weaknesses." List under the appropriate headings both the positive physical aspects and the negative physical aspects you perceived yourself to have at age 13.
3. Divide into groups of four to six persons. Discuss at least some of the physical strengths and weaknesses you perceived in yourself during adolescence. You will have approximately 10 minutes for this discussion.
4. Small groups come together for a large-group discussion. The large group considers the following questions:
   a. What does it feel like to be an adolescent?
   b. What specific physical changes tend to be the most striking and have the greatest effects on the developing personality?
   c. How do these physical changes and their effects on individual personalities relate to the research and factual material presented in the text? On what issues did the small groups and the text agree? Where were there differences?

A. Brief description

You will choose a partner; one person plays a social worker and the other a 16-year-old adolescent trying to decide what type of contraception to use. Various alternatives, and their strengths and weaknesses, are examined during the role-play. A group discussion follows.

B. Objectives

You will:

1. Identify the various methods of contraception.
2. Assess the positive and negative aspects of each.
3. Examine steps in decision making about means of contraception to use.
4. Recognize the differences between personal opinion and professional objectivity.
5. Examine your own values and opinions concerning birth control.

C. Procedure

1. Review the various methods of birth control presented in the text and the advantages and disadvantages of each.
2. Write down your personal opinion about which method of contraception is best. There is no one best method; the choice is personal.
3. Choose a partner; one person role-plays a 16-year-old adolescent and the other an adult acquaintance of that adolescent.

> **IF THE ADOLESCENT IS A FEMALE:** Frankie is 15 years old and confused. She has been going steady with Johnnie for four months now. Two weeks ago they started having sexual intercourse. They have not been using any form of birth control. Although Frankie has avoided admitting it to herself, she has finally accepted the fact that she is sexually active. She's afraid of getting pregnant and wants to use some form of birth control. The problem is that she doesn't know which one to use. She goes to an adult she knows and whom she trusts will keep their conversation confidential. She asks the adult what the best form of birth control would be for her to use.
>
> **IF THE ADOLESCENT IS A MALE:** Focus attention on Johnnie, the 16-year-old boyfriend. Everything about the role-play remains the same except for the fact that it is the male in the couple who is seeking birth-control advice.

4. Review the basic suggestions for doing a role-play. The adult role-player is not a professional social worker or counselor but only a friend who can give information and ask questions. The adult role-players:
    a. Ask the adolescent what he or she knows about birth-control methods.
    b. Provide information about forms of contraception available.
    c. Help the adolescent examine the pros and cons of each birth-control alternative and come to a final decision about what type to use.
    d. Remember that choosing a birth-control method is the adolescent's decision. Try to be objective.
5. You will have 10 to 15 minutes to complete the role-plays. Pairs role-play simultaneously.
6. Class discussion follows the role-playing:
    a. How did the adolescent and the adult differ in their views of "the best" method of birth control?
    b. What advantages and disadvantages of the various methods were most important to the adolescent?

    c.   How did the adult role-players feel when their views differed from the adolescent's feelings about various contraceptive methods?

    d.   How did the adolescent arrive at a final decision concerning what type of contraception to use?

Exercise 6.3: How Did You First Learn About Sex?

A.   Brief description

The group is broken down into smaller groups of four to six. The small groups are asked to discuss how individual members first learned about sex. Major points of each group's discussion and the total group's discussion are summarized.

B.   Objectives

You will:

1.   Identify and describe the circumstances under which you first learned about sex.
2.   Explore the issue of how comfortable parents feel providing sex education to their children.
3.   Examine the need for sex education and relate it to your own experience.

C.   Procedure

1.   Form groups of four to six members. Select a group of people with whom you feel at ease.
2.   Address the following questions:
    a.   How did you first learn about sex? What were the circumstances? Who was it that talked to you about it?
    b.   How comfortable did your parents feel discussing sex with you?
    c.   What kind of sex education did you receive in school?
    d.   What is your opinion about the need for sex education?
3.   You have 10 to 15 minutes to discuss the questions.
4.   One representative of each group summarizes that group's discussion and shares this summary with the larger group.
5.   Finally, formulate a summary statement regarding the conclusions of the entire class.

Exercise 6.4: Sex Education for an Adolescent

A.   Brief description

The instructor will role-play an adolescent and ask the entire class to respond to questions.

B.   Objectives

You will:

1.   Identify gaps in basic sexual information given to adolescents.
2.   Appraise your own levels of sexual knowledge and formulate answers to questions in a simulated situation.
3.   Recognize the difficulty of sharing sexual information clearly and simply.
4.   Examine your own ability to talk about sexual issues.

C.   Procedure

1.   The instructor role-plays a 14-year-old adolescent who asks various questions about sex.
2.   Class members call out the answers.
3.   Questions asked may include the following:
    a.   When is the right time to start having sex?
    b.   Can boys pull out in time?

c. What does an orgasm feel like?

d. Does it hurt the first time you have sex?

e. Can a person get any STIs from oral sex? If so, what kinds?

f. What do boys want?

g. What do girls want?

4. The instructor responds to group members' answers as an adolescent might. Group members' words should be clear and simple. Explanations should be specific.

5. Discuss your reactions to the experience.

Study Outline

I.   **A Perspective**

II. **Identity Formation**

    A.   Concept Summary Box: Erikson's Eight Stages of Development

    B.   Erikson's psychosocial theory

        1.   Stage 1: Basic trust versus basic mistrust

            a.   For infants up to 18 months of age, learning to trust others is the overriding crisis

            b.   Later in life, people may apply this concept of trust to friends, an intimate partner, or their government

        2.   Stage 2: Autonomy versus shame and doubt

            a.   The crisis of autonomy versus shame and doubt characterizes early childhood, from 18 months to 3 years

            b.   Accomplishing various tasks provides children with feelings of self-worth and self-confidence

            c.   If children of this age are constantly downtrodden, restricted, or punished, shame and doubt will emerge instead

        3.   Stage 3: Initiative versus guilt

            a.   Preschoolers aged 3 to 6 years must face the crisis of taking their own initiative

            b.   Preschoolers who are encouraged to take initiative to explore and learn are likely to assimilate this concept for use later in life

            c.   Preschoolers who are consistently restricted, punished, or treated harshly are more likely to experience the emotion of guilt

4. Stage 4: Industry versus inferiority

    a. School-age children 6 to 12 years old must address the crisis of industry versus inferiority. Children in this age group need to be productive and succeed in their activities

    b. Mastering academic skills and material is important. Those who do learn to be industrious master activities

    c. Children who experience failure in school, or even in peer relations, may develop a sense of inferiority

5. Stage 5: Identity versus role confusion

    a. Adolescence is a time when young people explore who they are and establish their identity. It is the transition period when people examine the various roles they play, and integrate these roles into a perception of self, an identity

    b. Role confusion: Occurs when people are unable to integrate their many roles and have difficulty coping with conflicting roles

6. Stage 6: Intimacy versus isolation

    a. Young adulthood is characterized by a quest for intimacy, which involves more than the establishment of a sexual relationship

    b. Intimacy includes the ability to share with and give to another person without being afraid of sacrificing one's own identity

    c. People who do not attain intimacy are likely to suffer isolation, and have often been unable to resolve some of the crises of earlier psychosocial development

7. Stage 7: Generativity versus stagnation

    a. Mature adulthood is characterized by the crisis of generativity versus stagnation. During this time of life, people become concerned with helping, producing for, or guiding the following generation

    b. Generativity: Involves a genuine concern for the future beyond one's own life track, although it does not necessarily involve procreating one's own children. Rather, it concerns drive to be creative and productive in a way that will aid people in the future

    c. Adults who lack generativity become self-absorbed. They tend to focus primarily on their own concerns and needs rather than on those of others. The result is stagnation

    d. Stagnation: A fixed, discouraging lack of progress and productivity

8.   Stage 8: Ego integrity versus despair

    a.   The crisis of ego integrity versus despair characterizes old age. During this time of life, people tend to look back over their years and reflect on them

    b.   Ego integrity: Appreciation for one's life and contentment with one's accomplishments. This is the ultimate form of identity integration

    c.   People who have ego integrity enjoy a sense of peace and accept the fact that life will soon be over

    d.   Others who have failed to cope successfully with past life crises and have many regrets experience despair

C.   Implications of identity formation in adolescence ✕ go to p299

    1.   Highlight 7.1: How to Determine Who You Are

        a.   What do I find satisfying, meaningful, and enjoyable?

        b.   What is my moral code?

        c.   What are my spiritual beliefs?

        d.   What are my employment goals?

        e.   What are my sexual mores?

        f.   Do I desire to have a committed relationship?

        g.   Do I desire to have children?

        h.   In what area of the country/world do I desire to live?

        i.   What do I enjoy doing with my leisure time?

        j.   What kind of image do I want to project to others?

        k.   What type of people do I enjoy being with, and why?

        l.   Do I desire to improve the quality of my life and that of others?

        m.   What types of relationships do I desire to have with relatives, friends, neighbors, and with people I meet for the first time?

        n.   What are my thoughts about death and dying?

        o.   What do I hope to be doing 5 years from now, 10 years, 20 years?

2.   Identity confusion: Expressed by delaying acting like a responsible adult; committing oneself to poorly thought-out courses of action; regressing into childishness to avoid assuming the responsibilities of adulthood. Cliquishness of adolescence and its intolerance of differences as defenses against identity confusion

3.   Experimentation with various roles that represent the many possibilities for their future identity

4.   Psychosocial moratorium: A period of free experimentation before a final sense of identity is achieved

5.   The crisis of identity versus role confusion is best resolved through integrating earlier identifications, present values, and future goals into a consistent self-concept

6.   Many adolescents are idealistic. If society can channel their energies constructively, adolescents' contributions can be meaningful. Unfortunately, some become disenchanted and apathetic after being continually frustrated with obstacles

7.   Importance of achieving identity—many people muddle through life and never arrive at well-thought-out identities

8.   The formation of identity

     a.   During the early years one's sense of identity is largely determined by the reactions of others

     b.   Looking-glass self: Persons develop their self-concept in terms of how others relate to them

     c.   In identity formation, it is important to remember that what we want out of the future is more important than past experience in determining what the future will be

D.   Marcia's categories of identity

1.   Identity achievement: To reach this stage, people undergo a period of intense decision making. The attainment of identity achievement is usually thought of as the most beneficial of the four status categories

2.   Foreclosure: People who fall into this category are the only ones who never experience an identity crisis as such. They glide into adulthood without experiencing much turbulence or anxiety. Decisions concerning both career and values are made relatively early in life

3.   Identity diffusion: People who experience identity diffusion suffer from a serious lack of decision and direction. Although they go through an identity crisis, they never resolve it. They are not able to make clear decisions concerning either their personal ideology or their career choice

4.   Moratorium: Includes people who experience intense anxiety during their identity crisis, yet have not made decisions regarding either personal values or a career choice. Instead of avoiding the decision-making issue, they address it almost constantly. They are characterized by strong, conflicting feelings about what they should believe and do. Moratorium people tend to have many critical, but as yet unresolved, issues

E.   Ethical Question 7.1: To what extent is there an ideal identity everyone should strive to acquire? How much individuality should be allowed or encouraged in identity formation?

F.   Critical thinking: The evaluation of theory and application to client situations

    1.   Both Erikson's and Marcia's theories provide interesting insights into people's behavior and their interaction with others, and provide a framework for better understanding "normal" life crises and events

    2.   Traditional theories of identity development such as Erikson's and Marcia's have limitations due to their Westernized perspective on how people *should* develop

    3.   Questions to help social workers evaluate theory and determine what theoretical concepts and frameworks are most suited for their own practice with clients

        a.   How does the theory apply to client situations?

        b.   What research supports the theory?

        c.   To what extent does the theory coincide with social work values and ethics?

        d.   Are other theoretical frameworks or concepts available that are more relevant to practice situations?

G.   Spotlight on Diversity 7.1: Race, Culture, Ethnicity, and Identity Development

    1.   Approximately one third of adolescents in the United States belong to an ethnic group that is a "minority"

    2.   Ethnic identity: Identifying with their ethnic group, feeling that they belong, and appreciating their cultural heritage

    3.   A parallel development for children from diverse ethnic groups that coincides with Marcia's four coping strategies for identity development

        a.   A person with a diffused identity demonstrates little or no involvement with his or her ethnic and cultural heritage and may be unaware of or disinterested in cultural issues

        b.   A person with foreclosed identity has explored his or her cultural background to a minor extent. However, his or her feelings about ethnic identity are vague. He or she most likely simply adopts the ideas of parents or other relatives without giving them much thought

c. Someone with a moratorium identity displays an active pursuit of ethnic identity. This stage reflects an ethnic identity crisis

d. A person who has achieved an ethnic identity has struggled with its meaning and come to conclusions regarding how this ethnic identity is an integral part of his or her life

4. An alternative model of racial and cultural identity development— Racial/Cultural Identity Development Model (R/CID) initially developed by Sue and Sue

a. Conformity stage: People identify closely with the dominant white society

b. Dissonance stage: Usually initiated by some crisis or negative experience. A person becomes aware that racism does exist, and that not all aspects of minority or majority culture are good or bad

c. Resistance and immersion stage: This stage is characterized by the resolution of the conflicts and confusions that occurred in the previous stage

d. Introspection stage: The individual discovers that this level of intensity of feelings is psychologically draining and does not allow time to devote energy into understanding one's racial/cultural group

e. Integrative awareness stage: People have developed an inner sense of security and can appreciate various aspects of their culture that make them unique. Greater control and flexibility are attained

5. Communities and schools can strengthen racial and cultural identity development for adolescents

a. Nuevo Puente (New Bridges): Initially designed to address substance abuse by Puerto Rican youth, a curriculum was developed including cultural pride

b. Community festivals can provide other avenues through which community residents can learn about and appreciate other cultures

c. Murals represent a community effort to utilize cultural symbols as a way of creating an impact internally and externally

H. Spotlight on Diversity 7.2: Lesbian and Gay Adolescents

1. Lesbian and gay adolescents in this culture suffer even more extreme obstacles to identity development than their heterosexual peers

2. Homophobia: An extreme and irrational fear of, and hatred toward, lesbian and gay people simply because they are lesbian and gay

3. Coming out: The process of a person acknowledging publicly that he or she is gay or lesbian

4. Social work practitioners must be especially sensitive to the issues facing lesbian and gay adolescents. Social workers need to:

   a. Evaluate their own homophobic attitudes

   b. Become knowledgeable about the needs and issues of lesbian and gay adolescents

   c. Understand that adolescence is a time for exploration of one's sexual identity

   d. Confront insulting, offensive, and belittling comments

   e. Provide accurate information about sexuality, sexual orientation, and safe sexual behavior

   f. Never assume that a person is heterosexual

   g. Advocate for the rights of lesbian and gay people when they are being violated

   h. Have resources about sexual orientation on hand, or advocate for schools to make them available

   i. Help lesbian and gay youth become connected with others of their own sexual orientation

   j. Help lesbian and gay youth navigate through the coming-out process

5. It is up to you as a social worker to scrutinize theories closely and use what you can from them. However, it is just as important to recognize limitations of theories

III. Moral Development

A. Morality: Involves a set of principles regarding what is right and what is wrong

B. Ethical Question 7.2: What are the major principles in your personal code of morality? How would you answer the following moral questions regarding what is right and what is wrong? Should there be a death penalty for monstrous crimes and, if so, how monstrous? Why or why not? Should there be national health insurance where all people receive medical services regardless of their level of wealth? If so, who should pay for it? Should corporal punishment be allowed in schools? Why or why not? Should prayer be allowed in schools? Why or why not?

C.	Kohlberg's theory of moral development

1.	Level 1: Preconventional (premoral): People usually experience this level from ages 4 to 10

    a.	Stage 1: Children do what they are told to in order to avoid negative consequences

    b.	Stage 2: Focuses on rewards instead of punishment; sometimes this involves an exchange of favors

2.	Level 2: Conventional: Moral thought is based on conforming to conventional roles; frequently, this level occurs from ages 10 to 13

    a.	Stage 3: Focuses on gaining the approval of others. Good relationships become very important

    b.	Stage 4: Emphasizes the need to adhere to law. Higher authorities are generally respected. "Law and order" are considered necessary in order to maintain the social order

3.	Level 3: Postconventional: Concerns developing a moral conscience that goes beyond what others say. At this level, people contemplate laws and expectations and decide on their own what is right and what is wrong. They become autonomous, independent thinkers. The needs and well-being of others become very important. At this level, true morality is achieved

    a.	Stage 5: Involves adhering to socially accepted laws and principles. Law is considered good for the general public welfare. However, laws are subject to interpretation and change

    b.	Stage 6: This stage is the ultimate attainment. During this stage, one becomes free of the thoughts and opinions expressed by others. Morality is completely internalized. Decisions are based on one's personal conscience, transcending laws and regulations. Examples of people who attained this level include Martin Luther King Jr. and Gandhi

D.	Concept Summary Box: Kohlberg's Three Levels and Six Stages of Moral Development

E.	Critical thinking: Evaluation of Kohlberg's theory

1.	Many questions have been raised concerning the validity and application of this theory; Kohlberg places primary emphasis on how people think, not what they do

2.	Dilemmas are posed in extremely abstract manner that requires a high level of verbal competence to answer. Are young children really premoral?

3.	The theory is culturally biased. Kohlberg himself has conceded that stage 6 may not be applied across all cultures, societies, and situations

F. Moral development and women: Gilligan's approach

1. Gilligan maintains that women fare less well according to Kohlberg's levels of moral development because they tend to view moral dilemmas differently than men

2. Women are more likely to adopt a care perspective that views people in terms of their connectedness with others and emphasizes interpersonal communication, relationships with others, and concern for others. Kohlberg's theory centers on a justice perspective in which each person functions independently and makes moral decisions on an individual basis

3. Women's moral development is often based on their personal interest and commitment to the good of others close to them. Goodness and kindness are emphasized

4. Gilligan's levels of moral development

    a. Level 1: Orientation to personal survival: Focuses purely on the woman's self-interest. The needs and well-being of others are not really considered. At this level, a woman focuses first on personal survival

    b. Transition 1: Transition from personal selfishness to responsibility: Involves a movement in moral thought from consideration only of self to some consideration of the others involved. During this transition, a woman comes to acknowledge the fact that she is responsible not only for herself but also for others, including the unborn. She begins to acknowledge that her choice will impact others

    c. Level 2: Goodness as self-sacrifice: Involves putting aside one's own needs and wishes. The well-being of other people becomes important. A woman at this level feels dependent on what other people think. Often a conflict occurs between taking responsibility for her own actions and feeling pressure from others to make her decisions

    d. Transition 2: From goodness to reality: Women begin to examine their situations more objectively. They draw away from depending on others to tell them what they should do. Instead, they begin to take into account the well-being of everyone concerned, including themselves

    e. Level 3: Morality of nonviolent responsibility: Involves women thinking in terms of the repercussions of their decisions and actions. At this level, a woman's thinking has progressed beyond mere concern for what others will think about what she does. Rather, it involves accepting responsibility for making her own decisions. She places herself on an equal plane with others, weighs the various consequences of her potential actions, and accepts the fact that she will be responsible for these consequences. The important principle operating here is that of minimizing hurt, both to herself and to others

G. Concept Summary Box: Gilligan's Theory of Moral Development for Women

H.   Critical thinking: Evaluation of Gilligan's theory

    1.   Some studies found that females consider moral dilemmas concerning caring aspects of social relationships more important and a greater moral dilemma than males do

    2.   A study found that girls were more likely than boys to use Gilligan's caring-based approaches when addressing dating predicaments

    3.   Other research has found that little if any difference exists between the moral reasoning of men and women

I.   Application of Gilligan's theory to client situations

    1.   Social work has a sound foundation of professional values expressed in the National Association of Social Workers (NASW) Code of Ethics

    2.   Gilligan's theory can provide some general ethical guidelines to which we can aspire in our day-to-day practice with clients

J.   A social learning theory perspective on moral development

    1.   The social learning perspective indicates that we gradually learn how to behave morally

    2.   Example of Waldo, a teenager and social learning theory

    3.   Ethical Question 7.3: What do you think is the moral thing for Waldo to do concerning his upcoming math test? What do you think Waldo would do? If you were Waldo, to what extent would you be tempted to cheat on the math test? What aspects in your upbringing would influence your decision?

K.   Fowler's Theory of Faith Development

    1.   Spirituality: One's values, beliefs, mission, awareness, subjectivity, experience, sense of purpose and direction, and a kind of striving toward something greater than oneself and may or may not include a deity

    2.   Religion: Refers to a set of beliefs and practices of an organized religious institution

    3.   Spotlight on Diversity 7.3: Social Work Practice and Empowerment Through Spiritual Development

        a.   Determining a client's spiritual beliefs and possible membership in an organized religion can lead to various means of empowerment

        b.   Spirituality and religious beliefs are an important aspect for clients who are coping with critical events in their lives

c.   Social workers should not impose their own values and spiritual beliefs on clients

d.   Faith-based organizations and ethical social work

4.   Faith is an integral, centering process, underlying the formation of beliefs, values, and meanings that gives direction to people's lives, links them to others, provides a broader, more meaningful frame of reference, and helps them tackle life's obstacles

5.   Fowler's seven stages that parallel Piaget's stages of intellectual growth

a.   Stage 1: Primal or Undifferentiated Faith (birth to 2 years): All people begin to develop their views of faith and the world from scratch. Infants learn early on whether their environment is safe or not, whether they can trust or not

b.   Stage 2: Intuitive-Projective Faith (ages 2 to 6): Children aged 2 to 6 continue developing their ability to glean meaning from their environments. What children are exposed to in terms of spiritual language and experiences is what they conceptualize on their faith. Their view of faith and religion lacks in-depth conceptualization and application to life experiences

c.   Stage 3: Mythic-Literal Faith (ages 6 to 12): Development of conceptual thought continues over this period. Stories are especially important as ways to help children develop their thinking about life and relationships. During this stage, children think more seriously about aspects related to faith, although their beliefs are literal and one dimensional

1)   People in this stage often develop a concept of God and assume that God rewards goodness and punishes evil

2)   They might exhibit either a kind of perfectionism or, on the other hand, they could be self-abasing, assuming they are inherently bad and will be punished

d.   Stage 4: Synthetic-Conventional Faith (ages 12 and older): During this stage, individuals develop their ability to conceptualize and apply information in new ways. Individuals view their faith as the one right, true, only way, any image of deity is seen as a companion and ally. Faith is rule bound and hierarchical with no questioning of the group's norms and beliefs

e.   Stage 5: Individuative-Reflective Faith (early adulthood and beyond): Critical thinking about the meaning of life characterizes stage 5. The focus of faith moves away from being viewed as the unifying concept of the group and more as making sense of the individual. People confront conflicts in values and ideas, and they strive to establish their individualized belief systems. Stage 5 marks the construction of a more detailed internal spiritual belief system that reflects an individual's critical evaluation of the physical and spiritual world

f.   Stage 6: Conjunctive Faith (mid-life and beyond): Only one-sixth of all respondents in Fowler's study reached stage 6, and never before age 30. They have integrated their own beliefs into their perception of the physical and spiritual universe. A person is willing to respect the validity of another's truth even when it contradicts one's own, while being able to communicate one's own authentic truth

g.   Stage 7: Universalizing Faith (mid-life and beyond): Universalizing faith is characterized by selfless commitment to justice on behalf of others. During this stage people confront discrepancies and unfairnesses, integrating them into their perception of how the world operates. An individual accepts and appreciates his own vulnerability, and seeks his own continued existence and salvation. Commitment may involve becoming a martyr on behalf of or devoting one's life to some great cause at the expense of personal pleasure and well-being. Only a tiny minority of people may reach this point. Martin Luther King Jr., Mother Teresa, and Joan of Arc are examples

6.   Critical thinking: Evaluation of Fowler's theory (Criticisms)

    a.   The theory provides a logically organized theory concerning the development of faith

    b.   Criticisms of the theory

       1)   The sample on which it was based is very limited concerning race and religious orientation. Questions can be raised regarding the extent to which it can be applied universally to non-Christian faiths worldwide

       2)   Concepts of human diversity, oppression, and discrimination are not taken into account. There is an inherent assumption that all people start out with a clean slate

       3)   How does the development of faith from an individual perspective fit into the overall scheme of the macro environment? How does faith development potentially affect organizational, community, and political life?

7.   Ethical Question 7.4: What are your personal beliefs about spirituality and religion? To what extent do you believe all people should also hold your views?

IV.   Significant Issues and Life Events: Assertiveness and Suicide

V. Empowerment Through Assertiveness and Assertiveness Training

A. Assertiveness: Involves behavior that is both straightforward and yet not offensive. It takes into account both your own rights and the rights of others

B. The relevance of assertiveness

   1. Assertiveness is an important skill to be acquired in adolescence and young adulthood; it is a critical aspect of establishing both a personal identity and a moral perspective toward other people

   2. Assertiveness helps social work practitioners recognize their own professional and personal rights in order to communicate effectively with clients and get the job done; also, it is important to recognize, respect, and appreciate your clients' rights and needs

   3. Clients may benefit from using an assertiveness perspective to understand their own actions and the effects of these actions on others. In your role as educator, you can teach your clients assertiveness principles to enhance their own interpersonal effectiveness

   4. Highlight 7.2: Each of Us Has Certain Assertive Rights

      a. You have the right to express your ideas and opinions openly and honestly

      b. You have the right to be wrong. Everyone makes mistakes

      c. You have the right to direct and govern your own life. In other words, you have the right to be responsible for yourself

      d. You have the right to stand up for yourself without unwarranted anxiety and make choices that are good for you

      e. You have the right *not* to be liked by everyone. (Do you like everyone you know?)

      f. You have the right to make requests and to refuse them without feeling guilty

      g. You have the right to ask for information if you need it

      h. You have the right to decide not to exercise your assertive rights. In other words, you have the right to choose not to be assertive

C.   Nonassertive, assertive, and aggressive communication

1.   Assertive communication takes into consideration both their own value system and the values of whoever is receiving their message

2.   Aggressive communication involves bold and dominant verbal and nonverbal behavior in which a speaker presses his or her point of view as taking precedence above all others

3.   Nonassertive communication involves speakers who feel that what the other person involved thinks is much more important than their own thoughts. They devalue themselves

D.   The advantages of assertiveness

E.   Assertiveness training

1.   Steps to establish assertive behavior

a.   Examine your own actions

b.   Make a record of those situations in which you felt you could have behaved more effectively

c.   Select and focus on some specific instance when you felt you could have been more appropriately assertive

d.   Analyze how you reacted

1)   Eye contact: Did you look the person in the eye?

2)   Body posture: Were you standing up straight or were you slouching?

3)   Gestures: Were your hand gestures fitting for the situation? Did you feel at ease? Or, were you tapping your feet or cracking your knuckles?

4)   Facial expressions: Did you have a serious expression on your face? Were you smiling or giggling uncomfortably, thereby giving the impression that you were not really serious?

5)   Voice tone, inflection, volume: Did you speak in a normal voice tone? Did you whisper timidly? Did you raise your voice to the point of stressful screeching? Did you sound as if you were whining?

6)   Timing: It is best to make an appropriately assertive response just after a remark is made or an incident happens

7)   Content: Did you choose your words carefully? Did your response have the impact you wanted it to have?

e.   Identify a role model and examine how he or she handled a situation requiring assertiveness

f.   Identify new assertive responses that could address the original problem situation you targeted

g.   Picture yourself in identified problematic situation

h.   Practice the way you envisioned yourself being more assertive

i.   Review new assertive responses. Emphasize your strong points and try to remedy your flaws

j.   Continue practicing

k.   Try out assertiveness in a real-life situation

l.   Continue to expand your assertive behavior repertoire until assertiveness becomes part of your personal interactive style

m.   Pat yourself on the back when you succeed in becoming more assertive

F.   Application of assertiveness approaches to social work practice

a.   Helping clients learn to be more assertive

b.   Good communication skills and a respect for others are basic necessities for social work practice

VI.   Suicide

A.   Incidence of suicide

1.   About 32,000 deaths are due to suicide in the United States each year

2.   The number of adolescent suicides in the United States and Canada tripled between the mid-1960s and mid-1990s, with a subsequent small decline since then

3.   Suicide is the third leading cause of death for people age 15 through 24 in the United States; second in Canada

4.   A survey found that 19 percent of adolescents in U.S. high schools thought seriously about suicide within the past year; one in 10,000 adolescents actually succeeds in committing suicide

5.   Native American adolescents are the most likely to commit suicide of any ethnic group in the U.S.

B.   Causes of adolescent suicide

   1.   Increased stress

      a.   These pressures might be related to current social and economic conditions

      b.   Unwanted pregnancy or even fear of unwanted pregnancy

      c.   Problems in peer relationships can contribute to stress; an adolescent may feel unwanted or isolated, that he or she simply does not fit in. Adolescents' lack of experience in coping with such situations may make it seem like life is over after losing someone they love

      d.   Teenagers who are overachievers experience greater stress and, therefore, are more likely to commit suicide

   2.   Family issues

      a.   Turbulence and disruption at home contribute to the profile of an adolescent suicide

      b.   Lack of a stable home environment contributes to the sense of loneliness and isolation for both boys and girls

      c.   Highlight 7.3: Joany—A Victim of Suicide

   3.   Psychological variables

      a.   Low self-esteem

      b.   Feelings of helplessness and hopelessness

      c.   Impulsivity, or a sudden decision to act without giving much thought to the action, is yet another variable related to adolescent suicide

C.   Lesbian and gay adolescents and suicide

   1.   There is some question about whether lesbian and gay youth are really at greater risk for suicide than their heterosexual peers; one study found 15 percent of gay and lesbian adolescents compared to 7 percent of heterosexual adolescents said they attempted suicide. Other research found only a slightly greater risk

   2.   Questions have been raised regarding the methodology used in studies establishing significant differences

D.   Suicidal symptoms

    1.   Highlight 7.4: Suicide Notes

    2.   SAD PERSONS Scale

        a.   **S**: Sex

            1)   Females are much more likely to try to kill themselves than males; however, males are four times more likely to succeed in their attempts

            2)   Males are more likely to choose a more deadly means of committing suicide such as firearms or a hanging

        b.   **A**: Age—Statistics indicate that people who are aged 15 to 24 or younger, or aged 75 or older are in the high-risk groups

        c.   **D**: Depression—Technically referred to as depressive disorder which involves a collection of characteristics, feelings, and behaviors that tend to occur in conjunction with each other

        d.   **P**: Previous attempts—People who have tried to kill themselves before are more likely to succeed than people who are trying to commit suicide for the first time

        e.   **E**: Ethanol and other drug abuse—People who abuse alcohol and other drugs are much more likely to commit suicide than people who do not

        f.   **R**: Rational thinking loss—People who suffer from mental or emotional disorders, such as depression or psychosis, are more likely to kill themselves than those who do not

        g.   **S**: Social supports lacking—People who feel that no one cares about them may feel useless and hopeless. Suicide potential may be especially high in cases in which a loved one has recently died or deserted the individual who's threatening suicide

        h.   **O**: Organized plan—The more specific and organized an individual's plan regarding when and how the suicide will be undertaken, the greater the risk. Additionally, the more dangerous the method, the greater the risk

        i.   **N**: No spouse—Single people are much more likely to commit suicide than married people. People who have never married are twice as likely; divorced and widowed people have the highest suicide rates of all

        j.   **S**: Sickness—People who are ill are more likely to commit suicide than those who are healthy. This is especially true for those who have long-term illnesses

3. Other symptoms

    a. Rapid changes in mood, behavior, or general attitude

    b. Giving away personal possessions

E. Spotlight on Diversity 7.4: Suicide and Adolescent Hispanic Families

    1. Sociocultural

        a. Discrepancies in acculturation between daughters and parents

        b. Acculturation: Accepting and adopting the cultural patterns and behaviors manifested by the dominant cultural group

    2. Family domain: Traditionally structured (that is, patriarchal and male-dominated) Hispanic families tend to emphasize restrictive, authoritarian parenting, especially with regard to girls. This traditionalism may affect a family's capacity to respond flexibly to a daughter during a developmental move toward autonomy and individualism, even when the father is absent

    3. Psychological domain: Because of the cultural prohibitions on women's direct expressions of anger, the adolescent Hispanic female also may be socialized by her own more tradition-bound parents to suppress her anger

F. How to use the SAD PERSONS scale

    1. Zero to 2 points: Send home with a follow-up

    2. 3 to 4 points: Close the follow-up; consider hospitalization

    3. 5 to 6 points: Strongly consider hospitalization, depending on confidence in the follow-up arrangement

    4. 7 to 10 points: Hospitalize or commit

    5. Highlight 7.5: SAD PERSONS scale

G. Guidelines for helping suicidal people

    1. Two levels of intervention

        a. Address immediate crisis

        b. Address other issues in person's life

    2. Reactions to a suicide threat

        a. Remain calm and objective

        b. Be supportive

        c.   Identify the immediate problem

        d.   Identify strengths

        e.   Decrease isolation

        f.   Explore past coping mechanisms

        g.   Latch on to the will to live

        h.   Avoid clichés

        i.   Examine potential options

3. Professional counseling of suicidal people

        a.   Make the environment safe

        b.   Negotiate safety

        c.   Plan for future support

        d.   Minimize loneliness and seclusion

        e.   Provide more intensive care via hospitalization

4. Cautionary note—Suicide prevention may not always be possible. All you can do is your very best to help a suicidal person hold on to life. The ultimate decision lies with him or her whether to continue living or not

H. Community empowerment: Suicide prevention and crisis intervention

1. Suicide prevention task forces

2. Crisis telephone lines

3. Peer helping programs

4. Suicide prevention training programs for community professionals and other caregivers

I. Ethical Question 7.5: Does a person have the right to take his or her own life? What if the person is terminally ill or in chronic, severe pain?

VII.   Summary

The following three exercises are designed to help you apply concepts used to assess suicide potential, identify concepts involved in identity formation, and explore assertiveness in response to difficult situations.

Exercise 7.1: Assessment of Suicide Potential

A.   Brief description
Two vignettes describing depressed people are presented. You will evaluate the suicide potential of each person on the basis of the SAD PERSONS scale.

B.   Objectives
You will:
1.   Recognize the variables that contribute to suicide potential.
2.   Apply knowledge about suicide potential to lifelike situations.

C.   Procedure
1.   Review the material concerning suicide presented in the text. Examine carefully each variable described by the SAD PERSONS scale.
2.   The instructor presents the following descriptions of potentially suicidal persons. These may be role-played or simply read by the instructor. After each vignette, you may ask further questions about the potentially suicidal person. These questions may be answered arbitrarily with any information the instructor wishes to include.

a.   Jerome, age 18, is depressed. He lives in one of the poor, inner city, African American neighborhoods of a large urban area. He finished high school, in a way. Reading and writing are not really some of his strengths. He managed to slip through each grade because he had a knack for playing basketball. He wasn't quite good enough for playing in the pros or even in college, but he had been good enough to play on the high school varsity team. Sports and connections with his family helped to keep him out of gang involvement.

Jerome is also bored. He has looked everywhere for a job but just can't find anything. He almost landed one as a janitor at a local supermarket. However, one of the prior employees returned to the city and got it instead. Even that job only paid minimum wage. It was hardly enough to move out of his parents' home and live on his own.

That's another thing. All his parents seem to do lately is nag. They want him to get out and do something useful. He tries to tell them how hard he has been looking for a job, but they don't seem to understand. His father has been working at a local clothing store for years. Jerome's family is poor but certainly not starving. His parents are also disappointed that he didn't go on to college. They have been hoping that Jerome's life would be better than their own in terms of opportunity and financial security.

Now Jerome has given up. The only thing left to do, it seems, is to sit around some of the local bars and drink with his old buddies who are in similar situations. How depressing. Lately, Jerome is considering ending it all. What is the use, anyway? He has no future. Things don't matter. Maybe he will just borrow a friend's old wreck of a car and drive off the Center Street Bridge. One of these days maybe he will do just that—end it all.

b.   Susie, age 17, has just started college this semester. She is depressed. All she seems to do is homework. She has opted to attend the major public university in her state. Her choice was based mostly on pressure from her high school steady boyfriend of two years who also wanted to attend this school. It is so big, scary, and lonely. It is also impersonal. She is just a freshman in classes of up to 300 other students. Sometimes she feels as if her entire identity is an identification number. The stark contrast with her high school experience makes it even worse. In high school, she had been very active in extracurricular activities and had scores of friends.

Her grades aren't very good either. She was accustomed to receiving almost straight A's in high school. Here she is barely maintaining a B average. She is taking an accelerated biology course that is baffling her with complicated theories. She is also taking an upper-level Spanish course that seems impossible to master. She might as well be taking ancient Russian. No matter how many hours she works, she can barely maintain a B- average in that course.

Another problem is her boyfriend. She used to think that she really loved him, but he just can't seem to find much time for her these days. He loves school. He is enjoying his studies and making new friends. Lately, whenever they get together, all they seem to do is fight. She is feeling like quite a "bitch" because of her incessant pleading that he give her more of his time.

Loneliness is another problem area. There are two or three people on her dormitory floor with whom she can talk a little and occasionally goes out for pizza. Susie doesn't do much else, though. All the other students seem to be having fun. But then, even if she did have friends, she couldn't do anything with them. She drives herself to study almost every waking hour.

Susie is very close to her family, who live in another city. Several weeks ago, her uncle died suddenly and unexpectedly. She had been very close to him and misses him very much. She knows she shouldn't keep calling her parents and crying to them on the phone about how depressed she is. They have their own problems.

Lately, she has been thinking about killing herself. She has thought about jumping off the top of her 15-story dorm, but she doesn't really know how to get up there. Maybe she can find some poison. Sometimes she thinks about what substances are poisonous. Cleaning fluid and ammonia don't appeal to her very much.

Life is certainly bleak. For Susie it is just too hard to live.

3.   Evaluate the person's suicide potential according to the SAD PERSONS scale. Do it silently and write down your conclusions.

4.   Discuss the following questions:
   a.   How did you rate each person's suicide potential?
   b.   What are the similarities and differences in their life situations?
   c.   How might you go about trying to help them?

Exercise 7.2: Forming an Identity

A.   Brief description
You will answer 18 questions designed to help you arrive at a sense of who you are and what you want out of life.

B. Objectives
You will:
1. Understand that forming a sense of who you are is one of the most important psychological tasks you face.
2. Examine the extent to which you have formulated a personal identity.
3. Identify specific areas you have to focus on in order to formulate a more thorough sense of who you are.

C. Procedure
1. Summarize the text material on the importance of arriving at an identity.
2. Write answers to the questions that appear at the end of this exercise.
3. After you have completed writing answers, the instructor will ask for volunteers to share what they wrote.
4. What questions caused the most struggle? (Some future class periods may be devoted to providing information about these areas.) What do you feel you learned from this process?

FORMING AN IDENTITY: ARRIVING AT A SENSE OF WHO I AM AND WHAT I WANT OUT OF LIFE

1. What do I find satisfying, meaningful, and enjoyable? (Only after you identify what is meaningful and gratifying will you be able to consciously seek involvement in activities that will make your life fulfilling and avoid those activities that are meaningless or stifling.)

2. What is my moral code? (One possible code is to seek to fulfill your needs and to do what you find enjoyable in a way that does not deprive others of the ability to fulfill their needs.)

3. What are my spiritual beliefs?

4. What are my employment goals? (Ideally, you should seek employment that you find stimulating and satisfying, that you are skilled at, and that provides you with enough money to support your lifestyle.)

5. What are my sexual mores? (All of us should develop a consistent code that we are comfortable with and that helps us to meet our needs without exploiting others. There is no one right code—what works for one may not work for another, due to differences in lifestyles, life goals, and personal values.)

---

6. Do I want to have a committed relationship? (If yes, with what type of person and when? How consistent are your answers here with your other life goals?)

7. Do I desire to have children? (If yes, how many and when? If you already have children, do you want to have more children? How consistent are your answers here with your other life goals?)

8. In what area of the country or world do I want to live? (Variables to be considered are climate, geography, type of dwelling, rural or urban setting, closeness to relatives or friends, and characteristics of the neighborhood.)

9. What do I enjoy doing with my leisure time?

10. What kind of image do I want to project to others? (Your image will be composed of your dressing style and grooming habits, emotions, personality, assertiveness, capacity to communicate, material possessions, moral code, physical features, and voice patterns. You need to assess your strengths and shortcomings honestly in this area and seek to make needed improvements.)

11. What type of people do I enjoy being with, and why?

12. Do I desire to improve the quality of my life and that of others? (If yes, in what ways? How do you hope to achieve these goals?)

13. What types of relationships do I desire to have with relatives, friends, neighbors, and people I meet for the first time?

14.   What are my thoughts about death and dying?

15.   What are the most severe stresses in my life at the moment?

16.   How am I handling these stresses? What strategies am I using to resolve them?

17.   What do I want to accomplish in the next 5 years?

18.   What are my plans for accomplishing the goals I listed in question 17?

Exercise 7.3: Are You Assertive?

A.   Brief description
Volunteers will be asked to role-play a series of situations before the entire class. Potentially assertive, nonassertive, and aggressive responses to these situations will be examined and discussed.

B.   Objectives
This exercise will enable you to:
1.   Recognize assertive, nonassertive, and aggressive responses (both verbal and nonverbal) to problematic situations.
2.   Examine the effectiveness of these types of responses.
3.   Propose specific effective assertive techniques.

C.   Procedure
1.   Following are a series of situations, each of which sets the stage for a role-play. In each role-play, two persons are described. One person is either making a request or doing something annoying. Your instructor will ask for two volunteers for each role-play to act out the characters. One volunteer plays the "annoyer." The other volunteer plays a person who's trying to act as assertively as possible in response:

a.
Ethel and Fred, both college students, have been dating steadily for the past eighteen months. Typically, they go to a movie or a sporting event on a Friday night and then out for pizza or subs afterward. Ethel really likes Fred and enjoys their evenings out together except for one thing. Every single Friday night while they're eating, Fred says something like, "You know, Ethel, you really shouldn't be eating such fattening food. It looks like you're gaining weight."

The scene is the local pizzeria. Ethel and Fred are midway through their pepperoni, mushroom, and black olive pizza when Fred makes his usual comment.

b.
Valerie and Nikki, best friends, are taking an upper-level sociology course that requires voluminous amounts of reading. Most of the reading is from supplementary sources that have been placed on reserve in the college library. Valerie has spent dozens of hours reading the material and taking copious notes in preparation for the upcoming cumulative exam. Nikki, on the other hand, has done some of the work. However, she really feels she isn't much good at taking notes, so she didn't. Nikki's had a good semester and has done a lot of partying. Valerie remembers some of her miserable weekend nights alone in the library while Nikki was out having fun.

The scene is the eve of the exam. Valerie and Nikki go to the library together to study. Nikki bluntly asks Valerie if she can study from the notes Valerie's been taking all semester while reading the reserve materials.

c.
Harry is standing in line at Randall's Country Market with a cart full of groceries. It's late Friday afternoon and the market is crowded. There are five people ahead of him in line. He thinks to himself that he has a knack for picking the slowest line possible. Harry is in a horrendous hurry as he has dinner reservations in an hour. The reservations were difficult to get and he is looking forward to the event very much. He's thinking how difficult it will be to make it to the restaurant on time. A woman with a crying child in her arms breaks in at the head of the line with a full cart of groceries and says, "Excuse me, but I have to get through."

d.
Tim works as a house parent at a group home for adults with developmental disabilities. He's going to school full-time with a social work major, while working at the group home part-time. He's supposed to work three evenings each week from 4:00 p.m. to midnight. He really likes his job and feels it will be good experience and look good on his resume when he gets his degree and looks for a full-time professional position. Sharon, his supervisor, has asked him to work an extra two to three nights each week for the past month. Another worker quit and she hasn't had time to fill the position yet. Tim wants to stay "on her good side" because he knows he will have to depend on her for a good reference someday. Therefore, each time she's asked him to work, he has. The problem is that he's starting to get tired and feels his schoolwork is suffering because of all the extra hours he's been working. Sharon approaches Tim and asks him if he could work an extra two nights next week. She initiates the request by saying how well he does his job and how she can always depend on him.

2.   Each role-play should continue for no more than about 10 minutes. The instructor will halt the role-play either at that time or when s/he feels that the scenario has been resolved.

3.   For each role-play, the class should focus discussion on the following questions:

    a.   In what ways, both verbally and nonverbally, was the response given in the scenario assertive, nonassertive, or aggressive?

    b.   In what ways were both individuals' rights taken or not taken into account?

    c.   What would be an aggressive response in the scenario, and why?

    d.   What would be a nonassertive response in the scenario, and why?

    e.   What would be the ideal way to resolve the situation assertively, and why?

Study Outline

I.   **A Perspective**

II.   **Social Development Changes in Adolescence**

    A.   Movement from dependence to independence

        1.   Young people are often in a conflict between wanting independence from parents and being dependent on them for basic needs

        2.   Children who are raised in families in which the parents have provided opportunities to learn self-reliance, responsibility, and self-respect tend to make a smoother transition from dependency to adulthood interdependence

        3.   A key to helping parents cope with thrusts of independence from their teenagers is to keep the lines of communication open

        4.   Social independence involves becoming self-directed rather than other-directed. Social independence does not mean becoming selfish. Socially independent people realize their best interests are served by becoming involved in political, civic, educational, religious, social, and community affairs

        5.   Highlight 8.1 Interaction in Families: Effective Communication Between Parents and Children

            a.   Active listening

                1)   It facilitates problem solving by young people, which fosters the development of responsibility

                2)   When a teenager feels his or her parents are listening, a by-product is that he or she will be more apt to listen to the parents' point of view

                3)   The approach helps a teen to explore, recognize, and express his or her feelings

            b.   I-messages

                1)   Solution message: Order, direct, command, warn, threaten, preach, moralize, or advise. This is a you-message

                2)   Put-down message: Blame, judge, criticize, ridicule, or name-call. This is a you-message

Instead of *put down*

Slow down you idiot
before you get us killed.

I feel frightened
when you drive
this fast.

3) I-message: Nonblaming messages that communicate only how the sender of the message believes the receiver is adversely affecting the sender

c. No-lose problem solving method

1) Step 1: Identifying and defining the needs of each person

2) Step 2: Generating possible alternative solutions *Brainstorm*

3) Step 3: Evaluating the alternative solutions

4) Step 4: Deciding on the best acceptable solution

5) Step 5: Working out ways of implementing the solution

6) Step 6: Following up to evaluate how it worked

d. Collisions of values

1) A parent can influence his or her offspring's values by modeling the values the parent holds as important

2) A parent can influence teenagers' values by acting as a consultant to them

3) A parent can modify his or her values to reduce tensions

B. Interaction in peer group systems

1. Adolescents have a strong "herd" drive and desire to be accepted by their peers

2. Kinds of peer groups vary according to a variety of factors (socioeconomic status, values derived from parents, the neighborhood one lives in, the nature of the school, special talents and abilities, and the personality of the adolescent)

3. Not all adolescents join cliques

4. Adolescents tend to identify with other teenagers, rather than with adults or younger children

5. Friends and peer groups help adolescents make the transition from parental dependence to independence

6. Spotlight on Diversity 8.1: Ethnic-Group Identity for Minority Adolescents

a. Ethnic identity involves not only knowing that one is a member of a certain ethnic group, but also recognizing that some aspects of one's thoughts, actions, and feelings are influenced by one's ethnic identity

b. Issues of ethnic identity may not become salient until early adolescence. "As minority children grow up, they tend to incorporate many of the ideals and values of the Anglo culture. Suddenly in adolescence, however, they may find themselves excluded from it

c. The more fully immersed minority adolescents are in the values and traditions of their ethnic culture, the more likely it is that they will experience a dual identity—for example, viewing themselves as an American and a Japanese American

C. Empowerment of homeless youth

1. Social workers can help homeless youth become more empowered by helping them progress through four stages

a. Understanding powerlessness: Young people must be allowed to express their despair, disappointment, fear, and hurt before social workers and others rush in to help them

b. Awareness and mutual education: After expressing feelings, homeless youth should be encouraged to talk about their experiences, as painful as they have been

c. Dialogue and solidarity: After telling their stories, continuing to exchange information and share feelings with others provides opportunities to learn from and support each other

d. Action and political identity: This involves a sense of self-confidence in one's ability to make progress, seek changes in conditions, and improve one's overall quality of life. Political identity is the sense that one has the right and power to seek improvements in life

III. Social Problems

A. Eating disorders

1. Anorexia nervosa: A disorder characterized by the excessive pursuit of thinness through voluntary starvation

a. Anorexics refuse to accept the fact that they are too thin. They eat very little, even when experiencing intense hunger

b. On the surface someone who is prone to develop anorexia appears to be a model child. She is eager to please, well-behaved, a good student, and someone who appears to get along well with her peers

c. The development of this disorder usually proceeds according to the following pattern

1) It begins with a diet

2) Dieting creates a feeling of control

   3) Exhausting exercise is added

   4) Health begins to fail. Weight loss and malnutrition begin, leading to mental and physical deterioration

  d. Anorexics, even in warm weather, tend to wear several layers of bulky clothing, or sweaters and baggy pants, to warm their cold bodies and to conceal their thinness

  e. Anorexics tend to maintain rigid control over nearly all aspects of their lives

  f. Ninety-five percent of those affected with anorexia nervosa are females

  g. To prevent death through starvation, hospitalization is frequently needed for anorexics

  h. Suicide following severe depression is also a danger

  i. The mortality rate for anorexia nervosa is thought to be higher than for any other psychiatric disorder

2. Bulimia nervosa: Derived from a Greek word meaning "ox-like hunger." But the binge-purge cycle that is characteristic of bulimics is triggered not by physical hunger but by emotional upset

  a. Pattern of disorder development

   1) Dieting leads to craving for food

   2) Overeating begins

   3) Guilt develops about weight gain

   4) Purging is discovered

   5) Binge-purge habit takes hold

  b. Bulimics binge to escape painful problems

  c. Health problems develop associated with disorder

  d. Bulimics tend to be people-pleasers

3. Compulsive overeating: Involves the irresistible urge to consume excessive amounts of food for no nutritional reason

  a. One out of five Americans are overweight

  b. Treatment is recommended for persons in excess of 20 percent over ideal body weight

c.   Compulsive overeaters are apt to display one or more of the following

    1)   Frequent diet plan failures

    2)   Avoidance of health warning signs

    3)   Social isolation

    4)   Nutritional ignorance

    5)   Selective eating amnesia

    6)   Overeating as a response to unwanted emotions

4.   Interrelationships among eating disorders

5.   Causes

    a.   Some may be genetically predisposed to these disorders

    b.   Are likely to have been brought up in middle-class, upwardly mobile families, where their mothers are overinvolved in their lives and their fathers are preoccupied with work outside the home

6.   Ethical Question 8.1: Do you have an eating disorder that you need to work on?

7.   Impacts of social forces

8.   Treatment

    a.   Goals

        1)   Resolution of the psychosocial and family dynamics that led to the development of the eating disorder

        2)   Provision of medical services to correct any medical problems that resulted from starving, bingeing and purging, or being obese

        3)   Reestablishment of normal weight and healthy eating behavior

    b.   Treatments must be comprehensive and multifaceted

    c.   Treatment approaches

        1)   Hospitalization

        2)   Individual psychotherapy

        3)   Family therapy

        4)   Group therapy

5)   Nutritional counseling

6)   Antidepressant medication

7)   Couples therapy

B.   Emotional and behavioral problems

     1.   Medical model: Views emotional and behavioral problems as a mental illness, comparable to a physical illness

     2.   Highlight 8.2: Major Mental Disorders According to the American Psychiatric Association

         a.   Disorders usually diagnosed in infancy, childhood, or adolescence: These include, but are not limited to, mental retardation, learning disorders, communication disorders (such as stuttering), autism, attention-deficit/hyperactivity disorders, and separation-anxiety disorder

         b.   Delirium, Dementia, and Amnestic and other cognitive disorders: These include delirium due to alcohol and other drug intoxication, dementia due to Alzheimer's disease or Parkinson's disease, dementia due to head trauma, and amnestic disorder

         c.   Substance-related disorders: This category includes mental disorders related to abuse of alcohol, caffeine, amphetamines, cocaine, hallucinogens, nicotine, and other mindaltering substances

         d.   Schizophrenia and other psychotic disorders: This category includes delusional disorders and all forms of schizophrenia (such as paranoid, disorganized, and catatonic)

            1)   Delusion: Something that is falsely believed or propagated

            2)   Schizophrenia encompasses a large group of disorders, usually of psychotic proportion, manifested by disturbances of language and communication, thought, perception, affect, and behavior that last longer than 6 months

[handwritten: onset approx 21 yr. more males]

         e.   Mood disorders: These include emotional disorders such as depression and bipolar disorders

            1)   Bipolar disorder: A major affective disorder with episodes of both mania and depression, which was formerly called manic-depressive psychosis

            2)   Bipolar disorders may be subdivided into manic, depressed, or mixed types, on the basis of current symptoms

f. Somatoform disorders:

  1) These are psychological problems that manifest themselves as symptoms of physical disease

  2) Hypochondria: A chronic preoccupation with shifting health concerns and symptoms, a fear or conviction that one has a serious physical illness, the search for medical treatment, inability to accept reassurance, and either hostile or dependent relationships with caregivers and family

g. Anxiety disorders: This category includes phobias, posttraumatic stress disorder, generalized anxiety disorder, acute stress disorder, and substance-induced anxiety disorder

  1) Phobia: Characterized by an obsessive, persistent, unrealistic, intense fear of an object or situation

  2) Common phobias include acrophobia (fear of heights), algophobia (fear of pain), and claustrophobia (fear of closed spaces)

h. Dissociative disorders: This category includes problems in which part of the personality is dissociated from the rest, such as dissociative identity disorder (formerly called multiple personality disorder)

i. Sexual and gender identity disorders: This category includes sexual dysfunctions (such as hypoactive sexual desire, premature ejaculation, male erectile disorder, male and female orgasmic disorders, and vaginismus), exhibitionism, fetishism, pedophilia (child molestation), sexual masochism, sexual sadism, voyeurism, and gender identity disorders (such as cross-gender identification)

j. Eating disorders: This category includes anorexia nervosa, bulimia nervosa, and compulsive overeating

k. Sleep disorders: This classification includes insomnia and other problems with sleep (such as nightmares and sleepwalking)

l. Impulse-control disorders: These disorders relate to the inability to control certain undesirable impulses (for example, kleptomania, pyromania, and pathological gambling)

m.   Personality disorders: This category refers to an enduring pattern of inner experience and behavior that deviates markedly from the expectations of the individual's culture, is pervasive and inflexible, has an onset in adolescence or early adulthood, is stable over time, and leads to distress or impairment

    1)   Paranoid: A pattern of distrust and suspiciousness, such that others' motives are interpreted as malevolent

    2)   Schizoid: A pattern of detachment from social relationships and a restricted range of emotional expression

    3)   Schizotypal: A pattern of acute discomfort in close relationships, cognitive or perceptual distortions, and eccentricities of behavior

    4)   Antisocial: A pattern of disregard for, and violation of, the rights of others

    5)   Borderline: A pattern of instability in interpersonal relationships, self-image, affects, and impulsivity

    6)   Histrionic: A pattern of excessive emotionality and attention seeking

    7)   Narcissistic: A pattern of grandiosity, need for admiration, and lack of empathy

    8)   Avoidant: A pattern of social inhibition, feelings of inadequacy, and hypersensitivity to negative evaluation

    9)   Dependent: A pattern of submissive and clinging behavior related to an excessive need to be taken care of

    10)   Obsessive-Compulsive: A pattern of preoccupation with orderliness, perfectionism, and control

n.   Other conditions: Parent-child relational problems; partner relational problems; sibling relational problems; child victimization of physical abuse, sexual abuse, and neglect; adult victimization of physical and sexual abuse; malingering; bereavement; academic problems; occupational problems; identity problems; and religious or spiritual problems

3.   Interactional model: Focuses on the processes of everyday social interaction and the effects of labeling on people

a.   Thomas Szasz categorized all of the so-called mental illnesses into three types of emotional disorders:

    1)   Personal disabilities: Excessive anxiety, depression, fears, and feelings of inadequacy

2) Antisocial acts: Bizarre homicides and other social deviati[on]

3) Deterioration of brain with associated personality Disorders labeled as mental illnesses in which person[ality] changes result following brain deterioration from such causes as arteriosclerosis, chronic alcoholism, general paresis, or serious brain damage following an accident

b. Ethical Question 8.2: Do you believe it is useful to society to label some people as being mentally ill? Do you believe labeling someone as mentally ill may be a factor in leading that person to continue to act irresponsibly?

c. The use of medical labels has severe adverse effects

d. The question of whether mental illness exists is important. The assignment of mental illness labels to disturbed people has substantial implications for how the disturbed will be treated, for how others will view them, and for how they will view themselves. Cooley's looking glass self-concept applies here

e. Adherents of the interactional approach believe that people get labeled mentally ill for two reasons—they may have an intense unwanted emotion, or they may be engaged in dysfunctional (or deviant) behavior

4. Assessing and treating unwanted emotions: Application of theory to client situations

a. Rational therapy approach: The primary cause of all our emotions is what we tell ourselves about events that happen to us

b. Events→Self-talk→Emotions

How we perceive it.

5. Changing unwanted emotions

6. Meaningful activity

7. Changing self-talk

8. Highlight 8.3: Format for a Rational Self-Analysis

9. Changing the distressing event

10. Destructive ways to change unwanted emotions

a. Alcohol and other drug use

b. Suicide

11. Assessing and changing deviant behavior: Application of theory to practice

12. Highlight 8.4: A Rational Self-Analysis to Combat Unwanted Emotions Following the Ending of a Romantic Relationship

13. Ethical Question 8.3: Do you sometimes engage in unethical or dysfunctional behavior because of your negative and irrational self-talk?

14. Highlight 8.5: Our Thinking Determines our Behavior and our Emotions

C. Macro system problems: Crime and delinquency

1. Crime: Violation of the criminal law

2. Ethical Question 8.4: Is it better to use a treatment approach, or a punitive approach, with criminal offenders?

3. Status offense: An act that is defined as illegal if committed by a juvenile but not if committed by an adult (e.g., running away or truancy)

4. Juvenile-court philosophy is one of treatment versus punishment

5. Reasons for committing crimes

6. Highlight 8.6: Self-Talk Explanation for Columbine Massacre

D. Macro system problems: Delinquent gangs

1. In recent years in the United States there have been increases in the number of gangs, the number of youths belonging to gangs, gang youth drug involvement, and gang violence

2. The inadequacy of the knowledge base about gangs is a major obstacle to developing effective intervention strategies

3. Morales' classification of youth gangs

   a. Criminal gangs: The primary goal is material gain through criminal activities. Drug trafficking of rock cocaine is presently a major source of income for criminal gangs

   b. Conflict gangs: These gangs are turf-oriented and will engage in violent conflict with individuals or rival groups that invade their neighborhood or that commit acts that they consider degrading or insulting. Respect is highly valued and defended. Hispanic gangs are heavily represented among conflict gangs

   c. Retreatist gangs: Focus on getting "high" or "loaded" on alcohol, cocaine, marijuana, heroin, or other drugs. Individuals tend to join this type of gang in order to secure continued access to drugs. In contrast to criminal gangs that become involved with drugs for financial profit, retreatist gangs become involved with drugs for consumption

d. Occult gangs: Some gangs become involved in "devil worship." However, not all occult groups are involved in criminal activity or in devil worship. Unlike the gangs mentioned earlier, which are primarily composed of juveniles, the majority of occult groups are composed of adults

4. Contradictions in conceptualizing gangs: At the present time there are inadequate statistical data on the number of gangs, the number and characteristics of members, and their criminal activities *unknown*

5. Sociological theories: Application of theories to gangs

   a. Differential association theory: Youth whose most admired person is a member of a gang involved in committing burglaries or in drug trafficking will seek to emulate this model, will receive instruction from gang members in committing these crimes, and will also receive approval from the gang for successfully committing these crime

   b. Anomie theory: Unable to achieve goals through society's legitimately defined channels, the individuals' and gangs' respect for these channels is weakened, and they seek to achieve the desired goals through illegal means

    c. Deviant subcultures theory: Asserts that lower-class culture is organized around six values—trouble, toughness, excitement, fate, smartness (ability to con others), and autonomy—and allegiance to these values produces delinquency. Therefore, the entire lower-class subculture is deviant in the sense that any male growing up in it will accept these values and almost certainly violate the law

    d. Control theory: Assumes that all people would "naturally" commit crimes and therefore must be constrained and controlled by society from breaking the law

6. Social work roles and intervention programs

   a. Intervention programs

      1) Detached worker programs

      2) Formal supervision of gang members through juvenile probation departments

      3) Group homes

      4) Residential treatment facilities

      5) Reform schools

      6) Drug treatment programs

7)   Programs to strengthen families

8)   School programs

    b.   Social work roles

        1)   Juvenile probation officer

        2)   Counselor

        3)   School social worker

        4)   Alcohol and other drug counselors

        5)   Enabler

        6)   Educator

        7)   Case manager

        8)   Broker

        9)   Detached worker

        10)   Group facilitator

        11)   Advocate

        12)   Negotiator

        13)   Mediator

        14)   Analyst and evaluator of community conditions

    c.   Community mobilization: A strategy that attempts to integrate and coordinate the collective resources of citizens and organizations in gang control. This appears to be the most effective strategy to reduce gang problems

IV.   Empowerment Through Social Work with Groups

    A.   Group: Two or more individuals in face-to-face interaction, each aware of his or her membership in the group, each aware of the others who belong to the group, and each aware of their positive interdependence as they strive to achieve mutual goals

    B.   Types of groups

        1.   Recreation groups: The objective is to provide activities for enjoyment and exercise

        2.   Recreation-skill groups: The objective is to improve a set of skills while providing enjoyment

3. Educational groups: The focus is to help members acquire knowledge and learn more complex skills

4. Task groups: These groups are formed to achieve a specific set of tasks or objectives

    a. Board of directors: An administrative group charged with responsibility for setting the policy governing agency programs

    b. Task force: A group established for a special purpose and is usually disbanded after the task is completed

    c. Committee: A group in an agency or organization that is formed to deal with specific tasks or matters

    d. Ad hoc committee: A group, like a task force, that is set up for one purpose and usually ceases functioning after completion of its task

5. Problem-solving and decision-making groups: Both providers and consumers of social services may become involved in groups concerned with problem solving and decision making. These may be considered a subcategory of task groups

6. Focus groups: Groups that are formed for a variety of purposes; to identify needs or issues, to generate proposals to resolve an identified issue, to test reactions to alternative approaches to an issue, and so forth

    a. Focus group: Specially assembled collection of people who respond through a semistructured or structured discussion to the concerns and interests of the person, group, or organization that invited the participants

    b. Representative group: Its strength is that its members have been selected specifically to represent different perspectives and points of view in a community

7. Self-help groups: Voluntary, small group structures for mutual aid and the accomplishment of a special purpose

    a. Powell's classification of self-help groups

        1) Habit disturbance organizations: Focus on a problem that is specific and concrete

        2) General purpose organizations: Address a wide range of problems and predicaments

        3) Lifestyle organizations: Seek to provide support for and advocate for the lifestyles of people whose members are viewed by society as being different (and the dominant groups in society are generally indifferent or hostile to that difference)

4) Physical handicap organizations: Focus on major chronic diseases and conditions

5) Significant other organizations: Members are parents, spouses, and close relatives of troubled and troubling persons

b. The American Self-Help Group Clearinghouse is a web-based database of over 1,100 national and international self-help support groups

c. Helper therapy principle: Helping others makes a person feel good and worthwhile; it also enables the helpers to put their own problems into perspective as they see that others' problems may be as serious, or even more serious, than their own

8. Socialization groups: Develop or change attitudes and behaviors of group members to become more socially acceptable

a. Spotlight on Diversity 8.2: The RAP Framework for Leading Multiracial Groups

1) **R**ecognizing crucial ethnic, cultural, and racial differences in any group requires the leader to be both self-aware and aware of the racial dynamics of the group

2) **A**nticipating how individual members will be affected by racial issues prepares the leader to respond preventively and interventively when racial issues arise

3) **P**roblem-Solve: When incidents related to racial issues do arise, the leader must intervene to resolve the issues

9. Therapy groups: Generally composed of members with rather severe emotional or personal problems

10. Encounter groups: A group experience in which people relate to each other in a close interpersonal manner, and self-disclosure is required (also called sensitivity-training groups)

C. Models of group development over time

1. Garland, Jones, and Kolodny model

a. Preaffiliation stage: Members are ambivalent about joining the group; interaction is guarded

b. Power and control stage: Patterns of communication within the group emerge, alliances and subgroups begin to appear, members begin to take on certain roles and responsibilities, norms and methods for handling group tasks develop, and membership questions arise. This is a transitional stage, with certain basic issues needing to be resolved

    c.   Intimacy stage: The group becomes more like a family, with sibling rivalry arising between members and the leader sometimes even being referred to as a parent

    d.   Differentiation stage: There is recognition of individual rights and needs and a high level of communication among members

    e.   Separation stage: The purposes of the group have been achieved, and members have learned new behavioral patterns to enable them to move on to other social experiences

2.   Tuckman model

    a.   Forming stage: In this stage members become oriented toward each other, work on being accepted, and learn more about the group

    b.   Storming stage: In this stage conflicts begin to arise as members resist the influence of the group and rebel against accomplishing the task

    c.   Norming stage: In this stage the group establishes cohesiveness and commitment, and in the process discovers new ways to work together

    d.   Performing stage: In this stage the group works as a unit to achieve its goals

    e.   Adjourning stage: In this stage the group disbands

3.   Schiller Model

    a.   A relational model of group development applicable to women's groups

    b.   Preaffiliation

    c.   Establishing a relational base

    d.   Mutuality and interpersonal empathy

    e.   Challenge and change

    f.   Separation

4.   Bales model

    a.   Recurring phase model, in contrast to the sequential-stage models

    b.   Groups continue to seek an equilibrium between task-oriented work and emotional expressions to build better relationships among group members

D.   Task and maintenance roles

    1.   Task roles

        a.   Information and opinion giver role: Offers facts, opinions, ideas, suggestions, and relevant information to help group discussion

        b.   Information and opinion seeker role: Asks for facts, information, opinions, ideas, and feelings from other members to help group discussion

        c.   Starter role: Proposes goals and tasks to initiate action within the group

        d.   Direction giver role: Develops plans on how to proceed and focuses attention on the task to be done

        e.   Summarizer role: Pulls together related ideas or suggestions, and restates and summarizes major point discussed

        f.   Coordinator role: Shows relationships among various ideas and harmonizes activities of various subgroups and members

        g.   Diagnoser role: Figures out sources of difficulties the group has in working effectively and the blocks to progress in accomplishing the group's goals

        h.   Energizer role: Stimulates a higher quality of work from the group

        i.   Reality tester: Examines the practicality of ideas, evaluates alternative solutions, and applies them to real situations to see how they will work

        j.   Evaluator: Compares group decisions and accomplishments with group standards and goals

    2.   Maintenance roles which strengthen social/emotional bonds within the group

        a.   Encourager of participation role: Warmly encourages everyone to participate, giving recognition for contributions and demonstrating openness to ideas of others; is friendly and responsive to group members

        b.   Harmonizer and compromiser role: Persuades members to analyze constructively their differences in opinions, searches for common elements in conflicts, and tries to reconcile disagreements

        c.   Tension reliever role: Eases tensions and increases the enjoyment of group members by joking, suggesting breaks, and proposing fun approaches to group work

        d.   Communication helper role: Shows good communication skills and makes sure that each group member understands what other members are saying

e. Evaluator of emotional climate role: Asks members how they feel about the way in which the group is working and about each other, and shares own feelings about both

f. Process observer role: Watches the process by which the group is working and uses the observations to help examine group effectiveness

g. Standard setter role: Expresses group standards and goals to make members aware of the direction of the work and the progress being made toward the goal, and to get open acceptance of group norms and procedures

h. Active listener role: Listens and serves as an interested audience for other members, is receptive to others' ideas, and goes along with the group when not in disagreement

i. Trust builder role: Accepts and supports openness of other group members; reinforces risk taking and encourages individuality

j. Interpersonal problem solver role: Promotes open discussion of conflicts between group members in order to resolve conflicts and increase group togetherness

3. Hersey and Blanchard situational theory of leadership

a. Asserts that when members have low maturity in terms of accomplishing a specific task, the leader should engage in high-task and low-maintenance behaviors

b. The task maturity of members increases as their experience and understanding of the task increases

E. Leadership theories

1. The trait approach: Assumes that leaders have personal characteristics or traits that make them different from followers. It also implies that leaders are born, not made, and that leaders emerge naturally rather than being trained. The trait approach has also been called the *great person theory* of leadership

2. Charisma: A charismatic leader must have a sense of mission, a belief in the social-change movement he or she leads, and confidence in oneself as the chosen instrument to lead the movement to its destination

3. Machiavellianism: Based on the concepts that followers: (1) are basically fallible, gullible, untrustworthy, and weak; (2) are impersonal objects; and (3) should be manipulated in order for the leader to achieve his or her goals

4. The position approach: Defines leadership in terms of the authority of a particular position and is focused on studying the behavior of people in high-level positions

5. The style approach

    a.   Authoritarian style: Leaders have more absolute power than democratic leaders. They alone set goals and policies, dictate the activities of the members, and set major plans

    b.   Democratic style: This style is slow in decision making and sometimes confusing, but frequently proves to be more effective because of strong cooperation that generally emerges with participation in decision making

    c.   Laissez-faire style: There is very little participation by the leader. The group members are primarily left to function (or flounder) with little input from the designated leader

6. The distributed functions approach: Disagrees with the great person theory of leadership. It asserts *any member* of a group will at times be a leader by taking actions that serve group functions. With this approach, leadership is viewed as being specific to a particular group in a particular situation

    a.   The needs and developmental stage of a group may at different times require a leader who can assume any of the previously described roles as well as those that follow:

        1)   Executive: Being the top coordinator of the activities of a group

        2)   Policymaker: Establishing group goals and policies

        3)   Planner: Deciding the means by which the group will achieve its goals

        4)   Expert: Serving as the source of readily available information and skills

        5)   External group representative: Being the official spokesperson for the group

        6)   Controller of internal relations: Controlling the structure as a way to control in-group relations

        7)   Purveyor of rewards and punishments: Determining promotions, demotions, and assigning pleasant or unpleasant tasks

        8)   Arbitrator and mediator: Acting as both judge and conciliator with the power to reduce or to increase factionalism within the group

        9)   Exemplar: Serving as a model of behavior to show what the members should be and do

10) Ideologist: Serving as the source of the beliefs and values of the members

11) Scapegoat: Serving as the target for ventilating members' frustrations and disappointments

V.   Summary

Experiential Exercises and Simulations

The following exercises are designed to help you: learn how to change unwanted emotions, assess intimate relationships, assess and treat dysfunctional behavior, understand the arguments about whether or not mental illness exists, and conduct trust walks.

Exercise 8.1: Changing Unwanted Emotions by Writing a Rational Self-Analysis

A.   Brief description
You will write a rational self-analysis.

B.   Objectives
You will:
1. Understand that unwanted emotions primarily result from negative and irrational thinking.
2. Change your unwanted emotions by challenging negative and irrational thinking with positive and rational self-talk.
3. Assist others in changing unwanted emotions by helping them to switch their negative and irrational self-talk to positive and rational self-talk.

C.   Procedure
1. Summarize the material in the text that indicates that unwanted emotions are caused primarily by negative and irrational thinking.
2. The instructor describes how to write a rational self-analysis. Look at the example presented in the text.
3. Write a rational self-analysis of an unwanted emotion currently or recently experienced.
4. The instructor may ask for volunteers to share what they wrote.
5. What difficulties did you experience in writing a rational self-analysis? What did you see as the strengths and shortcomings of writing such an analysis?

Exercise 8.2: Assessing and Treating Dysfunctional Behavior

A.   Brief description
You will assess dysfunctional behavior by identifying underlying thinking patterns of the perpetrators and then discuss various treatment approaches for changing these underlying thinking patterns.

B.   Objectives
You will:
1. Understand the principle that thinking processes primarily determine behavior, including dysfunctional behavior.
2. Apply the rational therapy approach to assessing and treating dysfunctional behavior.

C. Procedure
   1. The instructor summarizes the material on rational therapy in the text, which asserts that the reasons for dysfunctional behavior occurring can be identified by determining what the perpetrator was thinking.
   2. Divide into subgroups of about five persons. Each subgroup is given a card that has one of the following dysfunctional behaviors written on it: compulsive gambling, date rape, prostitution, suicide, alcoholism, anorexic behavior, bulimic behavior, child abuse, and wife abuse. Each subgroup receives a different dysfunctional behavior and tries to identify the thinking processes that would lead a person to engage in this behavior.
   3. Identify the interventions that you believe would be most effective in changing the thinking patterns of a person with this problematic behavior so that the person would be unlikely to continue engaging in such dysfunctional behavior.
   4. Each subgroup reports to the class on the thinking patterns of the dysfunctional behavior and the intervention approaches it identified. After each subgroup makes its presentation, the rest of the class is given an opportunity to add to the information being reported by the subgroup.
   5. Discuss the merits and shortcomings of assessing behavior by identifying the thinking patterns of the perpetrator.

Exercise 8.3: Mental Illness Debate

A. Brief description
A debate will be held in class about whether or not mental illness exists.

B. Objectives
You will:
   1. Understand the arguments regarding whether mental illness exists.
   2. Understand the effects of labeling someone "mentally ill."

C. Procedure
   1. Read the material in the chapter related to the medical model approach and the interactional model approach to emotional and behavioral problems. At a class session, select some students to form two panels, one to argue that mental illness exists and the other that it is a myth. Panel members should be given a few days to gather additional information to prepare for a debate. Panel members may choose to interview counselors and therapists in the community. Panel members should definitely read reference material related to this topic; the instructor may serve as a resource for such material.
   2. On a day selected by the class, a debate is held. At the end of the debate, the students who were not involved in the debate summarize the strong points made by the debaters.

Exercise 8.4: Trust Walk

A. Brief description
You and other students in class become involved in trust walks.

B. Objectives
You will:
   1. Learn how to conduct a trust walk.
   2. Get in touch with aspects of yourself that you are unaware of.

C. Procedure

1. The instructor informs the class of the objectives of the exercise. The instructor has the students form groups of two. (If a student is without a partner, the instructor can be a partner.)

2. One member of your subgroup closes his or her eyes, and keeps the eyes closed for the first part of this exercise. The "seeing" partner then leads the "blind" partner down corridors, around the room, and perhaps outside. The "seeing" partner can lead the "blind" partner with verbal directions and by taking a hand. The "seeing" person has the responsibility to watch that the "blind" partner does not run into objects, fall, stumble, or get hurt in any way.

3. After 8 to 10 minutes, the partners reverse roles and continue the exercise for another 8 to 10 minutes.

4. You and other students, as a class, then discuss the feelings experienced while doing this trust walk.

What makes a good leader?
What traits in a leader would you like to see?

When can a leader be problematic?
What may be the warning signs?

Chapter 9
Gender, Gender Identity, Gender Expression, and Sexism

I.   **A Perspective**

II.   **Gender, Gender Identity, and Gender Expression**

    A.   Definition of terms

        1.   Gender: The social and psychological characteristics associated with being female or male

        2.   Gender identity: A persons' internal psychological self concept of being either a male or a female, or possibly, some combination of both

        3.   Gender roles: The attitudes, behaviors, rights, and responsibilities that society associates with being male or being female

        4.   Gender role socialization: The process of conveying what is considered appropriate behavior and perspectives for males and females in a particular culture

        5.   Sex: The biological distinction between being female and being male, usually categorized on the basis of the reproductive organs and genetic makeup

    B.   The social construction of gender

        1.   Social constructionist approach: The process by which people's perception of reality is shaped largely by the subjective meaning that they give to an experience (how people think about situations as they interact with others becomes what is real to them)

        2.   Social construction of gender: Looks at the structure of the gendered social order as a whole and at the processes that construct and maintain it

        3.   It assumes that traditional gender expectations are not facts carved in stone, but rather perceptions and expectations that can be changed

    C.   The complexity of gender, gender identity, and gender expression

        1.   Money's six physical and two psychological variables in the concept of gender

            a.   Gender designated by chromosomes, XX for females and XY for males

            b.   Presence of testes or ovaries

            c.   Prenatal response in gender and brain development to the presence of testosterone for males and to the lack of it for females

d. Presence of internal organs related to reproduction including the uterus, fallopian tubes, and vagina in females, and the seminal vesicles and prostate in males

e. Appearance of the external genitals

f. Hormones evident during puberty (estrogen and progesterone in the female, and testosterone in the male

g. Gender assigned at birth ("It's a boy!" or "It's a girl!")

h. Gender identity, a person's internal psychological self concept of being either a male or a female

2. An estimated 1 out of every 1500 to 2000 babies born has some combination of physical characteristics demonstrated by both sexes

3. Pseudohermaphrodite or intersex: A person who has some mixture of male and female predisposition and configuration of reproductive structures

4. Hermaphrodite: A person born with fully formed ovaries and fully formed testes

5. The Intersex Society of North American (ISNA) questions the right of parents and physicians to make arbitrary decisions about surgically altering a child without that child's knowledge and consent

6. Ethical Question 9.1: When infants are born with an ambiguous or unclear gender, should they be assigned to one gender or the other? At that time, should they be physically altered to more closely resemble the assigned gender? If so, who should be responsible for making this decision? To what extent might children with ambiguous genitals (even after being given an assigned gender as ISNA suggests) fit in with their peers and be able to function well socially? Would it be better to wait until children reach adulthood to determine gender and/or to do any relevant surgery? Why or why not? Should society become more open-minded and expand its views of sex and gender to include more variations of male and female (a proposal that ISNA does not support)?

7. Spotlight on Diversity 9.1: Other Forms of Gender Expression

a. Transgenderism: Includes people whose appearance and/or behaviors do not conform to traditional gender roles, who live full- or part-time in the other gender's role, and derive psychosocial comfort in doing so

1) Transsexuals: People who feel they are imprisoned in the physical body of the wrong gender. Many prefer to be referred to as transgender people as transsexual emphasizes sex instead of gender, which they say is the real issue

2) Transvestites: Those who derive sexual gratification from dressing in the clothing of the opposite gender; almost all are heterosexual males

3) Drag queens: Gay men who dress up as women

4) Drag kings: Lesbians who dress up in traditionally masculine clothing

5) Female impersonators: Men who dress up as women, usually for the purpose of providing entertainment; they may be heterosexual or gay

III. Gender Role Stereotypes

A. From the moment they're born, boys and girls are treated very differently

B. Childhood

1. Parents generally treat male children in a more physical manner than female children. Parents tend to respond positively to boys who behave actively and to girls who talk calmly or touch gently

2. Boys are discouraged from external expression such as crying; the tragic result of this is that as adults, males often maintain this façade

3. Boys are drawn to "masculine" toys such as guns and trucks, whereas girls tend to prefer "feminine" playthings like Barbies

C. Adolescence

1. Early adolescence is characterized by gender intensification (a period of increased pressures for gender-role conformity)

2. Masculinity includes being strong, stable, aggressive, competitive, self-reliant, and emotionally undemonstrative

3. Femininity involves characteristics described as intuitive, loving, nurturing, emotionally expressive, and gentle

D. Adulthood

1. Women are often taught that they should be fulfilled by becoming wives and mothers

2. Men are often taught that their main source of self-satisfaction should come from their jobs

3. Three disadvantages for women that are associated with traditional gender-role socialization and stereotypes

    a. Women are encouraged to enter fields segregated by gender where they earn significantly less money than men do

Do you think these still exist?

b. Even when women work outside the home, they are still expected to do the majority of the housework and provide most of the child care (this is true regardless of social class, the status of the woman's job, or rural or urban residence)

c. The potential stress generated from the demands of being beautiful and attractive (women are surrounded on all sides by images of perfect female beauty)

4. Three repercussions for men that are associated with traditional gender-role socialization and stereotypes

a. Men are expected to be doers who are competent, aggressive, and successful

Do you think women have as much stress? ?

b. Pressure not to express emotions (intimacy is more difficult for men than women, perhaps due to how they were socialized)

c. Men have an average life span that is significantly less than that of women (the traditional male role may produce more stress)

5. Gender stereotypes pressure people to conform and don't allow much room for individuality and creativity

6. Highlight 9.1: The Special Issues and Needs of Men

a. Special issues experienced by men

1) Society attempts to socialize men to conform to male gender role stereotypes

Why ?, 2) Men risk greater health problems than women

3) Men who experience major disturbances or losses in their lives such as divorce or death of a loved one may have difficulty turning to others for emotional support and help

4) Men of color experience even greater difficulty

5) Men are more likely to use detrimental coping mechanisms such as turning to substance abuse and denial

b. Recommendations regarding social work practice with men

1) Practitioners should strive to be aware of any gender role stereotypes and expectations they harbor toward men

2) It is important to be aware of the wide range of diversity and "masculinities" among men

3)   It is important to focus on strengths (the extent to which a man is an active problem-solver and doer should be used to his advantage instead of disadvantage)

7.   Spotlight on Diversity 9.2: Cross-Cultural Perspectives on Gender Role Development

    a.   Chinese heritage

        1)   Sons were more highly valued than daughters; family lineage was passed through the male, while females were absorbed into the families of their husbands

        2)   The first-born son, the most valued child, received preferential treatment as well as more familial responsibilities

        3)   Females often did not come into positions of authority or respect until they assumed the role of mother-in-law

        4)   China continues to enforce the policy that most couples may have only one child. Because male infants are valued much more highly than females, many parents choose to give their infant girl up for adoption and try again for a boy

    b.   Mexican Americans (traditional families adhere to strict separation of gender roles)

        1)   Men are to be heads of the household and women should submit themselves to their husbands

        2)   The adolescent female is likely to remain much closer to the home than the male and to be protected and guarded in her contacts with others beyond the family, so as to preserve her femininity and innocence

        3)   The adolescent male, following the model of his father, is given much more freedom to come and go as he chooses and is encouraged to gain worldly knowledge outside the home in preparation for the time when he will assume the role of husband and father

    c.   African Americans

        1)   African-American children are often taught to assume more egalitarian roles

        2)   African American women, who often are more actively religious than their mates, tend to be regarded as all sacrificing and the strength of the family. Their identity often is tied to their role as mothers. Historically, they have worked outside the home, sometimes as the sole wage earners, particularly in times of high unemployment

      d.   An individual does not automatically conform to the gender role traits that often characterize their ethnic or racial group. Any individual may experience some degree of acculturation

      e.   Acculturation: An ethnic person's adoption of the dominant culture in which he or she is immersed

IV. Male-Female Differences

A. Ability level

1. Sometimes females display better verbal skills than males in some areas at some ages, but differences are so small they often don't matter

2. Males display a better grasp of spatial manipulation and understanding. Differences in some areas surface in childhood, and some continue into adulthood

3. In the past males scored higher than females on standardized math tests; however, currently males and females perform similarly on such tests, although girls get better grades in math classes

4. Some studies indicate that females are better at remembering things than their male counterparts, although possibly in some areas such as recalling where items are placed

5. The nature-nurture controversy: To what extent are such abilities innate and to what extent are they the result of the differential treatment of boys and girls

6. The important thing is not to make assumptions regarding an individual's ability on the basis of gender

B. Communication styles

1. Men and women interrupt at about the same rate in same-sex conversations. In mixed groups men interrupt more than women and are more likely to interrupt women than to interrupt men. It is about power

2. Feminine speech tends to work toward maintaining relationships, developing rapport, avoiding conflict, and maintaining cooperation. Masculine speech is more likely oriented toward attracting and maintaining an audience, asserting power and dominance, and giving information

3. Women are more likely to give information or make self-disclosures than are men

4. The less people adhere rigidly to traditional gender role stereotypes, perhaps the more flexible they are in their levels of self-disclosure

5. Women are better at understanding nonverbal cues and reading other people's emotions than are men

C. Ethical Question 9.2: What, if any, qualities do you think are biologically innate for females and males? To what extent are the gender-related behavior and traits of females and males due to influences in the environment as they're growing up?

V. People as Individuals

A. Men and women are more similar than dissimilar; cutting through and obliterating gender stereotypes and sexism will give people as individuals more freedom

B. Confronting the hidden rules that pressure people to conform on the basis of gender will allow individuals a better chance of being the way he or she naturally is comfortable being

VI. Significant Issues and Events in the Lives of Women

VII. Economic Inequality

A. Women earn about 81 percent of what men earn. For all races, women earn significantly less than men do at every educational level

B. Spotlight on Diversity 9.3: Gender/Racial Comparison of Median Weekly Earnings

C. The median income for women with a bachelor's degree or more is less than 63 percent of what men with a college education or more earn

D. The average annual income for women with a high school education is less than 72 percent of what correspondingly educated men earn

E. Almost 60 percent of all women age 16 and over work outside the home

F. Women and men tend to be clustered in different kinds of occupations; occupations more likely to be characterized by men usually pay higher salaries

G. Table 9.1: Employment Positions Held by Women

H. Women earn less in every occupational classification cited by the Bureau of Labor Statistics

I. Female physicians on the average earn less than 70 percent of what male physicians make

J. Female lawyers are less likely to be in criminal law and more likely to practice family law and make about 70 percent of male lawyers' salaries

K. Women are far less likely to get to the top of their professions or corporations due to barriers such as the glass ceiling

L. Women with Master's degrees in social work earned an average of $12,000 less than men; even when various factors were controlled, women earned 14 percent less than men

M.	Women make up only 24.4 percent of full professors when looking at all colleges and universities; women earn 80.7 percent of what men earn when considering all ranks at all colleges

N.	As of this writing, 87 women are serving in the U.S. Congress, making up 20 percent; of these, 16 are U.S. senators, making up 16 percent of the 100 senators

## VIII.	Sexual Harassment

A.	The highest number of sexual harassment complaints filed with the Federal Equal Employment Opportunity Commission was 15,889 in 1997; 12,510 complaints were filed in 2007

B.	Title VII of the Civil Rights Act of 1964 outlaws discrimination on the basis of sex along with discrimination on the basis of race. In 1991, the Civil Rights Act was amended to allow juries to award compensatory and punitive damages to people seeking legal action concerning sexual harassment in employment-related civil cases

C.	The definition of sexual harassment: Unwelcome sexual advances, requests for sexual favors, and other verbal or physical conduct of a sexual nature constitute sexual harassment when this conduct explicitly or implicitly affects an individual's employment, unreasonably interferes with an individual's work performance, or creates an intimidating, hostile, or offensive work environment

D.	Strengthening the definition: A macro system response

1.	A U.S. Supreme Court decision in late 1993 reinforced the seriousness of a hostile and offensive working environment as one aspect of sexual harassment

2.	The U.S. Supreme Court has made rulings that determine appropriate new parameters of behavior in the school or workplace

a.	An employee can successfully claim sexual harassment even though she has been treated well on the job

b.	A manager can be held accountable for a harasser's action, if the company does not have a strong system of handling harassment issues

c.	A victim of harassment must tell someone with decision-making power if she is being harassed

E.	The extent of sexual harassment

1.	Studies in the United States and Great Britain reveal that from 42 to 88 percent of female workers have experienced sexual harassment at work

2.	Between 20 and 49 percent of faculty women and about 30 percent of female students have been subjected to some form of sexual harassment

3. A massive study undertaken by the U.S. Merit Systems Protection Board used a stratified random sampling procedure involving more than 23,000 federal employees

   a. Of the female employees surveyed, 42 percent stated that they were victims of sexual harassment of some kind during the 2-year period before the survey

   b. Only 1 percent reported being victims of actual sexual assault

   c. Twenty-nine percent indicated that severe sexual harassment had occurred to them

   d. Twelve percent experienced less severe harassment

   e. Fifteen percent of the men in the MSPB study felt that they also had been harassed

   f. Variables that made victimization more likely according to the research

      1) Youth—A woman under age 20 was twice as likely to be sexually harassed as one between age 20 and 40

      2) Marital status—Divorced and single women were more likely to be harassed than women who were married or widowed

      3) Education—Sexual harassment was more likely to occur to women with higher levels of education. Perhaps this finding was due to the fact that more highly educated women were more aware of sexual harassment issues and also to the fact that they assumed job positions traditionally not held by women

F. Effects of sexual harassment

   1. Fear of retaliation, fear of not being believed, feelings of shame and humiliation, a belief that nothing can or will be done, and a reluctance to cause problems for the harasser. In many ways, a woman who reports sexual harassment is viewed as a troublemaker or whistle-blower and is treated accordingly

   2. A major study indicated that only about 6 percent of respondents pursued a formal complaint process regarding their being harassed

   3. The personal and emotional costs placed on the victims themselves cannot even be measured

G. Highlight 9.2: Confronting Sexual Harassment

   1. Ignoring the harasser, avoiding the harasser, or asking the harasser to stop. This is the most common approach women choose, however it has limited effect in the long run. Asking the harasser to stop may be more effective

   2. A victim needs to know her or his rights

3. Suggestions that can be applied to most situations where sexual harassment is occurring

    a. Confront your harasser

    b. Be assertive

    c. Document your situation

    d. Talk to others about the problem

    e. Get witnesses

    f. Follow the established complaint procedure

H. Ethical Question 9.3: Why do people sexually harass other people?

IX. Sexist Language

A. Sexist language can include jokes with inappropriate sexual connotations. It can also include derogatory comments about ability based on gender

B. Sexist structure of English language that reflect an aura of sexism and unfairness (e.g., mankind, chairman, salesman, congressman, and the best man for the job)

C. Proper titles for men and women (e.g., Mr. makes no reference to the status of a man's personal life; however, Miss or Mrs. clearly establishes her marital status)

D. Highlight 9.3: Using Nonsexist Language

    1. Replace the word man with other more inclusive terms such as human or person

    2. Use the term Ms. instead of Miss and Mrs.

    3. Phrase sentences so that the masculine pronouns *he, him,* and *his* can be avoided

        a. Eliminate pronouns altogether

        b. Statements can frequently be rephrased into the plural

        c. Masculine pronouns can be replaced with *one, you*, or *his or her*

    4. Avoid using patronizing and derogatory stereotypes

X.   Rape and Sexual Assault

A.   Rape: Sexual intercourse without mutual desire. It is generally seen as forced (or threat of forced) penetration of a body orifice, including the mouth, rectum, and vagina, and the use of objects or other body parts, such as fingers

B.   Refer to people who have survived sexual assault as *survivors*, not *victims*. Instead of focusing on a woman's weakness, which the word *victim* implies, the term *survivor* emphasizes a woman's survival strengths

C.   Incidence of rape

1.   Approximately 2,000 rapes (or about one every 5 minutes) are committed in the United States every day

2.   One study found that 20 percent of women college students said they had been forced to have sexual intercourse, most often by someone known to them

3.   A long-term study found that almost 70 percent of college women reported experiencing some type of forced sexual interaction since age 14

4.   A range of studies indicate that a woman has a 14 to 25 percent chance of being raped sometime during her life, and that the number of rapes being reported is only 12 to 28 percent of those actually committed

5.   Spotlight on Diversity 9.4: Cultural Differences in the Incidence of Violence Against Women

a.   Among Asian/Pacific Islander women, 6.8 percent reported being raped at some point in their lifetime; 17.7 percent of White women, 18.8 percent of African American women, 24.4 percent of mixed race women, and 34.1 percent of Native American/Native Alaskan women reported being raped. Among Hispanic women, 19.6 percent reported being raped

b.   Among Asian/Pacific Islander women, 49.6 percent reported being physically assaulted at some point in their lifetime; 51.3 percent of White women, 52.1 percent of African American women, 57.5 percent of mixed race women, and 61.4 percent of Native American/Native Alaskan women reported physical assault. Among Hispanic women, 53.2 percent reported physical assault

c.   Native American/Native Alaskan women were most likely to report rape and physical assault. Asian/Pacific Islander women were least likely to report victimization, although many did talk about violence as a significant concern

d.   Women of all races and Hispanic and non-Hispanic women were about equally vulnerable to violence by an intimate

e.   Rape/sexual assault rates increased as household income decreased

6. Women fail to report being raped for many reasons

    a. Survivors whose bodies have been brutally violated often desperately want to forget that the horror ever happened.

    b. Survivors fear retribution from the rapist

    c. Survivors feel that people around them will think less of them because they've been raped

D. Theoretical views of rape

    1. Victim-precipitated rape: Assumes that the survivor is actually to blame for the rape—that the woman "asked for it"

    2. Rapist psychopathology: Proposes that the rapist is emotionally disturbed or mentally unbalanced. This view places virtually none of the blame on society or on social attitudes

    3. The feminist perspective on rape: Emphasizes that rape is the logical reaction of men who are socialized to dominate women. Rape is seen as a manifestation of men's need to aggressively maintain power over women. It has little to do with sexuality

E. Common myths about rape

    1. Rapes tend to occur in dark alleys—Fact: Many rapes occur in a woman's own resident. In cases occurring indoors, especially in their own homes, survivors are very likely to know the rapist

    2. Only strangers are potential rapists—Fact: One study indicated that over three-quarters of all women aged 18 and older who reported that they had been raped named their significant other or a "date" as the perpetrator (known as acquaintance or date rape). Date-rape drugs such as Rohypnol and gamma hydroxbutyrate (GHB) pose great threats for women

    3. Women really want to be raped—this myth supports the misconception that a woman enjoys being raped because she sexually surrenders and it perpetuates the belief that rape is a sexual act rather than a violent one

    4. Women ask for it because of their behavior and the way they dress—this places the responsibility for the violent and aggressive act on the victim, not the perpetrator. A woman has the right to dress the way she wants and be attractive. Actually most rapes are premeditated and planned by the perpetrator. Opportunity is the critical factor in determining when a rapist will rape

F. Highlight 9.4: Suggestions for Rape Prevention

    1. Be aware of the things around you

    2. Be aware of your own behavior—try not to appear vulnerable or preoccupied

3. Don't be afraid to look behind you

4. Park in well-lighted areas and have your car keys ready to use

5. Check the backseat before getting in

6. Keep your doors locked and your windows partly rolled up

7. Keep enough gas in your car to avoid running out

8. If you have car trouble, pull over and stay in the car with doors locked and windows raised. When no one is around open your hood. It is best to wait for police. If a man volunteers to help, ask him to contact the police

9. Do not hitchhike

10. At home outside entrances and hallways should be well lighted. Doors should have dead-bolt locks and windows should have locks

11. If a service man knocks on your door, ask to see his identification and call his company for verification

12. If you are attacked, try to run and scream. Weapons are easily taken away from you by the attacker. Carry whistles, hat pins, etc.

13. To fight back, aim for the face, which is more sensitive to pain, loud screams in the attacker's ear will stun him. A kick aimed at his knees might be effective

G. Profile of a rapist

1. There is no clearly defined profile of a rapist in terms of the work they do, their educational level, whether they're married or not, their prior criminal history, or even their reasons for committing rape

2. A number of variables can predispose men to rape

   a. Rapists tend to come from hostile, violent family environments

   b. Perpetrators are more likely to have a history of delinquency

   c. Rapists tend to be sexually promiscuous

   d. Rapists tend to have a hostile, masculine personality defined as one scorning traits that might be construed as feminine characteristics such as empathy or nurturance

3. Rapists tend to believe in rape myths that they can use as a rationale for their behavior

4. They may ignore personal space, abuse alcohol or other drugs, sexualize conversations, are dominant/aggressive, have rigid gender roles, use threats in displays of anger, have a quick temper, are sadistic/narcissistic, and are impersonal/aloof emotionally

5. Rapists often harbor anger toward women, maintain hardened attitudes toward women, adhere to traditional gender-role stereotypes, and view women as owing them sexual favors. Their exaggerated sense of self-importance may facilitate their ability to rationalize their behavior

6. Three basic categories of rapists

   a. Anger rapist—may inflict substantial injury on victims ranging from verbal abuse to brutal beatings to murder, although the latter is rare

   b. Power rapist—often has a sexual dysfunction or an obvious physical deformity for which he is trying to compensate. By being demeaning towards his victim, using moderate force, and a blitz style attack, he rapes to assert his power and control over his victim and dominate her

   c. Sadistic rapist—is motivated to assault in order to live out his sexual and aggressive fantasies and resembles the angry rapist except for three things

      1) He often does considerably more planning to orchestrate an attack designed to live out a specific fantasy

      2) He derives gratification from hurting the victim

      3) Anger may or may not be involved

7. Date rape

   a. The vast majority of date rapes go unreported; many of the female survivors of sexual assault did not label it as such. Somehow, because they had been "in love" with the perpetrator, rape was within the realm of acceptable behavior

   b. One study reported that 70 percent of women who had been date-raped had been drinking or taking drugs prior to the rape, and 71 percent said their assailant had been drinking or taking drugs

   c. There is a mythical idea that women really love being raped, that they "really want it" so when she says "no," she really means "yes". There is also the idea that "she shouldn't have started it or let it go so far if she wasn't ready to go all the way"

8. Ethical Question 9.4: Why do you think men rape?

H.   Survivors' reactions to rape

1.   Posttraumatic stress disorder (PTSD): A psychological reaction occurring after a highly stressing event that is usually characterized by depression, anxiety, flashbacks, recurrent nightmares, and avoidance of reminders of the event

2.   Rape trauma syndrome: Serious psychological effects that can persist for a half year or more following a rape. Now considered to be a specific aspect of posttraumatic stress disorder

a.   Acute phase of rape trauma syndrome: Involves the woman's emotional reactions immediately following the rape and up to several weeks thereafter

1)   She may show her emotions by crying, expressing anger, or showing fear

2)   She may try to control these intense emotions and keep them from view

3)   Two primary emotions experienced during the acute phase are fear and self-blame

4)   Physical problems include difficulties related directly to the rape, also stress-related discomforts such as headaches, stomach difficulties, or inability to sleep

b.   Long-term reorganization and recovery phase of rape trauma syndrome: The emotional changes and reactions of this phase may linger on for years

1)   Most rape survivors feel that the rape has changed their lives in one way or another

2)   Reactions included fear of being alone, depression, sleeplessness, and an attitude of suspicion toward other people

3)   Some women avoided involvement with men, and suffered various sexual dysfunctions such as lack of sexual desire, aversion to sexual contact, or difficulties in having orgasms

I.   Suggestions for counseling rape survivors: Keys to empowerment

1.   Emotional issues

a.   Collier's three stages in counseling survivors of rape

1)   Provide the survivor with immediate warmth and support

        2)   Elicit support from others

        3)   Rebuild the survivor's trust in herself, in the environment around her, and in other personal relationships

2.   Reporting to the police

    a.   Many survivors choose not to call the police for various reasons

        1)   Fear that the rapist will try to get revenge

        2)   Fear of public embarrassment and derogation

        3)   An attitude that it won't matter anyway because most rapists get off free

        4)   Fear of the legal process and questioning

    b.   Only about 48 percent of men arrested for rape are released on bail; of all people accused of rape, 80 percent face a felony prosecution. About half of all men arrested for rape are convicted (usually of a felony rape)—most after a guilty plea

    c.   Over two-thirds of convicted defendants received a prison sentence; the average term was 14 years, another 19 percent were sentenced to terms in local jails, and 13 percent were placed on probation. Convicted rapists typically serve about half of their prison terms before release

    d.   Twenty states currently have laws that confine sex offenders without release dates, they allow the civil commitment of some sex offenders after their criminal sentences have ended by arguing in civil court that these offenders possess a mental disorder that makes them likely to offend again

    e.   In the event that a survivor decides to report, she should not take a shower. In counseling situations, it's important to emphasize the reason for not washing immediately

3.   Medical status of the victim

    a.   Survivor, at some point, needs to attend to the possibility of pregnancy

    b.   Survivor should be encouraged, at some point, to be screened for sexually transmitted infections, including HIV

J.   Ethical Question 9.5: What should be the consequences for men who rape?

X. Battered Women

A. Battered Woman Syndrome: The systematic and repeated use of one or more practices against a woman by her husband or lover (e.g., slapping, punching, knocking down, choking, kicking, hitting with objects, threatening with weapons, stabbing, and shooting)

B. Myths about battered women

1. Battered women aren't really hurt that badly

2. Beatings and other abuses just happen; they aren't a regular occurrence

3. Women who stay in such homes must really enjoy the beatings they get

4. Wife-battering only occurs in lower-class families

C. Incidence of violence toward women in intimate relationships

1. An estimated 2 to 3 million women are assaulted by male partners in the U.S. each year and that at least half of these women are severely assaulted

2. As many as 21% to 34% of women will be assaulted by an intimate partner during adulthood. Thirty-three percent to 50% are also the victim of partner rape. Studies have shown that 22% to 40% of the women who seek health care at clinics or emergency rooms are victims of battering

3. Approximately 66% of family violence deaths are women killed by their male partners; over 50% of all murders of women are committed by current or former partners. In contrast, only 6% of male murder victims are killed by wives or girlfriends

4. More than half of Canadian women (51 percent) have been physically or sexually assaulted at least once in their adult lives; more than half of them said they'd been attacked by dates, boyfriends, husbands, friends, family members, or other men familiar to them. One in ten Canadian women had been attacked in the past year

5. Over 90 percent of heterosexual partner-abuse cases involve men abusing women. Men tend to use violence as a means of control; women tend to use violence in self-defense or when they fear being attacked

6. Battering is not limited to poor families or any particular racial, ethnic, or cultural background, although it occurs more frequently in families with very low incomes and economic problems. Women of color are also more likely to be abused—they are overrepresented in impoverished populations

D. The abusive perpetrator

1. Tend to adhere to common masculine gender role stereotypes such as failing to display emotion or sensitivity to others, because they perceive these as reflecting weakness

2. May be insecure and jealous

3. Stress from job loss or poverty, or emotional distress like depression, can contribute to the potential for violence

4. It can be stressful for some men to have wives with higher-status occupations because the men have learned that they are supposed to be superior to their wives

5. Alcohol use is linked to violent episodes

E. The battering cycle

1. First phase involves building up stress and tension

2. The second phase is the explosion, this is when the battering occurs. It is generally the shortest of the three phases

3. The third phase involves making up—because a man's tension has been released, he now adamantly states that he is truly sorry and swears he will never do it again

F. Why does she stay?

1. Economic dependence—Many battered women are financially dependent on the abuser as the primary wage earner for themselves and their children

2. Lack of self-confidence—It takes initiative and courage to muster the self-confidence required to leave a painful situation and strike out for the unknown

3. Lack of power—A battered woman views herself as having significantly less power in her relationship with an abusive man than does a woman with a partner who is nonviolent

4. Fear of the abuser—It is logical for a battered woman to fear brutal retaliation by the perpetrator if she leaves him

5. Guilt—Many battered women feel that it is their own fault that they are abused

6. Feeling isolated with nowhere to go—Battered women often try to keep the facts of their battering a secret. They may feel isolated from friends and family. Frequently, the perpetrator strongly discourages his female partner's interactions with friends and family

7. Fear for her children—She might be worried about her ability to support them financially on her own. She may firmly adhere to the traditional belief that children need a father. She may even fear losing custody of her children

8. Love—Many battered women still love their abusive husbands

9. Spotlight on Diversity 9.5: Battering in Gay and Lesbian Relationships

G. Community responses to empower battered women: Their alternatives

1. The police, social policy, and battered women

   a. In the past, police have been generally lenient to batterers. Now many police departments are taking an increasingly active interest in addressing family violence

   b. Violence Against Women Act (VAWA)—includes increased funding for shelters and programs, a mandate for harsher penalties for batterers, and making the crossing of state lines in pursuit of a fleeing partner a federal offense

   c. Mandatory arrest laws are implemented in some states

   d. Suggestions for improving policy and empowering battered women

      1) Training about domestic violence for criminal justice system personnel

      2) Laws prohibiting the carrying of weapons by perpetrators

      3) Legal services with expertise in domestic violence issues to help survivors

      4) Restraining orders should be enforced

      5) Change the patriarchal practices that undermine female victims' opportunities to lead violence-free lives

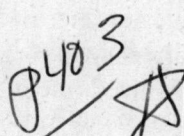

   e. Case of Karen and Richard Graves

   f. Ethical Question 9.6: What could and should have been done to protect Karen Graves?

2. Shelters for battered women

   a. Typical maximum stay at a domestic violence shelter is 30 days

   b. Most shelters have a policy that they will not pick women up from their homes, as doing so could result in danger to the woman and/or shelter volunteer. It also minimizes the risk of perpetrators following the car to the shelter

   c. Other services offered include crisis phone lines, counseling, advocacy, public education, legal advocacy, children's services, support groups, and batterer's intervention programs

d.   Transitional housing programs: Programs designed to help survivors and their children as they make the transition from domestic violence shelter to a more permanent residence

e.   Many other innovative resources are available

3.   Counseling strategies for empowerment

a.   The initial interview

1)   The counselor should try to make the survivor as comfortable as possible and emphasize that she doesn't have to talk about anything she doesn't want to

2)   It is important that the counselor put personal feelings aside, and not pressure the battered woman into any particular course of action

3)   The counselor needs to assure the survivor that no information will be given to anyone without her consent

4)   The counselor should make an effort to downplay any embarrassment by emphasizing that the woman is a survivor of victimization and that her situation has nothing to do with her character or with her intrinsic human value

b.   Offer support—A battered woman needs someone to empathize with her and express genuine concern

c.   Encourage expression of feelings—The counselor needs to encourage the survivor to get all of her emotions out in the open

d.   Focus on strengths—One aspect of counseling that is very easy to forget is focusing on the survivor's strengths. She probably needs help in identifying her positive characteristics

e.   Furnish information—Information about available legal, medical, and social services may open up alternatives to the survivors to better enable them to help themselves

f.   Review alternatives—A survivor may be so overwhelmed that alternatives other than surviving in her abusive situation may not even have occurred to her

g.   Establish a plan—A survivor needs to clearly understand and define what she chooses to do. This choice may include formulating major goals such as divorcing her husband. It may involve setting smaller subgoals such as developing a list of existing day-care centers she can call to find out available child-care options

h.   Advocate—Seek out information, and help the survivor get in touch with services, and especially advocate for changing legal macro systems

XII. Working with and Empowering Women

A. Social workers can help women regain their senses of having power and of being in control of their lives

B. Social workers can teach women about assertiveness and how to develop assertiveness skills

C. Social workers can also encourage women to express their anger instead of holding it in

D. Social workers can encourage women to take care of themselves

E. Spotlight on Diversity 9.6: Strategies for Empowering Women and Achieving Sexual Equality

    1. Become conscious of the gender role stereotypes affecting people from birth on

        a. Don't force boys to be little men who must be actively aggressive and never dare cry when they're sad or hurting

        b. Don't force girls to be little ladies who must wear frilly pink dresses, play with dolls, and be passive and submissive

        c. Androgyny: Implies that each individual, regardless of gender, be allowed to develop positive personal qualities

    2. Throughout life, place less emphasis on the need to conform with gender-based stereotypes

    3. To combat the discriminatory effects of sexism on women, encourage women to develop their assertiveness skills, enhance their self-confidence, and learn to develop and appreciate analytical and spatial manipulation skills

    4. Encourage more freedom in adult domestic relationships. Allow couples to negotiate both household tasks and outside work career goals without external pressure and criticism

    5. Confront laws and regulations that are discriminatory and restrictive on the basis of gender

XIII. Summary

Chapter 9
Gender Roles and Sexism

Experiential Exercises and Simulations

The following five exercises are designed to help you identify some of the common gender-role stereotypes for men and women, question the usefulness of some of these stereotypes, assess the impacts of sexism on both men and women, and examine your own attitudes and sexist biases.

Exercise 9.1: Media Craze

A.   Brief description
You are shown various magazine advertisements, and are asked to discuss how gender roles and sexist ideas are portrayed by the pictures.

B.   Objectives
You will:
1.   Identify how the media depict men and women.
2.   Examine common sexist biases.
3.   Propose alternative, nonsexist approaches to advertising.

C.   Procedure
1.   While looking at each picture, discuss the following questions:
    a.   What does this picture convey about how women and men are or should be?
    b.   What are your reactions as to how these attitudes relate to you?
    c.   How might the product be portrayed in a nonsexist manner?

Exercise 9.2: Have Things Really Changed?

A.   Brief description
You will discuss specific questions about current gender role expectations.

B.   Objectives
You will:
1.   Examine some issues concerning the equality or lack of equality of gender roles.
2.   Evaluate some current gender role expectations.
3.   Propose suggestions for correcting discrepancies between the gender roles that you judge to be unfair.

C.   Procedure
1.   Divide into groups of four to six persons.
2.   Discuss each of the following questions, one question at a time:
    a.   Should women ask men for dates?
    b.   Is there still a double standard concerning premarital sex?
    c.   Should mothers work outside the home or try to stay home with their young children?

3. You have approximately 10 minutes to discuss each question. After each question, a volunteer from each group summarizes its conclusions for the class, and a short discussion follows.
4. After addressing each question, the entire class addresses the following questions:
    a. Are there any differences between how you think things should be and what you would actually do yourself if involved in situations similar to those discussed?
    b. In regard to the situations you discussed in small groups, to what extent do you think things have changed from the traditional ways?
    c. What things might be done to increase the equality between men and women?

Exercise 9.3: Girls Are This Way, Boys Are That Way

A. Brief description
You will examine and discuss how traditional gender-role stereotypes characterize both females and males and evaluate the effects of these stereotypes.

B. Objectives
You will:
1. Identify stereotypes and characteristics traditionally associated with the respective gender roles.
2. Appraise the effects of these stereotypes on people's right to individuality.

C. Procedure
1. As an introduction to lecturing about and discussing sexism, the instructor will write the following open-ended statements on the board:
    Females are ____.
    Males are ____.
2. Call out some of the characteristics that males and females traditionally are supposed to have. The instructor writes the responses on the board.
3. Discuss the following questions:
    a. To what extent do these stereotypes apply to people's behavior today?
    b. How do these stereotypes affect people's right to individuality—the right to be themselves without uncomfortable pretense?

Exercise 9.4: The Fishbowl

A. Brief description
You will form two groups according to gender and discuss various aspects you find attractive in the opposite gender. Discussion will follow regarding the perceptions.

B. Objectives
You will:
1. Describe your feelings regarding positive qualities of the opposite gender.
2. Examine some of your misconceptions about the opposite gender.
3. Assess similarities and differences in the perceptions of each gender.

C. Procedure
1. Form two groups, one including all the females and the other all the males.
2. The females sit in an inner circle in the center of the classroom. The males position themselves in an outer circle around the females.

3. The females discuss what **physical, emotional, and behavioral** characteristics they find attractive in males. The males remain silent. The discussion continues for 10 to 15 minutes.

4. Reverse positions; males should sit in the inner circle and females in the outer one. The males discuss what **physical, emotional, and behavioral** characteristics they find attractive in females. This time, the females remain silent.

5. You will have 10 to 15 minutes of discussion. Then the entire class discusses the following questions:
   a. What did you learn about the opposite gender from this exercise?
   b. Were there any surprises?
   c. What were some of the similarities and some of the differences between females' and males' perceptions?

Exercise 9.5: Life Questions

A. Brief description
You will be given a variety of thought-provoking questions concerning male and female gender roles and asked to discuss your own opinions.

B. Objectives
You will:
1. Recognize your personal opinions and biases on a number of gender issues including treatment on the job, leadership, pregnancy, and household tasks.
2. Examine the distribution of power and opportunity between genders on these issues and assess the extent to which the situations are fair.
3. Formulate suggestions for addressing these issues.

C. Procedure
1. Form small groups of four to six persons.
2. Discuss the following questions. Write down your opinions on the question sheet. At the end of the exercise, a volunteer from each group will summarize your findings and ideas for the entire class.

LIFE QUESTIONS

1. Treatment on the Job

   a. Should men and women be treated equally on the job?

2. Leadership

   a. When you get a job, would you prefer a man or a woman as a supervisor?

   b. What are the reasons for your answer?

---

3. <u>Pregnancy</u>

    a.   Should a working woman be granted a leave of absence for pregnancy?

    b.   Why or why not?

    c.   If so, for how long?

    d.   Should the leave be with or without pay?

    e.   Do you think mothers of young children should stay home to take care of them?

    f.   Should fathers of newborn infants be given leaves of absence? If so, this should occur under what circumstances (e.g., length of time, paid or unpaid)?

4. <u>Household Tasks</u>

    a.   Do married men and women share household tasks equally these days (for example, taking out the garbage, cleaning the bathroom, doing the laundry, washing dishes, cooking, grocery shopping, taking care of the kids)?

    b.   Do you think household tasks should be shared equally by a male and female living together as spouses or partners?

    c.   If you marry (or are married), do you plan to share household tasks equally? Explain why or why not.

3.   A volunteer from your group should summarize your findings for the entire class. The class then addresses the following questions:

    a.   Are power and opportunity distributed fairly between genders? Why or why not?

    b.   What are your opinions and biases about these issues? How do these coincide with professional social work values?

    c.   In those instances where you perceive inequities, what changes should be made?

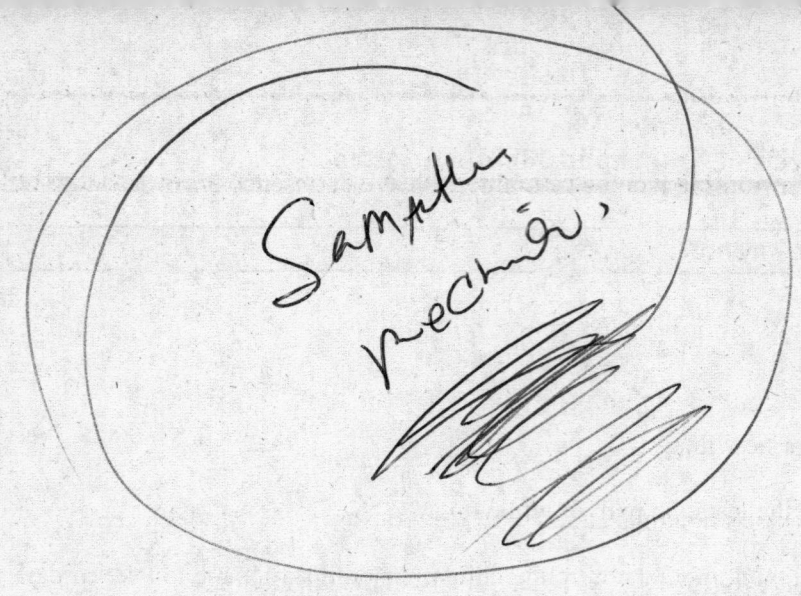

I.   **A Perspective**

II.   **Young Adulthood**

    A.   Physical development

        1.   Maximum muscular strength is attained between the ages of 25 and 30

        2.   After age 30, decreases in strength occur mostly in the leg and back

        3.   Top performance speed for tasks is reached at about age 30, as well as highest levels of manual agility

        4.   Eyesight and hearing are sharpest at age 20; however, a decline isn't significant until age 40 or 45

    B.   Health status

        1.   Ninety-three percent of people aged 15 to 44 perceive their health as being either good or excellent

        2.   Ethical Question 10.1: Are you taking good physical care of yourself?

        3.   Highlight 10.1: Breast Cancer

            a.   Approximately 1 of 8 women will develop breast cancer during her lifetime and about 1 in 35 will die from it

            b.   Benign lumps: Eighty percent of all breast lumps are benign. They are usually either cysts (pouches of fluid) or fibroadenoma (more solid, rounded growth of cells resembling scar tissue)

            c.   Symptoms: Any change in appearance; discharges from the nipple or discoloration, pain, dimpling or puckering of the nipple or skin; or any swelling of the upper arm or lymph nodes under the arm

            d.   Risk factors

                1)   Age: About two-thirds of women with breast cancer are age 55 or older by the time the cancer is discovered

                2)   Family history: Risk doubles for women who have a mother, sister, or daughter who has breast cancer. (However, about three-quarters of all women with breast cancer do not have it in their family history)

3)   Prior history: Prior history of breast cancer increases the chances of developing a new cancer in the same or the other breast

4)   Race: White women are slightly more likely to get breast cancer than are African-American women, but African-Americans are more likely to die of this cancer

5)   Radiation: Women whose breast has been exposed to radiation treatment in the chest area at some earlier time have greater risk

6)   Menstruation: Risk increases a bit for women who started menstruating before age 12 or who went through menopause after age 55

7)   Childless women and women having their first child after age 30: Risk increases slightly

8)   Contraceptive pills: The risk is not yet understood

9)   Postmenopausal hormone therapy (PHT): Long-term use increases the probability of breast cancer and of dying from the disease

10)   Alcohol consumption: In greater quantities on a regular basis increases risk

11)   Overweight: Increases risk

e.   Suspicion of breast cancer

1)   Mammogram: X-ray of the breast

2)   Magnetic resonance imaging (MRI) scans: Use radio waves and strong magnets instead of x-rays

3)   Ultrasound: Picture of an internal area by the use of sound waves

4)   Biopsy: Extracting some amount of tissue to examine for cancerous cells

5)   Fine needle aspiration biopsy: An extremely fine needle extracts fluid from the lump that is then evaluated

6)   Stereotactic biopsy: A larger needle is used that removes several cores of tissue for analysis

7) Mammotome and Advanced Breast Biopsy Instrument: New methods that entail removing larger cores of tissue than stereotactic biopsies

8) Surgical biopsy: A portion of a suspicious mass or the entire mass along with some of the surrounding tissue is removed

f. Treatment of breast cancer

1) Lumpectomy: Only the tumor and a small portion of the surrounding tissue are removed

2) Partial mastectomy: A portion of the breast containing the cancerous tumor is taken out along with some of the muscle tissue right below it and breast skin above it

3) Simple or total mastectomy: The entire breast is removed, but not the lymph nodes under the arm

4) Modified radical mastectomy: The breast and some of the underarm lymph nodes are removed. This is the most common procedure when the entire breast requires removal

5) Radical mastectomy: Removal of the breast, the underlying chest muscles, and all related lymph nodes. This procedure has become rare

6) Reconstructive surgery is an option that involves an artificial breast. Approximately 68,000 women undergo breast reconstruction each year

7) Chemotherapy: Administering cancer-fighting drugs either by injecting them into a vein or taking them in pill form

8) Radiation therapy: High-energy rays are used to kill or shrink cancer cells. Administered by a machine outside the body or by placing radioactive substances inside the tumor

9) Hormone therapy: Administration of drugs that block or decrease the effects of the female hormone estrogen in those women where estrogen encourages the development of breast cancer

10) Aromatase inhibitors: Drugs for women past menopause whose cancers have been found to respond positively to estrogen

       g.   Highlight 10.1: Early detection of breast cancer

           1)   Women should have an annual mammogram beginning at age 40. High risk women could begin earlier and potentially have an annual MRI

           2)   Beginning in their 20s or 30s, women should begin having a clinical breast exam performed by a health care practitioner every 3 years

           3)   Breast self-examination beginning in your 20s

       h.   Figure 10.1: Breast Self-Exam

    4.   Women should become experts on their own bodies

    5.   If a lump is found, women should seek help immediately and become knowledgeable about alternative remedies

C.   Lifestyle and good health

    1.   Eating regular meals; no smoking; moderate exercise; adequate sleep; moderate alcohol

    2.   Controlling stress

    3.   Spotlight on Diversity 10.1: Differential Incidence of Death

       a.   The leading causes of death among young adults in the United States age 15 to 24 are accidents, homicide and legal intervention, suicide, and cancer, respectively

       b.   Death rates for men age 15 to 24 are almost three times higher than those for women

       c.   Death rate for African American males age 15 to 24 is almost double that of their white counterparts. Murder is the number one cause of death

       d.   The U.S. homicide rate is six times the rate in Holland, five times the rate in Canada, and eight times the rate in Europe

       e.   Included in the top ten causes of death for African American women and Latinas are conditions connected to pregnancy and childbirth, probably partially due to decreased access to adequate health care

       f.   Twenty-five percent more African American women die in their twenties than do white women as a result of HIV/AIDS, maternal mortality, drug use, and homicide

g. Native American women aged 15 to 24 show a 50 percent higher death rate than white women of the same age for similar reasons

h. Poverty is linked to poor health status

III. The Age Span of Middle Adulthood

A. Middle age has no distinct biological markers

B. The beginning of middle adulthood has been identified by different writers as ranging from 30 to 40, and the ending of this age period has been viewed as ranging from ages 60 to 70

IV. Physical Changes in Middle Age

A. Changes in physical functioning

1. A major change is a reduction in reserve capacity, which serves as a backup in times of stress and during a dysfunction of one of the body's systems

2. Middle-aged adults also have less capacity to do physical work. Middle-aged adults are best at tasks that require endurance rather than rapid burst of energy

B. Health changes

1. Diabetes, hypertension, heart problems, and cancer have higher rates of occurring during the middle adult years as compared to the younger years

2. The three leading causes of death for those between the ages of 35 and 54 are, in order: cancer, heart disease, and accidents. Between ages 55 and 64 the leading causes of death are cancer, heart disease, and strokes

C. Changes in physical appearance

1. Grey hairs begin to appear, the hair may thin, wrinkles gradually appear, and the skin may become dry and lose some of its elasticity

2. Having a physically attractive body has become a cult in our society. The body-beautiful cult leads those who judge themselves to be attractive to feel that they are superior to those they judge to be less attractive physically

D. The double standard of aging

1. Grey hair, coarsened skin, and "crow's feet" wrinkles are considered attractive in men; yet, the same physical changes in women are viewed as unattractive indicators that they are "over the hill"

2. Today the double standard of aging is waning—both men and women encounter age discrimination in looking for a job

3.   Men are more apt than women to feel old before their time if they have not achieved career or financial success

4.   Ethical Question 10.2: If you were an employer, would you be reluctant to hire someone who was 50 or older?

E.   Changes in sense organs

    1.   Many middle-aged adults develop presbyopia (they become far-sighted)

    2.   During middle age there is a gradual hardening and deterioration of the auditory nerve cells

    3.   Presbycusis: Reduction in hearing acuity for high frequency tones. Middle-aged men generally have significantly greater losses in high frequency tones than middle-aged women

    4.   There are generally some minor changes in taste, touch, and smell as a person grows older

F.   Changes in physical strength and reaction time

    1.   Physical strength and coordination are at their maximum in the 20s and then decline gradually in middle adulthood

    2.   Some sports figures who have been applauded and worshiped by fans may experience an identity crisis in middle adulthood when they no longer are as competitive

    3.   Highlight 10.2: An Identity Crisis: When the Applause Stops

    4.   Simple reaction time reaches its optimum at around age 25 and is maintained until around age 60, when the reflexes gradually slow down. The improvement that comes from experience outweighs minor declines in physical abilities

    5.   Middle-aged workers are less likely to have disabling injuries on the job—which is probably due to learning to be careful and learning to use good judgment

G.   Changes in Intellectual Functioning

    1.   Mental functions (if used) peak in middle age

    2.   If a person is mentally active, that person will continue to learn well into later adulthood. Practically all cognitive capacities show no noticeable declines in middle adulthood

    3.   People in middle adulthood who use their verbal abilities regularly further develop their vocabulary and verbal abilities. There is some evidence that middle-aged adults may be slightly less adept at tests of short-term memory, but this is usually compensated by wisdom gained from a variety of past experiences

4. Creative productivity is at its optimum point in middle age. Scientists, scholars, and artists have their highest rate of output generally in their 40s—and their productivity tends to remain high in their 60s and 70s

5. Middle-aged adults tend to think in an integrative way. They tend to interpret what they see, read, or hear in terms of its personal and psychological meaning—they filter information through their own learning and experience. This enables middle-aged people to create inspirational legends and myths by putting truths about the human condition into symbols that younger generations can turn to for guidelines in leading their lives

6. Integrative thinking enables people in their 40s and 50s to be at the peak of their practical problem solving capacities

7. In the past few decades an increasing proportion of middle-aged adults have been returning to college

V. Female Menopause

A. Menopause: The event in every woman's life when she stops menstruating and can no longer bear children

B. The median age when menopause occurs is 51 years, although the event may occur in some women as young as 36, or may not occur until a woman is in her mid 50s

C. Climacteric: Time span ranging from two to five years during which a woman's body undergoes physiological changes that bring on menopause

D. Symptoms of the beginning of menopause include a change in a woman's menstrual pattern; the usual pattern is skipped periods, with the periods occurring farther and farther apart

E. Biological changes occurring during menopause

1. The ovaries become smaller and no longer secrete eggs regularly

2. The fallopian tubes become shorter and smaller

3. The vagina loses some of its elasticity and becomes shorter

4. The uterus shrinks and hardens

5. The hormone content of urine changes

6. The reduction of activity of the ovaries affects other glands and may produce disturbing symptoms in some women

7.   Spotlight on Diversity 10.2: Cultural Differences in Women's Experience of Menopause

a.   Only 12.6 percent of Japanese women who were beginning to experience irregular menstruation reported experiencing hot flashes in a 2 week period compared to 47.4 percent of Canadian women. Fewer than 20 percent of Japanese women had ever had a hot flash compared to almost 65 percent of Canadian women. The lack of a specific Japanese word for a hot flash supports the finding of a low incidence of what most Western women report as the most troubling symptom of menopause

b.   Mayan women in Mexico do not report having any symptoms related to menopause

c.   Symptoms of menopause are uncommon among Native American women. In Native American cultures menopause is viewed as an important rite of passage signifying entrance into the highly respected state of elderhood, and opening up the opportunity to assume important new social rules

8.   The most common symptom of menopause is the "hot flash" which affects approximately 50 percent of menopausal women

a.   A hot flash generally occurs quite rapidly, involves a feeling of warmth over the upper part of the body, and is usually accompanied by perspiring, reddening, and perhaps dizziness

b.   Some women have hot flashes infrequently (once a week or less), while others may have them every few hours

c.   Hot flashes may last just a few seconds and be fairly mild, or they may last for 15 minutes or more

d.   Hot flashes tend to occur more often during sleep than during waking hours

e.   Hot flashes appear to be due to a malfunction of temperature control mechanisms in the hypothalamus. Estrogen deficiency contributes to this malfunction and generally disappears after a few years

9.   Other changes may occur during menopause, most of which are due to reduced estrogen

a.   The hair on the scalp and external genitalia may become thinner, the labia may lose their firmness, and the breast may lose some of their firmness and become smaller

b.   There is a tendency to gain weight, and the body contour may change, though some women lose weight

c.   Some muscles, particularly in the upper legs and arms, may lose some of their elasticity and strength

d.   Growth of hair on the upper lip and at the corners of the mouth may appear

e.   In approximately one of four women who are postmenopausal, the decrease in estrogen leads to osteoporosis

f.   Highlight 10.3: Osteoporosis

      1)   As a result of a drop in blood calcium level, bones become thin and brittle, with a consequent reduction in bone mass

      2)   Osteoporosis is a major factor leading to broken bones in later life

      3)   Women who are white, thin, and smokers, and those who do not get enough exercise or calcium are much more susceptible to osteoporosis. Also women who have had their ovaries surgically removed in middle age are also more susceptible to osteoporosis

      4)   One of the dangers of osteoporosis is fractures of the vertebra, which can lead to those affected becoming stooped from the waist up, with a height loss of 4 inches or more. Osteoporosis also often leads to hip fractures in elderly women

      5)   The most important preventive measures include exercising, getting more calcium, and avoiding smoking

      6)   It is recommended that women should get between 1,000 and 1,500 milligrams (or more) of calcium daily, beginning in their youth

      7)   Hormone-replacement therapy (HRT) is now seldom recommended for preventing osteoporosis after a study found that women suffered more strokes, heart attacks, blood clots, and higher rates of invasive breast cancer

F.   Psychological reactions

1.   If a woman is well adjusted emotionally before menopause, she is unlikely to experience psychological difficulties

2.   If a woman sees this change as simply being one of many life changes, she is not apt to have any adverse difficulties

3.   Some women believe menopause is a signal they are losing their physical attractiveness, which they further erroneously interpret as meaning an ending of their sex life

4.   If a woman viewed her main role in life as being a mother and raising children, they now may feel a sense of rolelessness

G. There is no clear-cut way to identify the exact time when menopause ends. Most authorities agree that the climacteric can be considered as ending when there has been no menstrual period for 1 year

H. Some doctors urge that some type of birth control be continued for 2 years after the last period in order to prevent pregnancy. "Change-of-life" babies are rare because conception, although possible, is unlikely to occur

I. Middle-aged pregnancies do present increased health risks, such as having a child with Down syndrome. The chances rise from 1 such birth in 2,000 among 25-year-old mothers to 1 in 40 for women over 45

VI. Male Climacteric

A. The term male climacteric is more accurate than male menopause, since the term menopause means the cessation of the menses. Men who have gone through male climacteric still retain the potential to reproduce

B. Sometime between the ages of 35 and 60 men reach an uncertain period in their lives that has been termed a "midlife crisis." A man going through male climacteric usually encounters some event that forces him to examine who he is and what he wants out of life

C. Biological factors

1. As a male grows older, his hair thins and begins to turn gray, he develops more wrinkles and tends to develop a "tire" around his waist. His physical energy gradually decreases. There are changes in his heart, his prostate, his sexual capacity, his chest size, his kidneys, his hearing, and his gastrointestinal tract

2. The production of testosterone gradually decreases, which stimulates activity such as hair growth and voice depth, and helps to prevent deterioration in the sex organs in later life

3. The decline in the number of sperm in an ejaculation and a reduction of testosterone present in the plasma and urine occur. The testes lose their earlier vigorous functioning and produce decreasing amounts of hormones

4. Older men generally take a longer time to achieve an erection. It also takes a longer time before an erection can be regained after an orgasm

D. Psychological factors

1. Many of the problems associated with male climacteric are due to a culture that worships youth

2. Some men fear aging, and also fear failure. A fear of death may be apparent as he realizes he has probably lived at least half of his life

3. Depression is often brought on when a man fears aging and recognizes that his sexual powers are waning. He also realizes that he will never achieve the successes that he envisioned for himself years earlier

4. A man at midlife is also apt to experience a growing dissatisfaction with his job

VII. Mid-Life Crisis: True or false?

A. The ease of panic with which a man faces his mid-years will depend on how he has accepted his faults and his strengths throughout life. Women go through similar psychological worries (for example, the empty-nest syndrome). With the right attitude, this time period can become a time of reappraisal, renewed commitment, and growth

B. Midlife is a time of transition and change. For some it is a crisis, but not for others. Men who undergo a midlife crisis are apt to have had adjustment problems for a long time

C. The life-events approach: Asserts that such events as divorce, remarriage, death of a spouse, and being terminated from employment involve varying degrees of stress, and therefore are likely to influence an individual's development

D. The contemporary life events approach: Asserts that how life events influence an individual's development depends not only on the life event itself, but also on a variety of other factors—mediating factors, the individual's skills at coping, and the sociohistorical context

VIII. Sexual Functioning in Middle Age

A. Sex in marriage

1. A close relationship exists between overall marital satisfaction and sexual satisfaction, particularly for men

2. Generally speaking, marriage partners report satisfaction with marital sex

3. Figure 10.2: Percentage Engaging in Sexual Intercourse

4. After the birth of their first child, couples report less sexual satisfaction on the average than childless couples

5. Married couples now use a greater variety of sexual techniques than couples in earlier generations

6. A study of 3,432 Americans by the University of Chicago's National Opinion Center found that the more active a person's sex life, the more likely it is that the person masturbates: 60 percent of the men and 40 percent of the women in the study had masturbated in the previous year; 25 percent of the men and 10 percent of the women reported they masturbated in the previous week. Sex therapists generally view masturbation to be a normal and useful sexual outlet

B. Extramarital sexual relationships

    1. Ten to 25 percent of husbands, and 5 to 15 percent of wives, reported having affairs

    2. For males, the frequency of extramarital coitus decreases with age, whereas with females there is a gradual increase up to around age 40

    3. Ethical Question 10.3: Do you believe an extramarital affair is sometimes justifiable? If you were married, and your spouse had an extramarital affair, would you seek a divorce?

    4. Surveys examining why a high percentage of married couples do not have extramarital affairs found that the most mentioned reason is that it would be a betrayal of trust in the love relationship

    5. The discovery of an extramarital affair may lead to a divorce. Sometimes the discovery is a crisis that forces a couple to recognize that problems exist in their marriage, and then seek to work on these to improve the marriage

    6. A few spouses react to an extramarital affair by gradually entering into a consensual extramarital relationship

    7. Mate swapping: Two or more couples get together and exchange partners, either retiring to a separate place to have sexual relations or having sex in the same room with various combinations of partners

    8. Ethical Question 10.4: Do you view mate swapping as being unethical?

C. Sex following divorce

    1. A great majority of formerly married persons become sexually active within a year after divorce

    2. Divorced people today are less concerned about hiding their sexual relationships from their children than were divorced people a generation ago

D. Sex in widowhood

    1. Widowers are more likely than widows to establish a new sexual relationship

    2. There is a greater cultural acceptance of older men dating younger women than vice versa

    3. Widows tend to receive more emotional support from friends and family and, therefore, may feel less need to form a new sexual relationship

E. Sex among the never-married

    1. Very little research has been conducted on the sexual lifestyles of never-marriage adults

    2. The attitudes of singles about their status vary widely

    3. Some contently become celibate. Others are highly involved in the singles scene. Some singles become involved in their careers or hobbies, and though they occasionally date, they do not want the restrictions of a marriage

    4. Some occasionally cohabit with the opposite sex

F. Celibacy

    1. A small minority of people choose to abstain from sexual intercourse

    2. Certain religious leaders are required to remain celibate

    3. Although some people find abstinence to be very difficult, others experience it as satisfying. Periods of celibacy may be important for self-exploration and recovery from broken romances

IX. **People Living with AIDS: A Population-at-Risk**

A. What causes AIDS?

    1. AIDS is caused by a type of virus called HIV (human immunodeficiency virus)

    2. Retroviruses: The reverse of the usual order of reproduction within the cells they infect

    3. The HIV virus invades cells involved in the body's normal process of protecting itself from disease and causes these cells to produce more of the virus

    4. HIV is a tiny delicate shred of genetic material. It prefers one type of cell—the T-helper cell in human blood. Outside of blood and other bodily fluids, the virus apparently dies

B. How is AIDS contracted?

    1. AIDS can be transmitted by sexual intercourse with someone who has HIV, by using hypodermic needles that were also used by someone who has the virus, and by receiving contaminated blood transfusions or other products derived from contaminated blood

    2. Babies may also contract the AIDS virus before or at birth from their infected mothers and through breast milk

    3. HIV has been isolated in semen, blood, vaginal secretions, saliva, tears, breast milk, and urine

4. Experts doubt whether there is enough of the virus present in tears and saliva to be transmitted in these fluids. Experts rule out casual kissing or swimming in pools as a means of contracting AIDS. Sneezing, coughing, crying, or handshakes also have not proven to be dangerous

5. Only the exchange of body fluids (for example, through anal, oral, or genital intercourse) permits infection

6. Few lesbians have contracted AIDS. Female-to-female transmission *is* possible, however, through vaginal secretions or blood

7. Women who use sperm for artificial insemination from an infected donor are also at risk of infection

8. When a person is exposed to the virus, the virus usually becomes inactive. To stay active it needs help which might include a history of infections with certain other viruses, general poor health, the abuse of certain recreational drugs, malnutrition, and genetic predisposition

9. Most people infected by HIV will eventually develop AIDS. The length of time between initial infection of HIV and the appearance of AIDS symptoms is called the incubation period. The average incubation period was estimated to be 7 to 11 years. The variation in this incubation period ranges from a few months (particularly for babies who are HIV-positive) to 20 years or more

10. High risk factors in contracting AIDS

    a. Having multiple sex partners without using safe sex practices

    b. Sharing intravenous needles

    c. Having anal intercourse with an infected person

    d. Having sex with prostitutes

11. Prevention

    a. Abstaining from sex

    b. Having sexual relations only with a faithful and uninfected partner

12. Although some people believe any contact with someone who is HIV-positive guarantees illness and death, such fears are not justified

13. The virus can be transmitted from the mother to the child in utero during the last weeks of pregnancy and at childbirth, as well as during breastfeeding

C. Diagnosis

    1. Tests detect the antibodies a person's immune system develops to fight the virus

    2. It generally takes 2 to 3 months before enough antibodies are produced to be detected after being infected with HIV

D. Origin of AIDS

    1. One theory postulates that the virus first developed in Africa in the 1970s. Some authorities have found that some species of monkeys have the AIDS virus, and that the virus may have been transmitted to humans through a monkey bite or perhaps through eating monkey meat

    2. Another theory is that some military research unit may have developed the virus as a way to exterminate large numbers of the population of "enemy" countries. Somehow, the virus may have escaped during experimental tests

    3. Another theory links the birth of AIDS to polio vaccine. This vaccine was made from weakened polio viruses grown in a culture of monkey kidney cells

    4. Some feel the advent of AIDS in the United States can be traced to a single individual, Gaetan Dugas (Canadian airline steward). Investigation of many of the men who began suffering from a rare form of skin cancer named Kaposi's sarcoma revealed that either they or someone with whom they had sexual relations had also been sexually involved with Dugas

E. The effects of HIV

    1. Persons with the AIDS virus are now classified as being either HIV-asymptomatic (without symptoms of AIDS) or HIV-symptomatic (with symptoms of the syndrome)

    2. HIV invades a group of white blood cells called T-helper cells, or T-4 cells. When HIV attacks T-4 helper cells, it stops them from producing immune cells, which fight off disease. Eventually the infected person's number of healthy T-4 cells is so reduced that infections cannot be fought off

    3. Initial symptoms include dry cough, abdominal discomfort, headaches, oral thrush, loss of appetite, fever, night sweats, weight loss, diarrhea, skin rashes, tiredness, swollen lymph nodes, and lack of resistance to infection

    4. Persons with AIDS become less capable of fighting off opportunistic diseases

        a. Kaposi's sarcoma: A rare form of cancer that accounts for many AIDS deaths

        b. Pneumocystic carinii pneumonia: A lung disease that is also a major cause of AIDS deaths

c. Other opportunistic infections include shingles, encephalitis, severe fungal infections that cause a type of meningitis, yeast infections of the throat and esophagus, and infections of the lungs, intestines, and central nervous system

d. Tuberculosis, a disease once nearly eradicated in the United States, has escalated rapidly in recent years due largely to the epidemic of HIV infection and AIDS

5. The Centers for Disease Control and Prevention has now broadened the definition of AIDS to anyone who is infected with HIV and has a helper T-cell count of 200 cells per cubic millimeter of blood or less, regardless of other symptoms that person may or may not have (normal helper T-cell counts in healthy people not infected with HIV range from 800 to 900 per cubic millimeter of blood)

6. AIDS-dementia complex: A deterioration of the brain caused by AIDS. This occurs gradually and includes the inability to concentrate, forgetfulness, inability to think quickly and efficiently, visuospatial problems, and slowed motor ability

7. Reactions of people who have been informed that they have HIV infection or AIDS typically progress through different stages: shock; denial; crisis; transition; fear; depression; panic; guilt; anger; self-pity; bargaining; search for meaning, and fighting, to a stage of sense of self, positive action, and acceptance

F. Treatment and prevention of AIDS

1. At this time there is no cure for AIDS. To prevent AIDS, people should abstain from activities and behaviors that put them at risk for contracting the disease

2. Ethical Question 10.5: If you knew someone who was HIV positive, would you be hesitant to interact with that person? If you had children, would you be hesitant to have them interact with children who are HIV positive?

3. Drugs for fighting AIDS

a. AZT (azidothymidine): Has been found to delay the progress of AIDS in some people (brand name is Retrovir)

b. DDI (didanosine): The Food and Drug Administration approved this drug for treatment of adults and children with advanced AIDS who cannot tolerate or are not helped by AZT

c. Protease inhibitors: Drugs which fight HIV by deactivating an enzyme which the virus needs to be able to infect human blood cells

The ABC approach to lower the risk of acquiring AIDS during sex

1) Abstinence or delay of sexual activity, especially for youth

2) Being faithful, especially for those in committed relationships

3) Condom use, for those who engage in risky behavior

G. Impacts of social and economic forces: AIDS discrimination and oppression

1. People who test positive to HIV or who have AIDS often are victimized by discrimination

2. Spotlight on Diversity 10.3: AIDS: A Global Epidemic

a. More than 40 million people worldwide are now infected with AIDS (most of them in the developing nations of Asia and Africa)

b. More than 25 million people have died of AIDS since 1981

c. In Sub-Saharan Africa an estimated 25 million people are living with HIV, and nearly 3 million people are infected each year. More than 12 million children have been orphaned by AIDS in this area

d. Over a quarter of the population of Botswana, Swaziland, and Zimbabwe are infected with the HIV virus, and several other countries have HIV infection rates of around 20 percent

d. In the next several years it is estimated that the number of AIDS deaths in Africa will exceed all of those killed in both World War I and World War II, and will be far greater than the 20 million people that were killed by the infamous bubonic plague that devastated Europe in the fourteenth century

f. Most of the infected people are poor and cannot afford the expensive new drugs that often hold the HIV infection at bay

3. Ethical Question 10.6: Do you believe the United States and other developed countries have a moral obligation to provide assistance to developing countries to empower them to more effectively prevent the transmission of HIV and to treat those who are HIV-positive?

H. Professional values and AIDS

1. Social work has traditionally supported and advocated for oppressed and disenfranchised groups in our country, and has an ethical obligation to combat the numerous injustices connected with AIDS

2. In June, 1998 the United States Supreme Court ruled that people infected by HIV (including those having AIDS) are covered by the 1990 Americans with Disabilities Act

I.   Social work roles: Empowering persons living with AIDS

1.   Services provided by social workers include testing and counseling people for HIV infection; educating the general public and high-risk groups to reduce risk behavior for HIV infection; and assisting HIV-affected persons to remain active and productive

2.   Services provided by social workers to persons with AIDS include information and education; crisis intervention; case management; facilitating groups; advocacy, and many others

3.   Empowerment: Involves feeling good about ourselves and feeling that we have some control and direction over our lives

   a.   Persons with AIDS should never be referred to as victims. Rather, they should be referred to as people *living with* AIDS, with an emphasis on living

   b.   Maintaining a meaningful quality of life is important for persons living with AIDS. Strengths should be emphasized

   c.   Social workers can help people with AIDS to reconnect with other people. Support systems are essential

   d.   Suicidal thoughts and plans should be discussed openly and the potential for suicide assessed. Sometimes medications to curb anxiety and depression are helpful

   e.   Support groups provide another excellent means of enhancing empowerment. Social workers can help to identify and emphasize coping skills to help empower people

   f.   Suggestions for helping social workers when dealing with AIDS-dementia

      1)   Use a variety of environmental aids

      2)   Structure can help people living with AIDS-dementia continue to function

      3)   The difference between initiation and motivation should be stressed

      4)   People who help take care of those with AIDS-dementia should be well educated about what the condition involves

      5)   Have a clinical assessment for depression performed and provide psychotherapy in those cases in which it would be useful

      6)   Legal contracts and estate planning should be initiated before the dementia progresses to the point that these are no longer feasible

4. Ethical Dilemma 10.1: Do You have a Duty to Inform a Person Who is at Risk of Acquiring HIV?

    a.   *Tarasoff v. Regents of the University of California* (1974)—Psychotherapists have a duty to warn a potential victim when the professional believes there is a clear danger, even if this means breaching confidentiality

    b.   NASW position—Each social welfare agency develop and disseminate policies and guides that will cover when and how the social worker has a duty to warn regarding danger to the public, including guidance about handling HIV-positive clients' information

5. Social work roles when working with persons with AIDS

    a.   Educator

    b.   Advocate

    c.   Mediator

    d.   Social broker

    e.   Enabler

6. Highlight 10.4: Persons Living with AIDS

X.   Summary

Experiential Exercises and Simulations

Six exercises are described. The first is regarding health. The second is a values-clarification exercise on extramarital relationships. The third is a values-clarification exercise on AIDS. The fourth is an AIDS policy quiz, and the fifth pertains to persons living with AIDS. The sixth provides you, and the other students, an opportunity to ask (and receive answers to) the questions that you have about AIDS, but were reluctant to ask.

Exercise 10.1: To Be Healthy or Not To Be Healthy: That Is The Question

A.   Brief description
Aspects of your own healthful behavior are examined. In small groups you will discuss how unhealthful behaviors are maintained and address the difficulties involved in changing poor health behaviors.

B.   Objectives
You will:
1.   Identify some of the life-style habits that contribute to good health and some that are hazardous to health.
2.   Examine the advantages and disadvantages of various poor health habits.
3.   Propose how the behaviors that are related to poor health might be changed.

4.   Assess the difficulties involved in changing poor health habits.
5.   Relate these difficulties to the difficulties clients have in changing their life-style habits.

C.   Procedure
1.   Review the material in the text that addresses life-style and good health.
2.   Place a check mark before any of the following poor health habits that you feel are a regular part of your life-style.

Do you:
_____ rarely if ever eat breakfast
_____ rarely if ever eat regular meals
_____ frequently snack between meals
_____ smoke cigarettes regularly
_____ rarely if ever participate in moderate physical exercise
_____ get less than 7 to 8 hours sleep each night on a regular basis
_____ drink alcoholic beverages frequently and in large quantities

---

3.   Break into groups of four to six persons. Discuss the following questions:
        a.   Why do people participate in each of the listed behaviors?
        b.   What are the advantages or benefits for them?
        c.   What are the disadvantages for people who participate in each of these behaviors?
        d.   How might people go about changing unhealthful habits and behaviors?
        e.   What are the difficulties involved in trying to change each of these behaviors?
4.   You will have approximately 20 minutes for discussion. All group members are encouraged to participate. You need not divulge any of your personal habits if you don't choose to.
5.   After 20 minutes all small groups join in a summary discussion. Choose a representative from your group to summarize information discussed by your group. Each group should report on one of the seven bad habits. Your representative should summarize the group's discussion concerning all five of the questions in relationship to one poor health habit.
6.   Summarize the difficulties in changing poor health habits. Relate this to how difficult it is for clients to change their life-style habits and behaviors.

Exercise 10.2: Extramarital Affairs

A.   Brief description
This is a values-clarification exercise about issues relating to extramarital sexual relationships.

B.   Objectives
You will:
1.   State your values about extramarital affairs and mate-swapping arrangements.

C.   Procedures
1.   Form subgroups of about five persons and seek a group consensus about the following questions (the questions should be written on the board).
   a.   Do you think extramarital affairs are ever justified (for example, when one's spouse is physically unable to have sex)? If yes, in what circumstances are they justified?
   b.   If you were married, would you want to participate in a mate-swapping arrangement? Why or why not?
2.   After you have arrived at answers, a representative from each subgroup shares the views of the subgroup.

Exercise 10.3: AIDS and Values Clarification

A.   Brief description
You will fill out a values-clarification questionnaire on issues related to AIDS.

B.   Objectives
You will:
1.   State your values about issues related to AIDS.
2.   Receive information that will enable you to be more objective about AIDS.

C.   Procedure
1.   On a separate sheet of paper anonymously mark your answers to the following questions:

AIDS QUESTIONNAIRE

1.   Would you be comfortable working in the same office with another employee that is known to be infected with HIV?
____ Yes   ____ Uncertain   ____ No

2.   If you were a parent, would you send your child to a school in which a classmate is known to be infected with HIV?
____ Yes   ____ Uncertain   ____ No

3.   Assume you are a social worker in a nursing home. Would you be comfortable working with residents who have AIDS?
____ Yes   ____ Uncertain   ____ No

4.   Would you feel comfortable in hugging someone who has AIDS?
____ Yes   ____ Uncertain   ____ No

5.   Do you believe that the peril of AIDS is a punishment from a higher being for homosexual behavior?
____ Yes   ____ Uncertain   ____ No

6.   If you were a parent, would you be comfortable seeing your children play with a neighborhood child who has tested positive for HIV?
____ Yes   ____ Uncertain   ____ No

7.   Would you feel comfortable living with a roommate who has HIV?
____ Yes   ____ Uncertain   ____ No

8. Do you believe AIDS can be transmitted by mosquito bites?
    ____ Yes   ____ Uncertain   ____ No

9. Would you hesitate to swim in a swimming pool in which someone else is swimming who you know has HIV?
    ____ Yes   ____ Uncertain   ____ No

10. Do you believe people should restrict their sexual activity to safe (safer) sex practices?
    ____ Yes   ____ Uncertain   ____ No

11. If you discovered that someone you were dating tested positive for HIV, would you seek to terminate the relationship?
    ____ Yes   ____ Uncertain   ____ No

12. If you tested positive for HIV, would you contemplate suicide?
    ____ Yes   ____ Uncertain   ____ No

13. If you discover your physician or dentist is HIV positive, would you discontinue receiving services from this physician or dentist?
    ____ Yes   ____ Uncertain   ____ No

2. While you are recording your answers, the instructor lists the 13 question numbers on the chalkboard according to the following format:

	Yes	Uncertain	No
1.			
2.			
3.			
etc.			

3. Anonymously hand in your answers. Volunteers will list the students' responses on the chalkboard.

4. The instructor reads each question out loud and then reviews student answers. The instructor may want to present objective information as these questions are being reviewed. Share your thoughts and feelings and ask any questions you have.

Exercise 10.4: AIDS Policy Quiz

A. Brief description
   You will take an AIDS POLICY QUIZ, which forces you to confront some of the complicated and difficult policy choices concerning AIDS.

B. Objectives
   You will:
   1. Recognize some of the disturbing and complex social policy issues involved in the AIDS epidemic.
   2. Examine your own values and opinions about AIDS and persons living with AIDS.
   3. Identify some of the issues facing persons with AIDS.

C. Procedure
    1.   The instructor reads aloud the following questions. As the instructor reads each question, you should read along in this Student Manual. After each question, the instructor asks for a show of hands indicating "yes" and "no" responses.

AIDS POLICY QUIZ

		Yes	No
1.	Should testing for HIV antibodies be made mandatory for hospital patients?	___	___
2.	Should the patient be required to pay for such testing?	___	___
3.	Should private insurance companies be required to pay for such testing for insured patients?	___	___
4.	If no other funding is available, should hospitals be required to pay for testing?	___	___
5.	Should physicians and other health care workers be required to treat HIV positive patients?	___	___
6.	If you had a cancerous brain tumor, would you want a physician to be forced to do the surgery against his or her will?	___	___
7.	Should all people be required to have HIV testing before they get married?	___	___
8.	Should all students at your college or university be required to get HIV testing as part of their entrance physical exam?	___	___
9.	Should students be required to pay for the testing as part of their fees?	___	___
10.	Should students who test positive be denied admission to your college or university?	___	___
11.	Should all HIV testing be anonymous?		
12.	Should positive results, along with the names of the persons who test positive, be reported to a state agency?	___	___
13.	Should these results and the names of persons testing positive be available to the public?	___	___
14.	Should people who test positive be required to submit the names of sexual partners to a state agency?	___	___
15.	Should these sexual partners be notified?	___	___
16.	Should these sexual partners be required to have HIV tests?	___	___

---

17. Should positive results for sexual partners, along with the names of these persons, be reported to a state agency? ___ ___

18. Should the sexual partners of persons testing positive be required to pay for their own testing? ___ ___

19. Should employers be given the names of persons testing HIV positive? ___ ___

20. Should employers be allowed to dismiss persons testing HIV positive? ___ ___

21. Should insurance companies be alerted when someone covered by their policies is tested HIV positive? ___ ___

22. Should insurance companies be allowed to drop coverage of persons testing HIV positive in view of the tremendous expenses likely to be incurred? ___ ___

23. Should insurance companies be given the option of denying coverage to those who have tested HIV positive just as they can deny coverage to those with prior conditions such as heart problems or back injuries? ___ ___

24. Should all insurance premiums be raised, taking money from all participants in the program, in order to cover the additional health expenses incurred by people with AIDS? ___ ___

25. Should people who know they test HIV positive and who have unprotected sexual relations or share IV drug needles with others without telling them that they're HIV positive be legally prosecuted? ___ ___

26. Should health care workers (such as physicians, dentists, and nurses) who test HIV positive be required to inform their patients of the results? ___ ___

27. Should all health care workers receive mandatory HIV testing? ___ ___

28. Should surgeons who test HIV positive be allowed to continue to perform surgery? ___ ___

29. If you discover your physician is HIV positive, would you discontinue receiving services from her or him? ___ ___

30. If you discover your dentist is HIV positive, would you discontinue receiving services from her or him? ___ ___

31. Assume you are a social worker for a client who reveals he just discovered he is HIV infected. The client refuses to inform his sexual partner of his HIV infection, for fear that the partner will end the sexual relationship. Would you break confidentiality and inform the sexual partner that the client has tested positive for HIV? ___ ___

32. Should free needles be distributed to intravenous drug users in an effort to reduce sharing of contaminated needles among IV drug users? ___ ___

33. Should condoms be distributed at no charge to adolescents at school in an effort to prevent the spread of HIV? ___ ___

34. Should surgeons be allowed to require that patients be tested for HIV prior to having surgery? ___ ___

35. Should all pregnant women be required to be tested for HIV, as there now is a treatment regimen (if started early in pregnancy) that reduces the chances that the child will be born infected with HIV? ___ ___

36. Should people testing HIV positive be required to wear an emblem in clear view at all times signifying that they are HIV positive? ___ ___

2. After you've finished the quiz, discuss your feelings and reactions to taking it. You might focus on the following questions:
   a. How did you feel about the questions on the quiz?
   b. Which questions and policy issues concerned you the most?
   c. What do you think are possible solutions to these questions?
   d. What will the costs be for solutions?
   e. What would you be willing to sacrifice financially to attain these solutions?
   f. As a social worker, how might you function as an advocate for persons with AIDS?

Exercise 10.5: Persons Living With AIDS

A. Brief description
Vignettes concerning persons living with AIDS are presented, and you are asked how a social worker might help these persons.

B. Objectives
You will:
1. Formulate plans to empower persons with AIDS in a variety of situations.
2. Propose laws and social policies that would be helpful to persons with AIDS.

C. Procedure
1. The instructor explains the concept of empowerment and then reads to you a series of vignettes that illustrate a variety of situations involving people with AIDS. Follow along in your Student Manual. After each vignette, answer the following questions:
   a. In what ways could empowerment take place?
   b. In what ways could a social worker be helpful in this situation?
   c. What laws and social policies would be helpful to the AIDS sufferers in their situations?

PERSONS WITH AIDS

A.   Mary has AIDS. She's 38 and used to have a lucrative law practice. She had been dating Norm and having intercourse with him for a year and a half before he told her that he was bisexual, that he had tested positively for HIV antibodies, and that she had better get tested, too. She dropped him immediately. The first time she had a test, the results were negative. However, the physician told her to come in once again in three months just to be sure. The second time she tested positive. Her rage was almost uncontrollable. It wasn't fair! She didn't "sleep around!" She didn't use intravenous drugs! Now Mary rarely leaves her apartment. She's terrified of being vulnerable to the multitude of diseases running rampant among all of the people out there. She knows that people are much more dangerous to her than she is to them. She desperately feels she needs to isolate herself. Her savings are dwindling. She can't afford to worry about the future.

B.   Harry has been diagnosed positive for HIV antibodies in his system. Harry is only 22 and likes to party. He can hardly remember how many women he's had sexual intercourse with over the past two years. He's tall and handsome. Women have found him attractive as long as he can remember. He's always left the birth control responsibility up to them. He thought they all must be on the pill anyway. He never thought of using a condom. He thought AIDS was a gay disease. He found out it is not. He doesn't know if or when he'll actually come down with AIDS, but he does know he's potentially contagious. He's very scared.

C.   Bill has AIDS. He's 28. He's been feeling rundown for the past few months and finally went to a doctor to have the purple splotches of skin on his back checked. It is Kaposi's sarcoma. He's been with Mike for almost three years, a relationship they are committed to as being permanent. However, before he met Mike, Bill dated a lot of men. He didn't think about such things as "safe sex" three years ago. He must've gotten AIDS from one of his many intimate partners. He wonders who. Now he's worried about Mike. They haven't been practicing "safe sex" either because they're monogamous. What if Mike has it, too? He truly loves Mike and prays that Mike is all right. Mike's going in for his test results tomorrow. Bill is very worried.

D.   Tonya has AIDS. She's 19. She comes from a very poor side of town where living is tough. It seemed everybody was "into" using intravenous drugs. "Shooting up" was easy. Heroin let her escape. Needles were expensive so she shared them with her friends. Now she's very sick. She's in the hospital for some kind of strange pneumonia. This time deep down she doesn't think she'll ever make it home again.

E.   Cheryl has AIDS. She's two months old. She got it from her mother who also has it. Cheryl's very weak now. She probably won't last very long.

2.   After soliciting your feedback for each vignette, the instructor summarizes what has been said.

Exercise 10.6 Everything You Wanted to Know About AIDS, But Were Reluctant to Ask

A.   Brief description
      You (and the other students) anonymously write down your questions related to AIDS, and the instructor answers them at the next class period.

B.   Objectives
      You will:
      1.   Receive answers to questions that you have about AIDS.
      2.   Better understand the importance of engaging in safe/safer sex practices.

C.   Procedure
      1.   At the end of a class period the instructor distributes note cards to you and the other students, and then asks you (and the other students) to write down questions that you have about AIDS. Students are instructed not to put their names on the cards so that anonymity may be retained.
      2.   At the next class period the instructor provides answers to the written questions, and also seeks to answer any additional questions that arise.

Chapter 11
Psychological Aspects of Young and Middle Adulthood

I. **A Perspective**

II. **Intimacy Versus Isolation**

   A. Intimacy: The capacity to experience an open, tender, supportive relationship with another person, without fear of losing one's own identity in the process of growing close

   1. Traditional socialization patterns in our society create different problems for males and females in the establishment of intimacy

   2. Boys are taught to be restrained in expressing their feelings and personal thoughts. Males are thus unprepared for intimate heterosexual relationships—which require that they express their feelings, be supportive rather than competitive, and have a commitment to continuing the relationship rather than piling up sexual trophies

   3. Traditionally, girls are socialized to be better prepared for the emotional demands of intimacy. They are socialized to express their feelings and personal thoughts and to be nurturant

   4. The women's movement has changed gender-role expectations and socialization practices for males and females

   B. Isolation: People who resist intimacy continually erect barriers between themselves and others. This may result from situational factors, or may result from diverging spheres of activity and interest

III. **Generativity Versus Stagnation**

   A. Generativity: Involves a concern and interest in establishing and guiding the next generation

   1. The crisis of generativity versus stagnation is perceived by a middle-aged adult to involve a commitment to improve the life conditions of future generations

   2. The achievement of generativity

   a. It involves a willingness to care about the people and the things that one has produced

   b. It involves a commitment to protecting and enhancing the conditions of one's society

       c.   It is important for the survival and development of any society

       d.   It involves having the adult members dedicating themselves to contributing their skills, resources, and creativity to improve the quality of life for the young

   3.   To some extent it is a reciprocity situation—when these adults were younger they were recipients of such services from other adults; now they are providers of such services

  B.   Stagnation: Indicates a lack of psychological movement or growth

   1.   Some adults are self-centered and seek to maximize their pleasures at the expense of others; such people are stagnated because they have difficulty in looking beyond their own needs or experiencing satisfaction in taking care of others

   2.   Having children does not necessarily guarantee generativity; adults who are unable to cope with raising children or with maintaining a household are likely to feel a sense of stagnation. Burnout has been identified as being one of the signs of stagnation

   3.   Different individuals manifest stagnation in different ways. A narcissistic individual who generally relates to others in terms of how others can serve him may be fairly happy until the physical and psychological consequences of aging begin to occur. Many of these individuals experience a conversion to finding other meanings in life

   4.   A depressed person is likely to perceive himself or herself as having insufficient resources to make any contribution to society

IV. Peck's Theories of Psychological Development

  A.   Four psychological advances critical to successful adjustment

   1.   Socializing versus sexualizing in human relationships: Peck suggests it is psychologically healthy for middle-aged adults to redefine the men and women in their lives so that they value them as individuals, friends, and companions, rather than primarily as sex objects

   2.   Valuing wisdom versus valuing physical powers: Peck viewed wisdom as the capacity to make wise choices in life. He suggests that well-adjusted middle-aged adults are aware that the wisdom they now have more than compensates for decreases in stamina, physical strength, and youthful attractiveness

   3.   Emotional flexibility versus emotional impoverishment: Emotional flexibility is the capacity to shift emotional investments from one activity to another, and from one person to another. Middle-aged adults are apt to experience breaking of relationships due to the deaths of friends, parents, and other relatives and the growing independence of children and their moving out of the home. Physical limitations may also necessitate a change in activities

4.   Mental flexibility versus mental rigidity: By middle age, most people have completed their formal years of education and have been sufficiently trained for their jobs or careers. They have also arrived at a set of beliefs about an afterlife, religion, politics, desirable forms of entertainment, and so on. Some middle-aged adults stop seeking new information and ideas and become set in their ways and closed to new ideas. Others are apt to continue to seek new experiences and be challenged by additional learning opportunities; such people are likely to view life as being meaningful, rewarding, and challenging

V.   Levinson's Theories of Life Structure, Life Eras, and Transitions for Men

A.   Life structure: The underlying pattern or design of a person's life at a given time

B.   A person's life structure shapes and is shaped by the person's interactions with the environment. Components include the people, institutions, things, places, and causes that a person decides are most important, as well as the dreams, values, and emotions that make them so. Other important aspects may include religion, racial identification, ethnic heritage, societal events, and hobbies

C.   Levinson asserts that people shape their life structures during the following four overlapping eras, and the transitional periods within some of the eras

    1.   Preadulthood: (Birth to age 22) The formative time from conception to the end of adolescence

    2.   Early adulthood: (Age 17 to age 45) The era in which people make choices that significantly influence their lives, and the era in which people display the greatest energy and experience the most stress

    3.   Middle adulthood: (age 40 to age 65) The era in which people tend to have reduced biological capacities but increased social responsibilities

    4.   Late adulthood: (age 60 and beyond) The final phase of life

D.   Table 11.1: Eras and Transitional Periods in Levinson's Theories of Adult Development (Males)

E.   Transitional periods

    1.   Early adult transition (ages 17 to 22): During this transition a person moves out of his or her parents' home and becomes more financially and emotionally independent

    2.   Entry life structure for early adulthood (ages 22 to 28): During this phase a young person becomes an adult and builds the entry life structure for early adulthood

        a.   Dream feature: Men often have a dream of their future, which is usually viewed in terms of a career

b.	Mentor feature: A mentor is older (usually by about 8 to 15 years). The relationship is a friendship with adult equality, but the mentor also performs the fatherly tasks of teaching, caring, criticizing, helping, and offering constructive suggestions in both career and personal matters

c.	Ethical Question 11.1: Our dream of our future often becomes a self-fulfilling prophecy. What is your dream of your future?

3.	Age-30 transition (ages 28 to 33): During this phase men may review whether the commitments made during the previous decade were premature, or they may consider making strong commitments for the first time

4.	Culminating life structure for early adulthood (ages 33 to 40): The person makes a concerted effort to realize youthful dreams. The apprenticeship is over. During this phase men make deeper commitments to family, work, and other important aspects of their lives

a.	Becoming one's own man (BOOM): During this phase a man often becomes independent of his mentor and may be at odds with his wife, boss, children, friends, lover, or coworkers

b.	During BOOM a man chafes under the authority of those who have power and influence over him, and seeks to break away and speak with his own voice

5.	Midlife transition (ages 40 to 45): During this transition a person is focused on completing the work of early adulthood while learning the ropes of middle adulthood

a.	People in this stage undergo a midlife reappraisal that often involves emotional turmoil. Previous values are reviewed

b.	People at this age need to become more compassionate, more reflective and judicious, less tyrannized by inner conflicts and external demands, and more genuinely loving of themselves and others

6.	Entry life structure for middle adulthood (ages 45 to 50): During this transition a man in his mid-40s begins a life structure that may involve new choices. The most successful people often find middle age to be the most gratifying and creative time of life as they utilize opportunities that arise to allow new facets of their personalities to flower

7.	Age 50 transition (ages 50 to 55): This transition is likely to be an especially difficult time for men whose midlife transition has been relatively smooth. Most men experience a moderate crisis at this time

8.	Culminating life structure for middle adulthood (ages 55 to 60): This phase is generally a stable transition in which men finish the framework of their life structure for middle adulthood

9.	Late adult transition (ages 60 to 65): This is a major transitional turning point, as it is a time for ending middle age and preparing for late adulthood

F.   Levinson primarily studied middle-aged men; as a result, he has only limited and speculative information of the transitions and adjustments that occur in late adulthood

G.   Spotlight on Diversity 11.1: Application of Levinson's Theories to Women: An Evaluation

1.   The women interviewed were from 28 to 53 years old, primarily white, and most were employed. The studies had a mix of married and unmarried respondents, with and without children

2.   These studies tend to support the idea that women undergo similar kinds of age-linked changes as men, but found some of the following differences

     a.   The mentor: Women were substantially less likely to have a mentor. If these women's patterns are typical, many women may be hampered in their career for lack of a mentor

     b.   The love relationship: All the respondents sought a "special man," but these women mostly saw themselves as supporting their special man's dreams, rather than wanting a special man who would support them in achieving *their* goals

     c.   The dream: Most respondents had dreams that were more vague, more complex, more tentative and temporary, and less career-oriented than those of men. Most women's dreams were split between achievement and relationships. While men tend to "find themselves" by separating from their families of origin and pursuing their own interests, women tend to develop their identity through the responsibilities and attachments of relationships

3.   Levinson and Levinson completed a study designed to focus on three subgroups: (1) 15 homemakers drawn randomly from the city directory of New Haven, CT; (2) 15 women who had careers in major corporate financial organizations in New York City; and (3) 15 women faculty members in colleges and universities. The latter two groups were struggling to combine career and family

     a.   A major finding was that women, similar to men, go through a predictable, age-linked series of developmental stages

     b.   A number of profound differences were found between how men and women develop throughout their lives

          1)   Gender splitting: The rigid division between male and female, including differences in traditional gender role expectations, and the splitting of the personal qualities identified as "feminine" and "masculine." (Levinson notes that the evolution of society in the past few centuries has been gradually reducing the splitting)

2)   The women in the homemaker sample sought, at a young age, to lead predominantly traditional, family-centered lives. They entered marriage with the belief that their primary role was to continue the traditional family, with the wife's role as homemaker, and the husband's role as being the provider

    a)   Only 1 homemaker of the 15 by midlife was not working outside the home

    b)   Fifty percent were legally divorced, and most of the rest were psychologically divorced

    c)   Many of these women, as they developed in their 30s and 40s, became more independent and sought to exist on more equal terms with men

    d)   Anti-traditional figure: A more modern lifestyle

    e)   Levinson concludes that a traditional marriage is no longer viable in our culture

c.   The study reveals considerable hardships for both the homemakers and the "career women"—anguish, stressful and traumatic experiences, marital difficulties, problems in raising their children, problems at work, and difficulties in personal relationships

d.   The difficulties and anguish reported by these female subjects appear more pronounced than those reported by Levinson in his earlier study of men

VI.   Maslow's Hierarchy of Needs

A.   Maslow viewed humans as having tremendous potential for personal development. He believed it was human nature for people to seek to know more about themselves and to strive to develop their capacities to the fullest

B.   Maslow believed that very few people fully attain a state of self-actualization. Rather, he saw most people as being in a constant state of striving to satisfy their needs

C.   Maslow's hierarchy of needs that motivate human behavior

1.   Physiological: Food, water, oxygen, rest, and so on

2.   Safety: Security; stability; and freedom from fear, anxiety, threats, and chaos. A social structure of laws and limits assists in meeting these needs

3.   Belongingness and love: Intimacy and affection provided by friends, family, and lover

4.   Self-actualization: The sense that one is fulfilling one's potential and is doing what one is suited for and capable of. This need results in efforts to create and to learn

D. Figure 11.1: Maslow's Hierarchy of Needs

E. Applied to social work practice, Maslow's theory indicates that social workers must first help clients meet basic needs. Once they are met, higher level needs can be dealt with

F. Striving for self-actualization is seen as a universal process that can be observed at nearly all ages. However, it is likely that there is some progression among age groups

VII. Emotional Intelligence

A. Emotional intelligence (EI): The ability to recognize and deal with one's own feelings as well as the feelings of others, and includes qualities such as empathy, motivation, social competence, optimism, and conscientiousness

B. A study found that those who rose to the top of the corporate ladder tended to score highest on EI

C. Competencies most closely associated with effective work performance

1. Self-awareness (accurate self-assessment, emotional self-awareness, and self-confidence)

2. Self-management (trustworthiness, achievement drive, initiative, adaptability, and self-control)

3. Social awareness (empathy, organizational awareness, and service orientation)

4. Relationship management (exerting influence, conflict management, leadership, communication, building bonds, teamwork and collaboration, being a catalyst for change, and developing others)

VIII. Mezzo System Interactions: Nonverbal Communication

A. Sigmund Freud noted that "he that has eyes to see and ears to hear may convince himself that no mortal can keep a secret. If his lips are silent, he chatters with his finger tips; betrayal oozes out of him at every pore"

B. Nonverbal cues (such as sweating, stammering, blushing, and frowning) convey information about feelings that we desire to hide. Because feelings stem from thoughts, nonverbal cues also transmit information about what people are thinking

C. The functions of nonverbal communication

1. Nonverbal messages may *repeat* what is said verbally

2. Nonverbal messages may *substitute* for verbal ones

3. Nonverbal messages may *accent* verbal messages

4. Nonverbal messages may serve to *regulate* verbal messages

5. Nonverbal messages may *contradict* verbal messages

D. Although nonverbal messages can be revealing, they can also be unintentionally misleading

E. The identical nonverbal behavior may be interpreted differently depending on the cultural/ethnic/racial background of the observer

F. Highlight 11.1: Nonverbal Behavior Among Poker Players

G. Examples of nonverbal communication

    1. Posture

        a. Watching the degree of tenseness has been found to be a way of detecting status differences

        b. Teachers and public speakers often watch the posture of listeners to gauge how the presentation is going—if the audience is slumping in their chairs it is a cue that the presentation is beginning to bomb

    2. Body orientation

        a. Body orientation is the extent to which we face toward or away from someone with our head, body, and feet

        b. The phrase "turning your back" on someone concisely summarizes the message that is sent when you turn away from someone

    3. Gestures

        a. People who are nervous tend to fidget

        b. When people want to express friendship or attraction, they tend to move closer

        c. Preening behavior: Includes rearranging one's clothing, combing or stroking one's hair, and glancing in a mirror. Conducting this research only on women may indicate a sexist bias

        d. Many people are unaware of the number of gestures they use, and then (if videotaped) are surprised to view the extent to which they communicate with gestures

4. Touching

   a. In the nineteenth century high proportions of children died in some orphanages and other child-care institutions. The deaths were not found to be due to poor nutrition or inadequate medical care, but instead to lack of physical contact with parents or nurses

   b. From this research came the practice of nurturing children in institutions—picking the baby up, holding her close, playing with her, and carrying her around several times a day. With this physical contact the infant mortality rate dropped sharply in institutions

   c. Adults also need physical contact. Unfortunately, we have been socialized to refrain from touching, except in sexual contacts

   d. A number of therapists have noted that communication and human relationships would be vastly improved if people reached out and touched others more

5. Clothing

   a. Clothes give messages about our occupations, personality, interests, sexuality, groups we identify with, social philosophies, religious beliefs, status, values, mood, age, nationality, and personal attitudes

   b. A problem often encountered by women is that they lack a socially dictated business uniform

   c. Clothes also affect our self-image. When we're feeling at a low tide, dressing up will make us feel better about ourselves and raise our spirits

6. Personal space

   a. We use distances to guide us in setting the type of interactions we want to have with others. Following are the four distances or zones that we set in our daily interactions

      1) Intimate zone: Begins with skin surface and goes out about 18 inches. We generally let only people we are emotionally very close to enter this boundary, and then mostly in private situations. When someone moves into this intimate zone without our wanting them to, we feel invaded and threatened

      2) Personal zone: Ranges from about 18 inches to approximately 4 feet. This is the distance at which couples stand in public. The far range (from about 2 ½ to 4 feet) is the distance in which we convey that we are seeking to keep the other person at arm's length. Interactions at this distance are much less personal than the ones that occur at a closer distance

3)   Social zone: Ranges from about 4 feet to about 12 feet. Business communications are frequently exchanged in this zone. The closer part of the zone is the distance at which people who work together usually converse. The 7-to-12-foot range is the distance for more impersonal and formal situations

4)   Public zone: Runs outward from 12 feet. Teachers and public speakers often use a distance of 12 to 18 feet from their audience. In the farther distances of this zone two-way communication is very difficult

H.   Territoriality: Behavior characterized by identification with an area in such a way as to indicate ownership and defense of this territory against those who may invade it

     1.   Students tend in each class to select a certain seat to sit in. If someone else should happen to sit in your chosen seat, do you feel your territory is being invaded?

     2.   What we acquire as property is a strong indicator of our interests and values

I.   Facial expressions

     1.   Facial expressions are often mirrors that reflect our thoughts and feelings

     2.   Six basic emotions that facial expressions reflect: fear, surprise, anger, happiness, disgust, and sadness

     3.   Because people are generally aware that their facial expressions reflect what they are feeling and thinking, they may seek to mask their facial expressions for a variety of reasons

J.   Voice

     1.   The tone of one's voice often has more influence than the actual words spoken

     2.   Paralanguage: Deals with how something is said and not with what is said

K.   Physical appearance

     1.   Research shows that outer beauty (physical attractiveness) plays an influential role in determining responses for a broad range of interpersonal interactions

     2.   Physically attractive people have been found to exceed less attractive people on a wide range of socially desirable evaluations

     3.   Less attractive people are at a disadvantage from early childhood on. Teachers interact less (and less positively) with unattractive children

     4.   Ethical Question 11.2: Do you sometimes discriminate against people who are less attractive? For example, do you seek to date only people who are physically attractive?

5. Unattractive men who are seen with attractive women are judged higher in a number of areas than are attractive men who are seen with attractive partners

6. Being physically attractive does *not* mean that a person will *be* more intelligent, more successful, better adjusted, and happier than less attractive people. Attractiveness *initially* opens more opportunities to be successful

7. Both overweight people and very thin people have been found to be discriminated against when seeking to obtain jobs, buy life insurance, adopt children, and be accepted into college

L. The environment

1. The attractiveness of a room shapes the kind of communication that takes place and also influences the happiness and energy of people working in it. Workers do a better job and generally feel better in an attractive environment

2. The color of rooms apparently affects mood and productivity

   a. The most arousing colors are, in order, red, orange, yellow, violet, blue and green

   b. The colors thought to have a calming effect are pink, baby blue, and peach

   c. Some prison and jail administrators are now painting cells in pastel colors, hoping that it will have a calming and relaxing effect on inmates

3. Businesses have found that they can control the rate of customer turnover by environmental design

4. Casino owners in Las Vegas build their facilities without windows or clocks so that customers will be less aware of how long they have been gambling

5. The shape and design of buildings affect interaction in many ways

   a. A round table suggests the officeholder is seeking to have the communication be seen as equalitarian, whereas a rectangular table suggests the communication should recognize status and power differentials

   b. A classroom in which the chairs are in a circle suggests the instructor wants to create an informal, discussion atmosphere. A classroom with the chairs in rows suggests the instructor wants to create a formal, lecture-type atmosphere

IX. Control Theory

A. All our behavior is our constant attempt to reduce the difference between what we want (the pictures in our heads) and what we have (the way we see situations in the world)

B. Glasser asserts that we begin to create our picture albums at an early age and that we spend our whole lives enlarging these albums. Pictures mean perceptions

C. Pictures in our albums do not have to be rational. To change a picture, we have to replace it with another that will at least reasonably satisfy the need in question. People who are unable to replace a picture may endure a lifetime of misery

D. Whenever there is a difference between the picture we now see and the picture we want, a signal is generated by this difference, which starts us behaving in a way to obtain the picture we want

E. Axioms of choice theory

    1. The only behavior we can control is our own

    2. All we can give or get from other people is information

    3. All we can do from birth to death is behave

    4. All long-lasting psychological problems are relationship problems

    5. Human brains are very creative

        a. Unhappiness is the force that inspires the creativity inherent in the brain to be a partial cause of symptoms described in the *DSM-IV*

        b. Highlight 11.2: Our Thoughts Impact our Physiological Functioning: Healing Thoughts Versus Disease-Facilitating Thoughts

    6. Barring untreatable physical illnesses or severe poverty, unsatisfying relationships are the primary source of crimes, addictions, and emotional and behavioral disorders

    7. It is a serious mistake (and irrational to expect positive results) to seek to control others by nagging, preaching, punishing, or threatening to punish them

        a. Ethical Question 11.3: Is it unethical to seek to control others by nagging, preaching or punishing them? Do parents sometimes need to nag, preach and punish their children?

    8. The unsatisfying (problematic) relationship is always a current one

    9. The solving circle is a good strategy for two people who know choice theory to use in redefining their freedom and improving their relationship

10. Painful events that happened in the past greatly influence what we are today, but dwelling on the painful past can contribute little or nothing to what we need to do now—which is to improve an important, present relationship

11. It is not necessary to know our past before we can deal with the present

12. We can satisfy our basic needs only by satisfying one or more pictures in our quality world

13. When we have difficulty getting along with other people, we usually make the mistake of choosing to employ external control psychology, attempting to coerce or control others by nagging, preaching, moralizing, criticizing, or by using put-down messages

14. Since relationships are central to human happiness, improving our emotional and physical well-being involves exploring how we relate to others

15. It is therapeutic to view our total behavior in terms of verbs

16. All total behavior is chosen, but we have direct control over only the acting and thinking components

17. Whenever you feel as if you don't have the freedom you want in a relationship, it is because you, your partner, or both of you are unwilling to accept that you can only control your own behavior

18. People choose to play the mentally ill roles described in the *DSM-IV*

19. Psychotropic drugs prescribed by psychiatrists and doctors may make you feel better temporarily

20. A mentally healthy person enjoys being with most of the people he or she knows—especially the important people, such as family and friends

X. Intuition

A. The cerebrum (the area of conscious mental processes of the brain) is composed of two cerebral hemispheres. (It should be noted that research on the location of different functions is somewhat speculative and, further, that there is considerable overlap in functions across the two hemispheres)

    1. The right hemisphere has been called the *right brain*

        a. Movements of the left side of the body are under the control of the right hemisphere

        b. The right hemisphere may be more centrally involved in creativity, musical abilities, intuition, and feelings

2. The left hemisphere has been called the *left brain*

    a. Movements of the right side of the body are controlled by the left hemisphere

    b. The left hemisphere is more centrally involved in rational thought processes, logic, deduction, and mathematical skills

B. Importance of intuition

    1. A strong body/personality structure is created by trusting your intuition and learning to follow its direction

    2. Most of us have been taught from childhood not to trust our feelings, not to express ourselves truthfully and honestly, not to recognize that at the core of our being lies a loving, powerful, and creative nature

    3. Through reeducating ourselves to listen to and trust our intuition, Gawain asserts that we will gain integrity, creativity, and wholeness

    4. Human intuition is similar (and perhaps identical) to the instinct in geese that guides them to fly south in fall and north in spring

XI. **Chemical Substance Use and Abuse**

A. Drug abuse: The regular or excessive use of a drug when, as defined by a group, the consequences endanger relationships with other people, are detrimental to a person's health, or jeopardize society itself (also referred to as chemical substance abuse)

B. Legal drugs, such as alcohol and tobacco, prescription drugs, and illegal drugs, are frequently abused

C. Specific drugs—What they are and what they do

    1. Highlight 11.3: Drugs of Abuse: Facts and Effects

    2. Depressant drugs

        a. Alcohol: A colorless liquid found in beer, wine, brandy, whiskey, vodka, rum, and other intoxicating beverages. The type of alcohol found in beverages is ethyl alcohol; it is also called grain alcohol because most of it is made from fermenting grain

b.   Who drinks

1)   American adults consume an average of 21.7 gallons of beer, 2.0 gallons of wine, and 1.3 gallons of distilled spirits a year

2)   Biological factors: Close relatives of an alcoholic are four times more likely to become alcoholics themselves, and this tendency holds true even for children who were adopted away from their biological families at birth and raised in a nonalcoholic family

a)   Some Asian populations have highly negative reactions to alcohol

b)   Native Americans in the Western Hemisphere have a lower tolerance for alcohol than other groups, which places them at a greater risk for alcoholism

3)   Socioeconomic factors: Drinking is more frequent among younger men who are positioned at higher socioeconomic levels, and less frequent among older women at lower levels

4)   Gender: Men are more likely to use and abuse alcohol than are women. The recent dramatic increase in alcoholism among adult women could be that cultural taboos against heavy drinking among women have weakened, as well as the changing roles of women in our society

5)   Age: Older people are less likely to drink than younger people. Heavy drinking is most common at ages 21 to 30 for men and ages 31 to 50 for women

6)   Religion: Nonchurchgoers drink more than regular churchgoers. Heavy drinking is more common among Episcopalians and Catholics, while conservative and fundamentalist Protestants are more often nondrinkers or light drinkers. Fewer Jews are heavy drinkers

7)   Urban-rural residence: Urban residents are more likely to drink than rural residents.

8)   Recently, there has been a marked decline in drinking, especially of hard liquor, in many segments of the American public; however, the rates remain extremely high

c.   What alcohol does

    1)   It acts as a depressant to the central nervous system, because it reduces functional activity of this system. It slows down mental activity, reasoning ability, speech ability, and muscle reactions

    2)   Five drinks (with each drink being 1 ounce of 86-proof alcohol, or 12 ounces of beer, or 3 ounces of wine) in 2 hours for a 120-pound person will result in a blood alcohol concentration of one-tenth of a percent, which is the legal criterion in most states for being intoxicated

    3)   Alcoholics have a life expectancy that is 10 to 12 years less than that of nonalcoholics. However, for some as yet unknown reason, the life expectancy for light-to-moderate drinkers exceeds that for nondrinkers

    4)   Cirrhosis of the liver occurs when alcohol destroys liver cells and replaces the cells with scar tissue. This is the eighth most frequent cause of death in the United States

    5)   Alcohol can seriously affect sexual response

d.   Combining alcohol with other drugs

    1)   Synergistic interaction—Drugs interact to produce an effect much greater than either would cause alone

    2)   Antagonistic response—One drug negates the effects of the other

e.   Barbiturates

    1)   Barbiturates were first synthesized in the early 1900s, and there are now more than 2,500 different barbiturates

    2)   Commonly used to relieve insomnia and anxiety. Also used to treat epilepsy and high blood pressure, and to relax patients before or after surgery

    3)   Prolonged heavy use can cause physical dependence, with withdrawal symptoms similar to those of heroin addiction. Many authorities believe barbiturate addiction is more dangerous than heroin addiction, and it is considered to be more resistant to treatment than heroin addiction

    4)   Overdose may cause convulsions, coma, poisoning, and sometimes death. Accidental deaths due to excessive doses are frequent

    5)   Barbiturates are the number one drug used for suicide

f. Tranquilizers

    1) Common brand names are Librium, Miltown, Serax, Tranxene, and Valium

    2) Users have moderate potential of becoming physically and psychologically dependent

    3) Withdrawal symptoms are similar to those from alcohol and barbiturates

    4) Highlight 11.4: Date-Rape Drugs

        a) In the mid-1990s Rohypnol became known as the date-rape drug. It often causes blackouts, with complete loss of memory. Female victims who were slipped the drug and then raped often cannot remember any details of the crimes

        b) Rohypnol is related to Valium, but ten times stronger. It is legally available in more than 60 countries for severe insomnia. It is illegal in the United States, but widely used and abused. Much of it is smuggled in from Mexico and Colombia

        c) Gamma hydroxy butyrate (GHB) is another drug that is increasingly being used as a date-rape drug. It is a central nervous system depressant that is approved as an anesthetic in some countries. It is made from a mixture of chemicals normally used for cleaning. Just one gram of GHB provides an intoxicating experience equivalent to 26 ounces of whisky

g. Quaalude

    1) Methaqualone (better known by its patent name Quaalude) has effects similar to barbiturates and alcohol, although it is chemically different. It has a reputation as a love drug, as users believe it makes them more eager for sex and enhances sexual pleasure

    2) Users can become both physically and psychologically dependent on Quaalude. Withdrawal symptoms are severe and unpleasant

3.   Stimulants

   a.   Caffeine

       1)   Caffeine is a stimulant to the central nervous system

       2)   Some authorities assert that our approach to caffeine should serve as a model for the way we react to other illegal drugs that they feel are no more harmful than caffeine

   b.   Ethical Question 11.4: Is it unethical to drink excessively and to abuse other drugs?

   c.   Amphetamines

       1)   Amphetamines are synthetic drugs, similar to adrenalin (a hormone from the adrenal gland that stimulates the central nervous system)

       2)   Users feel euphoric, stronger, and have an increased capacity to concentrate and to express themselves verbally

       3)   The amphetamine high is often followed by mental depression and fatigue. Continued use leads to psychological dependence. It is unclear whether amphetamines are physically addictive, as the withdrawal symptoms are uncharacteristic of withdrawal from other drugs

       4)   One of the legal uses of certain amphetamines is in the treatment of hyperactivity in children. Ritalin is an example that has a calming and soothing effect on hyperactive children—the exact opposite effect occurs when Ritalin is taken by adults

       5)   Methamphetamine hydrochloride, known on the street at "meth" or "ice." In liquid form it is often referred to as "speed." As a last resort, methamphetamine hydrochloride (Desoxyn) is legally used to treat obesity as one component of a weight-reduction regimen. A serious side effect is that the user's appetite returns with greater intensity after withdrawal from the drug

   d.   Cocaine and crack

       1)   Cocaine is obtained from the leaves of the South American coca plant. It is rapidly replacing other illegal drugs in popularity

       2)   Although legally classified as a narcotic, it is in fact not related to the opiates from which narcotic drugs are derived

       3)   Larger doses, or extended use, may result in hallucinations and delusions

4) Formication: An effect of cocaine abuse which produces the illusion that ants, snakes, or bugs are crawling on or into the skin

5) Physical dependence on cocaine is considered to be a low to medium risk. However, the drug appears to be psychologically habituating

6) A few people who overdose may die if their breathing and heart functions become too depressed

7) Crack, also called "rock," is obtained from cocaine by separation of the adulterants from the cocaine by mixing it with water and ammonium hydroxide. The water is then removed from the cocaine base by means of a fast drying solvent, usually ether. The resultant mixture resembles large crystals, similar to rock sugar

8) Crack is highly addictive. The "rush" is more immediate than cocaine, and the drug gives an intensified high

9) An overdose is more common when crack is injected than when it is smoked

10) Highlight 11.5: Babies Who are Crack Exposed

a) Cocaine causes blood vessels in a pregnant woman to constrict, thus reducing the vital flow of oxygen and other nutrients to the fetus

b) Only the most intensive care after birth will give these babies a fighting chance to have a "normal" life

c) Cocaine exposure affects brain chemistry as well. The drug alters the actions of neurotransmitters, the messengers that travel between nerve cells and help control a person's mood and responsiveness

d) A few crack exposed babies have severe physical deformities from which they will never recover

e) Crack exposed children often ring up huge bills for medical treatment and other care

f) The best way to rescue a crack child is to rescue the mother as well

e. Amyl nitrate and butyl nitrate

    1) Amyl nitrate is prescribed for patients who risk certain forms of heart failure

    2) The drug is supposedly sold only by prescription, but the illicit drug market distributes it

    3) Butyl nitrate is legally available in some states without a prescription and has an effect similar to amyl nitrate's. Trade names under which it is sold are Rush and Locker Room. It is available at some sexual aid and novelty stores

    4) Both these drugs have been used as aphrodisiacs and as stimulants while dancing

4. Narcotics

a. The most commonly used narcotic drugs in the United States are the opiates (such as opium, heroin, and morphine)

b. The term *narcotic* means sleep-inducing. In actuality, drugs classified as narcotics are more accurately called *analgesics*, or painkillers. The principal effect produced by narcotic drugs is a feeling of euphoria

c. The opiates are all derived from the opium poppy, which grows in Turkey, Southeast Asia, and Colombia

d. Opium is the dried form of a milky substance that oozes from the seed pods after the petals fall from the flowers. It has been used for centuries

e. Morphine is the main active ingredient of opium. It was first identified early in the 1800s, and has been used extensively as a painkiller

f. Heroin was first synthesized from morphine in 1874. It was once thought to be a cure for morphine addiction, but later was also found to be addictive. Heroin is a more potent drug than morphine

g. "Mainlining" (injecting into a muscle or into a vein) maximizes the drugs' effects. Users rapidly develop a tolerance

h. The withdrawal process is very unpleasant. Addiction to opiates is extremely difficult to break

i. Heroin is the most widely abused opiate. Contrary to popular belief, most heroin users take the drug infrequently and do not, as a rule, become addicted

j. Heroin was first discovered in the late 1880s and was used as a painkiller. A number of people became addicted, and in the early 1900s laws were passed to prohibit its sale, possession, and distribution

k.   Heroin abuse continues to be regarded by some Americans as our most serious drug problem. This does not appear warranted because only a tiny fraction of the U.S. population has ever tried heroin

l.   Heroin users are thought to be "dope fiends" who commit many violent crimes; however, addicts are unlikely to commit violent crimes such as rape or aggravated assault. They are more apt to commit crimes against property in order to support their habit

m.   Unsanitary injections of heroin may cause hepatitis and communal use of needles can spread AIDS

n.   Because the price of illicit narcotic drugs is so high, organized crime has made huge profits in the smuggling and distribution of these drugs

5.   Hallucinogens

a.   Hallucinogens were popular as psychedelic drugs in the late 1960s. These drugs distort the user's perceptions, creating hallucinations consisting of sensory impressions of "sights and sounds" that do not exist

b.   The six hallucinogens most commonly used in this country are mescaline (peyote), psilocybin, psilocin, LSD, PCP, and ecstasy. All are taken orally

c.   Peyote is derived from a cactus plant. Mescaline is the synthetic form of peyote

d.   Psilocybin and psilocin are found in approximately 90 different species of mushrooms. They have been called "magic mushrooms"

e.   Both peyote and psilocybin have had a long history of use by certain Native-American tribes. Members of the Native American Church, a religious organization, have won the legal right to use peyote on ceremonial occasions

f.   One of the most popular hallucinogen is LSD (lysergic acid diethylamide). It is a synthetic material derived from a fungus (ergot) that grows on rye and other plants. It is one of the most potent drugs known; a single ounce will make up to 300,000 doses

g.   Users of LSD become highly suggestible and easily manipulated. Some users have developed severe emotional disturbances that resulted in long-term hospitalization. Flashbacks sometimes occur after the actual drug experience; they may happen at any time and place, with no advance warning

h.   There is no evidence of physical or psychological dependence on LSD among users

i. Phencyclidine (better known as PCP) was developed in the 1950s as an anesthetic. This was soon terminated because patients displayed symptoms of severe emotional disturbance after receiving the drug

j. PCP is used legally today to tranquilize elephants and monkeys, as they apparently do not have the adverse side effects

k. Ecstasy was developed and patented in the early 1900s as a chemical forerunner in the synthesis of pharmaceuticals. Chemically, ecstasy is similar to a stimulant, amphetamine, and to a hallucinogen, mescaline, as it can produce both stimulant and psychedelic effects

l. Chronic use of ecstasy can produce long-lasting, perhaps permanent, damage to the neurons that release serotonin, and consequent memory impairment

6. Tobacco

a. The use of tobacco has now become recognized as one of the most damaging drug habits in the United States

b. Tobacco is the number-one killer drug. It contributes to far more deaths than all other drugs combined. It is estimated to contribute to more than 400,000 deaths per year in the United States

c. In 1988, the then surgeon general of the United States, C. Everett Koop, declared that tobacco is as addictive as heroin or cocaine

d. Tobacco is highly habit-forming. Nicotine is the primary drug in tobacco

e. At the same time that the government is widely publicizing the hazards of drugs, the Department of Agriculture is subsidizing tobacco farmers

f. The biggest civil settlement in the United States history—tobacco companies agreed in 1998 to pay over $240 billion to 50 states to settle claims against the industry for health-care costs blamed on tobacco-related illnesses

7. Marijuana

a. Marijuana, or "grass" or "pot," comes from a variety of the hemp plant, *Cannabis sativa*. The main use of the plant now, however, centers on its dried leaves—marijuana—and on its dried resin—hashish. Hashish is several times more potent than marijuana

b. Many of the effects are produced because marijuana has sedative properties and creates in the user a sense of relaxed well-being and freedom from inhibition

c. The threat of physical dependence is rated low, while the threat of psychological dependence is rated as moderate

d. Frequent users may have impairments of short-term memory and concentration, and of judgment and coordination

e. The attempt to restrict the use of marijuana through legislation has been described as a "second prohibition," which has had results similar to those of the first, because a large number of people are using the drug in a disregard of the law. Such laws foster the development of organized crime and the illicit drug market

f. In 1996 voters in California and Arizona approved the medical use of marijuana. However, the Clinton administration threatened sanctions against doctors who prescribed it. In 1997 a panel of experts convened at the National Institutes of Health stated that marijuana shows promise in treating painful symptoms of some diseases and urged that its medical use should be studied further. Several other states soon passed legislation that allowed marijuana to be used for medical purposes

g. In 2001 the U.S. Supreme Court ruled that federal law definitely classifies the use of marijuana as illegal, and that marijuana has no medical benefits worthy of an exception. The high court did not strike down state laws, but it left those distributing the drug for that purpose open to prosecution

h. In 2005 the U.S. Supreme Court upheld the power of Congress to legislate to prohibit the possession and use of marijuana for medical purposes, even in the 11 states that permit it

8. Ethical Question 11.5: Do you know someone who is abusing one or more drugs? If yes, what might you do or say to help this person?

9. Anabolic steroids

a. Anabolic steroids are synthetic male hormones

b. Although steroids have been banned for use by athletes in organized sports competition, they are still being used by some people

c. Steroids can cause temporary acne and balding, upset hormonal production, and damage the heart and kidneys. Doctors suspect they may contribute to liver cancer and atherosclerosis

d. Steroid drug users are prone to moodiness, depression, and irritability. Users are apt to experience difficulty in tolerating stress

e. Steroid users generally experience considerable difficulty in terminating steroids after prolonged use

f. Highlight 11.6: Steroid Use in Baseball

D.   Dependence on alcohol and other drugs

    1.   Dependence: A tendency or craving for the repeated use or compulsive use (not necessarily abuse) of a chemical

    2.   Physical dependence: User experiences physical withdrawal symptoms when drug use is terminated

    3.   Psychological dependence: User feels psychological discomfort if use is terminated

    4.   Tolerance: User needs increasing amounts over time to achieve a given effect

    5.   Addiction: An intense craving for a drug that develops after a period of heavy use

    6.   Why do people use and abuse alcohol and other drugs?

        a.   The effects of using drugs range from feeling light-headed to death through overdose

        b.   Many drugs have a beneficial effect when used responsibly

        c.   Reasons for use and abuse

            1)   The media glamorize the mind-altering effects

            2)   Taverns and cocktail lounges have become centers for socializing, and promote drinking

            3)   Americans have become socialized to accept drug usage as a part of daily living. Socialization patterns lead many people to use drugs

            4)   Attitudes toward drug use also encourage abuse

            5)   Some people build up a tolerance to a drug, and then increase the dosage to obtain a high

            6)   For many abusers their drug of choice becomes their best friend because they tend to personalize it and value it more highly than they value their friends

            7)   Most abusers deny their drug usage is creating problems for them. They *rationalize* adverse consequences of drug abuse by twisting or distorting reality to explain the consequences of their behavior while under the influence

            8)   Drug abusers *minimize* the adverse consequences of their drug use. They use *projection* to place the blame for their problems on others

d. Theories about drug use

1) Biological theories: Assert that physiological changes produced by the drugs eventually generate an irresistible craving for the drug. Some biological theorists postulate that some people are predisposed by their genetic structure to abuse certain types of drugs

2) Behavioral theories: Hold that people use drugs because they find them pleasurable and continue to use them because doing so prevents withdrawal distress

3) Interactionist theories: Maintain that drug use is learned from interaction with others in our culture. They assert that those who use such illegal drugs as marijuana or cocaine have contact with a drug subculture that encourages them to experiment with illegal drugs

7. Interaction in family systems: A theoretical approach to drug abuse

a. Rules that tend to characterize the families of drug abusers

1) The dependent person's alcohol use becomes "the most important thing in the family's life"

2) Alcohol is not the cause of the problem. Denial is paramount

3) The dependent person is really not responsible for his or her behavior and that the alcohol causes the behavior. There is always someone or something else to blame

4) No one should rock the boat, no matter what. Family members strive to protect the family's status quo, even when the family is miserable

5) Discussion of the family problem is forbidden either within or outside of the family

6) Consistently avoid stating one's true feelings

b. Roles that are typically played by family members of a chemically dependent person

1) Chemically dependent person

2) Chief enabler: Main purpose is to assume the primary responsibility for family functioning. The chief enabler takes more and more responsibility and begins making more and more of the family's decisions. This is often the parent or spouse of the chemically dependent person

3)   Family hero: Often the person who does well at everything he or she tries. The hero works hard at making the family look like it is functioning better than it is. The family hero provides the family with self-worth

4)   Scapegoat: This person's role is to distract attention away from the dependent person and onto something else. This helps the family avoid addressing the problem of chemical dependency

5)   Lost child: This is the person who seems rather uninvolved with the rest of the family, yet never causes any trouble. The lost child's purpose is to provide relief to the family from some of the pain it is suffering

6)   Mascot: The person who probably has a good sense of humor and appears not to take anything seriously. Despite how much the mascot might be suffering inside, he or she provides a little fun for the family

8.   Application of theory to client situations: Treatment for the chemically dependent person and his or her family

    a.   One of the first tasks in treatment is for the chemically dependent person to take responsibility for his or her own behavior

    b.   Family members eventually learn to confront the chemically dependent person and give him or her honest information about his or her behavior

    c.   The family needs to learn about the progression of drug dependence

    d.   Figure 11.2: Alcohol Addiction and Recovery

    e.   Eventually, the dependent person hits rock bottom. Nothing seems to be left but despair and failure, and the dependent person admits complete defeat. Either he or she will continue on the downward spiral to a probable death, or may desperately struggle. Typically during this period vicious cycles of drinking and stopping are often apparent

    f.   Finally, the dependent person may express an honest desire for help. Support from others at this time in the process of recovery is especially critical

    g.   Alcoholics Anonymous (AA) is a self-help organization that has provided the support, information, and guidance necessary for many dependent people to continue on in their recovery

    h.   Highlight 11.7: An AA Meeting

    i.   Other organizations that provide support for other family members include Al-Annon for families of alcoholics, and Al-Ateen—specifically for teenagers within these families

j. Social work roles in treating addicts and family members include: counselor, group facilitator, broker, program initiator, and educator

k. Highlight 11.8: Working with Alcoholic Clients: The Problem of Denial

9. Understanding and treating codependency

a. Codependency: Unhealthy behavior learned amid chaos

b. Many codependent people grow up in a dysfunctional family (some are adult children of alcoholics)

c. To some extent, the addict fills the needs of the codependent ones—needs such as caretaking, loneliness, and addiction to destructive behavior such as excessive partying and thrill seeking. Codependency can be viewed as a normal reaction to abnormal stress

d. If the addict terminates the use of his or her drug of choice, the codependent's dysfunctional behaviors generally continue, unless he or she receives treatment

e. For many codependent people, treatment involves recognition that they have a life and an identity separate from the addict

f. Social work roles in treating codependency: Counselor, educator, facilitator, broker, and program initiator

10. Ethical Dilemma: Punishing or Treating Users of Prohibited Drugs?

11. Relationship between knowledge and assessment

a. Social workers need to know some of the dynamics involved in the behavior of chemically dependent individuals and families, and they need to understand the concept of enabling

b. Social work skills can also be used to encourage the family to realign responsibility

XII. Summary

Experiential Exercises and Simulations

Five exercises are described. In the first, you assess human behavior while using six different theoretical frameworks. The second focuses on nonverbal communication. The third provides answers to some of your questions about drug use and abuse. The fourth focuses on how the sense of sight affects communication. The fifth introduces you to the concept of personal space zones.

Exercise 11.1: Assessing Human Behavior

A.   Brief description
You will assess the underlying reasons for unusual behavior you have engaged in using Maslow's theoretical framework, control theory, intuition theory, and the self-talk approach described in chapter 8.

B.   Objective
You will:
1.   Assess unusual human behavior in terms of Maslow's theoretical framework, game analysis, script analysis, control theory, intuition theory, and the self-talk approach.

C.   Procedure
1.   Identify something that you did that was highly unusual or bizarre. You need not share what you focus on unless you choose to do so. Your task is to identify the underlying reasons why you did what you did in terms of the following six approaches: (1) Maslow's hierarchy of needs framework, (2) control theory, (3) intuition theory, and (4) self-talk.
2.   The instructor briefly describes each of these four approaches. (You should also read the material about these approaches in the text, prior to participating in this exercise.)
3.   Silently spend about 15 minutes identifying and writing down the underlying reasons why you did what you did.
4.   Volunteers are asked to share what they did and how some or all of these approaches were useful in identifying the underlying reasons for the action.

Exercise 11.2: Assessing Nonverbal Communication

A.   Brief description
You will assess the nonverbal communication of a relative you dislike and of a relative you like.

B.   Objectives
You will:
1.   Identify the various ways in which people communicate nonverbally.
2.   Identify nonverbal cues you like and dislike.

C.   Procedure
1.   The instructor begins by describing the purpose of this exercise. Brainstorm about the various ways that people communicate nonverbally, and list these on the chalkboard. A list might include:

Clothing	Gestures and other body movements
Eye movements	Paralanguage
Facial expressions	Use of time
Posture	Eyebrow movements
Physical appearance	Touch
Distance between people communicating	Silence and pauses
Voice tone	Blushing

2. Select a relative you disliked greatly in the past and another you especially liked. Describe on a sheet of paper as specifically as possible what you liked and disliked about the nonverbal communication of each. Avoid listing verbal communication cues, but focus only on nonverbal cues. It is crucial that you do not reveal the names of these relatives in your description, in order to avoid a violation of confidentiality.

3. Volunteers read what they have written. After each description is read, discuss which aspects of the description are nonverbal communication cues and which are not. Also you should seek to arrive at a consensus as to desirable and undesirable nonverbal behaviors for a relative.

Exercise 11.3: Everything You Always Wanted to Know About Drug Use and Abuse But Were Afraid to Ask

A. Brief description
You will write questions you have about drug use and abuse, which the instructor will answer at the next class period.

B. Objective
You will:
1. Obtain answers to your personal questions about drug use, abuse, effects, and treatment.

C. Procedure
1. At the end of a class period, anonymously write on a notecard or sheet of paper one or two questions about drugs that you would like answered. Examples of possible questions are:
   a. What are the adverse effects of cocaine use?
   b. How does LSD affect a person?
   c. How do you get a friend or relative to acknowledge a drinking problem?
   d. Is marijuana use more dangerous than use of alcohol?
   e. What kinds of treatment programs are available for those who abuse alcohol or cocaine?
   f. What are the adverse effects of using anabolic steroids?
   g. How can a woman prevent a date rape drug being slipped into her drink?
2. Prior to the next class period the instructor will obtain answers from references or by calling drug counselors.
3. At the next class period the instructor will answer each question, one at a time. You are encouraged to participate in the discussion.

Exercise 11.4: Communicating While Blindfolded

A. Brief description
You will discuss a controversial topic in a subgroup while your eyes are closed.

B. Objectives
You will:
1. Better understand how communication is affected when the sense of sight is not used.
2. Be more aware of how nonverbal cues are used in communicating.

C. Procedure
1. The instructor explains that nonverbal communication is heavily dependent on the sense of sight. We watch other people's facial expressions, posture, hand gestures, eyes, and body movements. The instructor describes the objectives of the exercise, and asks the class to form circles of five or six students each. Each subgroup receives a controversial topic to discuss (for example, whether physician-assisted suicide should be legalized in our society). The topic may or may not be the same for each subgroup. All participants are blindfolded and discuss the topic for ten to fifteen minutes. (As an alternative to blindfolding, the instructor may ask the students to keep their eyes closed during the discussion.)
2. At the end of the discussion, the students open their eyes (or remove the blindfolds). One large circle is formed, and the class is asked to discuss the following questions:
   a. How did it feel to communicate with your eyes closed?
   b. How did not being able to see affect the communication?
   c. Did not being able to see interfere with being able to concentrate on what was said?
   d. Did not being able to see result in your missing parts of the verbal messages communicated by others?
   e. Do you think you gestured more or less than you usually do?
   f. During this exercise did you become more aware of anything that you had not noticed before?
   g. Does not being able to see the people you are talking to substantially hamper communication? If yes, in what ways?

Exercise 11.5: Personal Space Zones

A. Brief description
Two volunteers talk to each other at varying distances from one another.

B. Objectives
You will:
1. Observe how the distance between communicators affects what people are thinking and feeling.
2. Better understand the concept of personal zones.

C. Procedure
1. The instructor explains the objectives of the exercise, and asks for two volunteers. The volunteers stand at the farthest corners of the room, away from each other. Their task is to slowly—very slowly—walk towards each other. As they are slowly walking towards each other, they engage in small talk about topics of their choosing. They should continue slowly walking and conversing until they touch. When they touch they should slowly start moving apart from each other (while continuing to talk). At the point where they are most comfortable in conversing, they should stop.
2. Other volunteers may be selected to repeat this exercise until interest wanes. The instructor then summarizes the distances at which the various pairs were most comfortable in conversing. The instructor then ends the exercise by discussing the concept of personal zones. The different personal zones are: intimate zone, personal zone, social zone, and public zone.

Study Outline

I. **A Perspective**

II. **Interaction in Family Systems: Choosing a Personal Lifestyle**

    A.   Marriage

        1.   One of the primary reasons for instituting the custom of marriage was to enable the two partners to enjoy sexuality as fully as possible with a minimum of anxieties and hazards

        2.   Close to 92 percent of all adults will get married in our society, and more than 90 percent of all married couples will have children

        3.   Highlight 12.1: Theories About Why People Choose Each Other as Mates

            a.   Propinquity theory: Asserts that being in close proximity is a major factor in mate selection

            b.   Ideal mate theory: Suggests we choose a mate who has the characteristics and traits we desire in a partner

            c.   Congruence in values theory: Holds that our value system consciously and unconsciously guides us in selecting a mate who has similar values

            d.   Homogamy theory: Suggests that we select a male who has similar racial, economic, and social characteristics

            e.   Complementary needs theory: Holds that we either select a partner who has the characteristics we wish we had ourselves or someone who can help us be the kind of person we want to be

            f.   Compatibility theory: Asserts that we select a mate with whom we can enjoy a variety of activities

        4.   Ethical Dilemma: Should You Marry Someone You Are Not in Love With?

        5.   Predictors of marital success

            a.   Highlight 12.2: Predictive Factors Leading to Marital Happiness/ Unhappiness

                1)   Factors for marital happiness

                      a)   Premarital factors

| | b) | Factors during marriage |

| | 2) | Factors for marital unhappiness |

| | | a) | Premarital factors |

| | | b) | Factors during marriage |

6. Benefits of marriage

    a. Marriage leads to the formation of a family, and the family unit is recognized as the primary unit in which children are to be produced and raised

    b. Marriage provides an available and regulated outlet for sexual activity

    c. Marriage is an arrangement to meet emotional needs of the partners, such as affection, companionship, approval, encouragement, and reinforcement for accomplishments

    d. Marriage correlates with good health. Married people live longer, particularly men. Widowed and divorced men have shorter life expectancies than single men, whose life expectancy is closest to the rate of married men

    e. The marriage relationship encourages personal growth; it provides a setting for the partners to share their inner-most thoughts

7. Highlight 12.3: Romantic Love versus Rational Love

8. Highlight 12.4: Guidelines for Building and Maintaining a Happy Marriage

    a. Keep the lines of communication open. Learn to bite the bullet on minor or unimportant issues

    b. Seek to foster the happiness, personal growth, and well-being of your spouse as much as you seek to foster your own happiness and personal growth

    c. Seek to use the no-lose problem-solving technique to settle conflicts with partners, rather than the win-lose technique

    d. Do not try to possess, stifle, or control your partner. Also do not seek to mold your partner into a carbon copy of your opinions, values, beliefs, or of your personal likes and dislikes

    e. Be aware that everyone has up and down mood swings

    f. Be affectionate, share pleasant events, be a friend and a good listener

    g. Make your spouse feel special

B. Cohabitation

1. Cohabitation: The open living together of an unmarried couple

2. People who cohabitated before marriage do not have better marriages than those who did not

3. Some problems are similar to those encountered by newlyweds, and others are unique to cohabitation

4. Closely related to cohabitating is a relationship in which the man and woman maintain separate addresses and domiciles, but live together for several days a month

5. In some instances courts have decided that cohabitating couples who dissolve their nonmarital living arrangements have certain legal obligations to one another

6. Ethical Question 12.1: If you are currently involved in a love relationship with someone, do you seek to make that person feel special? Does your partner seek to lead you to feel good about yourself?

C. Single life

1. Some people choose to remain single; they like being alone and prefer not being with others much of the time. Others end up being single because they do not find a partner they want to marry or because they are in relationships with a partner who chooses not to marry

2. There are advantages and disadvantages of being single

D. Parenthood

1. Highlight 12.5: Parental Gender Preferences

2. The birth of a baby signals to parents that they are now adults and no longer children; they now have responsibilities not only to themselves, but also in caring for someone who needs 24-hour care

3. Women generally assume the majority of both household and child-care responsibilities

4. One study found one-third of mothers view mothering as both enjoyable and meaningful, a third find it unpleasant and not meaningful, and another third report mixed experiences

5. Today, children are an economic liability, rather than an economic asset

6. Parenthood has many rewards and many joyful moments; it also has many demands and stresses

7.   Children are less likely to lower marital satisfaction in families where the parents desired to have children, and where the parents have outside resources for helping to care for the children

8.   Even when parenting has a negative influence on marital satisfaction, it often has a positive effect on the self-concepts of the parents and on their work roles

9.   Developmental stages of parenting

    a.   Anticipation stage: Occurs during pregnancy when the expectant parents think about how they will raise their children, how their lives will change, and the meaning of parenthood

    b.   Honeymoon stage: Occurs after the birth of the first child and lasts for a few months. It is a time of adjustment and learning, as attachments are formed between parents and child, and family members learn new roles in relation to one another

    c.   Plateau stage: Occurs from infancy through the teenage years. Frequent adjustments must be made by the parents, as parents adapt their parenting behavior to the level of the child

    d.   Disengagement stage: Occurs at the time when the child disengages (for example, when the child marries). Because the child disengages, the parents should also change their behavior and disengage from the child. Relationships change from parent-child in nature to adult-adult

E.   Childless couples

1.   The societal value of having children is no longer as strongly held as it once was

2.   There are many reasons couples decide not to have children

3.   It is estimated that a middle class family can expect to spend a quarter-million dollars to raise a child from birth through age 17

F.   Ethical Question 12.2: Given the high cost of raising a child, how many children do you want to have?

G.   Unwanted children are adversely affected in a variety of ways. If couples do not want to have children, it is probably in their best interest and that of society for them not to do so

III.   Macro Social System Theories

A.   Micro system theories seek to make sense of the effects of group life on individuals

B.   Macro system theories seek to make sense of the behavior of large groups of people and the workings of entire societies

C. The functionalist perspective

1. Theory views society as a well-organized system in which most members agree on common values and norms

2. Society is viewed as a system composed of interdependent and interrelated parts. Functionalism asserts that the components of a society, similar to the parts of the human body, do not always work the way they are supposed to work

3. According to the functionalist perspective, all social systems have a tendency toward equilibrium—maintenance of a steady state in which the parts of the system remain in the same relationship to one another

4. Manifest functions: Those that are obvious to everyone

5. Latent functions: Those that are hidden and unintended

6. Social disorganization: Occurs when a large organization or an entire society is imperfectly organized to achieve its goals and maintain its stability. When this occurs, the organization loses control over its parts

7. Rapid social change disrupts the balance of society

8. Cultural lag: When technological advances occur at such a pace that other parts of the culture fail to keep pace. This is viewed as one of the major sources of social disorganization

9. Criticism of functionalism

   a. It is a politically conservative philosophy, as it takes for granted the idea that society as it is (the status quo) should be preserved

   b. The approach is value laden, because one person's disorganization is another person's organization

   c. It is a philosophy that works for the benefit of the privileged social classes, while perpetuating the misery of the poor and those who are being victimized by discrimination

D. The conflict perspective

1. Conflict theory: Views society as a struggle for power among various social groups. Conflict is thought to be inevitable and in many cases actually beneficial to society

2. Society is viewed as an arena for the struggle over scarce resources

3. Norms have emerged that determine what types of conflict are allowable for which groups

4. Functionalists assert that most people in society share the same set of values and norms; in contract, conflict theorists assert that modern societies are composed of many different groups with divergent values, attitudes, and norms, and that conflicts are bound to occur

5. Criticisms

   a. Has been criticized as too radical. If there were as much conflict as these theorists claim, society would have disintegrated long ago

   b. Encourages oppressed groups to revolt against the existing power structure, rather than seeking to work within the system

6. Ethical Question 12.3: Do you believe it is better for oppressed groups to revolt against the existing power structure, rather than work within the existing system to address their concerns?

E. The interactionist perspective

   1. Focuses on individuals and the processes of everyday social interaction between them rather than on larger structures of society. It views behavior as a product of each individual's social relationships

   2. Asserts that people are the products of the culture and social relationships in which they participate

   3. Cooley asserts that we learn what kind of person we are by seeing and hearing how others react to us; the "looking glass" concept

   4. Social reality is what a particular group agrees it is. The reality we construct is mediated through symbols

   5. Symbol: Any object, word, or event that stands for, represents, or takes the place of something else

   6. Characteristics of symbols

      a. The meaning of symbols derives from social consensus

      b. The relationship between the symbol and what it represents is arbitrary—there is no inherent connection

      c. Need not be tied to physical reality. We can use symbols to represent things such as justice, or to stand for things that do not exist at all, such as unicorns

   7. Labeling theory: A direct offshoot of the interactionist perspective; this theory holds that the labels assigned to a person have a major impact on that person's life. Labels often become self-fulfilling prophecies

IV.   Poverty: Impacts of Social and Economic Forces

A.   The rich and the poor

    1.   Poverty and wealth are closely related

    2.   Income: The amount of money a person receives in a given year

    3.   Wealth: A person's total assets

    4.   Social stratification: There are social classes, and the upper classes have by far the most access to the pleasures money can buy

B.   Spotlight on Diversity 12.1: Personal Income Disparities are Astounding

C.   Income and wealth differences

    1.   Some of the job opportunities in the U.S. are being out-sourced to areas where extremely poor people are willing to accept work at almost any wage

    2.   The huge gap between the haves and the have-nots is a major factor leading to political instability in some countries, as well as leading to terrorism and violence

    3.   In the United States the wealthiest one percent of all households hold over one third of all personal wealth

    4.   Wealthiest 20 percent of households in the United States receive nearly 50 percent of all income; whereas the poorest 20 percent receive less than 5 percent of all income

    5.   Net worth: The value of all assets minus debts

D.   The problem

    1.   About 13 percent of the population in the United States is living below the poverty line

    2.   Poverty line: The level of income that the federal government considers sufficient to meet basic requirements of food, shelter, and clothing

    3.   Poverty does not simply mean that poor people in the United States are living less well than people of average income

    4.   The infant mortality rate of the poor is almost double the rate of the affluent

    5.   Poverty often leads to despair, low self-esteem, and stunting of physical, social, emotional, and intellectual growth

6.   Highlight 12.6: The Ideology of Individualism

    a.   Wealth is generally inherited in this country. There are few individuals who actually move up the social status ladder

    b.   Myth of individualism

        1)   Each individual should work hard and strive to succeed in competition with others

        2)   Those who work hard should be rewarded with success (seen as wealth, property, prestige, and power)

        3)   Because of widespread and equal opportunity, those who work hard will, in fact, be rewarded with success

        4)   Economic failure is an individual's own fault and reveals lack of effort and other character defects

    c.   The poor are blamed for their circumstances in our society

E.   Who are the poor?

1.   Prior to the twentieth century a majority of the population lived in poverty. In 1962, one-fifth of the population were living in poverty. Now 13 percent of the people are estimated to be below the poverty line

2.   Poverty is concentrated in certain categories: one-parent families, children, the elderly, large-size families, people of color, and the homeless

3.   A college degree is an excellent predictor of avoiding poverty, as only a small proportion of those with a college degree live in poverty

4.   People who live in rural areas have a higher incidence of poverty than people who live in urban areas

5.   People who live in urban, deteriorated areas constitute the largest geographical group in terms of number of poor people

6.   Poverty is extensive on Native American reservations and among seasonal migrant workers

7.   Spotlight on Diversity 12.2: Poverty Perpetuates Poverty

8.   Marginalization: The poor

    a.   Marginalized groups: Relatively powerless people who, because they belong to a certain socioeconomic class, age cohort, labor organization, political affiliation, gender, racial or ethnic group, or religious group, are seen as being of little importance by the dominant cultural group

F.   What causes poverty?

    1.   Large number of causes

    2.   Eliminating causes would require a large number of social programs

    3.   Poverty interacts with other social problems

    4.   Figure 12.1: A Macro System Problem: The Cycle of Poverty

G.   The culture of poverty: Evaluation of the theory and its application to client situations

    1.   The culture of poverty arises after extended periods of economic deprivation in highly stratified capitalistic societies

    2.   Economic deprivation leads to the development of attitudes and values of despair and hopelessness

    3.   Ethical Question 12.4: Do you believe the poor are poor because they have a distinct culture or lifestyle?

    4.   Once developed, this culture continues to exist, even though the economic factors that created it no longer exist. These attitudes, norms, and expectations of the poor serve to limit their opportunities and prevent their escape

    5.   A major reason they remain locked into their culture is that they are socially isolated

    6.   Criticisms of the theory

        a.   The distinctive culture of the poor is not the cause but the result of their continuing poverty

        b.   Instant gratification is a result of being poor rather than the cause, because it makes no sense to defer gratification when a person is pessimistic about the future. Deferred gratification is a rational response only when one is optimistic that postponing pleasure today by saving the money will reap greater benefits in the future

        c.   Because of poverty, the poor are forced to abandon middle-class attitudes and values, because such values are irrelevant to their circumstances

        d.   A classic example of "blaming the victim." Blaming the poor for their circumstances is a convenient excuse for avoiding developing the programs and policies thought necessary to eradicate poverty

H.   Poverty is functional

1.   Ethical Question 12.5: Is it functional for a society to have a segment of the population that is poor?

2.   Eleven functions provided by the poor for affluent groups

a.   They are available to do the unpleasant jobs that no one else wants to do

b.   By their activities, they subsidize the more affluent (an example of such an activity is domestic service for low pay)

c.   Jobs are established for those people, such as social workers, who provide services to the poor

d.   They purchase goods, such as those of poor quality, that otherwise could not be sold

e.   They serve as examples of deviance that are frowned on by the majority and that thereby support dominant norms

f.   They provide an opportunity for others to practice their "Christian duty" of helping the less fortunate

g.   They make mobility more likely for others because they are removed from the competition for a good education and good jobs

h.   They contribute to cultural activities by providing, for example, cheap labor for the construction of monuments and works of art

i.   They create cultural forms (for example, jazz and the blues) that are often adopted by the affluent

j.   They serve as symbolic opponents for some political groups and as constituents for others

k.   They often absorb the costs of change (for example, by being the victims of unemployment that results from technological advances)

3.   Denigrating the poor has the psychological function of making those who are not poor feel better about themselves

4.   The United States has the resources to eliminate poverty—but not the will

I.   Application of functionalism to poverty

    1.   Functionalists view poverty as being due to dysfunctions in the economy

        a.   Rapid industrialization has caused disruption in the economic system

        b.   The welfare system, which is intended to solve the problem of poverty, has a number of dysfunctions

            1)   Social welfare programs are sometimes established without sufficient funds to meet the needs of potential clients

            2)   Some bureaucrats are reluctant to bend the rules to help a deserving family that is technically ineligible for assistance

            3)   Social welfare programs at times have design dysfunctions in meeting the needs of recipients

            4.   Inadequate information systems fail to inform the poor about benefits to which they are entitled (in addition to the deliberate withholding of information due to prejudice)

    2.   According to functionalists, the best way to deal with poverty is to make adjustments to correct these dysfunctions

    3.   Many functionalists view some economic inequality as being functional. According to functionalists, poverty becomes a social problem when it no longer performs the function of motivating people to make productive contributions to society

    4.   Poverty is functional as the poor do the demeaning, difficult, and low-paying jobs that are essential but that no one else wants to do

J.   Application of conflict theory to poverty

    1.   There is so much wealth in modern societies that all should have their essential needs met

    2.   Poverty exists because the power structure wants it to exist, and the working poor are being exploited by being paid poverty-level wages so that their employers can reap higher profits

    3.   Wealthy people are apt to cling to the ideology of individualism, because they tend to view unemployment and poverty as stemming from a lack of effort rather than from social injustice or from circumstances beyond the control of the individual

    4.   Conflict theorists see charity and government welfare programs as a force in perpetuating poverty and economic inequality, as such programs quell political protests and social unrest that threaten the status quo

5.   Conflict theorists assert that many poor people eventually come to accept the judgments passed on to them by the rest of society and adjust their aspirations and self-esteem downward

6.   They see poverty as arising because some groups benefit from the poverty of others

7.   Poverty can best be dealt with by the poor becoming politically aware and organizing to reduce inequality through government action. Poverty can be reduced only through political action that receives at least some support from concerned members of the power structure

K.   Application of interactionist theory to poverty

1.   Poverty is viewed as being relative, because it depends on what it is compared to. A successful person in some neighborhoods is someone who knows where the next meal is coming from

2.   Instant gratification: People are not inclined to defer immediate rewards so that long-range goals, such as a college education, can be reached

3.   Interactionists view poverty as a matter of shared expectations. The poor are negatively judged by influential groups, and those who are the objects of such labeling are stigmatized and may begin to behave in accordance with those expectations

4.   To resolve the poverty problems, interactionists urge that the stigma associated with poverty be eliminated

V. Family Mezzo System Problems

A.   Empty-shell marriages

1.   Empty-shell marriages: The spouses feel no strong attachments to each other. Outside pressures keep the marriage together

2.   Three types of empty-shell marriages

    a.   Devitalized relationship: Husband and wife lack any real interest in their spouse or their marriage. Boredom and apathy characterize this marriage

    b.   Conflict-habituated relationship: Husband and wife frequently quarrel in private. They may also quarrel in public or put up a façade of being compatible. The relationship is characterized by considerable conflict, tension, and bitterness

    c.   Passive-congenial relationship: The partners are not happy, but are content with their lives and generally feel adequate. They may have some interests in common, but these interests are generally insignificant. This type of relationship generally has little overt conflict

3. Ethical Question 12.6: Is it better to get a divorce than live in an empty-shell marriage?

4. Highlight 12.7: Conflict Resolution Strategies

   a. Conflict is inevitable in interpersonal relationships. It is not only a natural component of any interpersonal relationship, but often desirable, because they have a number of potential payoffs

   b. Strategies for resolving conflicts

      1) Win-lose approach: The two sides engaged in the conflict attempt to sell their own solution without really listening to the other side. Both sides usually end up losing

      2) Problem-solving approach: Asserts that it is almost always possible for both sides to have their needs met in a conflict situation. Both sides have the right to have their needs met; and what is in conflict between the two sides is almost never their needs but their solutions to those needs. There are six steps in the problem-solving approach

         a) Identify and define the needs of each opposing side

         b) Generate possible alternative solutions

         c) Evaluate the merits and shortcomings of the alternative solutions

         d) Decide on the best acceptable solution

         e) Work out ways of implementing the solution

         f) At a later date, evaluate how well the solution is working

      3) Role reversal: Each person expresses his or her opinions or views only after restating the ideas and feelings of the opposing person. Role reversal can result in a reevaluation and a change of attitude concerning the issue by both parties

      4) Empathy: Involves putting yourself in the shoes of the person you are in conflict with, and expressing your understanding of what he is thinking and saying

      5) Inquiry: Involves using gentle, probing questions to learn more about what the other person is thinking and feeling. Tone of voice is very crucial in this technique

      6) Being assertive: Being able to express yourself in a confident, nonaggressive manner

7) "I"-messages: Tend to foster open communication, as they are nonblaming messages that simply communicate how the sender of the message believes the receiver is affecting the sender

8) Disarming: Involves finding some truth in what the other person (or side) is saying and then expressing this "agreement"

9) Stroking: Saying something genuinely positive to the person (or side) you are in conflict with, even in the heat of battle

10) Mediation: Involves the intervention of an acceptable impartial, neutral third party who has no authoritative decision-making power to assist contending parties in voluntarily reaching their own mutually acceptable settlement of issues in dispute

c. What if these strategies don't work?

1) Perhaps the other person wants to be in conflict with you in order to make your life uncomfortable

2) Law of Requisite Variety: States that if you continue to creatively come up with new ways of responding to the "daggers being thrown" at you, eventually the other person will grow tired of the turmoil and will finally decide to "bury the hatchet"

5. Both spouses have to put considerable effort into making a marriage work in order to prevent an empty-shell marriage from gradually developing

B. Divorce

1. Our society places a higher value on romantic love than most other societies. This happily-ever-after ideal rarely happens

2. About one of two marriages ends in divorce. Before World War I divorce was comparatively rare

3. Divorce is very stressful. Divorce people have a shorter life expectancy. Suicide rates are higher for divorced men

4. Reasons for divorce

a. Partners do not meet expectations

b. Lack of effort to make marriage work

c. Unwillingness of some men to accept changing status of women

d. Growth of individualism

e. Growing societal acceptance of divorce

f. Fewer family functions

5. Highlight 12.8: Analyzing Love Relationships

    a. Attraction/infatuation: When we meet someone who comes close to having the characteristics we desire, we tell ourselves that this is an "ideal" potential partner

    b. Appreciation: The two persons are a couple who are seriously dating, living together, or even married

    c. Habituation: Involves being comfortable and secure with dependability and familiarity

    d. Expectation: The difference between duty and pleasure often rears its ugly head in this phase. Many of the things that one did and were appreciated by one's partner now become an expectation

    e. Disappointment/disillusionment: The partners become increasingly disappointed because each is failing to fulfill the other's expectations

    f. Threshold/perceptual reorientation: This is reached when one or both partners decide the relationship is over

    g. Verification: In this stage the partner who has decided to end the relationship focuses on observing the other's behaviors and qualities to find evidence that warrants termination. Usually one of the partners reaches this stage sooner than the other

    h. Termination: At this stage one or both partners decide to end the relationship

    i. We often tend to treat strangers with more respect than the people close to us. A major suggestion for improving intimate relationships is to seek to treat a partner with the same kind of respect given to strangers

6. Highlight 12.9: Facts About Divorce

    a. Age of spouses: Divorce is most likely to occur when the partners are in their 20s

    b. Length of engagement: Divorce rates are higher for those having a brief engagement

    c. Age at marriage: People who marry at a very young age are more apt to divorce

    d. Length of marriage: Most divorces occur within 3 years after marriage. There is also an increase in divorce shortly after the children are grown

    e. Social class: Divorce occurs more frequently at the lower socioeconomic levels

f. Education: Divorce rates are higher for those with fewer years of schooling. Divorce occurs more frequently when the wife's educational level is higher than the husband's

g. Residence: Divorce rates are higher in urban areas than in rural areas

h. Second marriages: The more often individuals have divorced, the more likely they are to divorce again

i. Religion: The more religious individuals are, the less apt they are to become divorced. Divorce rates are higher for Protestants than for Catholics or Jews. Divorce rates are also higher for interfaith marriages than for single-faith marriages

7. Consequences of divorce

a. Both members of the couple experience grief at the loss

b. People may feel anger, anxiety, self-blame, and guilt

c. A sharp decline in the standard of living for women

d. Usually, divided assets do not include occupational assets such as years of experience in full-time employment, health insurance, and future earning-power potential

e. Older women who have not worked outside of the home have had no opportunity to acquire skills and experiences. Because of their age, they find it difficult to get jobs that can support them

f. In most divorce cases, mothers are awarded custody of the children. The income for the divorced mother and her children often plunges below the poverty level

g. There is currently a trend toward joint custody

h. Ethical Question 12.7: Is it desirable for mothers to be awarded custody of the children when divorce occurs? Does this tradition discriminates against fathers?

8. Children of divorce

a. Annually, over 1 million children under the age of 18 experience a divorce in their family

b. Within 5 years after a divorce, three-quarters of all divorced people are remarried

c. Children appear to react more severely to a divorce than they do to the death of a parent

d.   When parents end a marriage, the children are apt to be fearful of the future, to feel guilty for their own role in causing the breakup, to be angry at both parents, and to feel rejected by the parent who moves out

e.   Immediately after a breakup there is considerable disruption and disorganization in family life

f.   A child's reaction to a divorce is affected by a variety of factors

    1)   The age and sex of the child

    2)   The length of time of severe discord in the marriage, and the length of time between the first separation and the formal divorce

    3)   How well the parents deal with the child's concerns, fears, questions, and anxieties

    4)   If one or both of the parents seek to turn the child against the other parent

g.   Children need to work through at least six major issues in order to maintain positive emotional adjustment

    1)   Accept the fact that their parents' marriage is over

    2)   Withdraw from any conflicts their parents might be having and get on with their own lives and activities

    3)   Cope with their loss

    4)   Acknowledge and cope with their strong feelings of anger at their parents and of self-blame

    5)   Understand that the situation is a permanent one

    6)   Maintain a realism about their own relationships with other people

h.   Divorce has significant negative effects on school achievement, behavior, adjustment, self-concept, and relations with both the remaining parent and the departed parent

i.   Highlight 12.10: The Effects of a Divorce on Children Depend on What Happens After the Divorce

9.   Social work roles: Marriage counseling

a.   Marriage counselors generally use a problem-solving approach

b. Marriage counselors try to see both spouses together during sessions c.	If some of the areas of conflict involve other family members, it may be desirable to include these other family members in some of the sessions

d.	Parents Without Partners serves divorced people, unwed mothers or fathers, and stepparents

e.	Divorce mediation helps spouses who have decided to obtain a divorce to resolve issues

C.	One-parent families

1.	About one child in four in the United States is raised with one parent. About 90 percent of these families are headed by women

2.	The rate of female-headed homes in African American families is nearly three times that in white families and is over 60 percent

3.	Research varies on the negative effects and positive effects of divorce on children

4.	Twenty-eight percent of female-headed families are living in poverty, compared to 5.4 percent for two-parent families

5.	White mothers who live in poverty most likely have been married. African American mothers in poverty, however, are more likely to have borne their children without having been married

6.	Highlight 12.11: Temporary Assistance to Needy Families (TANF)

a.	In 1996 President Clinton and the Congress compromised on welfare reform and passed the Personal Responsibility and Work Opportunity Reconciliation Act. This abolished the Aid to Families of Dependent Children (AFDC) program, and replaced it with TANF

b.	The key provisions of TANF

1)	The federal guarantee of cash assistance for poor families with children is ended. Each state now receives a capped block grant to run its own welfare and work programs

2)	The head of every family has to work within 2 years, or the family loses its benefits. After receiving welfare for 2 months, adults have to perform community service unless they have found regular jobs. (States can choose not to have a community service requirement)

3)	Lifetime public welfare assistance is limited to 5 years. (States can establish stricter limits.) Hardship exemptions from this requirement are available for up to 20 percent of the recipients in a state

4)   States can provide payments to unmarried teenage parents only if a mother under 18 is living at home, or in another adult-supervised setting, and attends high school or an alternative educational or training program as soon as the child is 12 weeks old

5)   States are required to maintain their own spending on public welfare at 75 percent of their 1994 level, or 80 percent if they failed to put enough public welfare recipients to work

6)   States cannot penalize a woman on public welfare who does not work because she cannot find day care for a child under 6 years old

7)   States are required to deduct from the benefits of welfare mothers who refuse to help identify the fathers. States may deny Medicaid to adults who lose welfare benefits because of a failure to meet work requirements

8)   A woman on public welfare, who refuses to cooperate in identifying the father of her child, must lose at least 25 percent of her benefits

9)   Future legal immigrants who have not yet become citizens are ineligible for most federal welfare benefits and social services during their first 5 years in the United States. SSI benefits and food stamp eligibility ended for noncitizens, including legal immigrants, receiving benefits in 1996

c.   Initial results of the early studies of TANF

1)   More single mothers are working

2)   Most mothers who leave the welfare rolls find jobs, but a large minority do not. Moreover, some of those who find jobs soon lose them and do not again appear on the welfare rolls

3)   Incomes are rising at the top, but not at the bottom. Even the more successful jobholders experience economic hardship and often must ask for help from family and friends. The long-term impact of welfare reform on both single mothers and their children could well turn out to be like the long-term impact of deinstitutionalization on the mentally ill

4)   There have been significant increases in the proportion of poor people, especially single mothers and their children, who are not covered by health insurance

5)   Almost all mothers who are working state they prefer work to welfare

6) Many working mothers report problems finding satisfactory child care

7) The TANF program was implemented at a time when the nation's economy was booming. If a serious recession occurs, no one knows what will happen to TANF participants if few jobs are available

8) The people who have been kicked off the welfare rolls are pushing down wages for low-skilled workers in the United States

9) States now have many more choices in determining whom they will assist, what requirements they will impose upon those who receive aid, and what noncash supports those families will receive

10) TANF has transformed the central question of American welfare policy—from how much to give single mothers who do not work, to how to support work among low-income families with children

11) Teenage birthrates have fallen in recent years

12) A majority of those who receive TANF do not make it above the poverty line

d. Some children will be better-off, and many children may be worse-off under TANF than under AFDC

e. There is a serious danger that many TANF recipients will be trapped into long-term poverty. There is no provision for TANF recipients to attain a higher level of education

D. Blended families: Any nontraditional configuration of people who live together, are committed to each other, and perform functions traditionally assumed by families

1. Various terms for two families that are joined together: Stepfamilies, blended families, reconstituted families, and nontraditional families

2. Many adjustments have to be made

3. Blended families are increasing in number and proportion in our society

4. People come into a blended family with ideas and issues based on past experiences

5. The area of greatest stress for most stepparents is that of childrearing

6.   Three myths about blended families

   a.   The "wicked stepmother"

   b.   "Step is less." In other words, stepchildren will never hold the same place in the hearts of parents that biological children do

   c.   The moment they become joined as one family, they will have "instant love" for each other

7.   Research literature on stepparenthood concluded the following

   a.   Integration tends to be easier in families that have been split by divorce than by death

   b.   Stepparents and stepchildren come to the blended family with unrealistic expectations that love and togetherness will rapidly occur

   c.   Children tend to see a stepparent of the opposite sex as playing favorites with their own children

   d.   Most children continue to miss and admire the absent biological parent

   e.   Male children tend to more readily accept a stepparent, particularly if the new parent is also a male

   f.   Adolescents have greater difficulty accepting a stepparent than young children or adult children

8.   Stepfamilies need to pursue at least four tasks in order to achieve integration

   a.   Acknowledging that losses from old relationships do exist

   b.   Creating new customs and traditions

   c.   Establishing new alliances within the family

   d.   Integrating the new family

9.   Suggestions to help parents in blended families increase the chances of positive relationships developing between adults and children

   a.   Understand emotions of their children

   b.   Allow time for loving relationships to develop between stepparents and stepchildren

        c.   Develop new rituals, traditions, and ways of doing things that seem right and enjoyable for all members

        d.   Seek social support. Parents in blended families should seek to share their concerns, feelings, frustrations, experiences, coping strategies, and triumphs with other stepparents and stepchildren

E.   Mothers working outside the home

    1.   Employment of married women with children under age 18 rose from 24% in 1950 to 40% in 1970, to 70% in 2006. Most working mothers work full-time

    2.   Many questions have been raised concerning the effects of working mothers (and single working custodial fathers) on the social and emotional development of children

    3.   Research on working mothers and their children conclude that if the mother is satisfied with her job and the provision for child care is reasonably good and suitable, there is no adverse effect on the child's development

    4.   Some questions have been raised concerning the effects on children under age 3 when mothers work outside the home

    5.   Indications are that good child care does not harm a child

    6.   The term maternal deprivation is commonly used, while the parallel term paternal deprivation is not. In reality, mothers, whether they work outside of the home or not, generally maintain the primary responsibility for child care in our society

F.   The "sandwich" generation

    1.   Sandwich generation: Middle-aged adults who provide care for their parents as well as their children

    2.   Stresses and demands are faced by adult children when their parents become dependent on them

    3.   The Family and Medical Leave Act (1993) guarantees family caregivers some unpaid leave for caregiving

VI.   Assessing and Intervening in Family Systems

A.   Verbal and nonverbal communication

B.   Family norms: Rules that specify what is considered proper behavior within the family group

    1.   It is important for families to establish norms that allow the family and each individual members to function effectively and productively

    2.   Social workers need to identify and understand family norms so that inappropriate, ineffective norms can be changed

C.   Family system assessment: The ecomap

      1.   Ecomap: A paper-and-pencil assessment tool used to assess specific troubles and plan intervention for clients. It is a drawing of the client/family in its social environment

      2.   The ecomap consists of a family diagram surrounded by a set of circles and lines used to describe the family within an environment context

      3.   Figure 12.2: Commonly Used Symbols in an Eco-Map

      4.   Figure 12.3: Setting Up an Eco-Map

      5.   Figure 12.4: Sample Eco-Map: Barb and Mike Haynes

      6.   A major value of an ecomap is that it facilitates both the worker's and the client's view of the client's family from a systems and an ecological perspective

D.   Family system assessment: The genogram

      1.   Genogram: A graphic way of investigating the origins of a client's problem by diagramming the family over at least three generations. It is essentially a family tree

      2.   The genogram is a useful tool for the worker and family members to examine problematic emotional and behavioral patterns in an intergenerational context

      3.   Figure 12.5: Commonly Used Genogram Symbols

      4.   Figure 12.6: Sample Genograms: The Chris and Karen Witt Family

      5.   Ecomap and genogram similarities

            a.   With both techniques, users gain insight into family dynamics

            b.   Some of the symbols used in the two approaches are identical

      6.   Ecomap and genogram similarities

            a.   The ecomap focuses attention on a family's interactions with groups, resources, organizations, associations, other families, and other individuals

            b.   The genogram focuses attention on intergenerational family patterns, particularly those that are problematic or dysfunctional

E. Family problems and social work roles

    1. Problems

        a. Marital problems between husband and wife

        b. Difficulties between parents and children

        c. Personal problems of individual family members

        d. Stresses imposed on the family by the external environment

    2. Social workers need to assess the many dimensions of the problem and the impacts on all family members

    3. Couple's Pre-Counseling Inventory: An assessment of couple's problems in which each member of the couple is asked to fill out the questionnaire separately. Later, answers can be shared during counseling, and misconceptions each has about how the other person feels can be clarified

    4. Parent Effectiveness Training (PET): Developed by Thomas Gordon as a tool for practitioners to help parents improve their control of children by assessing the individual family situations and teaching parents some basic behavior modification techniques

    5. Social workers need to advocate, support, or even help to develop appropriate resources for their clients

VII. Social Work with Organizations

A. Organizations are "(1) social entities that (2) are goal directed, (3) are designed as deliberately structured and coordinated activity systems, and (4) are linked to the external environment"

B. Highlight 12.12: Analyzing a Human Services Organization

C. Autocratic model: Uses one-way communication—from the top to the workers. Management believes that it knows what is best. The employee's obligation is to follow orders

    1. This model has been in existence for thousands of years. The model depends on *power*. An employee who does not follow orders is penalized, often severely

    2. Most military organizations throughout the world are formulated on this model. It was also used successfully during the Industrial Revolution

3.   Disadvantages of the autocratic model

    a.   Workers are often in the best position to identify shortcomings in the structure and technology of the organizational system, but one-way communication prevents feedback to management

    b.   The model fails to generate much of a commitment among the workers to accomplish organizational goals

    c.   The model fails to motivate workers to put forth an effort to further develop their skills (skills that often would be highly beneficial to the employer)

D.   Custodial model: Employees are able to express their feelings and thoughts to employers

1.   Employers began to provide welfare programs, including pension programs, child-care centers at the workplace, health insurance, and life insurance

2.   The custodial approach leads to employee dependence on the organization

3.   Employees working under a custodial model tend to focus on their economic rewards and benefits. They are happier and more content than under the autocratic model

4.   Possible disadvantages

    a.   Employees do not have a high commitment to helping the organization accomplish its goals

    b.   Tend to give *passive cooperation* to their employer

    c.   Most employees are producing substantially below their capacities. They are not motivated to advance to higher capacities. Most such employees do not feel fulfilled or motivated at their place of work

    d.   Contented employees (which the custodial model is designed to generate) are not necessarily the most productive

E.   Scientific management model: Focuses on the need for managers to conduct a scientific analysis of the workplace, including how each job could be best accomplished, and provide incentives to increase productivity

1.   Piece-rate wage: Theoretically used to provide incentives to increase productivity

2.   Criticisms:

    a.   The model tends to treat workers as little more than cogs in a wheel. Forcing the same work approach on different workers may actually decrease both productivity and worker satisfaction

b.   Taylor's approach has limited application to human services providers, because each client is unique, and each situation has to be individualized; therefore, it is difficult (if not impossible) to specify the "one best way" to provide service

F.   Human relations model: The level of production is set by social norms; noneconomic rewards and sanctions significantly affect the behavior of the workers; workers do not act or react as individuals but as members of groups; and the role of leadership is important in understanding social factors in organizations

1.   Hawthorn effect: When subjects know they are participants in a study, this awareness may lead them to behave differently and substantially influence the results

2.   Results of studies led some researchers to conclude that the key variables impacting productivity are social factors

3.   Workers who are capable of greater productivity often will not excel because they are unwilling to exceed the "average" level set by the norms of the group, even if this means earning less

4.   Mangers who succeed in increasing productivity are most likely responsive to the workers' social needs

5.   Criticisms of the model

a.   It tends to manipulate, dehumanize, oppress, and exploit workers. The model allows for concentrated power and decision making at the top. It is not intended to empower employees in the decision-making process or to assist them in acquiring genuine participation in the running of the organization

b.   A happy workforce is not necessarily a productive workforce, because the norms for worker production may be set well below the workers' levels of capability

G.   Theory X and Theory Y

1.   Theory X managers: View employees as being incapable of much growth. Employees are perceived as having an inherent dislike for work and attempting to evade work whenever possible

a.   They believe they must control, direct, force, or threaten employees to make them work; employees are viewed as having relatively little ambition, wishing to avoid responsibilities, and preferring to be directed

b.   Theory X managers spell out job responsibilities carefully, set work goals without employee input, use external rewards to force employees to work, and punish those who deviate from established rules

      c.   Work becomes so structured that it is monotonous and distasteful

      d.   Theory X managers adhere to an autocratic model of organizational behavior

2.   Theory Y managers: View employees as wanting to grow and develop by exerting physical and mental effort to accomplish work objectives to which they are committed. They believe that the promise of internal rewards, such as self-respect and personal improvement, are stronger motivators than external rewards (money) and punishment

      a.   They believe that under proper conditions, employees will not only accept responsibility but seek it

      b.   Most employees are assumed to have considerable ingenuity, creativity, and imagination for problem solving; they are therefore given considerable responsibility to test the limits of their capabilities

      c.   Mistakes and errors are viewed as necessary phases of the learning process, and work is structured so that employees have a sense of accomplishment and growth

      d.   Employees who work for Y-type managers are generally more creative and productive, experience greater work satisfaction and are more highly motivated than employees who work for X-type managers

3.   Under both management styles, expectations often become self-fulfilling prophecies

H.   The Collegial model: Emphasizes a team concept, and involves employees working closely together and feeling a commitment to achieving a common purpose

1.   University departments, research laboratories, and most human services organizations have a goal of creating a collegial atmosphere to facilitate achieving their purposes. (Sadly, many such organizations are unsuccessful in creating such an atmosphere)

2.   Creating a collegial atmosphere is highly dependent on management's building a feeling of partnership with employees

3.   In this environment, employees are more apt to have a sense of fulfillment, to feel self-actualized, and to produce higher-quality work

I.   Theory Z: Involved and committed workers are the key to increased productivity. Ideas and suggestions about how to improve the organization are routinely solicited, and implemented where feasible

1.   Japanese approach to management. According to Theory Z, a business organization in Japan is more than the profitability-oriented entity that it is in the United States. It is a way of life. It provides lifetime employment

2. Quality circle: Employees and management routinely meet to brainstorm about ways to improve productivity and quality

3. Experiments designed to transplant Japanese-style management to the United States have resulted in mixed success

J. Management by Objectives

1. Management by Objectives (MBO): Instead of focusing on employee needs and wants, or on organizational structure, as ways to increase efficiency and productivity, begin with the desired outcome and work backwards

   a. In many areas, including human services, the MBO approach can be applied to the cases serviced by each employee. Goals are set, tasks to meet these goals are determined, and deadlines are set for the completion of these tasks. The degree of success of each case is then determined at a later date (often when a case is closed)

   b. An adaptation of this approach, called strategic planning and budgeting (SPB), became popular in the 1990s, and is still widely used

   c. Advantages of the model

      1) Produces clear statements about the objectives and the tasks that are expected to be accomplished in specified time periods

      2) Provides a guide for allocating resources and a focus for monitoring and evaluating organizational efforts

      3) Creates diversity in the workplace

K. Total Quality Management (TQM): The integration of all functions and processes within an organization in order to achieve continuous improvement of the quality of goods and services. The goal is customer satisfaction

1. W. Edwards Deming most closely associated with developing this concept. He along with J. Juran are recognized as laying the groundwork for Japan's industrial and economic boom

2. 85/15 rule: Asserts that 85 percent of the problems in an organization can only be corrected by changing systems; and that less than 15 percent of the problems can be solved by individual workers

3. Key principles of TQM

   a. Employees asking their external and internal customers what they need, and providing more of it

   b. Instilling pride into every employee

   c. Concentrating on information and data to solve problems, instead of concentrating on opinions and egos

d.   Developing leaders, not managers, and knowing the difference

e.   Improving every process (everyone is in a process), checking this improvement at predetermined times, then improving it again if necessary

f.   Helping every employee enjoy his or her work while the organization continues to become more productive

g.   Providing a forum or open atmosphere so that employees at all levels feel free to voice their opinions when they think they have good ideas

h.   Receiving a continuous increase in those suggestions, and accepting and implementing the best ones

i.   Utilizing the teamwork concept, because teams often make better decisions than individuals

j.   Empowering these teams to implement their recommended solutions and learn from their failures

k.   Reducing the number of layer of authority to enhance this empowerment

l.   Recognizing complaints as opportunities for improvement

L.   Summary comments about models of organizational behavior

VIII.   Value Orientations in Organizational Decision Making

A.   Decisions made are largely based on values and assumptions

B.   Value orientation: An individual's own ideas about what is desirable and worthwhile

C.   Value orientations described by Edward Spranger

     1.   Theoretical: Strives toward a rational, systematic ordering of knowledge. The theoretical person places value on simply knowing what exists—and why

     2.   Economic: Places primary value on the utility of things, and practical uses of knowledge are given foremost attention. If the costs outweigh the benefits, the economically oriented person is not likely to support the plan

     3.   Aesthetic: Grounded in an appreciation of artistic values, and personal preferences for form, harmony, and beauty are influential in making decisions

     4.   Social: An empathetic orientation that values other people as ends in themselves. Concern for the welfare of people pervades the behavior of the socially oriented decision maker

5.   Political: A concern for identifying where power lies. Conflict and competition are seen as normal elements of group activity

6.   Religious: Directed by a desire to relate to the universe in some meaningful way. Personal beliefs about an "absolute good" or a "higher order" are employed to determine the value of things, and decisions and their outcomes are placed into the context of such beliefs

D.   Ethical Question 12.8: When you make major decisions, which of these value orientations do you tend to use?

IX.   Liberal, Conservative, and Developmental Perspectives on Human Service Organizations

A.   Conservative perspective: Emphasis on tradition and belief that rapid change usually results in more negative than positive consequences

1.   Conservatives feel that the government should not interfere with the workings of the marketplace. A free market economy is thought to be the best way to ensure prosperity and fulfillment of individual needs. Conservatives embrace the old adage "that government governs best which governs least"

2.   Conservatives generally view individuals as being autonomous, as being self-governing. Poverty and other personal problems that people have are seen as being the result of laziness, irresponsibility, or lack of self-control

3.   Conservatives generally advocate the residual approach to social welfare programs. Residual view: Holds that social welfare services should be provided only when an individual's needs are not properly met through other societal institutions, primarily the family and the market economy

4.   If government funds are provided for health and social welfare services, conservatives advocate that such funding should go to private organizations, which are thought to be more effective and efficient than public agencies in providing services

5.   Conservatives revere the "traditional" nuclear family and try to devise policies to preserve it. They oppose abortion, sex education in schools, rights for homosexuals, public funding of day-care centers, birth control counseling for minors, and other measures that might undermine parental authority or support alternative family forms such as single parenthood

6.   The Republican party is considered to be relatively conservative

7.   Ethical Dilemma: Are the Poor to Blame for Being Poor?

B. Liberal perspective: Believe change is generally good as it brings progress; moderate change is best. They view society as needing regulation to ensure fair competition between various interests

    1. Liberals feel government regulation and intervention are often necessary to safeguard human rights, to control the excesses of capitalism, and to provide equal chances for success. They emphasize egalitarianism and the rights of minorities

    2. Liberals generally adhere to an institutional view of social welfare. The institutional view: Holds that social welfare programs are accepted as a proper legitimate function of modern industrial society in helping individuals achieve self-fulfillment

    3. They assert that because society has become so fragmented and complex, and because traditional institutions have been unable to meet human needs, few individuals can now function without the help of social services

    4. Liberals believe that the personal problems encountered by someone are generally due to causes beyond that person's control

    5. Liberals view the family as an evolving institution, and therefore they are willing to support programs that assist emerging family forms—such as single-parent families and same-sex marriages

C. Developmental perspective: A process of planned social change designed to promote the well-being of the population as a whole in conjunction with a dynamic process of economic development

    1. This approach appears to have appeal to liberals, conservatives, and to the general public

    2. It supports the development and expansion of needed social welfare programs

    3. It asserts that the development of certain social welfare programs will have a positive impact on the economy

    4. The general public would be apt to support this approach

    5. The developmental perspective's global relevance began in the Third World in the years of decolonization after World War II

    6. Characteristics of the developmental approach

        a. Advocates social interventions that contribute positively to economic development. It promotes harmony between economic and social institutions

b.   Regards economic progress as a vital component of social progress, and it promotes the active role of government in economic and social planning

c.   Focuses on integrating economic and social development for the *benefit of all* members of society

X.   Summary

Experiential Exercises and Simulations

Several exercises are presented. The first assesses intimate relationships. The second is regarding romantic love versus rational love. The third is a values-clarification exercise about marriage and divorce. The fourth focuses on applying the macro system theories of functionalism and conflict theory to poverty. The fifth focuses on the two prominent political theories in the United States: liberalism and conservatism. The sixth asks you to identify problems encountered by blended families and recommend social services to help families handle these problems. The seventh has you prepare an eco-map of your family, and the eighth, a genogram of your family. The ninth asks you to analyze a love relationship. The tenth focuses on resolving interpersonal conflicts. The eleventh assists you in understanding an approach to analyzing a human services organization. The twelfth introduces you to two contrasting management styles.

Exercise 12.1: Assessing Intimate Relationships

A.   Brief description
You will evaluate some aspects of an intimate relationship you have had by answering various questions confidentially. Discussion then focuses on critical issues involved in the assessment of relationships.

B.   Objectives
You will:
1.   Identify some of the basic issues involved in intimate relationships.
2.   Examine the difficulty of relationship assessment.
3.   Relate your own life experience to the experience of others.

C.   Procedure
1.   Picture a time in your life (which may be the present) when you were involved in an intimate relationship. Complete the following statements and answer the questions on the basis of that relationship. The questions resemble those often used to assess the functioning of a couple that has requested counseling. It is helpful to discuss and complete each section independently.

SECTION A: EXPLORATION

1.   If I were to describe our relationship in one word, it would be ___.
2.   My partner and I are alike in the way that we ___.
3.   My partner and I are different in that we ___.
4.   If our relationship were a television movie, the title would be ___.
5.   The needs my partner fulfills for me are ___.
6.   The needs that my partner does not fulfill for me are ___.
7.   The things my partner does that please me include ___.

---

8. The things my partner does that annoy me include ___.
9. I am proud of my partner when ___.
10. My partner is proud of me when ___.
11. I feel that my partner's and my ability to talk and communicate with each other is ___.
12. The things I would like to talk to my partner about, but don't, include ___.
13. My major concern in our relationship is ___.
14. I think my partner's major concern in our relationship is ___.
15. When my partner and I have conflicts, we ___.
16. I wish my partner would tell me ___.
17. The thing I think my partner would like to know about me is ___.
18. I have the most fun with my partner when ___.
19. I have the least fun with my partner when ___.
20. I would like our relationship to ___.

SECTION B: SPECIFYING STRENGTHS AND WEAKNESSES
My major strengths are:

1.

2.

3.

4.

5.

My partner's major strengths are:

1.

2.

3.

4.

5.

My major weaknesses are:

1.

2.

3.

4.

5.

My partner's major weaknesses are:

1.

2.

3.

4.

5.

SECTION C: CHANGES AND GOALS

The changes I would like to see in our relationship (in order of priority) are:

1.

2.

3.

The changes I think my partner would like to see (in order of what I think my partner's priorities would be) are:

1.

2.

3.

Immediate goals I would like to strive for in our relationship are:

1.

2.

Long-term goals I would like to strive for in our relationship are:

1.

2.

2.   After each section, answer the following or similar questions:
a.   What are your reactions to the exercise?
b.   How did you feel while answering the questions?
c.   How difficult did you think the exercise was?
d.   What were the reasons for any difficulties you encountered?
e.   How might a couple seeking counseling because of relationship problems feel when asked such questions?
f.   What did you learn from doing this exercise?

Exercise 12.2: Romantic Love Versus Rational Love

A.   Brief description
You will analyze a current or past love relationship to determine whether the attraction was primarily a romantic love relationship or a rational love relationship.

B.   Objectives
You will:
1.   Learn how to analyze the positives and negatives in love relationships.
2.   Assess the nature of attraction in love relationships.

C.   Procedure
1.   Write down on a sheet of paper the following information about someone with whom you are currently "in love." If you are not currently in a love relationship, then write about someone you were "in love" with in the past. The information you write will be confidential. You will not be asked to share this information with anyone.

The items or characteristics that I find (or found) attractive about this person are:	The items or characteristics that I find (or found) irritating about this person are:
1.	1.
2.	2.
3.	3.
4.	4.
5.	5.
6.	6.

2. The instructor explains the characteristics of romantic relationships and rational love relationships, and describes the pitfalls of romantic love. (This material is presented in the text.)

3. Examine what you wrote, and silently assess whether your relationship is (was) primarily one of romantic love or rational love. If you listed all positives about your partner, you probably are idealizing your partner, and therefore the relationship is apt to be a romantic love relationship. If you listed both positives and irritants, you are apt to be in a rational love relationship. If you listed all irritants, then your love relationship may have ended, or be near ending.

4. Discuss the merits and shortcomings of analyzing love relationships in terms of the conceptualization of romantic love versus rational love.

Exercise 12.3: Attitudes Toward Marriage and Divorce

A. Brief description
    You will anonymously fill out an attitudinal questionnaire, and the responses will then be discussed.

B. Objectives
    You will:
    1. Become more aware of your attitudes and values toward marriage and divorce.
    2. Become more aware of your attitudes toward physical abuse.

C. Procedure
    1. You are asked questions related to your attitudes toward marriage, spouse abuse, and divorce. Paper or 5" by 7" notecards are distributed on which to record the answers. Number from 1 through 15 on the response sheet. DO NOT write your name on the sheet.
    2. The instructor reads the following questions, giving you time to record your responses.

a. If a man is drunk and yelling obscenities at his wife, do you think the woman has a right to slap his face in order to get him to stop yelling obscenities?
    _____ Yes   _____ No

b. If a woman discovers that her husband is having an affair with someone else, do you think she has a right to show her indignation by slapping his face?
    _____ Yes   _____ No

c. If you were in an empty-shell marriage, would you choose to get a divorce over maintaining the marriage?
    _____ Yes   _____ No

d. In a marriage where there is considerable tension and discord, are the children generally better off psychologically if a divorce is obtained?
    _____ Yes   _____ No

e. If you were married to someone and discovered that your spouse had had several affairs while married, would you seriously consider getting a divorce?
    _____ Yes   _____ No

f. If you were married to someone who became permanently paralyzed from the neck down in an automobile accident, would you seriously consider getting a divorce?

  _____ Yes   _____ No

g. If you were married to someone who became chronically depressed and suicidal, would you seriously consider getting a divorce?

  _____ Yes   _____ No

h. If you were married to someone who periodically physically abused you or other family members, would you seriously consider getting a divorce?

  _____ Yes   _____ No

i. If you were married to someone and then discovered your spouse was primarily homosexual in sexual orientation, would you seriously consider getting a divorce?

  _____ Yes   _____ No

j. If you were married to someone who developed such a severe drinking problem that he or she was unable to hold a job, would you seriously consider getting a divorce?

  _____ Yes   _____ No

k. If you were married to someone who tested HIV positive and you are HIV negative, would you seriously consider getting a divorce?

  _____ Yes   _____ No

l. If a man discovers that his wife is having an affair with someone else, do you think the man has a right to show his indignation by slapping his wife's face?

  _____ Yes   _____ No

m. If a woman is drunk and is yelling obscenities at her husband, do you think the husband has a right to slap the woman's face in order to get her to stop yelling obscenities?

  _____ Yes   _____ No

n. Have you ever been slapped or hit by someone you were romantically involved with?

  _____ Yes   _____ No

o. Have you ever slapped or hit someone you were romantically involved with?

  _____ Yes   _____ No

3. The instructor collects the responses. The letters a through o are listed on the board. Volunteers record the responses of the students.

4. The instructor reads each question aloud and the responses are noted and discussed.

Exercise 12.4: Poverty: Functionalism Versus Conflict Theory

A. Brief description
You will discuss questions about poverty that are generated by functionalism and conflict theory.

B. Objectives
You will:
1. Describe functionalism and conflict theory.
2. Analyze poverty in terms of functionalism and conflict theory.

C. Procedure
1. The instructor describes the vast differences in income and wealth that exist in our society. He or she defines functionalism and conflict theory, summarizes the proposals of each for reducing poverty, and describes the controversial notion that poverty may be functional for the rich.
2. The instructor writes the following questions on the board, or you may read the questions in this manual:
   a. Do you believe poverty is functional for our society?
   b. Since poverty could virtually be eliminated in our society by a redistribution of wealth and income from the rich to the poor, do you believe the existing power structure really wants to eliminate poverty?
   c. Do you believe the poor are largely to blame for being poor, or do you believe poverty is largely due to societal factors that are beyond the control of the poor?
   d. Which do you believe has better ideas on how to reduce poverty in our society—functionalism or conflict theory?
3. Form groups of five or six. You have 10 to 15 minutes to arrive at answers to these questions. Then share your opinions. After each subgroup presents its positions, discuss the merits and shortcomings of these positions.

Exercise 12.5: Liberalism Versus Conservatism

A. Brief description
You will discuss the two prominent political philosophies in the United States: liberalism and conservatism. You will also discuss the applications of these two approaches to resolving social problems. Finally, you will discuss the developmental perspective which is an emerging perspective that has appeal to both liberals and conservatives.

B. Objectives
You will:
1. Understand and describe liberalism, conservatism, and the developmental perspective.
2. Present arguments as to which approach has the most potential for resolving contemporary social problems.

C. Procedure
1. Read the descriptive material on liberalism, conservatism, and the developmental perspective in the text. The instructor may choose to begin the exercise by summarizing the basic postulates of these philosophies. (Have your textbook available in class to use for reference.)

2.   Form subgroups of five or six persons. The instructor distributes a notecard with a social problem written on it to each subgroup. Each subgroup is given a different social problem. You have 20 minutes to arrive at a consensus as to how liberals, conservatives, and those who adhere to the developmental perspective would combat the social problem listed on your notecard. Each group should also arrive at a consensus on whether liberals, conservatives, or those who adhere to the developmental perspective have the better approach for resolving the specified social problem.

3.   One or two representatives from each group present to the class (a) the liberal, conservative, and developmental approaches to resolving the specified social problem, and (b) the group's views as to which of these three perspectives have the better approach to resolving the social problem.

Exercise 12.6: Needed Services for Blended Families

A.   Brief description
You will identify problems encountered by blended families and then recommend needed services to assist blended families in handling these problems.

B.   Objectives
You will:
1.   Become more knowledgeable about the needs of blended families.
2.   Become more aware of services to meet these needs.

C.   Procedure
1.   Blended families are becoming a typical family form in our society, and there is only limited information available on the problems encountered by these families and on the social services needed by these families. The instructor will either have you read the material on blended families in the text or will summarize this material in a brief lecture.
2.   Form groups of about five persons. First identify what you view as being the four or five most difficult or serious problems encountered by blended families. After you have completed this task, identify the social services that would help blended families handle these problems.

Exercise 12.7: An Ecomap of My Family

A.   Brief description
You will draw an ecomap of your family. Volunteers will share their ecomap with the class.

B.   Objectives
You will:
1.   Practice this family system assessment technique.
2.   Gain insight into the dynamics of your family.

C.   Procedure
1.   The instructor distributes large sheets of paper and magic markers. Using the symbols and instructions in the text, draw an ecomap of your family.
2.   Volunteers describe their ecomaps.

Exercise 12.8: A Genogram of My Family

A.   Brief description

A genogram is essentially a family tree. You will draw a genogram of your family. Volunteers will share their genograms with the class. (The instructions for this exercise are similar to Exercise 7. There are a number of similarities between eco-maps and genograms.)

B.   Objectives

You will:

1.   Comprehend the family system assessment value of a genogram.
2.   Gain insight into dynamics of your family and its history.

C.   Procedure

1.   The instructor distributes large sheets of paper and magic markers to you and the other students. Using the symbols and instructions in the text, draw a genogram of your family.
2.   Volunteers share and describe their genograms.

Exercise 12.9: Analyzing the Stages in a Love Relationship

A.   Brief description

Analyze a love relationship in terms of Cameron-Bandler's framework, which is described in the text, and reflect on suggestions for improving love relationships.

B.   Objectives

You will:

1.   Analyze love relationships.
2.   Become aware of guidelines or suggestions for improving love relationships.

C.   Procedure

1.   The instructor describes Cameron-Bandler's framework of the stages in a love relationship (described in the text). Reflect on a love relationship you currently have or had in the past. Silently identify to yourself what stage you are now at in the relationship.
2.   The instructor summarizes suggestions (described in the text) for improving love relationships. Silently reflect on whether any of these suggestions are useful for improving your current relationship or might have been useful in improving a relationship you had in the past.
3.   Form small groups of about five and share only what you feel comfortable in sharing related to your responses to the questions that were asked in the above steps.
4.   After this discussion, the instructor asks if any subgroup wants to share with the class what it discussed. Are there any comments on the merits and shortcomings of this exercise?

Exercise 12.10: Resolving Interpersonal Conflicts

A. Brief description

Examine a recent interpersonal conflict, and then reflect on whether other conflict resolution strategies would be more effective in resolving the conflict.

B. Objectives

You will:
1. Become aware of a variety of conflict resolution strategies.
2. Become more skillful in resolving future interpersonal conflicts.

C. Procedure
1. Students are instructed to write down on a sheet of paper a summary of a recent interpersonal conflict that they had—perhaps involving a friend, a relative, another student, or a faculty member. The summary should include who the conflict was with, what was at issue, and how it was resolved. (If the issue has not been resolved, the summary should contain a description of the current status of the conflict.)
2. The instructor describes the following conflict resolution strategies and lists them on the chalkboard: the win-lose approach, the problem-solving approach, role reversal, empathy, inquiry, assertiveness, I-messages, disarming, stroking, and mediation.
3. The class forms into subgroups of three students each. The subgroups share with each other the nature of the interpersonal conflicts they summarized in step 1. (Students have a right not to reveal what they wrote.) For each conflict that is shared in the subgroup, the members discuss whether <u>needs</u> or <u>solutions</u> of the people involved in the conflict were primarily at issue. The subgroups also discuss whether any of the following strategies were used (or would have been helpful to use) in resolving the various conflicts: the problem-solving approach, role reversal, empathy, inquiry, assertiveness, I-messages, disarming, stroking, and/or mediation.
4. The class re-forms, and students are given an opportunity to ask questions about conflict resolution. Some students may want to share a complicated unresolved conflict situation they are now experiencing in order to obtain feedback on how it may be effectively resolved.

Exercise 12.11 Analyzing a Human Services Organization

A. Brief description

You visit a human services organization and gather information to write a report, according to formatted questions, about the organization.

B. Objectives

You will:
1. Learn an approach to analyzing a human services organization.
2. Acquire valuable information about the agency you visit.

C. Procedure
1. Each student visits (perhaps in groups of two or three) a human services agency and writes a report covering the following information. (Some agencies may not have information or data on one or more questions. If the information in unavailable, the students should indicate this in their reports.)

a.   What is the agency's mission statement?

b.   What are its clients' major problems?

c.   What services does the agency provide?

d.   How are client needs determined?

e.   What percentage of clients are people of color, women, gays or lesbians, elderly, or members of other at-risk populations?

f.   What was the total cost of services for the past year?

g.   How much money is spent on each program?

h.   What are the agency's funding sources?

i.   How much and what percentage of funds are received from each source?

j.   What types of clients does the agency refuse?

k.   What other agencies provide the same services in the community?

l.   What is the organizational structure of the agency? For example, is there a formal chain of command?

m.   Is there an informal organization (that is, people who exert a greater amount of influence on decision making than would be expected for their formal position in the bureaucracy)?

n.   How much decision-making input do the direct service providers have on major policy decisions?

o.   Does the agency have a board that oversees its operations? If yes, what are the backgrounds of the board members?

p.   Do employees at every level feel valued?

q.   What is the morale among employees?

r.   What are the major unmet needs of the agency?

s.   Does the agency have a handbook of personnel policies and procedures?

t.   What is the public image of the agency in the community?

u.   In recent years what has been the rate of turnover among staff at the agency? What were the major reasons for leaving?

v.   Does the agency have a process for evaluating the outcomes of its services? If yes, what is the process, and what are the outcome results?

w.   What is the student's overall impression of the agency? For example, if the student needed services that this agency provides, would she or he want to apply at this agency? Why, or why not?

2.   The reports are handed in, on a specified date, to the instructor.

Exercise 12.12 Theory X Versus Theory Y

A.   Brief description

You will analyze the benefits and shortcomings of two contrasting management styles—Theory X versus Theory Y.

B.   Objectives

You will:

1.   Gain an understanding of two contrasting management styles.

2.   Be able to analyze management styles in terms of these two contrasting theories.

C. Procedure
1. The instructor explains the objectives of this exercise and describes both Theory X and Theory Y styles of management, providing examples of personal employment under a manager who used one or the other style.
2. You (and the other students in the class) are encouraged to describe examples of employment experiences you have had under these styles and to share your feelings about these contrasting styles.
3. You (and the other students) are encouraged to discuss the merits and shortcomings of these contrasting styles.

Study Outline

I. **A Perspective**

II. **Homosexuality and Bisexuality**

    A. Stereotype: A fixed mental image of a group that is frequently applied to all its members

    B. Highlight 13.1: Stereotypes About Gay and Lesbian People

        1. The queen and the butch

            a. These stereotypes may sometimes prove accurate, but they do not apply to the majority of homosexual people

            b. The stereotypes about how gay and lesbian people look is the result of confusion between two central concepts

                1) Gender identity: Refers to a person's internal psychological self-concept of being either a male or a female

                2) Sexual orientation: A person's erotic and emotional orientation toward members of his or her own gender or members of the other gender

            c. Most gay men think of themselves as being men

            d. A woman may feel like a woman and think of herself as a woman, yet still be attracted to women

        2. Playing male and female roles—Any individual, homosexual or heterosexual, may play a more dominant or more submissive role depending on his or her particular mood, activity, or the interaction involved

        3. The myth of child molesting

            a. Eighty percent of all child molesting is done to young girls by heterosexual men who usually are people trusted and close to them. Heterosexual men are eleven times more likely to be child molesters than are gay men

            b. There are indications that lesbians are much less likely to molest children than heterosexual or gay men

4.   The stereotype "If they're gay, they must have AIDS"

    a.   Because gay men were among the first groups hit by the epidemic, the public has some tendency to identify them with the virus. In reality, the spread of AIDS is growing in other population groups

    b.   More than one quarter of all new AIDS cases are women, most contracted it from high-risk heterosexual contact. Worldwide, about half of people living with AIDS are women

    c.   Seventy-one percent of new AIDS cases are diagnosed among racial and ethnic minorities. Approximately 70% to 75% of new HIV infections are in women of color—even though women of color represent only roughly 24% to 25% of all women in the U.S.

    d.   Nearly 27% of people living with AIDS in the U.S. are 50 or older

    e.   Forty-four percent of senior women in Florida with AIDS, and 18 percent of men over 50 there, are known to have been infected through heterosexual sex

    f.   Gay men have been extremely active in AIDS prevention, education, and advocacy for research and resources

    g.   AIDS is not a "gay disease." Its transmission has nothing to do with being gay. Sexual and other behaviors can put anyone at greater risk

5.   Ethical Question 13.1: Do you harbor any stereotypes about lesbian or gay people? If so, what are they? What, if anything, do you plan to do about them?

C.   What does being a homosexual mean?

1.   Homosexual: A person who is attracted primarily to people of the same gender to satisfy sexual and affectional needs

2.   Sexual orientation: Sexual and romantic attraction to persons of one of both genders

3.   The concept of having a same-gender sexual orientation might be an ever-emerging social construction of reality that changes as social conditions and expectations change

4.   An important aspect of any definition of homosexual is that, above all else, a homosexual is a person

5.   Homophobia: The irrational hatred, fear, or dislike of homosexuals and bisexuals

6. Figure 13.1: The Personality Pie

   a. The homophobic perception of homosexuality: Other aspects of the personality disappear

   b. In reality, the fact that a person is lesbian or gay is only one slice in a person's personality pie

7. Highlight 13.2: The Ethical Problems of Conversion Therapy

   a. Conversion therapy (also referred to as reparative or reorientation therapy) used to convert people who are gay or lesbian to heterosexuals

   b. Today's approaches tend to focus on cognitive-behavioral techniques in an attempt to suppress an individual's attraction to others of the same sex

   c. Cognitive-behavioral therapy: Involves the modification of thoughts and actions by influencing an individual's conscious patterns of thought

   d. There is no credible empirical support for the success of conversion therapy in actually changing sexual orientation

   e. The National Association of Social Workers Policy Statements state that conversion therapy is unethical

   f. Ethical Question 13.2: What ethical issues do you think are involved in conversion therapy? Explain your reasons.

8. The word *homosexual* is derived from the Greek root *homo*, meaning "same." The word *homosexual* itself was not used until the late 1800s

9. Gay men prefer the term *gay* instead of *homosexual* because it has neither the direct sexual connotations nor the demeaning implications frequently associated with the word homosexual

10. The word *lesbian* derived from around the year 600 B.C., when a woman named Sappho lived on the Greek island of Lesbos in the Aegean Sea (from which the term *lesbian* originates). Although Sappho was married, she remains famous for the love poems she wrote to other women

11. Many lesbians have expressed concern that men are given preference over women when the term *gay* is used to refer to both men and women

12. There is some indication that the media is now beginning to use the terms gay men and lesbians

13. Gender identity: A person's internal psychological self-concept of being either a male or a female, or, possibly, some combination of both

D.   Spotlight 13.1: Transsexual and Transgender People

1.   Transsexual people: Those whose gender identity is the opposite of their biological gender. Often transsexual people prefer to be referred to as transgender people, because the term transsexual emphasizes "sex," and gender identity involves so many more facets of an individual's personality

2.   Transgender people: Preferred term as gender identity involves so many more facets of an individual's personality and circumstances

3.   Many transgender people pursue surgery to enhance their physical appearance as people of the opposite gender—a process that usually involves four steps

   a.   They enter counseling to make certain that they are aware of their true feelings and that they understand the potential ramifications of changing genders

   b.   They undergo a "real-life test" where they actually live and undertake their daily activities as a person of the opposite gender

   c.   They receive extensive hormone treatments to align their bodies with the opposite gender as much as possible—a process that they must continue for the rest of their lives

   d.   They undergo surgery where genitals and other areas of the body are surgically altered to more closely resemble the opposite gender. The changes are primarily cosmetic because construction of internal organs is impossible

      1)   Genital tissue is used to create a penis-like organ and scrotum for female-to-male transgender people, and a vaginal canal and labia for male-to-female transgender people

      2)   Other physical alterations might include breast implants or breast removal, or decreasing the size of a biological male's Adam's apple

      3)   Female-to-male surgery is generally more complex

4.   The National Association of Social Workers (NASW) Policy Statement on Transgender and Gender Identity Issues states that people of diverse gender—including those sometimes called "transgender"—should be afforded the same respect and rights as any other person

5.   Ethical Question 13.3: Should transgender people have the right to physically alter themselves to better resemble their true gender identity? If so, who should pay for it? The individuals themselves? Insurance companies? The public?

E.   Definition of a bisexual

    1.   Bisexual person: A person who is sexually attracted to members of either gender

    2.   Thirty-seven percent of the men in a study sample of 5,300 had at least one sexual experience with another male, to the point of orgasm, after reaching age 16

    3.   In a study of 5,940 women, it was found that between 8 and 20 percent had some type of homosexual contact between ages 20 and 35

    4.   A significantly smaller percentage of each group had exclusively homosexual experiences throughout their lifetimes

    5.   Because it was so difficult to place people into distinct categories, Kinsey and his associates developed a six-point scale that placed people on a continuum concerning their sexual experiences

    6.   Figure 13.2: Conceptualizations of Homosexuality and Heterosexuality

        a.   0—Exclusively heterosexual

        b.   1—Mostly heterosexual with incidental homosexual experience

        c.   2—Heterosexual with substantial homosexual experience

        d.   3—Equal heterosexual and homosexual experience

        e.   4—Homosexual with substantial heterosexual experience

        f.   5—Homosexual with incidental heterosexual experience

        g.   6—Exclusively homosexual

    7.   Storm developed a two-dimensional scheme to reflect sexual orientation

        a.   Homoeroticism: Sexual interest in and/or experiences with those of the same gender

        b.   Heteroeroticism: Sexual interest in and/or experience with those of the opposite gender

        c.   Individuals who express high interest in both sexes are considered bisexual. Those persons who have a very low sexual interest in either gender are considered asexual

F.   A matter of terms

    1.   GLBT—Gay, lesbian, bisexual, and transgender people

    2.   Sometimes only one or some of the groups will be the focus of reference

G. Numbers of lesbian and gay people

    1. Based on Kinsey's work, many authors have used 10 percent as the proportion of men who are gay

    2. Kinsey found that, although more than one-third of American men had homosexual experiences leading to orgasm during their adolescent or adult lives, only 10 percent of men were exclusively homosexual for a 3-year period between ages 16 and 55. Only about 4 percent were gay throughout their lives

    3. Two to three times as many men as women have a homosexual orientation. Kinsey found that 19 percent of American women had homosexual experiences by the age of 40, although only 2 to 3 percent of these remained lesbian throughout their lives

    4. Ten Percent Society: A gay and lesbian organization that maintains lesbian and gay people make up 10 percent of the population

    5. Somewhere between 2 percent and 10 percent of the population appears to be gay or lesbian

III. Why Are Some People Lesbian or Gay?

A. Biological theories

    1. Genetic factors

        a. Bailey and Pillard compared groups of identical twins, fraternal twins, and brothers who were adopted

            1) Identical twins were studied, and found that when one brother was gay, 52 percent of the identical twins were also gay

            2) Among only 22 percent of fraternal twins and 11 percent of adoptive brothers were both brothers gay

            3) They concluded that the degree of genetic contribution to homosexuality could vary from 30 to 70 percent

        b. Another study looked at 108 lesbians who had either identical or fraternal twin sisters, and at another 32 lesbians who had adopted sisters

            1) They found that among almost half of the identical twins, both were lesbians

            2) Only 16 percent of fraternal twins and 6 percent of the unrelated sisters were both lesbians

            3) These results support the idea that there is a genetic component to homosexuality

  c. There is evidence that gay and lesbian sexual orientations run in families; however, a specific gene linked to homosexuality has not been identified

 2. Brain (anatomical) factors

  a. LeVay studied the brains of 41 cadavers: 19 of gay men, 16 of supposedly heterosexual men, and 6 of supposedly heterosexual women and found the anterior hypothalamus (a marble-sized cluster of cells that regulates sexual activity in addition to appetite and body temperature) in gay men was only half the size as that in heterosexual men. There are many concerns about these findings

  b. More recent studies failed to find any differences between the brains of gay and heterosexual men

 3. Hormonal factors

  a. This theory suggests that hormonal type and level cause homosexuality

  b. Research has established no relationship between hormonal levels and sexual orientation either during the prenatal period or in adulthood

B. Psychosocial theories

 1. Psychosocial or behavioral theories emphasize that homosexual behavior is learned, just as any other type of behavior is learned

 2. Early in life, homosexual behavior might be positively reinforced by pleasurable experiences and thereby strengthened; or such behavior may be punished by negative, punitive experiences and, as a result, be weakened

C. The evaluation of theory: What is the answer?

 1. If some researchers postulate that genetic rationales explain some component or percentage of why people are gay, then what explains the remaining components or percentages?

 2. If people are gays or lesbians because of some hormonal impact, why aren't all people lesbians or gays who experienced similar hormonal impacts?

 3. Shortcomings with respect to psychosocial theories of homosexuality

  a. There is a tremendous amount of negative feedback about homosexuality. How homosexual behavior would be reinforced and would increase in frequency, in view of such punitive circumstances, might be questioned

  b. Learning theory implies that a person must first have a homosexual experience. Might it not be the case that individuals who have homosexual desires seek out sexual experiences with the same gender in the first place?

D. Interactionist theory: Focuses on the interaction of biological predisposition and the effects of the environment

1. The development of a homosexual orientation is related to the rate at which people mature during preadolescence

2. The sex drive for some people emerges earlier than for others. If children who mature earlier are still in same-sex groupings, they may have positive sexual experiences with persons of the same gender

3. If early maturers do not have these experiences, they continue later to develop a heterosexual orientation as they begin interacting with people of the opposite gender

4. Many experts agree that homosexuality probably results from some mixture of both biological and psychosocial variables

E. Ethical issues related to theory

1. Gelman and his colleagues found that people were generally more accepting of lesbian and gay people if they felt such people were "born that way" instead of *choosing* or *learning* that lifestyle

2. Might potential parents be more likely to abort a fetus determined to be lesbian or gay if they learn about the homosexuality early in the gestational process?

F. Other research on the origins of homosexuality

1. Bell, Weinberg, and Hammersmith and the Alfred C. Kinsey Institute for Sex Research study

   a. They studied 979 lesbians and gay men, and compared them to 477 heterosexual women and men. They were asked extensive questions about many aspects of their lives

   b. Path analysis: A statistical method that was used to allow researchers to explore possible causal relationships between variables, such as prenatal characteristics and family relationships, and the development of sexual orientation

   c. Several of the variables proposed by other theories were found not to be related to homosexuality. They found no relationship between being gay and having been seduced by a person of the same gender when young

   d. Three findings of special significance

      1) Sexual orientation appears to emerge by the time both males and females reach adolescence. The average gay person now comes out just before or after graduating high school

2)   Lesbian and gay people have a similar amount of heterosexual experience during childhood and adolescence when compared to heterosexual people. There was one basic difference—despite the fact that lesbian and gay people participate in heterosexual activity, they do not enjoy it very much

3)   Gender nonconformity was a much stronger causal factor for gay men than for lesbians. Other factors such as family relationships have a stronger causal relationship with lesbianism

4)   Gender nonconformity: Refers to a child's preference for play and activities that our society generally assumes appropriate for children of the opposite gender

e.   This research indicates that sexual orientation develops very early in life. Whether a person is gay or lesbian or heterosexual is not a matter of choice

f.   Many lesbian and gay people externally assume heterosexual roles for appearance sake because of homophobic stigmas that are placed on gay or lesbian people

G.   Spotlight on Diversity 13.2: Discrimination and the Impacts of Homophobia

1.   Homophobia: The irrational hatred, fear, or dislike of homosexuals and bisexuals

2.   It is not clear how homophobia originated. Maier postulates that it may be people's attempts to deny homosexual feelings in themselves

3.   The American Psychiatric Association didn't remove homosexuality from the list of mental illnesses until 1974

4.   One Gallup poll found that 43% of Americans surveyed responded that they did not consider homosexuality an acceptable alternative lifestyle

5.   Social workers must confront their own homophobia and learn more about the special issues of lesbian and gay clients

H.   Ethical Question 13.4: Why do you think people are lesbian, gay, or bisexual? To what extent does a person's sexual orientation matter to you, and why?

IV.   **Lesbian and Gay Lifestyles**

A.   Lesbian and gay relationships

1.   When examining heterosexual married, heterosexual couples, and gay male and lesbian couples, there are striking similarities across family forms in terms of what is valued, issues to be negotiated, problems confronted, problem-solving strategies adopted, and so on

2.   Given the lack of legal sanction or social recognition, lesbians' relationships are often marked by stability and longevity

3.   There is some evidence that gay men have a greater number of partners than heterosexual men and that gay partners are more likely to accept nonmonogamy than their heterosexual counterparts. There is also evidence that many gay men establish long-term relationships

4.   Major social and legal obstacles exist that prevent lesbian and gay people from establishing long-term relationships

B.   Sexual interaction

1.   The physiological responses of gay and lesbian people are exactly the same as those of heterosexuals

2.   One difference between gay and lesbian people and straight people is that gay and lesbian people tend to be more open to new techniques, take more time, and pay more attention to the ways in which they interact sexually

3.   Perhaps many heterosexual couples could learn a thing or two from lesbian and gay couples

V.   Significant Issues and Life Events

A.   The impacts of social and economic forces: Legal issues

1.   Legislation against homosexual acts in the United States and the prevailing homophobia in American culture have caused many gay and lesbian persons to fear revealing their sexual orientation

2.   In 2003 the U.S. Supreme Court in *Lawrence et al. v. Texas* struck down a Texas sodomy law that made private sexual contact between homosexuals illegal. Several other states overturned similar laws

3.   Spotlight on Diversity 13.3: Gay and Lesbian Pride and a Sense of Community

4.   Employment

    a.   In 1976 the federal government's personnel manual changed to forbid discrimination against lesbian and gay people in hiring or terminations unless the public agency involved could prove that homosexual behavior affected work completion

    b.   Other than for federal government jobs, there are no federal statutes that prohibit employers from discriminating against lesbian and gay people

    c.   Some states have passed laws prohibiting some kinds of discrimination based on sexual orientation

    d.   Major progress has been made in implementing antidiscrimination policies in corporate America, although this progress is not reflected in many small businesses

e. 8,250 American companies offer domestic partner benefits, 92.2 percent of Fortune 500 companies have anti-discrimination policies based on sexual orientation. However, only 57 percent feel that homosexuality is an acceptable alternative lifestyle

f. About a third of the population think that lesbians and gays experience significant discrimination, and only 29 percent indicate that the government should expend effort in establishing and defending gay rights

g. Lesbian and gay people's perception differs—60 percent feel that significant discrimination exists, and 83 percent want the government to protect their rights and prohibit discrimination

h. Ethical Question 13.5: What, if anything, should be done to protect lesbian, gay, and bisexual people from discrimination in employment?

5. The military

a. Lesbian and gay people historically have been prohibited from joining the CIA, the FBI, and the armed forces

b. In January 1993, President Clinton announced a plan to revoke the 50-year-old ban on gay and lesbian people in the military. However, Congress so eroded the plan that the final version entailed an uncomfortable "don't ask, don't tell, don't pursue" guideline

1) More than 10,000 service members have been fired for homosexuality since 1994

2) 1,250 gay men and lesbians were discharged from the military in 2001, after they had announced their sexual orientation or homosexual behavior—up from 1,212 discharges in 2000

3) In 2006 there were 612 such discharges

4) The armed services in numerous other countries allow gay men and lesbians to serve

c. Currently 46 percent of Americans support lesbians and gay serving openly in the military, 36 percent feel they should continue serving under the current policy, and 15 percent feel they should serve under any circumstances

d. It is estimated that 65,000 lesbian and gay Americans are currently serving in the military. What if they were all discharged?

e. Ethical Question 13.6: What policy should the military adopt about inclusion or exclusion of lesbian and gay personnel? What are your reasons?

6. Personal relationships, finances, and same-sex marriage

   a. In May 2008, the Supreme Court of California struck down a state law limiting marriage to a union between a man and a woman, making California the second state that allows same-gender marriages. Massachusetts became the first state in the nation to legalize gay marriage

   b. Eight states have constitutional amendments banning gay marriage specifically and another 18 states have broader anti-gay constitutional amendments banning relationships in addition to marriage

   c. Thirty-three states have statutes banning same-sex marriages, 6 states have statutes banning same-sex marriage in addition to other legal same-sex relationships. Some states have both constitutional amendments and state statutes concerning the issues

   d. A civil union is a legally recognized union that is similar to marriage in some or many respects. Vermont passed a law in 2000 allowing gay and lesbian people to form civil unions that provide essentially the same rights and responsibilities as those in a heterosexual marriage. These civil union rights are not transferable to other states should a couple move. Connecticut, New Jersey, and New Hampshire have implemented civil unions

   e. A domestic partnership is a legal agreement where two people live together, establish a personal relationship intended to be permanent, and share a domestic life together without being in a marriage or civil union. Oregon, the District of Columbia, Maine, and Washington have domestic partnership laws

   f. Hawaii has a legal reciprocal beneficiary arrangement with limited rights

   g. A recent Gallup poll indicated that 56 percent felt same-sex marriage was not valid, 40 percent felt it was, and 4 percent held no opinion. Forty-nine percent are in favor of civil unions for same-sex couples, but not marriages

   h. Countries with legal same-sex marriages—Canada, Spain, South Africa, Belgium, and the Netherlands. Many nations allow some form of legal same-sex partnerships

   i. Same-sex couples experience numerous disadvantages

   j. Ethical Question 13.7: Should lesbian and gay people be given the right to marry?

7. Child custody and visitation rights

    a. Numerous courts have denied parents custody simply because of being lesbians or gays. Some state courts have ruled that child custody could not be denied purely on the basis of parental homosexuality unless it was proven that such sexual orientation would hurt the child

    b. Judges presiding over custody disputes can make arbitrary judgments concerning what is in the child's best interests

    c. Myths about lesbian and gay parenthood

        1) Lesbian or gay parents will influence their children to become gays or lesbians

        2) Children will be damaged by growing up in lesbian or gay homes

        3) Gay and lesbian people's parenting skills are inadequate

        4) Children of lesbians and gay men are sexually abused by adults, ostracized by peers, and isolated in single-sex homosexual communities

    d. The American Association of Pediatrics endorsed its support of gay and lesbian parents adopting a partner's children

    e. The odds for gaining custody may still not be good

8. The future of lesbian and gay rights

    a. Their struggle for equality is sometimes characterized by the phrase "Remember Stonewall!" Stonewall was a gay bar in New York City's Greenwich Village. In 1969, the police stormed and raided the bar; however, the people fought back, and the struggle continued in the street for hours

    b. People involved in gay/lesbian liberation have provided much impetus to progress made in gay and lesbian legal rights

    c. Social workers need to attend to gay and lesbian rights issues

B. Community responses: Violence against lesbian and gay people

1. Matthew Shepard, a gay college student, died in Laramie, Wyoming after being beaten and left tied to a fence

2. Hate crimes: Crimes motivated by hatred of someone's religion, sex, race, sexual orientation, disability, or ethnic group (also known as message crimes)

3. Victimization surveys on homophobic violence in a number of English-speaking countries found that 70 to 80 percent of lesbians and gay men reported experiencing verbal abuse in public, 30 to 40 percent reported threats of violence, 20 percent of gay men reported physical violence, and 10-12 percent of lesbians reported physical violence

4. Potential solutions to halt victimization of lesbians and gay men

   a. Gay and lesbian civil rights legislation must be passed

   b. Passage of laws that specifically address crimes committed because of hatred and prejudice toward specific groups

   c. Educating the police, and people working in the criminal justice system, about homophobia, gay and lesbian victimization, and the needs and rights of gay people

   d. Establish crisis centers for victims

5. Ethical Question 13.8: How can violence against lesbian, gay, bisexual, and transgender people be stopped?

C. Coming out

   1. Coming out: Refers to the process of a person acknowledging publicly that she or he is lesbian or gay

   2. Four stages of coming out described by the Boston Women's Health Book Collective include

      a. Coming out to oneself

      b. Getting to know other people within the gay and lesbian community

      c. Sharing with family and friends that one is lesbian or gay

      d. Coming out of the closet—openly and publicly acknowledging one's sexual orientation

   3. A more thorough examination of these stages include the following

      a. Signification: The first stage of coming out, which involves thinking about oneself as a person who is lesbian or gay instead of as one who is heterosexual

         1) Intervention strategies for human service professionals when helping lesbian and gay clients during their coming out period

            a) Provide the client with information about what being lesbian or gay is really like

b)   Address the issue of self-concept

c)   Realistically identify and evaluate the alternatives open to a lesbian or gay person; address advantages and disadvantages

     b.   The second phase involves meeting and getting to know other lesbian and gay people. It is important to establish a social support system made up of people who understand what it is like to come out

     c.   The third phase involves telling friends and family. The potential consequences need to be realistically examined

     d.   The fourth phase involves publicly acknowledging that one is a lesbian or a gay person. It is important to evaluate the potential positive and negative consequences of each alternative

4.   Many people choose not to come out of the closet

5.   Spotlight on Diversity 13.4: Ethnicity and Sexual Orientation

6.   Highlight 13.3: Cheryl's Exploration of Her Self-Identity and Sexual Orientation

D.   Empowering lesbian and gay adolescents

1.   Most gay men indicate they realized that they were gay between ages 9 and 15

2.   Lesbian and gay adolescents are six times more likely to attempt suicide than their heterosexual counterparts

3.   Principles to guide social workers when trying to help lesbian and gay youth

     a.   Simply admit to yourself that some adolescents are lesbian or gay

     b.   Increase your own awareness and that of your agency regarding how to provide accessible services to lesbian and gay youth

     c.   Do not allow antigay, homophobic sentiment to get in the way of providing lesbian and gay youth with the services they need

E.   Lesbian and gay parents

1.   Estimates of lesbian and gay adults with children vary from 1.5 to 5 million; it is also estimated that the number of children raised in lesbian or gay homes is between 8 and 10 million

2.   During the past decade, lesbians have increasingly turned to bearing children through artificial or donor insemination

3. Suggestions for social workers and other human service professionals in their efforts to help lesbian and gay people cope with parenthood

    a. Help the lesbian or gay parents identify and appreciate the joys of parenthood

    b. Help lesbian and gay parents address the issue of coming out to children

    c. Assist lesbian or gay parents in dealing with new partners

    d. Help parents identify and evaluate ways to help children with issues of prejudice and discrimination

4. Teach children situational ethics—that it is more appropriate to refer to and talk about sexual orientation in some situations than in others

5. Providing psychosocial support for families of GLBT people may include providing families with accurate information and information on how to access local agencies and other support organizations

F. As lesbians and gay men age

1. Most older lesbian and gay people are relatively well-adjusted

2. The adjustment levels and the psychosocial needs of older lesbian and gay people are more similar to those of heterosexuals than dissimilar

3. Lesbian and gay people may adjust better to aging than heterosexual people based on two principles

    a. Mastery of independence: Means that being independent is nothing new to lesbian and gay people. They have had to fend for themselves and experience a lifetime of independence

    b. Mastery of stigma: Means that lesbian and gay people are probably better at coping with the stigma of old age because they have experience coping with stigma and rejection

4. Suggestions to social workers for their interventions with lesbian and gay clients

    a. Know something about what homosexuality is like and also about the local gay and lesbian communities

    b. Confront your own biases and ideas about homosexuality and sexuality of the elderly

    c. Work to develop new services for older lesbian and gay people and also help them receive better service from existing traditional agencies

G. Gay and lesbian people and AIDS

    1. Homophobic responses by heterosexual people and the idea that AIDS is a punishment for bad behavior may have been a contributing factor to the relative inaction on the part of the government to AIDS

    2. Gay people can be thanked for much of the publicity about AIDS, the new resources directed to research for a cure, and the strong emphasis on prevention

    3. Any social worker who works with a gay or lesbian client needs to be aware of the ramifications and emotional impacts AIDS has had

H. Spotlight 13.5: Social Work with Lesbian and Gay People: Promoting Optimal Well-Being

    1. Counseling

        a. It is very important to confront one's own homophobia

        b. Become familiar both with the lesbian and gay lifestyles and with the lesbian and gay communities

    2. Agency provision of services

        a. Advantages for mainstreaming services for lesbian and gay people into already existing social service agencies

            1) A large traditional agency can provide a wider variety of services and serve more specific individual needs

            2) Lesbian and gay people do not have to be segregated from the rest of society

            3) Mainstreaming provides the opportunity for heterosexual practitioners to interact with practitioners who are familiar with the issues of gay or lesbian life and serve a gay or lesbian clientele

        b. Social workers need to apply social work values to lesbian and gay clients; learn about resources available, and make appropriate referrals; educate others about the special issues confronting lesbian and gay people; and act as advocates for the rights of lesbian and gay people

VI. **Summary**

Experiential Exercises and Simulations

The following four exercises are intended to help you identify stereotypes about lesbian and gay people, examine your own attitudes toward them, and propose strategies to combat discrimination against them.

Exercise 13.1: If I Woke Up Gay Tomorrow Morning . . .

A. Brief description
The class will divide into small groups. You will discuss how you would feel if you woke up lesbian or gay tomorrow morning. Implications are discussed.

B. Objectives
You will:
1. Identify some of the issues confronting lesbian and gay people today.
2. Examine your own feelings and ideas about homosexuality.
3. Formulate and evaluate some of the viable alternatives available to lesbian and gay people today.

C. Procedure
1. Form groups of four to six people.
2. Discuss the following questions. It's important that all group members participate in the discussion and share answers. Choose one person to summarize responses to share with the class.
    a. "How would your life be different if you woke up tomorrow morning and discovered you were lesbian or gay?"
    b. "How would this affect your relationships with friends, family, and colleagues?"
    c. "To whom would you come out and how?"
    d. "How would this affect your social and work life?"
3. You will have 10 to 15 minutes to discuss the question.
4. Ask a volunteer to summarize your group's discussion and share this summary with the larger group.
5. Finally, formulate a summary statement regarding the conclusions of the entire class.

Exercise 13.2: Am I Homosexual?

A. Brief description
The instructor will read a series of vignettes. You are then asked whether you think the vignettes are about homosexuals. Discussion follows.

B. Objectives
You will:
1. Question some of your basic assumptions about being lesbian or gay.
2. Evaluate your stereotypes about being lesbian or gay.
3. Examine the difficulty involved in defining homosexuality.

C.   Procedure
    1.   The following vignettes are read to the class:

> a.   I am a 30-year-old female librarian. I love my work and consider myself a dedicated professional. I'm not really very attractive and am about twenty-five pounds overweight. I'm shy and don't have many friends. I'm pretty lonely most of the time. I dated a man in college, but he dropped me to go out with somebody else. I really have never had any other boyfriends. A woman I work with has approached me about having a sexual relationship with her. I'm kind of afraid, but I'm really considering getting involved with her. It sure gets lonely on Saturday nights. Am I a lesbian?

> b.   I am a 30-year-old man. I've been in prison for six years now for murder. I'm serving a life sentence and really don't know if I'll ever get out on parole. I'm married and still love my wife. We had a good sexual relationship before I came to jail. Here I've had hundreds of sexual relationships with men. I have to admit I do enjoy them and get sexual satisfaction out of them. Am I gay?

> c.   I am a 30-year-old married man. My wife takes very good care of me sexually on a regular basis. I enjoy our sexual relationship very much. Whenever I have sex with her I like to fantasize about having sex with a man. I also like to watch male wrestlers on television. It's sexually exciting to me. They really turn me on. Am I gay?

    2.   After you have discussed each vignette, join a general discussion concerning the difficulty of defining homosexuality and the many gradations of homosexual and heterosexual behavior that are possible.

Exercise 13.3: My Friend is Coming to Visit

A.   Brief description
You will be asked to participate in a role-play: a college junior announces to his or her roommates that a lover of the same gender is coming to visit. Class discussion follows observation of the role-play.

B.   Objectives
You will:
    1.   Recognize some of the difficulties in "coming out" to those close to you.
    2.   Examine some of the dynamics involved in homophobia.
    3.   Confront and assess your own values concerning gay and lesbian people.

C.   Procedure
    1.   Six volunteers are needed to dramatize a "coming out" situation.
    2.   Focus on the following six roles:

> **The Person Coming Out**: You are a college student living in the same house with five other students. Although you all have been housemates for a year, none of the others knows that you are gay. You have invited your lover, who is of the same gender, to stay the weekend with you. You need to tell your housemates about it.

Housemate 1: You don't know much about homosexuality, although you've heard many dirty jokes about it. You really don't know how you feel about it because you've never knowingly met a lesbian or gay person.

Housemate 2: You are very religious and belong to a conservative denomination. You believe that homosexuality is a sin.

Housemate 3: You are a psychology major who sees homosexuality as a *paraphilia* ("recurring, intense, unconventional sexual fantasies, urges, or behavior that is obsessive and compulsive") or illness (Hyde & Delamater, 2008, p. G-6). You think that lesbian and gay people need counseling so that they can become "normal."

Housemate 4: You see sexual orientation as something an individual has the right to choose. You have several gay friends of both sexes. Their sexual orientation is irrelevant to you. You see homosexuality as simply one aspect of an individual's personality.

Housemate 5: You have never really thought much about homosexuality. However, in general you feel that it restricts people's relationships and their life-style. You feel sorry for people who are "that way."

3. Role-players should put themselves into their respective parts and play each individual's attitudes as closely to the part as possible. They may add any other facts as they wish. It's important to remain in the respective roles until the role-play is over. The role-play should last for approximately 15 minutes.

4. After terminating the role-play, both role-players and class observers can discuss the following questions:

   a. What were the reactions of role-players to their respective roles?

   b. How did it feel and how did you think it might feel to be the person coming out? What were the observers' reactions to each respective role?

   c. What are your perceptions of the individual rights, group rights, and social pressure involved?

   d. What do you think would be the "right" thing for each of the role-players to do in such a situation?

Exercise 13.4: What it Means to be Lesbian or Gay

A. Brief description
You will be asked to identify some aspect of your life that is very important to you and examine how you would feel if you had to give it up.

B. Objectives
You will:

1. Begin to recognize the difficulty gay and lesbian people have living in a heterosexual world.

2. Examine what being gay or lesbian means to an individual.

C.   Procedure

    1.   Think carefully about what aspect of your life is the most meaningful to you. It could be an activity you heartily enjoy, a goal you are sincerely committed to achieve, a very special person, or some personality characteristic about which you are very proud. Take a piece of scratch paper and jot the life aspect down.

    2.   Now imagine that you have to live without that part of yourself or your life forever. What would it be like? How would you feel? What would you do without it?

    3.   You have two or three minutes to think about what giving up such a significant part of your life would be like. Then begin a class discussion focusing on the following questions and issues:

        a.   What part of your life did you choose to give up?

        b.   How meaningful is that life aspect to you?

        c.   How did it feel to even think about giving it up?

        d.   Did you think about the potential painfulness of living without this part of your life?

        e.   To what extent do you think giving up the life aspect that is particularly important to you would be like giving up being gay or lesbian?

    4.   Discuss how difficult it would be to change something that is a part of your core self. To what extent could you change your orientation, for any reason? The research indicates that regardless of why people are gay, their orientation is something that is an integral part of their total selves.

REFERENCES

Hyde, J. S., & DeLamater, J. D. (2008). *Understanding human sexuality* (10th ed.). New York: McGraw-Hill.

Chapter 14
Biological Aspects of Later Adulthood

Study Outline

I.   **A Perspective**

II.   **What Is Later Adulthood?**

A.   When our Social Security Act was passed in 1935, the United States followed the German model by selecting 65 as the age of eligibility for retirement benefits

B.   Gerontologists: Doctors who specialize in medical care of older people

C.   In primitive societies, old age was generally determined by physical and mental conditions rather than by chronological age

D.   Spotlight on Diversity 14.1: Internationally Noted Individuals Prove that Age Need Not be a Barrier to Being Productive

E.   A new view on aging—people today are living longer and faring better than at any time in history. In Japan, old age is a mark of status

F.   Senescence: The normal process of bodily change that accompanies aging

    1.   Appearance

    2.   Senses

       a.   The sense of touch declines due to drying, wrinkling, and toughening of the skin

       b.   The sense of hearing gradually deteriorates. The ability to hear very high tones is generally affected first

          1)   An impairment in hearing is five times as common in persons aged 65 to 79 as it is in individuals between the ages of 45 and 64 years

          2)   Men are more apt to experience hearing impairments than women

       c.   Most people over age 60 need glasses or contact lenses to see well. Half of the legally blind persons in the United States are over 65

          1)   Cataracts: Clouding of the lens of the eye or its capsule that obstructs the passage of light. With the development of corrective lenses and new surgical techniques for removing cataracts and implanting artificial lenses, many vision losses are fully or partially restored

2)   Glaucoma: Occurs when fluid pressure in the eye builds up. If this disease is detected through routine vision checkups, it can be treated and controlled with eyedrops, medication, and surgery, or laser treatments

3)   Macular degeneration: Occurs when the center of the retina gradually loses the ability to sharply distinguish fine details. Smokers are about 2½ times as likely to develop this condition

d.   The senses of taste and smell have reduced functional capability during advancing years. Much of this reduced sensitivity appears to be related to illness and poor health

e.   Vestibular senses: Function to maintain posture and balance. These senses also lose some of their efficiency

3.   Teeth: Periodontal disease (a disease of the gums) becomes an increasing problem

4.   Voice: Changes are partly due to the hardening and decreasing elasticity of the laryngeal cartilages

5.   Skin: Some of the subcutaneous muscle and fat disappears, resulting in the skin hanging in folds and wrinkles

6.   Psychomotor skills: A key factor in the high accident rates of older people is a slowdown in the processing of information by the central nervous system. Physical exercise and mental activity appear to reduce losses in psychomotor skills

7.   Ethical Question 14.1: Do you believe most older people will gradually become senile? If you answered yes, does this belief affect how you relate to an older person?

8.   Intellectual functioning

a.   The notion that there is a general intellectual decline in old age is largely incorrect. It could well be that while the elderly show a decline in performance on IQ tests, their actual intellectual competence may not be declining

b.   The terminal drop: Sudden drop in intellectual performance occurring a few weeks or a few months before death from a terminal illness

c.   Highlight 14.1: Values and Aging: The Myth of Senility

1)   Senility: An irreversible mental and physical deterioration associated with later adulthood.

2)   Senility is not a true medical diagnosis, but a wastebasket term for a range of symptoms

9. Height and joints

    a. The maximum height of a person is reached by the late teens or early 20s

    b. In older people there may be a small reduction in overall height due to a progressive decline in the discs between the spinal vertebrae

    c. Joint movements become stiffer and more restricted, and the incidence of disease (such as arthritis) affecting the joints increases with age

10. Homeostasis: The stabilizing mechanisms become sluggish, and the physiological adaptability of the person is reduced

11. Muscular structure

    a. After age 30, there is a gradual reduction in the power and speed of muscular contractions, and the capacity for sustained muscular effort decreases

    b. After the age of 50, the number of active muscle fibers gradually decreases, resulting in the older person's muscles being reduced in size

    c. The hand grip strength of a 75-year-old man is only about 55 percent that of a 30-year-old man

    d. The ligaments tend to harden and contract, and sometimes result in a hunched-over body position

12. Nervous system

    a. Although there is little functional change in the nerves with increasing age, some of the nerve tissue is gradually replaced by fibrous cells

    b. The total number of brain cells may decrease, but the brain continues to function normally unless its blood supply is blocked

    c. The brain weight of an average 75-year-old person is similar to that of a middle-aged person

13. Digestive system: Complaints about digestive disorders are among the most common complaints of the elderly. The regularity of bowel movements is also more of a problem in later adulthood

14. Respiration: As people age, their lungs decrease in size, resulting in a decrease of oxygen utilization. The maximum breathing capacity and maximum oxygen intake in a 75-year-old are about 40 percent of those of a 30-year-old

15. Heart

    a.   The heart and the blood vessels are the bodily parts in which aging produces the most destructive changes

    b.   The heart and arteries are the weakest links in the chain of life, as most of the other organs would probably last for 150 years if they received an adequate blood supply

    c.   With age, the heart shrinks in size, the heart muscles tend to become stringy and dried out, and deposits of a brown pigment in the cells of the heart partly restrict the passage of blood and interfere with the absorption of oxygen through the heart walls. The elasticity in the valves of the heart is reduced, and deposits of cholesterol and calcium in heart valves also decrease valve efficiency

    d.   The heart of an older person pumps only 70 percent as much blood as that of a younger person

    e.   The coronary artery has a tendency to harden and become narrow; this is the site of many heart attacks that are brought on by increased emotional stress or physical effort. Hardening of the coronary artery may also increase blood pressure and may reduce the flow of blood to many parts of the body

16. Reserve capacity: A backup capacity of organs and body systems that can be used during times of stress

    a.   Younger adults have reserve capacities that put forth four to ten times as much effort as usual

    b.   The reserve capacities of older people decrease; as a result, they cannot respond to stressful demands as rapidly as younger adults

    c.   As the reserve capacity continues to diminish, those affected become less able to care for themselves and more dependent on others

17. Sexuality: Conceptualizing sexual response

    a.   Myotonia: Muscle tension resulting from individual stimulation

    b.   Vasocongestion: Blood engorgement

    c.   Ethical Question 14.2: Should older people be sexually active?

    d.   Four stages of sexual response in males

        1)   Excitement: Blood flows into the erectile tissue of the penis (vasocongestion), resulting in erection. The scrotum (the sac surrounding the testicle) becomes thicker, more wrinkled, and the testicles move up closer to the body

2)   Plateau: Characterized by the continuation of erection, although it often waxes and wanes during sex play. The testicles become fully elevated, rotate toward the front, and become blood-engorged, causing expansion in their size. The Cowper's gland secretes a small amount of clear fluid that comes out at the tip of the penis. The purpose of this fluid is generally thought to be to cleanse the urethra of urine, thereby neutralizing the chemical environment for the passage of sperm

3)   Orgasm: Consists of two phases in men. The first is ejaculatory inevitability, a short period during which the stimulation sufficient to trigger orgasm has occurred and the resulting ejaculation becomes inevitable. The second phase, ejaculation, results from rhythmic contractions (myotonia) forcing sperm and semen through the urethra. Simultaneous with this is the very pleasant physical sensation of orgasm

4)   Resolution: Represents the return to the unstimulated size. The penis loses its erection and the testicles lose their engorgement and elevation

e.   Four stages of sexual response in females

1)   Excitement: The process of vaginal lubrication begins. This response is analogous to the male erection, and is physiologically a blood-engorgement response. The uterus and cervix begin to move up and away from the vagina. The clitoris and labia minora (inner lips) enlarge and the labia majora (outer lips) spread. Breast size increases slightly and the nipples become erect

2)   Plateau: The uterus continues in its movement up and back, the vagina lengthens and balloons at the rear, and the outer third of the vagina contracts, causing a gripping effect. The clitoris retracts under its hood, making it seem to disappear

3)   Orgasm: The uterus and vagina become involved in wavelike muscular contractions. This response, as well as the subjective pleasure of orgasm, are very similar to the experience of the male

4)   Resolution: The cervix and uterus drop to their normal position and the outer third of the vagina returns to normal, followed by the inner two-thirds. The clitoris and the breast also return to normal

f.   Extragenital physical responses: Muscle tension responses such as facial grimaces, spastic contractions of the hands and feet, and pelvic thrusting

g.   Extragenital blood engorgement responses: Sex flush, blood pressure and heart-rate increases, and perspiration on the soles of the feet and the palms of the hands

h.   Figure 14.1 Effects of Aging on Sexual Response in Men

i.   Figure 14.2 Effects of Aging on Sexual Response in Women

18.   Values and sexuality

     a.   Sexual interest and sexual activity gradually decline among older people. However, many older people continue to engage in sexual activity

     b.   Women over 60 are much less likely to have a sexual partner available; so they report lower frequencies of partnered activity

     c.   About 24 percent of the women and about 31 percent of the men ages 60 to 74 reported having intercourse at least weekly

     d.   For women 75 and over, 6.6 percent reported having intercourse at least weekly, compared to 19.1 percent for men 75 and over

     e.   If sexual behavior declines in later years, it probably is due to social rather than physical reasons

     f.   Attitudes of younger adults, as to what is appropriate sexual behavior for the elderly, commonly create problems. Older people, like other age groups, have a right to sexual expression as long as they do not hurt anyone

     g.   Many of the current living arrangements for older people (group homes, nursing homes, assisted living facilities, and foster homes) have overlooked the need for privacy

G.   What causes aging?

1.   Genetic theories

     a.   Cellular genetic theory of DNA damage: Asserts that damages or changes to DNA molecules alter the genetic information and result in the cell being unable to manufacture essential enzymes

     b.   Running-out-of-program theory: Asserts that there is a set amount of basic genetic material (DNA molecules) in each cell. As the cells age, the DNA is used up and the cells die

     c.   The somatic-mutation-by-radiation theory: Asserts that aging is due to an accumulation of errors involved in the transmission of information from the DNA molecule to the final protein product. Such an accumulation of errors results in an "error catastrophe," which eventually leads to the death of the cells

2. Nongenetic cellular theories

   a. The deprivation theory: Assumes that aging is caused by vascular changes that deprive cells of essential nutrients and oxygen

   b. The accumulation theory: Asserts that aging results from the accumulation of harmful substances in the cells of an organism. When the accumulation builds up, the cells eventually begin to die

   c. The wear-and-tear theory: Asserts that cells begin to die after long use and exposure to stressful elements during the process of living. In this theory the human body is comparable to a machine whose parts eventually wear out

   d. The free-radical theory: Hypothesizes that there are chemicals, called free radicals, that contain oxygen in a highly activated state and that react with other molecules in their vicinity. Such reactions are postulated to damage and kill some cells

   e. The cross-linkage theory: Asserts that cross-linkages or bonds develop between molecules or between components of the same molecules. These bonds supposedly change the chemical and physical properties, which cause some cells to function improperly and gradually die

3. Physiological theories

   a. The single organ system theory: Asserts that aging is due to an essential system breaking down. The precise system that is thought to control aging has not been identified, but various systems have been suggested

   b. The endocrine control system theory: Postulates that hormones control the aging process. There is evidence that hormones are involved in puberty and menopause

   c. The stress theory: Asserts that aging is due to the accumulation of the effects of the stresses of living. Each stress encountered is thought to leave a small residual of accumulants and impairments, which results in bodily systems then aging

   d. The immunological theory: Assumes that changes in the immune system result in aging. The immune system protects the body from invading bacteria, microorganisms, and atypical mutant cells that may form. As a person grows older, it is hypothesized that fewer antibodies are produced, which decreases the protective ability of the immune system

   e. The control-mechanisms theory of the central nervous system: Asserts that mechanisms in the central nervous system are responsible for aging. A variety of mechanisms may be involved

4. Evaluation of theories of aging: As yet, sufficient evidence has not been presented to prove which (if any) theory is valid

H.   Factors that influence the aging process

   1.   Illness

   2.   "Biological insults": accidents, broken bones, severe burns, severe psychological stress, and severe alcohol or drug abuse

   3.   Poor eating habits

   4.   Environmental factors: A positive outlook (positive thinking) tends to slow down the aging process

   5.   Genetic inheritance

   6.   Highlight 14.2: Health Practices and Longevity

      a.   Eating breakfast

      b.   Eating regular meals and not snacking

      c.   Eating moderately to maintain normal weight

      d.   Exercising moderately

      e.   Not smoking

      f.   Drinking alcohol moderately or not at all

      g.   Regularly sleeping seven to eight hours a night

      h.   Avoiding the use of illegal drugs

      i.   Learning to cope with stress

      j.   Leading a healthy sexual life

III.   **Diseases and Causes of Death Among Older People**

   A.   The most frequently occurring chronic conditions are arthritis, hypertension, hearing impairments, heart disease, orthopedic impairments, cataracts, diabetes, visual impairments, and sinusitis

   B.   The medical expenses of an older person average four times more than those of a young adult

   C.   Ethical Dilemma: Is Genetic Testing Desirable?

   D.   The physical process of aging is a factor in the elderly having a higher rate of health problems. It has also been demonstrated that personal and social stresses also play major roles in causing diseases

E.   Highlight 14.3: Leading Causes of Death Among Older People

    1.   Diseases of the heart (30.4%)

    2.   Malignant neoplasma [cancer] (22%)

    3.   Cerebrovascular diseases [stroke] (7.4%)

    4.   Chronic lower respiratory diseases [lung diseases] (6%)

    5.   Alzheimer's disease (3.5%)

    6.   Diabetes (3.1%)

    7.   Pneumonia and influenza (3%)

    8.   All other causes (24.6%)

F.   The majority of older people are reasonably healthy. People over 65 have a health advantage over younger persons in a few areas—they have fewer flu infections, colds, and acute digestive problems

G.   Highlight 14.4: Alzheimer's Disease

    1.   Alzheimer's disease: A degenerative brain disorder that gradually causes deterioration in intelligence, memory, awareness, and ability to control bodily functions. In its final stages, Alzheimer's leads to progressive paralysis and breathing difficulties

    2.   Over a period lasting from as few as 5 years to as many as 20, the disease destroys brain cells

    3.   Researchers have identified at least several different genes as being linked to the disease, yet having one or more of these genes does not necessarily mean one will develop this disorder. Therefore, researchers believe there must be some as yet unidentified "triggers"

    4.   Scientists are investigating the finding that victims of Down syndrome who survive into their 30s frequently develop symptoms indistinguishable from Alzheimer's. A recent clue is the discovery of fragments of amyloid in brains of persons who died from the disorder. Possibly abnormal patches of this protein in the brain set up a chain reaction that progressively destroys brain cells

    5.   Cholinesterase inhibitors can stabilize or slow symptoms for 6 months to a year in one third to one half of patients

    6.   Scientists at the University of Wisconsin in 2004 discovered that mice who naturally produce an increased amount of the protein called transthyretin do not develop Alzheimer's disease

IV.   Life expectancy

A.   The average life expectancy in ancient Rome and during the Middle Ages was between 20 and 30 years. Infant mortality was very high, and famine, diseases, and wars took the lives of many more

B.   In the middle of the nineteenth century, Americans lived for an average of 40 years. At the turn of the twentieth century, the average was 49 years

C.   The average life expectancy in 2007 was 78 years

D.   Ethical Question 14.3: If it were possible, would you want to know the year in which you will die?

E.   Two life events found to be significant in predicting the death of an older person: death of a spouse and moving to a nursing home

F.   Significant sex differences found in life expectancies

    1.   In 2006, females in the United States had a life expectancy at birth of 80 years while males had a life expectancy of only 75 years

    2.   Environmental factors

        a.   Men are more likely to die from suicide, accidents, and homicides

        b.   Sex role stereotypes allow women to be more expressive of their feelings than men. Suppression of feelings may result in an increased number of stress-related disorders in men, and then shorten their life span

    3.   Biological factors: The higher mortality rate among males in the fetal stage and in infancy supports the notion of an inborn difference in resistance

    4.   In 2007 there was a sex ratio, among those who were 65 and over, of 141 women for every 100 men

G.   Factors that influence longer life expectancy

    1.   Parents and grandparents lived to 80 or more

    2.   Being married for most adult years

    3.   Not being overweight

    4.   Exercising regularly

    5.   Light drinking

    6.   Not smoking

    7.   Being basically happy and content with life

8.   Graduating from college

9.   Living in a rural environment

10.   Having regular medical checkups and regular dental care

11.   Routinely using stress management techniques

H.   Ethical Question 14.4: How many years would you like to live?

I.   Factors associated with a shorter life expectancy

1.   Parents and grandparents died of an illness fairly early in their lives—such as a heart attack or a stroke before age 50

2.   Parents or grandparents had diabetes, thyroid disorders, breast cancer, cancer of the digestive system, asthma, or chronic bronchitis

3.   Being unmarried for most adult years

4.   Overweight

5.   Not exercising regularly

6.   Having a sedentary job

7.   Heaving drinking (more than four drinks per day)

8.   Smoking

9.   Being aggressive, intense, and competitive

10.   Often being unhappy, or worried, or feeling guilty

11.   Not completing high school

12.   Living in an urban environment that has moderate to high levels of smog

13.   Frequent illnesses

14.   Experiencing high levels of stress without routinely using stress management techniques

15.   Engaging in activities that are high risk for the AIDS virus

J.   Spotlight on Diversity 14.2: Longevity: Cross-Cultural Research on Centenarians

1.   There are now an estimated 80,000-plus centenarians (people living to be 100 or older) in the United States

2.   One personality characteristic that appears to be shared by this group is the ability to manage stress

3. A study was conducted in a remote region of Italy on 40 centenarians. Most of these people continued to perform physical tasks and activities associated with daily life. They had very low levels of depression, and were functioning well mentally. Significantly, they continued to feel important and valued in their culture

4. Sadly, our society has tended to devalue the contributions of older people in our society

5. Five behaviors in old, old men that were found to be associated with living into extreme old age, and with good health and independent living

    a. Abstaining from smoking

    b. Weight management

    c. Blood pressure control

    d. Regular exercise

    e. Avoiding diabetes

V. Wellness: The Strengths Perspective

A. Physical exercise: There is evidence that, as people grow older, continued exercise reduces the degree of physical and mental slowness that occurs in many older people

B. Mental activity: Our society needs to put more emphasis on ensuring that older people are exposed to intellectual stimulation

1. Elderhostel offers low-cost courses designed for people over 55

2. Some public universities also have provisions for those over 65 to attend regular classes with either reduced or no tuition

3. Traveling is another way for the elderly to stay mentally active. The American Association of Retired Persons (AARP) and Elderhostel offer travel tours within the United States and to other parts of the world

4. Most authorities on aging now believe that an intellectual decline in later adulthood is largely a myth

C. Sleep patterns

1. It appears that older people in fairly good health require no more sleep than those in middle adulthood

2. Sleep disturbances that older people experience tend to be a result of anxiety, depression, worry, or illness. Restless sleep is common for those who are inactive, those who catnap too much, and those who have physical discomforts

3. Normal changes that occur in sleep patterns for older people

    a. Deep sleep virtually disappears for older people

    b. They generally take a longer time to fall asleep and have more frequent awakenings

    c. They distribute their sleep somewhat differently. They generally have several catnaps of 15 to 60 minutes during the day

4. People develop their sleep patterns according to their physical needs and according to the responsibilities and activities they have

D. Nutrition and diet

1. The elderly are the most undernourished group in our society

2. Some older people have a tendency to overeat. The caloric requirements decrease somewhat in the later years

3. To improve the nutritional health of older people, some programs have been developed, such as Meals on Wheels

E. Stress and stress management

1. Learning how to manage stress is important for the physical and emotional health of all age groups, and is a contributing factor in a wide variety of emotional and behavioral difficulties, as well as most physical illnesses

2. Conceptualizing stress

    a. Stress: Physiological and emotional reactions to stressors

    b. Stressor: A demand, situation, or circumstance that disrupts a person's equilibrium (internal balance) and initiates the stress response

    c. Selye's theory of a three-stage reaction to stress (general adaptation syndrome: GAS)

        1) Alarm phase: The body recognizes the stressor and responds by preparing to fight or flee

        2) Resistance phase: The body seeks to repair any damage caused by the stressors

        3) Exhaustion phase: Occurs only when the body remains in a state of high stress for an extended period of time. If exhaustion continues, a person is apt to develop a stress-related illness

      d.   Two components of a stressor

          1)   Experiences or events that are encountered

          2)   Thoughts and perceptions about these events

3.   Highlight 14.5: Conceptualizing Stressors, Stress, and Stress-Related Illnesses

4.   Not all stress is bad; life without stress would be boring

5.   Distress: The kind of stress that is harmful

6.   Table 14.1: Stress Signals

7.   Empowerment approaches to stress management: Application of theory

      a.   Three constructive approaches to stress management

          1)   Changing the distressing event

          2)   Changing one's thinking about the distressing event

          3)   Taking one's mind off the distressing event, usually by thinking about something else

      b.   Two destructive ways that some people use to relieve stress

          1)   Resorting to alcohol, other drugs, or food

          2)   Committing suicide

      c.   Changing a distressing event: Confront the distressing event directly and try to improve the situation

      d.   Changing one's thinking about a distressing event

          1)   Positive thinking: Having a philosophy of life that allows us to take crises in stride

          2)   Sharing concerns with someone helps to vent emotions

          3)   Having a social support group

      e.   Taking one's mind off the distressing event, usually by thinking about something else

f. Relaxation approaches

    1) Deep-breathing relaxation: Helps you to stop thinking about day-to-day concerns and to concentrate your thinking on your breathing processes

    2) Imagery relaxation: Involves switching your thinking from your daily concerns to focusing your thinking (for 10 to 15 minutes) on your ideal relaxation place

    3) Progressive muscle relaxation: Tightening and relaxing a set of muscles. With practice, the capacity to relax, simply by visualizing the muscles, is developed

    4) Meditative approaches

        a) Being in a quiet environment free from external distractions

        b) Being in a comfortable position

        c) Having an object to dwell on, such as a word, sound, chant, phrase, or imagery of a painting

        d) Having a passive attitude in which you stop thinking about day-to-day concerns (the key element in inducing the relaxation response)

    5) Use of biofeedback equipment that measures the levels of functioning of numerous physiological processes, such as blood pressure, hand temperature, muscle tension, heartbeat rate, and brain waves

g. Exercise: Through exercise we can use up fuel in the blood, reduce blood pressure and heartbeat rate, and reverse the other physiological changes set off during the alarm state of the general adaptation syndrome

h. Pleasurable goodies: Relieve stress, change our pace of living, are enjoyable, make us feel good, and are, in reality, personal therapies

8. Application of theory to client situations

a. Social work roles in stress management

    1) Educator

    2) Counselor

    3) Broker

    4) Initiator and consultant

VI. Summary

Experiential Exercises and Simulations

Three exercises are described in this section. The first increases your awareness that later adulthood can be rewarding. The second is designed to give you an appreciation of what it is like to be an older person in our society. The third is an exercise in which you learn how to meditate.

Exercise 14.1: Later Adulthood Can Be Rewarding

A.   Brief description
You will contact an older person to gather information, which is then shared in class.

B.   Objectives
You will:
1.   Have a greater appreciation that later adulthood can be enjoyable and rewarding.
2.   Identify factors that contribute to good physical and mental health.

C.   Procedure
1.   Talk to an older friend or relative who appears to be enjoying life and who is in fairly good health. (If you cannot meet with this person, telephone him or her.) Ask (a) what activities make this person's life enjoyable, and (b) to what does he or she attribute his or her good health?
2.   At the designated class period, form subgroups of four or five persons. Describe positive qualities and characteristics of the person you talked to and then summarize their responses to the questions.
3.   A representative of each group presents a summary of activities that make the respondents' lives enjoyable and to what they attribute their good health.
4.   Discuss the consistency between the chapter presentation of factors that promote good health and those mentioned by the respondents.

Exercise 14.2: Interviewing an Older Person

A.   Brief description
The instructor asks for a volunteer (for which extra credit is given) to invite and interview in class an older person who is still active and who has had interesting life experiences.

B.   Objectives
You will:
1.   Gain an appreciation of what it is like to be an older person in our society.
2.   Be motivated to have more contact and communication with the older persons who are relatives, friends, and acquaintances.

C.   Procedure
1.   Suggested questions for the volunteer to ask the older person follow. The volunteer should follow up on comments, probe as necessary, and ask for clarification. The other students in the class should also be encouraged to ask questions.

QUESTIONS

1.   How old are you and where were you born?
2.   What did you do for a living? (Can include housewife and mother.)
3.   How old do you feel—younger than your age, older?

2.   When the interview ends, the volunteer should thank the older person.

3.   At some later class session, the instructor may ask for another volunteer to invite and interview a different older person.

Exercise 14.3: Meditation

A.   Brief description
The instructor will lead you in three forms of meditation.

B.   Objectives
You will:
1.   Experience the enjoyable effects of being deeply relaxed.
2.   Learn to describe the harmful effects of stress, and to identify when you are experiencing high levels of stress.
3.   Be able to use one or more of these meditative techniques in the future in order to relax when stress levels mount.

C.   Procedure
1.   Using the material in the chapter, the instructor briefly summarizes what stress is and indicates that prolonged high levels of stress lead to emotional disorders, behavioral disorders, and stress-related illnesses. It is important for each person to learn some ways to reduce stress.
2.   Many people are unaware of moderately elevated levels of stress. By becoming more conscious of your body signals, you can learn to identify when stress levels are too high. Look at the section below, "Signals for a Good Level of Stress and for Too High a Level of Stress." With practice you can learn awareness of body signals that indicate when levels of stress are too high.

SIGNALS FOR A GOOD LEVEL OF STRESS AND FOR
A TOO-HIGH LEVEL OF STRESS

Good Level of Stress	**Level of Stress Too High**

1. Feelings

Excitement, exhilaration	Anxiety, fear, timidity
Pleasure, enjoyment	Anger, resentfulness, dissatisfaction, bitterness
Relaxation, calmness	Confusion, feelings of being overwhelmed or swamped
Feeling of confidence	Helplessness or powerlessness
	Fear of inadequacy or failure
	Tension or tightness
	Depression, weariness, feeling fed up
	Paranoia

2. Behaviors

Smile, laugh, joke	Engage in wasted motion and activity
Act intelligent and knowledgeable	Irritable—put people down
Sensitive to others, appreciate others, and recognize contributions of others	Unpleasant to be around
Get a lot done—productive	Let little things get to you
Able to listen to others	Impatient
Generally successful	Tend to be easily startled by small sounds
Friendly	Unable to concentrate
Creative; make good decisions	Stutter
	Smoke to excess
	Overeat or overdrink (e.g., coffee)
	Poor work quality
	Not creative
	High-pitched nervous laughter

3. Body Reactions

Coordinated body reactions	Various aches and pains in head, muscles, back, neck
Absence of ill health	Ulcers or upset stomach
Absence of aches and pains	Sleep problems
Unaware of your body, which functions smoothly	Skin rashes, itches, skin irritations
Sleep soundly	Breathing irregularities or asthma
	Tense or tight muscles
	High blood pressure
	Frequent colds, flu
	Feelings of weakness or dizziness
	Trembling, nervous tics
	Sweating, frequent need to urinate
	Diarrhea or vomiting; loss of appetite; accident prone

3. Learning to meditate is one way to reduce stress. The instructor leads you in three meditative exercises. The purpose is to demonstrate that through meditating you can become deeply relaxed.

You can do these exercises by yourself, whenever you are anxious and want to relax. For example, you can use them to relax prior to taking an important exam or giving a speech. You may also want to do these exercises before going to bed at night in order to fall asleep faster. The instructor slowly reads the following to the class, pausing occasionally. (The instructor is free to modify what is said to the class.)

Herbert Benson, who wrote *The Relaxation Response*, has identified four key elements common to meditative approaches that help people to relax. These four elements are: (1) being in a quiet place; (2) getting in a comfortable position; (3) having an object to dwell on, such as your breathing, or thinking about your ideal relaxation place, or a neutral word or phrase that you continually repeat silently; and (4) having a passive attitude in which you let go of your day-to-day concerns by no longer thinking about them. Having a passive attitude is the key element in helping you to relax.

Now, I want you to form a circle. [Wait until a circle is formed.] I will lead you in three types of meditation. First, we will do a deep breathing exercise. Then, we will repeat the word "Relax" silently to ourselves. Third, I'll have you focus on visualizing your most relaxing place. We will move directly from the first to the second, and then from the second to the third without stopping. When we do this exercise, don't worry about anything unusual happening. There will be no tricks. Concentrate on what I'm telling you to focus on, while taking a passive attitude where you let go of your everyday thoughts and concerns. Everyday thoughts and concerns may occasionally enter your mind, but seek to let go of them when they do.

Before we start, I want each of you to identify one of your most relaxing scenes. It may be lying in the sun on a beach or by a lake. It may be sitting in warm water in a bathtub reading a book. It may be sitting by a warm fireplace. Is there anyone who hasn't identified a relaxing scene? [Wait until everyone has identified one.]

OK, we're ready to start. [If possible, dim the lights, or turn out some of them.] First, I want you to close your eyes and keep them closed for the entire exercise. Next, get in a comfortable position. If you want, you can sit or lie on the floor. [Take five or six minutes for each of the three meditative exercises. Speak softly and slowly. Pause frequently, sometimes for twenty seconds or more without saying anything. Feel free to add material to the following instructions.]

First, I want you to focus only on your breathing. Breathe in and out slowly and deeply...Breathe in and out slowly...as you breathe out feel how relaxing it feels...While exhaling, imagine your concerns are leaving you...as you're breathing in and out, feel how you're becoming more calm, more relaxed, more refreshed...Just keep focusing on breathing slowly in and out...Don't try to be in sync when I'm talking about breathing in and out...Find a breathing rhythm that's comfortable for you...Breathe in slowly and deeply, and then slowly breathe out...You've got the power within you to get more and more relaxed...All you have to do is focus on your breathing...Breathe in slowly and deeply, and then slowly breathe out...If other thoughts happen to enter your mind, just let them drift away as effortlessly as possible...The key to becoming more relaxed is to let go of your day-to-day concerns...To do this, all you need to do is simply focus on your breathing...Breathe in slowly and deeply, and then breathe out.

Now we will switch to repeating silently to yourself the word "Relax." Keep your eyes closed...just keep repeating to yourself the word "Relax"...Keep repeating "Relax" to yourself silently and slowly...If day-to-day thoughts enter your mind, seek to stop thinking about them...Keep repeating "Relax" to yourself...All of us encounter daily stressors...It is impossible to avoid daily stressors...The important thing to remember about stress management is not to seek to avoid daily stressors but to find ways to relax when we are under high levels of stress...An excellent and very simple way to learn to relax is to sit in a quiet place, in a comfortable position, and silently repeat to yourself the word "Relax"... "Relax" ... "Relax"...By simply repeating the word "Relax" to yourself, you have the power within you to become more and more relaxed...Find a nice comfortable pace for repeating the word "Relax" to yourself...The pace should be slow enough so that you can relax...But not be so slow that thoughts about your day-to-day concerns enter your mind...Remember, the key to relaxing is letting go of your day-to-day concerns...If such concerns begin to enter your mind, focus more of your attention on repeating "Relax" silently and slowly to yourself...By repeating "Relax" to yourself, you will find it will appear to have magical powers for you, as you will find yourself becoming more and more relaxed and refreshed...[Have the members repeat "Relax" for five or six minutes.]

Now, we will switch to focusing on your most relaxing scene. Don't open your eyes...Focus on being in your most relaxing place...Feel how good and relaxing it feels...Just dwell on how relaxing it feels...Enjoy everything about how calm and relaxing this place is...Feel yourself becoming calmer, more relaxed...Enjoy the peacefulness of this place...Feel yourself becoming more relaxed, more renewed and refreshed...Enjoy all the sights and sounds of this special place for you...Notice and cherish the pleasant smells and aromas...Feel the warmth, peacefulness, and serenity of this very special place for you...Whenever you want to become more relaxed, all you have to do is close your eyes, sit quietly, and visualize yourself being in this very relaxing place...The more you practice visualizing being in your relaxing place, the quicker you will find yourself becoming relaxed...It will appear to you that your relaxing place has magical, relaxing powers for you, but in reality you are simply relaxing yourself by letting go of your day-to-day concerns and instead focusing on enjoying the peacefulness of your most relaxing place...If you have to give a speech, or are facing some other stressful situation, you can learn to reduce your level of anxiety by simply closing your eyes for a short period of time and focusing your thoughts on being in your most relaxing place... You always have the power within you to reduce your level of anxiety...All you have to do is close your eyes and visualize being in your very special relaxing place...Continue to visualize, now, being in this very relaxing place...Feel yourself becoming more relaxed, refreshed, and calm...If you're feeling drowsy, that's fine...Feeling drowsy is an indication that you're becoming more and more relaxed...You're doing fine...Just keep on visualizing being in your very relaxing place...You will become more and more relaxed by simply letting go of your day-to-day concerns and by enjoying this very special relaxing place...[Pause, then continue this exercise for five or six minutes.]

Unfortunately, in a minute or so, it will be time to return to this class, but there is no hurry. I will slowly count backward from 5 to 1, and then ask you to open your eyes shortly after we reach 1... 5. Enjoy how relaxed you feel. You may now feel warmer, drowsy, and so relaxed that you feel you don't even want to move a muscle...Enjoy this very special feeling...It is so healthy to become this relaxed as your immune system functions best when you are relaxed... 4. Slowly begin to return to this class...There is no rush...There is no hurry...Take your time to become more alert. Anytime you want to relax, all you need to do is use one of these three meditative approaches. With practice, you will gradually get better at relaxing by using these approaches... 3. You should now focus on returning in a short time to this class...Take your time...We still have a half-minute or so...Examine whether you want to make a commitment to use relaxation exercises to reduce the daily stress you encounter... 2. We are nearly at the time to return to this class...You should now work toward becoming more and more alert... 1. Slowly open your eyes...There is no hurry...Take your time to get oriented. A word of caution: If you have to drive some place soon, please walk around for several minutes before trying to drive a car, as you may be so relaxed now that you may not be alert enough to drive safely.

4.   What do you think of these three approaches? How relaxed did you get? Did you have trouble getting relaxed? If yes, why? Which of the three approaches did you like best and why?

Chapter 15
Psychological Aspects of Later Adulthood

Study Outline

I. **A Perspective**

II. **Developmental Tasks of Later Adulthood**

    A.   Retirement and lower income

    B.   Living with one's spouse in retirement

    C.   Affiliating with individuals of one's own age group or with associations for older people

    D.   Maintaining interest in friends and family ties

    E.   Continuing social and civic responsibilities

    F.   Coping with illness and loss of a spouse and/or friends

    G.   Finding satisfactory living arrangements at the different stages of later adulthood

    H.   Adjusting to changing physical strength and health and overcoming bodily preoccupation

    I.   Accepting the prospect of death

III. **Theoretical Concepts about Developmental Tasks in Later Adulthood**

    A.   Integrity versus despair

        1.   Integrity: An ability to accept the facts of one's life and to face death without great fear

        2.   Despair: A feeling of regret about one's past, including a continuous nagging desire to have done things differently

        3.   Men, particularly older men, are more apt to commit suicide than are women. Men are more apt than women to view their chosen career as providing the primary source of meaning in life

    B.   Three key psychological adjustments

        1.   Self-differentiation: The older person has to adjust to the fact that she or he will no longer go to work and needs to find a new identity and new interests

2. Body transcendence: Health problems increase for older people, and energy levels decrease. Those who make this transcendence have generally learned to define comfort and happiness in terms of satisfying social relationships or creative mental activities. Many older people become preoccupied with their state of health and their appearance

3. Self-transcendence: The inevitability of death must be dealt with

C. Life review

1. The two key elements in this review are: Concluding that the past was meaningful and learning to accept the inevitability of death

2. A reorganization of the past may provide a more valid picture for the individual, providing a new and significant meaning to his or her life

3. Ethical Question 15.1: In a review of your life from birth to the present time, would you view your past as meaningful or meaningless?

D. Self-esteem

1. If older people are treated by others as if they are old-fashioned, senile, dependent, and incompetent, they are apt to view themselves in the same way

2. Privacy is a factor in furthering competence and self-esteem

E. Life satisfaction: A sense of psychological well-being in general or of satisfaction with life as a whole

F. Low status and ageism

1. Older people suffer psychologically because our society has been generally unsuccessful in finding something important or satisfying for them to do

2. In most primitive and earlier societies, older people were respected and viewed as useful to their people to a much greater degree than is the case in our society. Their experiences enabled them to supervise planting and harvesting and to pass on knowledge about hunting, housing, and crafts. Older people also played key roles in preserving and transmitting the culture

3. Our society does not allow many of our older people to experience their later years positively. We don't respect older people for their experience and wisdom, but instead dismiss their ideas as being irrelevant and outdated

4. Ethical Question 15.2: Do you have negative images of, and negative attitudes toward, being old?

5. Ageism: Having negative images of, and attitudes toward, people simply because they are old

G.   Spotlight on Diversity 15.1: Triple Jeopardy: Being Female, African American, and Old

      1.   Despite their positive status in the African American family and culture, African American women over the age of 70 are the poorest population group in the United States

      2.   Three out of five older African American women live alone; most of them are widowed

      3.   Even though many of these women are struggling financially, socially, and physically, they have shown remarkable adaptiveness, resilience, coping skills, and responsibility

      4.   African American churches have provided avenues for meaningful social participation, social welfare services, feelings of power, and a sense of internal satisfaction

H.   Depression and other emotional problems

      1.   Depression is the most common emotional problem of older people. Those who have had unresolved emotional problems earlier in life will generally continue to have them when older

      2.   Two major barriers to good mental health in the later years are failure to bounce back from psychosocial losses and failure to have meaningful life goals

      3.   Older people respond well to both individual and group counseling

I.   Spirituality and religion

      1.   Spirituality and religion are important components in the lives of older people

      2.   In recent years there has been a renewal of interest, in the social work profession, in recognizing the importance of spirituality and religion

      3.   In a study of 100 well-educated white women and men aged 58 to 80, heading the list of coping strategies were behaviors associated with religion

      4.   A study of 836 older adults found that people who were religious had a higher level of morale, better attitude toward aging, and were more satisfied and less lonely than those who were not affiliated with any religion

      5.   Ethical Question 15.3: Do you respect the religious beliefs of people who adhere to a different religion than yours?

      6.   As people grow older and reflect about death and the meaning of their lives, they are apt to focus more on spiritual matters

7. Spotlight on Diversity 15.2: Spirituality and Religion

    a. It is essential that social workers comprehend the influence of religion and spirituality in human lives. The Educational Policy and Accreditation Standards of the Council on Social Work Education now require that accredited social work programs provide practice content in the area of religion and spirituality

    b. Spirituality: The general human experience of developing a sense of meaning, purpose, and morality

    c. Social work originated under the inspiration of the Judeo-Christian religious traditions of its philanthropic founders

    d. There is a danger that those who believe that their religion is the "one true religion" will tend to view people with divergent religious beliefs as ill-guided, evil, mistaken, or in need of being "saved." More wars have been fought over religious differences than for any other cause

    e. The goal of incorporating religious and spiritual beliefs in social curricula should include a broad array of knowledge of many different religious and spiritual beliefs, primarily to expand students' understanding and sensitivity

    f. Judaism

        1) Judaism is the religion of the Jews. Jews believe in one God, the creator of the world

        2) The Hebrew Bible is the primary text of Judaism. (The Hebrew Bible was adopted by Christians as part of their sacred writings, and they now call it the Old Testament.) God is believed to have revealed his law (Torah) to the Jewish people; part of this law was the Ten Commandments, which were given to Moses by God

        3) Next in importance to the Hebrew Bible is the Talmud, an influential compilation of rabbinic traditions and discussions about Jewish life and law

        4) Abraham (who lived roughly 2,000 years before Christ) is viewed as an ancestor or father of the Hebrew people. Abraham is regarded by Judaism, Christianity, and Islam as an important ancestor or father of their religion

        5) All Jews see themselves as members of a community whose origins lie in the time in which Abraham lived. The family is the basic unit of Jewish ritual, although the synagogue has come to play an increasing important role

6) The Sabbath, which begins at sunset on Friday and ends at sunset on Saturday, is the central time of religious worship. A rabbi is primarily a teacher and a spiritual guide

7) There is an annual cycle of religious festivals and days of fasting

   a) Rosh Hashanah: The Jewish New Year, which falls in September or October

   b) Yom Kippur: The Day of Atonement, the holiest day in the Jewish year. This comes at the end of 10 days of penitence following Rosh Hashanah. It is a day devoted to fasting, prayer, and repentance for past sins

   c) Hanukkah: Held in December, commemorating the rededication of Jerusalem after the victory of Judas Maccabees over the Syrians

   d) Pesach: The Passover festival, occurring in March or April, which commemorates the exodus of the Israelites from Egypt; the festival is named after God's passing over the house of Israelites when he killed the first-born children of Egyptian families

g. Christianity

1) This religion is centered on the life and work of Jesus of Nazareth, and developing out of Judaism. The earliest followers were Jews, who, after the death and resurrection of Jesus, believed him to be the Messiah or Christ, as promised by the prophets in the Old Testament. He was declared to be the Son of God

2) During his life he chose 12 men as disciples, who formed the nucleus of the church. This communion of believers believed that Jesus would come again to inaugurate the "Kingdom of God"

3) God is believed to be one in essence but threefold in person, comprising the Father, the Son, and the Holy Spirit or Holy Ghost (known as the Trinity). The Holy Spirit represents the touch or "breath" of God that inspires people to follow the Christian faith. The Bible is thought to have been written under the Holy Spirit's influence

4) Jesus Christ was the son of Mary and Joseph, yet also the Son of God, created by a miraculous conception by the spirit of God. He was born in Bethlehem, but began his ministry in Nazareth

5)   The main records of his ministry are the New Testament Gospels, which show him proclaiming the coming of the Kingdom of God and, in particular, the acceptance of the oppressed and the poor into the kingdom. The duration of his public ministry is uncertain, but from John's Gospel, one gets the impression of a 3-year period of teaching. He was executed by crucifixion under the order of Pontius Pilate, a Roman ruler. Jesus was believed to be in his early 30s

6)   At the heart of the Christian faith is the conviction that through Jesus' death and resurrection, God has allowed humans to find salvation. Many Christians believe that those who ask for forgiveness of their sins will join God in heaven, while nonbelievers who do not ask for forgiveness of their sins will be consigned to hell

7)   The Gospel of Jesus was proclaimed at first by word of mouth, but by the end of the first century A.D., it was written down and became accepted as the authoritative scripture of the New Testament. The Christian faith spread through the Greek and Roman worlds, and in 315 A.D., was declared by Emperor Constantine to be the official religion of the Roman Empire

8)   Since the Middle Ages, major divisions of Western Christianity have formed as a result of differences in doctrine and practice

h.   Islam

1)   Islam is the Arabic word for "submission" to the will of God, Allah. Islam is also the name of the religion originating in Arabia during the seventh century through the prophet Muhammad. Followers of Islam are known as Muslims, or Moslems

2)   Muhammad was born in Mecca. He was the son of Abdallah, a poor merchant of the powerful tribe of Quaraysh, hereditary guardians of the shrine of Mecca. Muhammad was orphaned at 6 and raised by his grandfather and uncle. His uncle, Abu Talib, trained him to be a merchant. He married a rich widow, and had six children. While continuing as a trader, Muhammad became increasingly drawn to religious contemplation

3)   Muhammad began receiving revelations of the word of Allah, the one and only God, by the angel Gabriel over a period of 20 years. They were eventually codified into the Quran (Koran)

4)   The Quran commanded that the numerous idols of the shrine should be destroyed and that the rich should give to the poor. This message provoked a great deal of hostility from those who felt their interests threatened. When his wife and uncle died, Muhammad was reduced to poverty, but he began making a few converts among the pilgrims to Mecca

5)   Muhammad migrated to Hegira. The name of this town was changed to Medina, "the city of the prophet." This migration marks the beginning of the Muslim era. After a series of battles with warring enemies of Islam, Muhammad was able to take control of Mecca, which recognized him as the chief and prophet. By 360 A.D. he had control over all of Arabia. Two years later he fell ill and died in the home of one of his nine wives. His tomb in the mosque at Medina is venerated throughout Islam

6)   The religion of Islam embraces every aspect of life. Muslims believe that individuals, societies, and governments should all be obedient to the will of God as set forth in the Quran. The Quran teaches that there is one God who has no partners. He is the Creator of all things and has absolute power over them. All persons should commit themselves to lives of praise-giving and grateful obedience to God, as everyone will be judged on the Day of Resurrection. Those who have obeyed God's commandments will dwell forever in paradise, while those who have sinned against God and have not repented will be condemned eternally to the fires of hell

7)   There are five essential religious duties, known as "the pillars of Islam"

    a)   Shahadah: (Profession of faith) is the sincere recitation of the two-fold creed: "There is no god but God" and "Muhammad is the Messenger of God"

    b)   Salat: (Formal prayer) must be performed at fixed hours five times a day while facing toward the holy city of Mecca

    c)   Zakat: ("Purification") Alms-giving through the payment of Zakat is regarded primarily as an act of worship and is the duty of sharing one's wealth out of gratitude for God's favor, according to the uses stated in the Quran

    d)   Saum: A duty to fast (Saum) during the month of Ramadan. (Ramadan is the ninth month of the Muslim year). Muslims abstain from eating and drinking between sunrise and sunset

    e)   Hajj: The pilgrimage (hajj) to Mecca is to be performed if at all possible at least once during one's lifetime

8)   Sariah is the sacred law of Islam, and applies to all aspects of life, not just religious practices. This is found in the Quran and the Sunnah (the sayings and acts of Muhammad)

i.   Buddhism

1)   Buddhism originated in India about 2,500 years ago. The religion derived from the teachings of Buddha (Siddharta Gautama). Buddha is regarded as one of the continuing series of enlightened beings

2)   At about age 30, Buddha (Gautama) left the luxuries of the court, his beautiful wife, and all earthly ambitions. He became an ascetic, and he practiced strict self-denial as a measure of personal and spiritual discipline. After several years he saw, in meditation and contemplation, the way to enlightenment. For the next 4 decades, he taught, gaining many followers and disciples. He died at Kusinagara in Oudh

3)   The teachings of Buddha are summarized in the Four Noble Truths, the last of which asserts the existence of a path leading to deliverance from the universal human experience of suffering

4)   A central tenet of Buddhism is the law of Karma, by which good and evil deeds result in appropriate rewards or punishments in this life or in a succession of rebirths. It is believed that the sum of a person's actions is carried forward from one life to the next, leading to an improvement or a deterioration in that person's fate

5)   The Buddha's path to deliverance is through morality (Sila), meditation (Samadhi), and wisdom (Panna). The goal is Nirvana, which is the "blowing out" of the fires of all desires and the absorption of the self into the infinite

6)   All Buddhas are greatly revered, with a place of special accordance being given to Gautama

7)   There are two main branches of Buddhism, dating from its earliest history

   a)   Theravada Buddhism adheres to the strict and narrow teachings of the early Buddhist writings; in this branch, salvation is possible for only the few who accept the severe discipline and effort to achieve it

   b)   Mahayana Buddhism is more liberal and makes concessions to popular piety; it teaches that salvation is possible for everyone. It introduced the doctrine of the bodhisattva (or personal savior). A bodhisattva is one who has attained the enlightenment of a Buddha but chooses not to pass into nirvana and voluntarily remains in the world to help lesser beings attain enlightenment

IV.   Theories of Successful Aging: The Strengths Perspective

A.   Activity theory: The more physically and mentally active one is, the more successfully one will age

B.   Disengagement theory

1.   Disengagement theory: A process whereby people respond to aging by gradually withdrawing from the various roles and social relationships they occupied in middle age

2.   Ethical Question 15.4: Is it functional for older people to gradually withdraw from the various roles and social relationships they occupied in middle age?

3.   Community disengagement theory: Refers not only to older people withdrawing from the community, but also to the community withdrawing from older people

4.   Evaluation of disengagement theory

a.   Research has found that some people do voluntarily disengage as they grow older

b.   Critics assert that disengagement is related less to old age itself than to the factors associated with aging

c.   Disengagement is neither universal nor inevitable. Contrary to the theory's predictions, most older persons maintain extensive associations with friends, and active involvement in voluntary organizations

d.   The disengagement theory at times advocates the exact opposite of the activity theory

5.   Ethical issues: A severe criticism of the disengagement theory is that it may be used to justify society's failure to help older people maintain meaningful roles

C.   Social reconstruction syndrome theory

1.   Social breakdown occurs for older people because of the effects of labeling

2.   Social reconstruction syndrome

a.   Our society should liberate older people from unrealistic standards and expectations

b.   Society should provide older people with the social services they need

c.   Society should find creative ways to give older people more control over their lives

V. The Impact of Life Events on Older People

A. Marriage

    1. Couples who are still married in their later years are less likely than younger couples to see their marriages as full of problems

    2. Being in love is still important for successful marriage in late adulthood

    3. People over age 70 tend to consider themselves less happily married than those aged 63 to 69

    4. Married older people are happier than the unmarried, and considerably happier than the widowed and the divorced

B. Death of spouse

    1. The more intertwined married couples are, the deeper the loss is apt to be felt

    2. The survivor's social life changes; gradually friends and family return to their own lives, leaving the widower or widow to form a new life

C. Widowhood

    1. Because women tend to live longer than men, and tend to be younger than their husbands, they are more likely to be widowed

    2. People who adjust best to widowhood are those who keep busy

D. Never married

    1. Only about 5 percent of older men and women have never been married

    2. People who have never been married tend to be more independent, have fewer social relationships, and express less concern about their age than older persons who have been married

E. Remarriage

    1. Our society has generally opposed the idea of older people dating and remarrying

    2. Remarriage in later adulthood is increasing

    3. Our society should change its negative attitude about remarriage in later adulthood

F.   Family system relationships

1.   Research suggests that most older adults' family relationships are generally quite positive

2.   In most instances, older people and their adult children do not live together; however, they tend to live close to them and to see them frequently

3.   The fact that many adults would rather see their parents cared for in a nursing home than living with them suggests that they do not feel as great an obligation to their parents as do members of primitive societies

4.   Most older people see their children quite often—an average of once or twice a week

5.   How parents help children

a.   Parents are usually the primary caregivers for adult children who have a mental illness, have a moderate cognitive disability, or who have some other disability

b.   In a study of 29 healthy, white, Midwestern, middle-class, and working-class married couples who were aged 60 and over, it was found that the subjects' children were a daily topic of conversation

c.   Another study found that when an adult moves into the home of his or her older parents, the parents report that they get along quite well

d.   Grandparents who are providing care to their grandchildren or to their adult children refute the societal myth that older adults are freed from active parenting and its stresses

G.   Grandparenthood

1.   Five major styles of grandparenting in our society

a.   Fun seeker: Playmate to the grandchildren in a mutual relationship that both enjoy

b.   Distant figure: Periodic contact with the grandchildren, generally on birthdays and holidays, but is quite uninvolved with their lives

c.   Surrogate parent: Assumes considerable caretaking responsibilities, usually because the grandchildren's parents are working, or because the mother is single and working

d.   Formal figure: Leaves all child-rearing responsibilities to the parents and limits his or her involvement with the grandchildren to providing special treats and occasional babysitting

e.   Reservoir of family wisdom: Takes on an authoritarian role and dispenses special resources and skills

2. The tacit "norm of noninterference" by grandparents tends to evaporate in times of trouble faced by their adult children and their grandchildren

3. Grandmothers tend to have closer and warmer relationships with their grandchildren and are more apt to serve as surrogate parents than are grandfathers, and the mother's parents are likely to be closer to the grandchildren than the father's parents

4. Grandmothers tend to be more satisfied with grandparenting than are grandfathers

H. Great-grandparenthood

1. Great-grandparents view great-grandchildren as a source of diversion and as evidence of their own longevity and of their family's renewal and continued survival

2. Because of age, declining health, and the scattering of families, great-grandparents tend to be less involved than grandparents in a child's life

VI. Guidelines for Positive Psychological Preparation for Later Adulthood: The Strengths Perspective

A. Highlight 15.1: Jimmy Carter: Stumbled as President, Excelled in Later Adulthood

B. Factors that are closely related to satisfaction in later adulthood

1. Close personal relationships

2. Finances

3. Interests and hobbies

4. Self-identity

5. Looking toward the future

6. Coping with crises

VII. Grief Management and Death Education

A. Death in our society: Impact of social forces

1. Spotlight on Diversity 15.3: The Cultural-Historical Context of Death and Bereavement

a. In ancient Greece, bodies of heroes were publicly burned as a symbol of honor. Public cremation is still practiced by Hindus in India and Nepal

b. Cremation is prohibited under Orthodox Jewish law, as it is believed that the dead will rise again for a "last judgment" and the chance for eternal life

c. To this day, some of the Polynesians that live in the Tahitian islands bury their parents in the front yard of their parents' home as a way of remembering them

d. In Malayan society (which prospered several centuries ago in Mexico and Central America), death was seen as a gradual transition. At first a body was given only a provisional burial. Survivors continued to perform mourning rites until the body decayed to the point where it was thought the soul left it and transcended into the spiritual realm

e. In Japan, religious rituals expect survivors to maintain contact with the deceased. Families keep an altar in their homes that is dedicated to their ancestors

f. Hopi (Native American tribe) fear the spirits of the deceased and try to forget, as quickly as possible, those who have died

g. Some modern cultural customs have evolved from ancient ones. The current practice of embalming evolved from the mummification practice in ancient Egypt and China that was designed to preserve a body so that the soul could eventually return to it

h. Muslims in Bali are encouraged to suppress sadness and to laugh and be joyful at burials. Muslims in Egypt are encouraged to express their grief through displaying deep sorrow

2. In our society we tend to shy away from thinking about death. We need to become comfortable with the idea of our own eventual death

3. Funerals are needed for survivors. They help initiate the grieving process so that people can work through their grief

4. Children should not be sheltered from death. They should be taken to funerals of relatives and friends and their questions answered honestly

5. It is generally a mistake for survivors to seek to appear strong and emotionally calm following the death of a close friend or relative

6. Many health professionals find death difficult to handle

B. The grieving process

C.   Kübler-Ross model

    1.   Stage one: Denial

    2.   Stage two: Rage and anger

    3.   Stage three: Bargaining

    4.   Stage four: Depression

    5.   Stage five: Acceptance

D.   Westberg model

    1.   Shock and denial

    2.   Emotions erupt

    3.   Anger

    4.   Illness

    5.   Panic

    6.   Guilt

    7.   Depression and loneliness

    8.   Reentry difficulties

    9.   Hope

    10.   Affirming reality

    11.   Figure 15.1 Westberg Model of the Grieving Process

E.   Evaluation of models of the grieving process: Kübler-Ross and Westberg note that some people continue grieving and never do reach the final stage, and they caution that it is a mistake to rigidly believe everyone will progress through these stages as diagrammed. There is considerable movement back and forth in these stages

F.   How to cope with grief

    1.   Crying is an acceptable and valuable expression of grief

    2.   Talking about the loss and about your plans is very constructive

    3.   Death often causes us to examine and question our faith or philosophy of life

    4.   Writing out a rational self-analysis on your grief will help you to identify irrational thinking that is contributing to your grief

5. Try not to dwell on how unhappy you feel. Become involved and active in life around you

6. Seek to accept the inevitability of death—yours and that of others

7. If the loss is the death of a loved one, holidays and the anniversaries of your loved one's birth and death can be stressful

8. You may feel that you have nothing to live for and may even think about suicide. Seek to find assurance in the fact that a sense of purpose and meaning will return

9. Intense grief is very stressful, and is a factor that leads to a variety of illnesses

10. Intense grief may lead to sleeplessness, sexual difficulties, loss of appetite, or overeating. You may find you have little energy and cannot concentrate. Don't be surprised if you dream the person is still alive

11. Medication should be taken sparingly and only under the supervision of a physician

12. Recognizing that guilt, real or imagined, is a normal part of grief. Learn to forgive yourself. All humans make mistakes

13. You may find that friends and relatives appear to be shunning you. Take the initiative and talk with them about your loss. Inform them about ways in which you would like them to be supportive of you

14. If possible, put off making major decisions until you become more emotionally relaxed

G. Application of Grief Management Theory to Client Situations

1. Initiator

2. Educator

3. Counselor

4. Group facilitator

5. Broker

6. Social workers need to become comfortable with their own eventual death

H. How to relate to a dying person

1. Highlight 15.2: Questions about Grief, Death, and Dying

2. You need to accept the idea of your own eventual death and view death as a normal process

3. Convey verbally that you are willing to talk about any concerns that the other person has. Touching or hugging the dying person is very helpful

4. Answer the dying person's questions as honestly as you can

5. A dying person should be allowed to accept the reality of the situation at his or her own pace

6. If people around the dying person are able to accept the death, the dying person is helped to accept the death

7. If you do have trouble about certain subjects involving death, inform the dying person of your limitations

8. The religious or philosophical viewpoint of the dying person should be respected. Your own personal views should not be imposed

9. Ethical Dilemma: Whether to Insert a Feeding Tube?

I. How to relate to survivors

1. If you are comfortable about your own death, you will be better able to calmly listen to the concerns being expressed by survivors

2. It is helpful to initiate the first encounter with a survivor by saying you are sorry, and then touching or hugging the person. Then convey that if he or she wants to talk or needs help, you're available

3. It is helpful to use active listening with both survivors and persons who are terminally ill

4. It is frequently helpful to share with a survivor pleasant and positive memories you have about the person who has died

5. Continue to visit the survivors if they show interest in such visits

6. The religious or philosophical viewpoint of survivors should be respected. You should not impose your views on the survivors

J. How to become comfortable with your own eventual death

1. Ethical Question 15.5: Are you comfortable with the fact that someday you will die? Most people are not. If you are not, what do you need to work on to become more comfortable?

2. Identify what your concerns are and then seek answers to these concerns

3. Taboos against talking about death and dying need to be broken in our society

4. It is probably accurate that we will never become fully accepting of the idea of our own death, but we can learn a lot more about the subject and obtain answers to many of the questions and concerns we have

5. Some people become more comfortable with their own death by studying the research that has been conducted on near-death experiences

6. View dying as the final stage of growth

7. Having a well-developed sense of identity is an important step in learning to become comfortable with our own eventual death

8. Highlight 15.3: Life after Life

VIII. Summary

Experiential Exercises and Simulations

Seven exercises are described in this section. The first helps you examine your attitudes about later adulthood. The second is designed to help you learn how to handle losses constructively. The third helps you become more comfortable with the idea of your own eventual death. The fourth has you write your own epitaph. The fifth is designed to help you examine your personal feelings and beliefs about death. The sixth helps you become more aware of the thoughts and feelings you will have when your death becomes imminent. The seventh is designed to assist you in respecting diverse religious beliefs.

Exercise 15.1: Attitudes Toward Later Adulthood

A. Brief description
You will complete an attitudinal questionnaire about later adulthood, and the responses will be discussed.

B. Objectives
You will:
1. Be more aware of your attitudes toward and values concerning later adulthood.
2. Be able to identify prejudicial statements about older people.

C. Procedure
1. Answer the following ten questions related to your attitudes about later adulthood. Write your answers on a sheet of paper or a five-by-seven-inch notecard. Do <u>not</u> write your name on the response sheet.
2. The instructor will slowly read the following questions, giving you time to record your responses. Alternatively, you may read the questions from this manual.

a. Do you currently have a friend or relative over age 65 with whom you frequently discuss your concerns?
_____ Yes _____ No

b. Do you believe that most people over age 65 are physically attractive?
_____ Yes _____ No

c. Do you believe that it is desirable for older people to be sexually active?
_____ Yes _____ No

3.   The instructor collects the responses and lists the letter of each question on the chalkboard, from (a) through (j). Volunteers record the responses.
4.   Reread each question, and discuss the responses.

Exercise 15.2: Learning to Grieve Constructively

A.   Brief description
Through a visualization exercise, you will review how you handle a significant loss. Volunteers will share their grieving experiences. Suggestions are given on how to handle significant losses constructively.

B.   Objectives
You will:
1.   Understand two models of the grieving process.
2.   Be able to more effectively handle past, present, and future losses.

C.   Procedure
1.   The instructor summarizes the Kübler-Ross and Westberg models of the grieving process. (As an alternative, you can read this material in the text.)
2.   This exercise is designed to help you get in touch with a grief experience that you have had. The exercise may become intense. If it becomes too intense, it is certainly acceptable if you leave the room temporarily.
3.   The instructor asks you (and the other students) to close your eyes. There will be no surprises in this exercise. The instructor reads the following slowly, pausing frequently:

First, I want to have you get as relaxed and comfortable as possible...Take several deep breaths, while breathing in and out slowly...I want you now to focus on the greatest loss you have experienced...It might be the death of someone close to you...It might be the end of a romantic relationship...It might be moving away from friends and family...It might be the death of a pet...It might be not getting as high a grade on a test or in a course that you had hoped for...Whatever it is, concentrate on it...

When you were first informed about the loss, were you in a state of shock?...Did you deny the loss?...Were you, at times, angry about the loss?...Did you, at times, seek to bargain about the loss?...If you did seek to bargain, whom did you seek to bargain with?...Were you, at times, depressed about the loss?...If you were depressed, why (specifically) were you depressed?...Did you at times have some fears or concerns about the loss?...If you had fears or concerns, what were these fears or concerns?...Did you at times have guilt about this loss?...If you did feel guilty, what specifically did you feel guilty about? Did you cry about this loss?...If you cried, do you know why you cried?...If you didn't cry, do you know why you didn't cry?...If you cried, was it helpful?...How deeply has this loss hurt you?...How long have you been hurting about this loss?...

Do you at times still grieve deeply about this loss?...Have you found that as time goes on you are grieving less deeply, and that your intense grieving periods are shorter in duration?...Do holidays, anniversaries, birthdays, special days still remind you of the loss?...If and when you are grieving deeply, how do you seek to handle this grief?...

Has the loss been so great that you thought about taking your life?...Many people think about taking their life when they are grieving deeply...Have you made attempts to take your life?...

Have you had some physical reactions to the loss, such as difficulty in sleeping, stomach problems, headaches, anxiety attacks, sexual difficulties?...Grieving is very stressful, and it is common to have physical reactions...Do you dream about the loss?...For example, it is common for people who have lost a loved one to dream that person is still alive...Often when someone awakes from such a dream, it is difficult to separate reality from the dream...

What aspects of the loss have you handled well?...What aspects could you have handled better?...What aspects are you still working on?...How have you gone about handling this loss?...How pleased are you with your efforts to handle this loss?...How have others close to you handled this loss?...How have you gone about helping them?...Have you grown from this loss experience?...What yet do you need to work on to handle this loss?...What specific efforts are you making to handle this loss?...OK...slowly open your eyes, and let's talk about grieving.

4. The instructor indicates that one of the best ways to handle grief is to talk about it. The instructor asks if someone wishes to share a loss he or she has experienced and describe what helped him or her to handle this loss. If no one begins to share a grieving experience, the instructor describes a personal loss and how it was handled.

5. The class discusses whether the Westberg model or the Kübler-Ross model of the grieving process can better describe the grief they experienced. The instructor ends the exercise by summarizing material given in the chapter on how to handle grief constructively.

Exercise 15.3: Becoming Comfortable With Your Own Death

A. Brief description
Through a visualization exercise, reflect on your reactions to being informed that you have a terminal illness. A discussion follows.

B. Objectives
You will:
1. Examine your fears about death and dying.
2. Become sufficiently comfortable with the concept of death so that you will be able to rationally contemplate your own eventual death.

C. Procedure
1. This is a visualization exercise. The instructor reads the following slowly:

> I want you to close your eyes and get as comfortable as possible. Take several deep breaths, while breathing in and out slowly. There will be no surprises in this exercise. (pause) Imagine that you haven't been feeling well for a period of time, and that you go to your doctor for a series of tests. The tests are taken, and you have an appointment to be informed about the results. The doctor has a concerned look and asks you to be seated. The doctor informs you that you have a terminal illness and estimates that you have about six or seven months to live. Does this scene seem believable? I know this scene may be difficult for some of you to imagine, as many of us like to think we will live for a very long time and don't want to think about our own death. If we are to become comfortable with our own death, we need to think about it and prepare for it. One way of doing so is through an exercise like this. Therefore, I ask you to concentrate as fully as you can on this scene in which you have just been informed you have a terminal illness.
>
> What are you thinking and feeling? Are you in a state of shock? Are you actively denying that this could happen? Are you breathing faster? Are your eyes watering? Is your heart beating faster? Are you numbed by this? Are you terrified? Do you have fears about the pain you may experience in your remaining months?
>
> What do you want to do? Are you interested in seeking more information about your illness from your physician? Do you want to leave the office? When you leave the office, what do you want to do—drive home? Tell friends or relatives? Be by yourself? What do you plan to do with the remaining months you have left to live? Do you want to travel? Would you seek to change your lifestyle? Would you seek to satisfy hedonistic desires such as sex or drugs? Would you become more withdrawn? Would you become more religious and pray more? Would you seek to complete projects and tie up loose ends? Would you become concerned about preparing dependents and friends about your death? Would you consider committing suicide?
>
> If it were possible, would you want to know the exact date on which you will die? What efforts do you believe ought to be made to keep you alive? All possible medical efforts even though there is no hope of returning to a quality life? Or, would you want medical efforts to be discontinued when there is little hope to return to a quality life?

What aspect of your own death is most distasteful to you? Is it that you will no longer have enjoyable experiences? Is it that you are afraid of what will happen to your body and mind after you die? Is it that you are uncertain as to what might happen to you if there is a life after death? Are you worried about what will happen to people who depend upon you? Are you concerned that your plans and projects might come to an end? Are you worried about your relatives and friends grieving about you? Are you worried about the pain you may experience before you die? Are you worried that your body may deteriorate as you die?

How would you want people to remember you? What would you like placed on your tombstone? If you want people to remember you in a certain way, are you living your life in such a way that they will remember you as you desire?

What kind of funeral do you want? Do you want a lot of people at your funeral? Or, do you want only close relatives and friends to be at your funeral? Do you want a church service? Do you want a lot of flowers at your funeral? Is there a certain song that you wish would be played? Do you think funerals are primarily for those who died, or for survivors to help them cope with the loss? Do you want a burial, or do you wish to be cremated? Have you considered donating parts of your body for organ transplants? Have you considered donating your body to a medical school or to science? If mystery surrounded your death, would you want an autopsy?

What does death mean to you? How is what happens after you die different from what life was like before you were born? Do you view death as the absolute end of life? Do you view death as being a transition to a new life? Do you view death as being a joining of your spirit with a cosmic force? Do you view death as being an endless sleep? Do you view death as the termination of this life, but with the survival of your spirit or soul? Do you believe that there is an afterlife?

If you would want to make changes in your life upon learning you have a terminal illness, what is preventing you from making these changes at the present time? OK, slowly open your eyes and let's talk.

2. The instructor discusses the exercise with the class, including the following questions:
   a. Did you have trouble visualizing the exercise as being real?
   b. If so, why do you think you had trouble?
   c. Do you think the exercise was helpful in getting you to think about, and become comfortable with, your eventual death?

Exercise 15.4: An Epitaph as a Guide to Living

A. Brief description
You will write an epitaph that is anonymously shared with the class.

B. Objectives
You will:
1. Better accept your eventual death.
2. Specify a broad-based statement as to how you want to live life prior to dying.
3. Compare your "guide to living" with that of others.

C. Procedure
1. A sheet of paper or a large notecard is distributed to each of you. Write down the epitaph you want placed on your tombstone. An epitaph is a brief statement or phrase describing the deceased. Do not put your name on the paper.
2. The instructor collects the epitaphs in a way that prevents them from being identified and reads them to the class.

Exercise 15.5: Questions About Grief, Death, and Dying

A. Brief description
You are asked to complete a questionnaire that forces you to confront personal feelings about death.

B. Objectives
You will:
1. Examine your personal feelings about death.
2. Increase your ability to empathize with persons who are coping with their own death or the death of a loved one.

C. Procedure
1. Fill out the following questionnaire:

QUESTIONS ABOUT GRIEF, DEATH, AND DYING
(For the multiple-choice questions, circle all of the items that apply to you)

1. Which of the following describe your present conception of death:
    a. Cessation of all mental and physical activity
    b. Sleep
    c. Existence in heaven or hell
    d. A pleasant afterlife
    e. Mysterious and unknown
    f. The end of all life
    g. A transition to a new beginning
    h. A joining of the spirit with an unknown cosmic force
    i. Termination of this physical life with survival of the spirit
    j. Something other than the above

2. Which of the following aspects of your own death do you find distasteful:
    a. What might happen to your body after death
    b. What might happen to you if there is a life after death
    c. What might happen to your dependents
    d. The grief that it would cause to your friends and relatives
    e. The pain you may experience as you die
    f. The deterioration of your body before you die
    g. All your plans and projects coming to an end
    h. Something other than the above

3. If you could choose, what age would you like to be when you die?

---

4. When you think of your own eventual death, how do you feel?
   a. Depressed
   b. Fearful
   c. Discouraged
   d. Purposeless
   e. Angry
   f. Pleasure in being alive
   g. Resigned, as you realize death is a natural process of living
   h. Other (specify)

5. For what, or for whom, would you be willing to sacrifice your life:
   a. An idea or moral principle
   b. A loved one
   c. The nation
   d. An emergency where another life could be saved
   e. Not for any reason

6. If you could choose, how would you prefer to die?
   a. A sudden violent death
   b. A sudden but nonviolent death
   c. A quiet and dignified death
   d. Death in the line of duty
   e. Suicide
   f. Homicide
   g. Death after you have achieved your life goals
   h. Other (specify)

7. If it were possible, would you want to know the exact date on which you would die?

8. Would you want to know if you had a terminal illness?

9. If you had six more months to live, how would you want to spend this time?
   a. Satisfying hedonistic desires such as sex
   b. Withdrawing
   c. Contemplating or praying
   d. Seeking to prepare loved ones for my death
   e. Completing projects and tying up loose ends
   f. Considering suicide
   g. Other (specify)

10. Have you seriously contemplated suicide? What are your moral views of suicide? Are there circumstances under which you would take your life?

11. If you had a serious illness, and the quality of your life had substantially deteriorated, what measures do you believe should be taken to keep you alive?
   a. All possible heroic medical efforts
   b. Medical efforts being discontinued when there is practically no hope of returning to a life with quality
   c. Other (specify)

12. If you are married, would you prefer to outlive your spouse? Why?

13. How important do you believe funerals and grief rituals are for survivors?

14. If it were up to you, how would you like to have your body disposed of after you die?
    a. Cremation
    b. Burial
    c. Donation of body parts for organ transplants
    d. Donation of body to medical school or to science
    e. Other (specify)

15. What kind of funeral would you prefer?
    a. A church service
    b. As large as possible
    c. Small with only close friends and relatives present
    d. A lavish funeral
    e. A simple funeral
    f. Whatever survivors want
    g. Other (specify)

16. Have you made a will? Why or why not?

17. Have you signed a living will? Why or why not?

18. Were you able to arrive at answers to most of these questions? Were you uncomfortable in answering these questions? If you were uncomfortable, what were you feeling, and what made you uncomfortable? For the questions you do not have answers to, how might you arrive at answers?

Exercise 15.6: Recognizing Life is Terminal

A. Brief description
Through giving up items you deeply cherish, you experience in simulated form feelings related to your own eventual death.

B. Objectives
You will:
1. Become more aware of the thoughts and feelings you will have when your own death becomes imminent.
2. Recognize life is terminal.

C.   Procedure

1.   The instructor begins by stating that many people do not like to attend funerals, nor do they like to think about their own eventual death. Many people avoid thinking about their own death—they have the irrational notion that their eventual death is so far in the future that they live like they think they will live indefinitely. Yet, grief management authorities assert we need to come to terms with our own death, and that our daily lives will be more meaningful if we become more comfortable with the fact that life is terminal from birth—as we will all die. The instructor then states the objectives of this exercise.

2.   The instructor distributes to each student a packet of twelve slips of paper. The students are instructed to write on each of the small slips of paper, one of the following twelve items:

- •   Three personal characteristics she is proud of.
- •   Three activities she enjoys participating in.
- •   The three possessions that she cherishes the most.
- •   The names of the three people that are the most important in her life.

Each student then arranges these twelve slips of paper in front of her on a desk or table so that she can see them all.

3.   The instructor states the following: Imagine that you haven't been feeling well for the past several months. You finally decide to see your doctor. The doctor administers a number of medical tests. Today is the day you go in to hear the results of the tests. As you walk in, the doctor has a very concerned look on her face. The doctor informs you that you have a terminal illness. <u>You have thirty seconds to tear up three of your slips of paper.</u>

4.   The instructor states the following: You leave the physician's office in a state of shock. You return home. Who is there to greet you? Who do you really want to be there to greet you? What do you say to these people? What do you want to hear from them? <u>Tear up another three slips of paper.</u>

5.   The instructor states the following: It is now two months later. You realize your health is deteriorating. Your symptoms are worsening and you are feeling weaker. Where are you now living? Have you made changes in your lifestyle? Are there projects and loose ends in your life that you are seeking to complete? What are you thinking and feeling about your terminal illness? <u>Tear up another two slips of paper.</u>

6.   The instructor states the following: It is now four months after you were informed you have a terminal illness. You are undeniably ill. You are in considerable pain, and you now need caregivers to stay alive. Where are you now living? Who is taking care of you? Who visits you? Who are the people you want to visit you and take care of you? <u>Tear up another two slips of paper.</u>

7.   The instructor states the following: Six months have now passed since you learned you have a terminal illness. You have very little energy left. The smallest activity of daily living takes most of your energy. A caregiver now has to attend to you 24 hours each day. You no longer can bathe yourself alone. How do you now feel about yourself? Where are you now living? <u>Please turn over your remaining two slips of paper, and I will take one.</u> (The instructor takes one from each student.)

8.   The instructor states the following: <u>Look at your last slip of paper, and then tear it up. You are now dead.</u>

9.   The instructor thanks the students for conscientiously participating in the first part of this exercise. The instructor then asks the students to form subgroups of about three persons. The members of each subgroup are asked to share their reactions to the following questions, which should now be listed on the blackboard. (If a student chooses not to share, that is his or her personal right.)

a.   Did the exercise seem real? If "yes," when did it become real? If "no," why didn't it seem real?

b.   What emotional reactions did you have to this exercise?

c.   What were the last two items on the slips of paper that you kept?

d.   What were your thoughts, feelings, and reactions to tearing up the last slip of paper?

The class as a whole then discusses the merits and shortcomings of this exercise.

Exercise 15.7: Respecting Religious Beliefs

A.   Brief description

You will briefly study religions that may differ from your own religious beliefs, and you will examine some religious questions.

B.   Objectives

You will:

1.   Begin to understand background information about diverse religions.

2.   Learn to respect religious beliefs that may differ from your own beliefs.

3.   Ultimately make progress in becoming more comfortable with your own religious beliefs.

C.   Procedure

1.   You first read the boxed material on "spirituality and religion" in the text. This material summarizes background information on Judaism, Christianity, Islam, and Buddhism.

2.   You then form subgroups consisting of approximately three students to a group and discuss the following five questions:

    a.   Some religions assert that God is all good, all knowing, and all powerful. If God has all three of these characteristics, why would he or she allow diseases like AIDS to occur, or send someone to eternal damnation?

    b.   What evidence is there that God existed and that he or she currently exists?

    c.   Most of the prominent religions in the world have a "bible," that is, a book of sacred scriptures. Is one of these bibles more accurate in being the word of God than the others? If you answer "yes"—what is it and what evidence do you have?

    d.   Is there a "one true religion"? If you answer "yes"—what is it and what evidence do you have?

    e.   If a social worker strongly believes his or her religion is the one true religion, can that worker fully accept clients who are members of some other religious faith?

3.   The instructor then asks each subgroup to share its answers with the class. If serious unanswered questions arise during the sharing, the instructor may invite a recognized authority (such as a clergy person or a religious studies professor) to the class to present his or her views on the unanswered questions.

4.   The instructor concludes the exercise by asking questions such as the following: Do you believe it is important to respect and understand the religious beliefs of people who hold somewhat different beliefs than what you have? Is intolerance of others' religious beliefs a factor that contributes to other forms of prejudice—such as racism?

Study Outline

I.   **A Perspective**

II.   **Older People: A Population-at-Risk**

    A.   Human societies have different customs for dealing with incapacitated older people

        1.   The Crow, Creek, and Hopi tribes built special huts away from the tribe where the old went to die

        2.   The Eskimos left the incapacitated older people in snowbanks or they went off in a kayak

        3.   The Siriono of the Bolivian forest simply left them behind when they moved on in search of food

    B.   Have we not also abandoned older people in our society?

        1.   When a person is urged to retire, his or her status, power, and self-esteem are lost

        2.   We seldom have a place for large numbers of older people; community facilities are oriented to serving children and young people

        3.   If older people are not able to care for themselves, we store them away from society in nursing homes

        4.   Our taking little action to relieve the financial problems of older people is another abandonment. About one out of 10 older people is living in poverty. The poverty rate for older adults is lower than that of the total population

        5.   Our abandonment of older people, in some ways, is more barbaric than that of tribal societies who are forced by survival pressures to abandon older people

    C.   Older people are subjected to various forms of discrimination

III. **Problems Faced by Older People**

    A.   Problems suffered by older people within the macro system context

        1.   Problems people as individual micro systems suffer within the macro environment include poverty, malnutrition, health difficulties, elder abuse, and lack of transportation

        2.   Problems affecting older people by macro systems include not providing them with support and services

B. Emphasis on youth: The impacts of social and economic forces

    1. Our society fears aging more than most other societies. We place a high value on youthful energy and action

    2. Spotlight on Diversity 16.1: High Status for Older People in China, Japan, and Other Countries

        a. Older people in these countries are integrated into their families much more than in the United States

        b. In Japan, more than 75 percent of older people live with their children, while in the United States most older people live separately from their children

        c. Older people in Japan are accorded respect in many ways

        d. Japan is becoming more urbanized and Westernized. As a consequence, the proportion of older people living with their children is decreasing, and older people there are now often employed in lower-status jobs

        e. Five factors for predicting high status for older people in a culture

            1) Older persons are recognized as having valuable knowledge

            2) Older persons control key family and community resources

            3) The culture is more collectivistic than individualistic

            4) The extended family is a common family arrangement in the culture, and older persons are integrated into the extended family

            5) Older persons are permitted and encouraged to engage in useful and valued functions as long as possible

C. The increasing older population

    1. Table 16.1: Composition of U.S. Population Aged 65 and Older

    2. There are now over ten times as many people age 65 and older than there were in 1900. The life expectancy of Americans was 49 years in 1900; in 2007 it was 78 years

    3. By 2030, 72 million people are projected to be age 65 and older, which is a 100% increase over 30 years, compared to a 30% growth in the total population in the same amount of time

    4. The birthrate is declining—fewer babies are being born, while more adults are reaching later adulthood

    5. The baby boom lasted from 1947 to 1960. Very soon, this generation will begin to reach retirement

6. After 1960, there was a baby bust. The average number of children per woman went down from a high of 3.8 in 1957 to the current rate of about 2.0

7. The increased life expectancy, along with the baby boom followed by the baby bust, will significantly increase the median age of Americans in future years

D. The fastest growing age group is the old-old

   1. People aged 85 and over constitute the fastest-growing age group in the United States; the number will increase by more than 500% by 2050, due largely to the aging of the 69 million baby boomers

   2. Those who are 75 and over are creating a number of problems and difficult decisions for our society

      a. Many suffer from multiple chronic illnesses

      b. The older an older person becomes, the higher the probability that he or she will become a resident of a nursing home

      c. The cost for care in a nursing home is over $40,000 a year per person

      d. Most frail older people still live outside institutional walls, being cared for by a spouse, a child, or a relative

   3. In 1984, Governor Richard Lamm of Colorado created controversy when he asserted the terminally ill have a duty to die

   4. Ethical Question 16.1: Do the terminally ill have a duty to end their lives as soon as they can?

E. Early retirement: The impacts of social and economic forces

   1. One instrument that our society used in the past to keep the work force reduced to a level in line with demand was mandatory retirement at a certain age, such as 65 or 70

   2. In 1986, Congress outlawed most mandatory retirement policies due to the fact they were overtly discriminatory against older people

   3. Although employers can no longer force a worker to retire, many exert subtle pressures on their older employees to retire

   4. Nearly 90 percent of Americans 65 and older are retired, even though many are intellectually and physically capable of working

   5. In our society, we still view people's worth partly in terms of their work. Retirement often diminishes people's social contact and their status, and places them in a roleless role

6. Research has shown that older workers have lower turnover rates, produce at a steadier rate, make fewer mistakes, have lower absenteeism rates, have a more positive attitude toward their work, and exceed younger employees in health and low on-the-job injury rates

7. Adjustment to retirement varies for different people. Retirement appears to have little effect on physical health, but it sometimes affects mental health

8. The two most common problems associated with retirement are adjusting to a reduced income and missing one's former job

F. Financial problems of older people

1. Many older people (one out of ten) live in poverty. Nine percent of older whites are poor, compared to 23.7 percent of older African Americans, and 19.5% of older Hispanics

2. Nearly half of older Hispanic women, and 4 out of 10 older African-American women, are living in poverty

3. Financial problems of older people are compounded by additional factors

   a. The high cost of health care

   b. Inflation—most private pension benefits do not increase in size after a worker retires. In 1974, Congress enacted an automatic escalator clause in Social Security benefits, providing a 3 percent increase in payments when the Consumer Price Index increased a like amount

   c. The percent of older adults who receive Social Security is 95%; for 18% of them, Social Security is their only income

   d. The percent of people age 65 and older who are in the paid labor force in the U.S. is 14%

G. The Social Security system

1. The Social Security system was not designed to be the main source of income for older people, yet for many of older people Social Security has become the major source of income for them

2. Some projections have the Social Security fund being depleted around 2030

3. Dependency ratio: The number of societal members who are under 18 or are 65 and over compared with the number who are between 18 and 64

4. Currently, there are 63 dependents for every 100 persons between 18 and 64. Authorities predict that by the year 2050 it is estimated that the dependency ratio will be 80 to 100

5. Ethical Question 16.2: Should Social Security benefits be expanded, reduced, or kept at the same level?

H.   Death

1.   Older adults' concern about dying is most often focused on the disability, the pain, or the long periods of suffering that may precede death. People generally would like a death with dignity

2.   The hospice movement is an attempt to foster death with dignity. Hospices originated among European religious groups in the Middle Ages who welcomed travelers who were sick, tired, or hungry

3.   Hospices view the *disease*, not the patient, as terminal. Their emphasis is on helping people use the time that is left, rather than trying to keep people alive as long as possible

4.   Ethical Dilemma: Should Assisted Suicide Be Legalized?

   a.   Increasingly, through "living wills," patients are able to express their wishes and refuse treatment

   b.   The Netherlands permits physicians to give qualifying terminally ill patients a lethal dose of drugs

   c.   Hemlock Society founder Derek Humphry has written a do-it-yourself suicide manual that has become a bestseller. The Hemlock Society promotes active voluntary euthanasia

   d.   Michigan doctor Jack Kevorkian made national news by building a machine to help terminally ill people end their lives and by assisting a large number of them to do so

   e.   In the Netherlands an informal, *de facto* arrangement made with prosecutors over 25 years ago allows physicians there to help patients die, as long as certain safeguards are followed

   f.   Oregon's Death with Dignity Act was passed by voters in 1994. It allows doctors to prescribe lethal drugs at the request of terminally ill patients who have less than 6 months to live. Doctors may only prescribe a lethal dose, not administer it

   g.   People in favor of assisted suicide argue that unnecessary, long-term suffering is without merit and should not have to be endured

   h.   Opponents assert that suicide is, at best, unethical and, at worst, a mortal sin for which the deceased cannot receive forgiveness. They view assisted suicide as assisted murder

   i.   In many states it is legal for physicians and courts to honor a patient's wishes to not receive life-sustaining treatment

   j.   In the Nancy Cruzan case in Missouri, the U.S. Supreme Court ruled that states could sanction the removal of food and water from hopelessly ill patients if there is "clear and convincing evidence" that the patient would have wished it

    k.   In June 1997, the U.S. Supreme Court ruled that terminally ill people do not have a constitutional right to doctor-assisted suicide

    l.   In 2001, then-Attorney General John Ashcroft issued a directive that Oregon's Death with Dignity Act violates the Federal Controlled Substances Act. The state of Oregon sued to prevent enforcement. In 2006, the U.S. Supreme Court ruled that the Bush administration's attempts to stop Oregon doctors from prescribing lethal doses were improper. Oregon doctors may continue to prescribe lethal doses without fear of federal penalty

    m.   What are your beliefs on these topics?

I.   Elder abuse

    1.   Elder abuse: Neglect, physical abuse, or psychological abuse of dependent older persons

    2.   Elder abuse is grossly underreported, but estimates of the number of cases each year range from 600,000 to more than 2 million. The number abused may involve as many as 5 percent of the older population

    3.   The typical victim is an older person in poor health who lives with someone. The abuser is more likely to be a spouse than a child, partly because substantially more older people live with spouses than with their children

    4.   Categories of elder abuse:

        a.   Physical abuse: The infliction of physical pain or injury

        b.   Psychological abuse: The infliction of mental anguish, such as intimidating, humiliating, and threatening harm

        c.   Financial abuse: The illegal or improper exploitation of the victim's assets or property

        d.   Neglect: Including deliberate failure or refusal to fulfill a caretaking obligation, such as denial of food or health care, or abandoning the victim

        e.   Sexual abuse: Nonconsensual sexual contact with an older person

        f.   Self-neglect: Behaviors of a frail, depressed or mentally incompetent older person that threaten her or his own safety or health

        g.   Violating personal rights: Rights that may be violated include the older person's right to privacy and to make her or his personal and health decisions

J.   Where older people live

      1.   Over 95 percent of older people do not live in nursing homes or any other kind of institution

      2.   Nearly 80 percent of older married couples maintain their own households, and nearly half of the single older people live in their own homes

      3.   Older people who live in rural areas generally have a higher status than those living in urban areas

      4.   Almost three-fourths of our population live in urban areas, and older people often live in poor-quality housing. At least 30 percent of older people live in substandard, deteriorating, or dilapidated housing

      5.   Fortunately, many mobile home parks, retirement villages, and apartment complexes geared to the needs of older people have been built throughout the country

      6.   The fastest growing facilities (in number) for older people are assisted-living quarters

K.   Transportation: The lack of convenient, inexpensive transportation is a problem faced by most older people

L.   Crime victimization

      1.   Many older people live in constant fear of being victimized, although reported victimization rates for older people are lower than rates for younger people. The actual victimization rates for older people may be considerably higher than official crime statistics indicate, because many older people feel uneasy about becoming involved with the legal and criminal justice systems

      2.   Some older people are hesitant to leave their homes for fear they will be mugged or fear their homes will be burglarized while they are away

M.   Malnutrition: Older people are the most uniformly undernourished segment of our population

N.   Health problems and cost of care

    1.   A national debate is raging over how to reduce the rate of increase of the funds the federal government spends on Medicare and Medicaid

    2.   Physicians are primarily trained in treating the young, and generally less interested in serving older people. Medical conditions of older people are often misdiagnosed, as physicians receive little specialized training in the unique medical conditions of older people

IV.   Current Services: Macro System Responses

A.   Older Americans Act of 1965

    1.   Created the Administration on Aging to operate the program

    2.   The basis for financial aid by the federal government to assist states and local communities to meet the needs of older people

    3.   Gerontology: The scientific study of the aging process from physiological, pathological, psychological, sociological, and economic points of view

    4.   Social insurance program: Financed by a tax on employees, or on employers, or on both. In our society, receiving these benefits is generally considered a right

    5.   Public assistance benefits: Paid from general government revenues, such as income taxes. In our society, receiving these benefits is usually considered charity and is stigmatized

B.   Old Age, Survivors, Disability, and Health Insurance (OASDHI)

    1.   A social insurance program created by the 1935 Social Security Act, and is usually referred to as Social Security

    2.   Payments to beneficiaries are based on previous earnings. Dependent husbands and wives over 62 and dependent children under 18 are also covered under the benefits

    3.   Is generally funded by a payroll tax (FICA—Federal Insurance Contributions Act) assessed equally to employer and employee

    4.   Eligibility for benefits is based on the number of years in which Social Security taxes have been paid and the amount earned while working

C.   Supplemental Security Income (SSI)

    1.   The federal government makes monthly payments to people in financial need who are 65 years of age or older or to persons of any age who are legally blind or disabled

    2.   Applicants must have no (or very little) regular cash income, own little property, and have little cash or few assets that could be turned into cash

    3.   Became effective on January 1, 1974, and sometimes supplements OASDHI monthly payments

D.   Medicare

    1.   Enacted in 1965 as Title XVIII of the Social Security Act to help older people pay the high cost of health care. The two parts include

        a.   Hospital insurance (Part A)

            1)   Everyone 65 or older who is entitled to monthly benefits under the Old Age, Survivors, and Disability Insurance programs gets Part A automatically, without paying a monthly premium

            2)   Disabled people under age 65 who have been getting Social Security benefits for 24 consecutive months or more are also eligible for Part A

            3)   Coverage is limited to 150 days in a hospital and to 100 days in a skilled nursing facility

            4)   Covers home health care on a part-time or intermittent basis if beneficiaries are homebound, in need of skilled nursing care or physical or speech therapy, and services are ordered and regularly reviewed by a physician

            5)   Covers up to 210 days of hospice care for a terminally ill Medicare beneficiary

        b.   Supplementary medical services (Part B)

            1)   This part is voluntary, and beneficiaries are charged a monthly premium

            2)   Disabled people under age 65 who have been getting Social Security benefits for 24 consecutive months or more are also eligible for Part B

3) Helps pay for physicians' services, outpatient hospital services in an emergency room, outpatient physical and speech therapy, a number of other medical and health services, and some ambulance services

4) Each beneficiary has the choice of selecting from an "alphabet soup" of health plans

c. Prescription drug assistance for seniors

1) Medicare Prescription Drug Improvement and Modernization Act (2003)

2) Program designed to assist older people, especially low-income older people, purchase prescription drugs at lower costs

E. Medicaid

1. Established in 1965 by Title XIX of the Social Security Act, and primarily provides medical care for recipients of public assistance

2. The federal government shares the expenses with the states on a 55-45 basis for recipients of public assistance

3. Medicaid benefits vary from state to state

F. Food stamps: A program designed to combat hunger, and available to public assistance recipients and other low-income families. The stamps are used to purchase groceries

G. Adult protective services

1. About one in every 20 older people probably needs some form of protective services, and this is expected to increase as the proportion of people over age 75 increases

2. Protective services are for adults who are being neglected or abused or for adults whose physical or mental capacities have substantially deteriorated

3. The aim is to help older people, and adults with disabilities, meet their needs in their own home if possible. Alternative placements include foster care, group home care, and older people housing units

4. Services provided include homemaker services, counseling, rehabilitation, medical services, visiting nursing services, Meals on Wheels, and transportation

5. Highlight 16.1: Adult Protective Services

H.   Additional programs

   1.   Meals on Wheels: Provides hot and cold meals to housebound recipients

   2.   Senior-citizen centers: Golden age clubs, and similar groups provide leisure time and recreational activities for older people

   3.   Special bus rates

   4.   Property tax relief

   5.   Housing projects: Built for older people by local sponsors with financing assistance by the Department of Housing and Urban Development

   6.   Reduced rates at movie theaters and other places of entertainment

   7.   Home health services: Provide visiting nurse services, physical therapy, drugs, laboratory services, and sickroom equipment

   8.   Nutrition programs: Provide meals for older people at group eating sites

   9.   Homemaker services: Provide household tasks that older people are no longer able to do for themselves

   10.   Day care centers: Provide activities that are determined by the needs of the group

   11.   Telephone reassurance: Volunteers telephone older people who live alone, to provide social contact and to ascertain whether any serious problems have arisen

   12.   Nursing homes: Provide residential care and skilled nursing care when independence is no longer practical for older people who cannot take care of themselves

   13.   Congregate housing facilities: Private or government-subsidized rental apartment complexes, remodeled hotels to meet the needs of independent older adults, or mobile home parks designed for older adults. They provide meals, housekeeping, transportation, social and recreational activities, and sometimes health care

   14.   Group homes: Provide housing for some older residents. A group home is usually a house that is owned or rented by a social agency

   15.   Assisted-living facilities: Allow older people to have semi-independent living. Older people live in their own rooms or apartments. Residents receive personal care, meals, housekeeping, transportation, and social and recreational activities

   16.   Foster-care homes: Usually single-family residences where the owners of the home take in an unrelated older adult and are reimbursed for providing housing, meals, housekeeping, and personal care

17. Continued care retirement communities: Long-term housing facilities which are designed to provide a full range of accommodations and services for affluent older people as their needs change

18. Nursing Home Ombudsman Programs: Investigate and act on concerns expressed by residents in nursing homes

I. Nursing homes

1. About 1.5 million older people now live in extended-care facilities. There are more patient beds in nursing homes than in hospitals

2. Range from residential homes that provide primarily room and board, with some nonmedical care, to nursing-care centers that provide skilled nursing and medical attention 24 hours a day

3. The costs per resident average more than $3,000 a month

4. About 3 percent of adults 65 years of age and older reside in a nursing home at any point in time

5. A study in 2001 found that a third of the nursing homes in the United States have been cited by state inspectors as being abusive to residents in 1999 and 2000

6. A number of nursing homes fail to meet food sanitation standards and have problems administering drugs and providing personal hygiene for residents

7. A nationwide investigation of nursing homes was conducted and concluded that the majority of nursing homes are safe, well-run institutions that take good care of the sick people entrusted to them, and some are superb

8. Ethical Question 16.3: If you were mentally competent but physically incapacitated, would you agree to being placed in a nursing home?

9. The cost of care for impoverished nursing home residents is largely paid by the Medicaid program

10. A danger of nursing home care is the potential abuse of the residents by staff members. A survey of 577 nurses and nurses' aides found that one-third of the respondents stated they had seen other staff members physically abusing patients. Ten percent acknowledged committing one or more of these acts themselves

11. Psychological abuse was even more common, with 81 percent of the respondents indicating they had seen other staff members yelling at patients, insulting them, isolating them unnecessarily, threatening them, or refusing to give them food. Forty percent of the respondents acknowledged committing such abuse themselves

12. Highlight 16.2: Community Options Program: Providing Alternatives to Nursing Home Placement

V. **Social Work with Older People**

A.   Brokering services

B.   Case management or care management

C.   Advocacy

D.   Individual and family counseling

E.   Grief counseling

F.   Adult day care services

G.   Crisis intervention services

H.   Adult foster care services

I.   Adult protective services

J.   Support and therapeutic groups

K.   Respite care

L.   Transportation and housing assistance

M.   Hospital and nursing home social services

N.   More employment opportunities in the future

VI.   **Older People Are a Powerful Political Force**

A.   Political activism

1.   American Association of Retired Persons (AARP): This group lobbies for the interests of older people at local, state, and federal levels of government

2.   Gray Panthers: This action-oriented group seeks to end ageism and to advance the goals of human freedom, human dignity, and self-development

3.   Older people are more likely to vote than younger people

VII.   **Changing a Macro System: Finding a Social Role for Older People**

A.   Older people who want to work and are still performing well should be encouraged to continue working past age 65 or 70

B.   Retired Senior Volunteer Program (RSVP): Offers people over age 60 the opportunity of doing volunteer service to meet community needs

C.   Service Corps of Retired Executives (SCORE): Offers retired businessmen and businesswomen an opportunity to help owners of small businesses and managers of community organizations who are having management problems

D. Foster Grandparent Program: Employs low-income older people to provide personal care to children who live in institutions. This program has been shown to be of considerable benefit to both the children and to the foster grandparents

E. Ethical Question 16.4: If you were physically and mentally healthy and in your 70s, would you continue to be employed?

F. Highlight 16.3: John Glenn, One of the Many Productive Older People

VIII. Summary

Experiential Exercises and Simulations

Three exercises are presented in this section. The first focuses on the financial health of the Social Security system, and the second is a values-clarification exercise about the living conditions of older people. The third relates to physician-assisted suicide.

Exercise 16.1: Keeping the Social Security System Healthy

A. Brief description
You will have small-group discussions aimed at ranking various alternatives for keeping the Social Security system solvent. Findings will then be summarized to the total group and discussed.

B. Objectives
You will:
1. Understand the financial aspects of the Social Security system.
2. Explain to others why the Social Security system in future years may not be able to financially maintain older people.
3. State alternatives for keeping the Social Security system solvent and evaluate the pros and cons of each.

C. Procedure
1. The instructor summarizes information contained in the chapter about: (1) the Social Security system's financial base; (2) there will be more recipients as people live longer; (3) monthly benefit payments are inadequate to totally financially maintain older people, but should they be?; and (4) Social Security taxes have increased dramatically over the years.
2. Form subgroups of five or six persons. Discuss and then rank from 1 to 6 the following alternatives for keeping the Social Security system healthy, with rank number 1 being the most preferred alternative.

a. Continue to raise the maximum tax on Social Security an average of $250 per year. This amount is roughly the current average increase. With this kind of increase, the maximum tax paid in the year 2010 would be $10,000 per employee.

b. Withhold highly expensive medical care from those over age 75. Less expensive medical care would continue to be provided.

c. For those over 85, do not provide medical treatment for life-threatening illnesses, such as cancer, heart attacks, or pneumonia. Treatment for minor ailments, such as colds and arthritis, would continue to be given.

d. Use physician-assisted suicide for those in a nursing home who meet both of the following conditions: (a) have no chance of returning to society, and (b) sincerely express (for at least a two-month period) a wish to die.

e. Sharply reduce the benefits paid out of the Social Security system. (With this approach, many of the current recipients would be deeply impoverished.)

f. Seek to increase the amount of money in the Social Security system by investing available funds in the stock market.

---

3. A representative from each small group lists the group's rankings on the board. A representative from each group explains the reasons for its rankings. Discuss these rankings.

Exercise 16.2: Hard Choices About Living Conditions for Older People

A. Brief description

You are asked to indicate (anonymously) your personal choices relating to difficult questions about living conditions for older people.

B. Objectives

You will:

1. Have a greater understanding of the complex questions that arise about living conditions for older people.

2. Identify and state your values about living conditions for older people.

C. Procedure

1. The instructor hands out sheets of paper or five-by-seven-inch notecards. Write your answers to the following ten multiple-choice questions on your paper or notecard. Do not sign your name.

QUESTIONS

a. If I were age 70, I would prefer to:
    1) Continue to work to maintain my standard of living
    2) Retire, which would mean a sharp reduction in my standard of living
    3) Uncertain

b. If I were age 75 and had a heart disease that was terminal, I would:
    1) Want a heart transplant to attempt to help me live longer
    2) Prefer the less painful way of saying no to a heart transplant and let nature take its course
    3) Uncertain

c. If I were age 80 and my mental and physical capacities had deteriorated substantially, I would want to:
    1) Be placed in a nursing home
    2) Continue living in my own home, where I would be unlikely to meet my basic needs and therefore might die
    3) Uncertain

d. If I were age 75, I would prefer:
    1) To die fairly suddenly, with my physical and mental capacities still intact
    2) To continue living for 20 more years in a nursing home, with deteriorated mental and physical capacities
    3) Uncertain

e. If I lived in a nursing home from age 80 to age 100, I think it would be _____ to younger taxpayers to have them pay my expenses through the Social Security system.
    1) Fair
    2) Unfair
    3) Uncertain

f. I think it is _____ to sign a living will in which I state that, if I am unconscious (for example, in a coma) and have no chance to return to a life of quality, I do not want heroic medical efforts used to keep me alive.
    1) Desirable
    2) Undesirable
    3) Uncertain

g. If one of my parents dies and the remaining parent becomes fairly disabled physically, I _____ allow that parent to live alone if he or she wanted to even though life-threatening conditions could arise.
    1) Would
    2) Would not
    3) Uncertain

h. I _____ believe that an older person who is terminally ill and in intense pain has an ethical right to commit suicide.
   1) Do
   2) Do not
   3) Uncertain

i. If I were married and had young children, and my only surviving parent became fairly disabled, mentally and physically, I would:
   1) Allow the parent to live with me, which would disrupt my family and force family members to provide 24-hour care each day
   2) Place the parent in a nursing home
   3) Uncertain

j. I think middle-aged adults _____ an obligation to physically take care of their parents, just as parents are obligated to take care of their children.
   1) Have
   2) Do not have
   3) Uncertain

2. Hand in your papers or cards anonymously. The instructor writes on the chalkboard the identifying letters of the questions and the numbers of the possible responses:

	1	2	3
a.			
b.			
c.			
d.			
e.			
f.			
g.			
h.			
i.			
j.			

A volunteer lists the responses.

3. The instructor rereads each question out loud and then leads a discussion about the responses.

Exercise 16.3: Physician Assisted Suicide

A. Brief description
You are asked two questions related to whether you believe physician-assisted suicide should be legalized.

B.   Objectives
      You will:
      1.   Identify the arguments on both sides of this issue.
      2.   Clarify your values on this national issue.

C.   Procedure
      1.   Form subgroups of four or five persons. Each subgroup discusses the following two
            questions:
            a.   If I were 75 years old, had a terminal illness, and were in severe pain, would I
                  consider physician-assisted suicide as being an option for coping with my
                  deteriorating condition? Why or why not?
            b.   Should physician-assisted suicide be legalized for older persons who have a
                  terminal illness, are in severe pain, and want to die? Why or why not?
      2.   A representative from each subgroup shares the diverse views of its members with the
            class.
      3.   The instructor ends the exercise by providing a summary of the views that are expressed.